Milk Teeth

Milk Teeth

A MEMOIR OF A WOMAN AND HER DOG

Robbie Pfeufer Kahn

Rutgers University Press

New Brunswick, New Jersey, and London

Library of Congress Cataloging-in-Publication Data

Kahn, Robbie Pfeufer, 1941—
Milk teeth : a memoir of a woman and her dog / Robbie Pfeufer Kahn.
p. cm.
ISBN 978–0–8135–4370–3 (hardcover : alk. paper)
ISBN 978–0–8135–4371–0 (pbk. : alk. paper)
1. Human-animal relationships—Case studies. 2. Puppies—Training—Case studies. 3. Puppies—Behavior—Case studies. 4. Parent and child—Case studies. 5. Interpersonal relations—Case studies. 6. Family—Case studies. 7. Kahn, Robbie Pfeufer, 1941– 8. Kahn, Robbie Pfeufer, 1941—Family. 9. Women sociologists—United States—Biography. I. Title.
QL85.K34 2008
301.092—dc22
[B]

2008000896

A British Cataloging-in-Publication record for this book is available from the British Library.

Visit our Web site: http://rutgerspress.rutgers.edu

Design by Karolina Harris

Manufactured in the United States of America

For

Judy, with whom I first loved words;

Nynke, muse of the written word;

Jan, who knows when a teacher should leave;

Laska, who knows many human words but chooses to mind only some of them;

and for Sarah, the one who came before

Contents

Acknowledgments

WHEN she was a small girl, my son's paternal grandmother thought that a book called *The Craft of Fiction* was about boats. To me, Reed was partly right. A memoir is not fiction, but it needs crafting, as I learned over many revisions. Additionally, I seemed to be journeying in a boat whose oars were not entirely within my control. What came from inside me was unforeseeable, as was the guidance and support I received from others.

Some people read early versions of the book, some read late ones, some read more than one revision. I thank deeply Clint Sanders, Stan Coren, Maury Stein, Phil Arkow, Joshua Chasan, Jerry Held, Barbara Zucker, Becky Sarah, Judy Teller, Philip Greven, Sue Silverman, Suzanne Arms, Tony Burbank, Laurie Matheson, three anonymous readers, and Susan Davidson. I give special thanks to Norman Denzin, whose advocacy was both unexpected and decisive (if you don't hear from a busy person for a year, it doesn't necessarily mean that he doesn't like your book). Clint Sanders also helped the book find a home.

Beth Mintz, my former chair in the Sociology Department, had read summaries of *Milk Teeth* in my yearly self-evaluations. One day she suggested Rutgers University Press to me and kindly sent the manuscript to my current editor, Adi Hovav. Adi took a liking to the book from the start (she herself is a dog lover), helped me pare the length down, provided a subtitle, generously extended the deadline, and continues to offer clear-eyed advice when my judgment fails. I am deeply grateful to Beth and to Adi. Leslie Irvine peer reviewed *Milk Teeth* for Rutgers. I thank her for her many-sided appreciation of the book.

Two women taught me the double meaning of craft—how to write a sustained personal narrative and how to keep the boat from capsizing. I thank literary agent Betsy Amster for my initial exposure to what story writing entails. In my first book, *Bearing Meaning: The Language of Birth,* I combined scholarship with personal narrative. Stories popped up, unbidden, and I included them (many people loved these sections best, and some confessed to reading *only* the stories). But incorporating bursts of storytelling is not the same thing as crafting an entire book. My former writers' group member Nynke Doetjes (poet, novelist, and creative writing teacher at the Maharishi University) guided draft after draft. I never sent Nynke the last version because I knew she'd want another go-round. Nynke's trust, sweet as her voice, saved me from silence.

When we were small girls, my cousin Judy and I had a dispute over her toy stuffed donkey, which today rests against a volume of Yeats's poetry in her library. Documented in a series of photographs, Judy and I had fought over whether the donkey's ears should pitch forward or back. We compromised—one ear each way. When I called upon my cousin for help with the title of the book and the pseudonyms, we collaborated as we had long ago. She provided "teeth"; I added "milk." Judy came up with all the pseudonyms; I changed half of them.

I am deeply indebted to the following people: Jan Bissonette, Lynn Mayo, Evelyn Cummings, Judy Kay, Jennifer Rupert, Don DeMercurio, David Boedy, Linda Steinman, and Martha Day. I also thank my students in several courses at the University of Vermont, including those in Sociology of Animals and Society. Some of the readings we shared became part of *Milk Teeth.*

A book can't get very far without assistance in manuscript preparation. Lynn Carew, Salli Griggs, and Barb Caron proofread the book, Lynn and Salli several times. Former student Matt Cropp helped me prepare the manuscript for Rutgers University Press. His intelligence and knowledge of the Internet allowed me to make the deadline. Ashley Ethier provided additional help of similar quality. Christina Brianik brought stamina and good cheer to the skilled work of acquiring permissions. Bobbe Needham copyedited *Milk Teeth.* I appreciate her subtle refinements in phrasing and astute questions. I am very thankful to Beth Kressel, Alicia Nadkarni, Allyson Fields, and other staff members at Rutgers University Press who have transformed *Milk Teeth* from a manuscript into a book.

I am most grateful to Gillian Randall for her photograph of Laska and me. Black dogs are hard to catch on camera successfully.

The University of Vermont, Lintilhac Foundation, and two anonymous feminist donors provided funding that sustained me during the sabbatical year Laska came along and I began this book. I thank the University of Vermont for the sabbatical.

I am more than grateful to my son, Levin Morrell Pfeufer, who allowed me to include him in a book for the second time. Many thanks to my sister, Karen, for her support during this project. I thank my mother for carrying me safely inside her. Levin and his wife, Amina, have blessed me with their love and their two children. Aziz and Aya have made "Grandma Hoppy" out of me. They both love "Laski" and visit her by webcam from London (and once in person).

I am lucky to have had the eidetic care of Dr. Siegel—Andy Siegel—who loves dogs too.

November 2007

A Note to the Reader

EARLY childhood memory is controversial. Certain stories from my childhood in *Milk Teeth* arise from emotional and bodily states; clues from present, daily experiences; early childhood objects and photographs; dreams; and flashbacks. These early childhood narratives should not be read as factual representations of what happened—they may or may not be real or accurate. I offer them to the reader because these early "memories" likely influenced my state of mind in the larger story of *Milk Teeth* and are important for that reason.

Some of the names of individuals in this book have been changed to protect their identity.

Milk Teeth

Prologue

May 1999

THE SETUP

YOU wouldn't find us on the couch together, this dog and me. First of all, I no longer allow dogs on furniture. But that isn't the real reason.

Every evening after supper I sit on a Breuer chair in the living room and invite Laska to join me so that I can pat her. Tonight we take up our customary positions, eyeing each other expectantly. Laska's looks strike me afresh and remind me of why they attract attention on our walks. Her springy step, the high carriage of her head, and her shiny coat that ripples down her back as if ocean waves had just left their trace, radiate life. These traits, combined with her shape, often cause people to mistake her for a puppy. In reality, her slender, compact body belongs to the British type of Labrador retriever. If we didn't walk so briskly, people might notice that Laska's face holds more dignity than a pup's. What looks like a thought furrow runs vertically down her forehead. Shepherds' crooks, ancient as the domestication of animals, could have inspired the curve of Laska's brow bones. Covered by rich black fur they catch the light, drawing attention to her eyes.

Though she's over two years old, the inside of Laska is less familiar to me than the outside. Tonight, I look into her wide-set brown eyes and notice for the first time that they are the color of wood streams running with iron. A stream we passed earlier today on our walk in the Vermont woods prompts the comparison. Iron seems the right metaphor, for Laska is a strong-willed dog. Suddenly I hear myself say out loud, "You are my *perfect* girl." My words surprise me because by "perfect," I do not mean her looks.

Laska's sturdy otter tail, as Labrador retriever breeders call it, circles like an airplane propeller. She scans my eyes.

I say, "Do you know why?"

More and faster wags, as if the plane is about to take off. Yet she holds her body poised, ears pitched forward.

Besides their wood stream color there is something else about her eyes I notice. They are discerning, inquiring, mischievous but not—no, never—soulful. The word "soulful" applies to the yearning look of my first Labrador, Sarah, who died four years ago. Unfairly, I often have measured Laska by the standard of Sarah.

Setting Laska free from the comparison I say, "Why are you my perfect girl? Because you are your *very* own self and no one else."

Is it possible that after two years I finally have accepted Laska for who she is? This turn of heart would be the greatest surprise of all.

I do not have time to answer the question. The buildup of my three excited comments is too much for my dog. She lunges at my face excitedly, the whites of her eyes showing.

No longer startled as I used to be by Laska's rude civility, I turn away from her in the chair and fold my arms. This gesture signals my lack of interest in her style of greeting. Firmly I say "Off," repeating the word several times before she drops back down on all fours. Then I stretch my hand out to pat her.

As usual, my touch agitates Laska. She wriggles frenetically, grabs my hand between her large white teeth, presents her rump for me to pet instead of her head, then jumps away as if in alarm.

I once read a scientific study that showed that patting a dog lowers your blood pressure, but these findings do not seem to apply to me. With Laska, my blood pressure always surges. To be fair, it seems hers does too when she receives my touch. Our misbegotten moments of affection are the real reason you would not find us hanging out together on the couch.

Despite this typically awkward encounter, my acceptance of Laska makes possible what happens next. I know that the moment I am about to describe also is the result of over two years' growth in her and in me. Yet curiously, there is an all-at-onceness to it, as when a cocoon bursts and a butterfly emerges. After it unfolds its beautiful wings, the butterfly allows them to dry in the sun, then floats upward and out of sight. How could this graceful creature once have been a creeping caterpillar? Most mysteriously, how, shrouded in a cocoon, could the transformation have taken place?

I get up out of my chair and proceed to create a "setup" for Laska, as my son used to call such arrangements of household objects in his childhood. It was a private family term for creating an environment. The young artist he later became would call it an "installation piece."

"Look, Mom," Levin said one day long ago, bringing me into a walk-in closet in our Cambridge apartment. Under the low slanted ceiling, a scale just right for kids, he had set up his oak table and chairs with bentwood legs.

"What a great idea," I replied, not realizing the secret space soon would become the location of the Bad Club, founded by a judge's son. The first-grade members of this new association were intent on doing "one bad thing a day." Learning the bylaws, I advised Levin to give up his membership. He would not listen. However, the day his father told him to quit the Bad Club, he did. I have read that dogs, too, listen more compliantly to men than to children or women.

I hope that my setup will allow Laska and me to become closer. I drag a narrow futon with an orange cover from upstairs and place it perpendicular to the broad birch wood frame of the living room couch. I double two thirds of the futon over for me to sit on. Laska can curl up on the remaining third that extends between my legs. I place a reading pillow against the couch frame to support my back, and sit down. What will happen?

In the past, whenever I got down to the same level as Laska, she lunged at me, roughhouse ready, putting my teeth, nose, and delicate wire-rim glasses at risk. I ask Laska to sit in front of me, and she complies. Presenting her with the palm of my hand I say sternly, "Stay."

To my surprise, Laska remains where she is, her eyes watching me with focused attention.

Cautiously, I settle onto my part of the futon. Once I get comfortable, I invite her to join me by exclaiming, "OK."

As if matching my up-and-down inflection, she pounces in a high arc, all four legs off the floor, more cat than dog, into my lap. A few minutes later, after some unruly wriggling, her tail slapping my chest, her open mouth making for my face, she curls up in the crook of my legs. Her graceful head, placed precisely between her two blunt black paws with ebony nails, rests on my thigh. She settles in with a back-and-forth motion of her chin, the same burrowing movement a puppy makes after flopping its head down onto the back of a littermate. I can feel the pulse in her throat flutter like a bird that might at any moment fly away. I force myself not to hold my breath for fear of disrupting a moment of intimacy I never imagined was possible.

I cannot see Laska's eyes, but watching her thick black lashes close from time to time, I can tell that she lies awake, listening. As my hand moves gently down the side of her muzzle, I can feel the ridges of her jagged molars under the skin. In a quiet voice I say, "Thank you for accepting me, too."

ORANGE, GRAY, AND GREEN

I awake in the middle of the night. Outside the east-facing bedroom window, the street lamp, which gives the sky an orange cast, has not yet been shut off. I am enfolded in deep night. Usually, I easily return to sleep, but tonight I lie awake. The unnatural light seems conjured strangely by a dream, reminding me that my unconscious is close.

Orange was the color of the primordial earth's atmosphere two billion years ago, before newly evolved blue-green algae released oxygen into the air, slowly changing the orange sky to blue. Like the ancient atmosphere, the unconscious seems both terrible and wonderful. Archaic, it can prove inhospitable to living in present time. As if it were an interior primordial flame, the unconscious holds the power to destroy, but also to transform and preserve.

Perhaps my comparison between the unconscious and the atmosphere is more than a metaphor. Cosmologist Brian Swimme and creation theologian Thomas Berry believe that outer nature awakens our inner nature and that the stories we tell always are records of our place in the universe. As they put it in *The Universe Story: From the Primordial Flaring Forth to the Ecozoic Era—A Celebration of the Unfolding of the Cosmos:* "Humans give voice to their most exalted and terrible feelings only because they find themselves immersed in the universe filled with such awesome realities. The inner depths of each being in the universe are activated by the surrounding universe."[1] The farthest objects in the universe belong to the deep past; the unconscious mind mirrors this relation between time and space. What is most deeply stowed away inside the self comes from farthest away—infancy.

Laska snores lightly on a bed of her own underneath mine, which is raised on cement blocks. I can smell her warm, yeasty scent. Until recently this dog, who now sleeps peacefully, plunged me into an emotional atmosphere as archaic as that of early earth. Steeped in a private orange, I felt *cut off* from the universe, which is one of the destructive aspects of the unconscious. Disconnection was familiar to me since childhood, but if I were to assign a color to those years I would call them gray. One image sets the tone for my memory of the years before puberty. Each day, on my way to grammar school, I passed a hotel on West End Avenue, between Seventy-third and Seventy-fourth Streets. Against my will, in a treadmill way, every day I repeated the letters printed on a regal awning above the entryway, Hotel Esplanade, in time to my steps on the gray cement squares. I did not know that I recited a wish—"esplanade" comes from the Latin *esplanare*, which means to explain. My day-to-day life in the 1940s and 1950s offered no explanation as to why I felt vague and smudged like a poorly done charcoal drawing. Often, when I returned to our apartment on the fourteenth floor, I found the door to my parents' bedroom shut; my mother slept a lot, face down, sealed off from me. I walked back into the living room, feeling adrift in the silent house. My father, who practiced dentistry, wouldn't be home until suppertime. Where was my younger sister? I don't remember being aware of her in the house. I sat down in a big armchair with wings, turned on the radio, and lost myself in the family world of a soap opera.

The gray extended into adolescence, when an eating disorder overtook me at age fourteen. Today there are words like "binge-eating syndrome" to describe the impulse; in the late 1950s there were not. All I knew was that when I started to overeat only bedtime could stop me, and the obsession might continue into the next day or string of days. I walked back and forth from the kitchen to the bedroom, dressed in a T-shirt and underpants, because the food, like an umbilical cord, held me fast to my parents' apartment. I called these my "eating days." Oddly, no one in my family commented on my strange habit. Whatever foods I devoured, for example, whole boxes of graham crackers at a time, my mother simply replaced. No one seemed to notice that my weight increased, by ten and then twenty pounds. I was alone with my compulsion. Trapped inside my body, I took to hanging out in the foyer of our apartment. The gray wall-to-wall carpeting mirrored my emotional state, yet the large, sparsely furnished room led to the front door and invited liberation.

Eventually, I escaped to college. After the all-girl environment of Hunter College High School, which I had attended since seventh grade, Brandeis University seemed to offer unlimited freedom. I hung out with a bohemian crowd and squandered study hours at Chumley's Coffee Shop, named for the campus photographer's dog. Suffering torment was the fashion, and torment was an emotion I did not have to fake. My women friends and I anguished over our relationships with men. In my first year I surrendered my virginity to a biology graduate student who was indifferent to me. I complained about his lack of feeling, but his lean body and prowling walk dazed me. He reminded me of the gamekeeper in *Lady Chatterley's Lover*, and so I trusted that this man would save me from the grayness, the way Mellors had rescued Lady Chatterley. After college I married another man, whom I also met at Brandeis. Tall and blond, Eric descended, on his mother's side, from the Mayflower Pilgrims. I held an unconscious yet powerful conviction: my self-prison and my Jewish ancestry would vanish when I became one flesh with Eric. Despite having gone to Brandeis, formally nondenominational but 70 percent Jewish, I suffered from anti-Semitism, a prejudice that the larger culture did little to discourage. This emotion added to my self-dislike. Neither my college lover nor my husband provided, nor could they provide, the escape I longed for.

The source of these unhappy years lay in infancy and early childhood—in experiences that were hidden away in my unconscious, as if boarded up in a cellar. Philip Greven, who applies a psychoanalytic perspective to history, explains that early memories may be forgotten, but they have not been left behind. In *Spare The Child: The Religious Roots of Punishment and the Psychological Impact of Child Abuse,* he writes: "The experiences of infancy and childhood are encoded in our memories permanently, in visual, tactile, and verbal forms. We too often fail to acknowledge that these memories persist throughout our lives, for most of them are buried and inaccessible to us despite our utmost efforts at recovery."[2] Most importantly, these experiences shape our actions in present time unless we can bring them into consciousness.

Throughout my twenties, memories of the remote past remained inaccessible. But when I was thirty years old, pregnancy and birth unexpectedly altered my inner life, turning gray to green. A short Buddhist saying, "Sitting quietly/doing nothing/spring comes/and the grass grows by itself," describes perfectly the joy I felt simply in being alive. In my seventh month of pregnancy, I visited Sylvann's Wood on Cape Cod. I walked on the rich, dark brown earth amongst fruit trees and euonymus shrubs with their strange, segmented branches. Poking up from the soft earth were early spring bulbs—English primroses, crocuses, daffodils, and cyclamen. I no longer felt separate from this abundance: as it bloomed, so did I.

If pregnancy was the chrysalis, birth burst the case. At the contractions' strongest, a flush rushed hotly over my face as if the life force, so long damped down, had returned all at once. When my son unfolded, wetly, out of me, he brought me with him, refreshed as if I too were newly born.

The day the milk came in, I sat out on our porch and admired the fiery orange nasturtiums, in wooden flower boxes, that had grown noticeably in my absence. I saw a gull glide on an air current, a row of poplar trees lean away from a breeze in the yard next to ours, and at the same time I became aware of the surge of milk in my breasts. These different currents (of milk, of air, of the sap in the trees and the flowers) seemed to me to flow into one another, so that I became part of them and they part of me.

Besides blessing me with sensations of connection and aliveness, childbearing became the wellspring of my intellectual life. First, I joined the women's health movement of the 1970s and contributed to the self-help classic *Our Bodies, Ourselves.* Then, at age thirty-five, I entered graduate school to research the social, cultural, and historical forces that impeded women from giving birth by their own powers and from breastfeeding their babies. The book that resulted, *Bearing Meaning: The Language of Birth,* wove my own story of childbearing into the book's scholarly material, like a leaf and vine motif, to make vivid the pleasures of maternity.

By the time the book came out, I was already in my early fifties—a mother, professor, and author. Yet, I lived in a certain ignorance of myself. Over the years, psychotherapy had helped me work *around* the past in pursuit of life goals. In *Bearing Meaning,* I recounted a dream that showed my partial awareness of my inner life: "I put my arm around a small girl—we are in a dream version of the movie *Bambi,* which was my favorite book when I was little—and tell her that we shouldn't yet go into the scary places, crumbling buildings with the carved figure of a woman on the lintel over the doors, her head in profile bent down leaning on her arm, as in images on Greek grave steles. I say, 'We should follow the master narrative' and not rush."[3]

In the dream I protected myself from encountering my past, both frightening and grief filled, until reason, the "master narrative," dictated the right time. All the same, the dream showed that I was, literally, on the threshold of self-discovery.

The only reader of *Bearing Meaning* to notice the unrevealed story was cultural scholar William Irwin Thompson, perhaps because he writes about *preliterate* Paleolithic and Neolithic goddess cultures in *The Time Falling Bodies Take to Light: Mythology, Sexuality, and the Origins of Culture.* In his e-mail to me on April 12, 1998, Thompson wrote:

> Just a note to let you know that I finally did finish your book, though it seems inadequate to call it a book because it is more like an archipelago than a continent: pieces of all the books you meant to write in your life floating as islands in a sea that is deep, silent, and mysterious in the way that it surrounds all your prose with a sense of wounding that is prehistoric to the emergence of the prose islands above the sea.

A year before Laska came into my life, I began to explore the crumbling buildings and Thompson's sea, which is another metaphor for the primordial orange of the unconscious. Secure enough in the present (with my son raised, book published, and tenure earned), I could look back at the gray past; it turned out to be far more alive than I had imagined. Meditation and psychotherapy, where I discussed dreams and old photographs, yielded vivid flashbacks, and these recollections inspired my sabbatical project in 1997–1998. As my motherhood gave birth to *Bearing Meaning,* I hoped that my new book, *Creatural Lessons: An Archaeological Memoir of the Body,* would grow from my childhood, a plan I have yet to complete. As with my first book, I would combine my personal story with scholarship as I explored the sociological and familial reasons that caused me, at an early age, to lose a sense of being alive. I would attempt to explain why bodily experiences of childbearing, sexuality, disability caused by rheumatoid arthritis, as well as bearing witness to the death of my dog Sarah, restored me to animate life. I intended to add my voice to the nature/culture debate in sociology. How much are we shaped by each force? I was convinced that nature, our "creatural" side, had more influence than sociologists were willing to admit.

But early in the sabbatical year my research and writing took an unexpected turn. I began a journal about my puppy Laska because when my first Labrador retriever, Sarah, died in 1995, I regretted that I had not written more about her. I originally called the journal *My Puppy, Myself,* words that implied a warm affiliation, two parts of a whole. The entries soon gave the title an ironic twist, for ours was far from a story about two pals who cuddled on a couch. Instead, I found myself recounting a mutually painful relationship. The journal began to claim more time than my sabbatical project. I reasoned that the journal might bridge my two scholarly books as I traveled, somewhat awkwardly, from motherhood back to childhood. Yet the impulse to write was deeper than logic; I felt compelled to record an experience as life changing as that of giving birth—my journey into the vast inner landscape of the unconscious to find out where my story began.

Such a quest is not so unusual for a person living in a modern society. In his book *Modernity and Self-Identity: Self and Society in the Late Modern Age,* social theorist Anthony Giddens explains that modernity destroys traditions that, for millennia, provided each person with a reliable place in their family, society, and even the cosmos. Modernists lack what Giddens calls "ontological security," a philosophical term that refers to the nature of what is. (Brian Swimme and Thomas Berry, whom I quoted earlier, try to comfort ontologically insecure moderns by telling us that our true home is in the great streams of the universe.) Giddens explains that modernity forces us to become self-reflexive; that is, we consciously review our lives as they unfold into the future. Giddens states: "The 'capable individual' today not only has a developed self-understanding, but is able to harmonise present concerns and future projects with a psychological inheritance from the past."[4] In the absence of tradition's story, we create our own life narratives.

Another sociologist, Adrian Franklin, builds upon Giddens's work. In his book *Animals and Modern Cultures: A Sociology of Human-Animal Relations in Modernity,* Franklin explains that the unwavering love of a companion animal can reduce ontological insecurity. He believes that moderns' attachment to pets undermines, for the good, the sharp boundary Western tradition sets between humans and animals. For example, many people in the United States who live with companion animals consider them to be members of the family.

My story with Laska fits right into Giddens's and Franklin's theories. I was engaged in a self-reflexive narrative typical of a modern person. Yet the insights into my past were intended to light the way to a good relationship with my puppy Laska to repair, build, and maintain trust.

Giddens believes that basic trust acquired during the first months and years of life is essential to withstand the destabilizing effects of modernity and hence to sustain a successful life trajectory. In *Bearing Meaning* I spoke of the culture of the newly born. By "culture" I meant that babies belong to a community that possesses knowledge even though they barely use language. If I resorted to sociological jargon, I would call the very young *prelinguistic.* The newly born teach us that there is never just a baby, but a baby and someone. Here, basic trust begins. As a child I did not feel connected to my mother. In our case, bottlefeeding expressed that estrangement (a state by no means shared by all who are bottlefed). So I became attached to a blanket that I named You-you; it was the "you" that comforted my "I." By contrast, my son, Levin, felt that he was connected to me. In fact, while still breastfeeding he seemed to see himself as part of a whole. He would use the pronoun "my" instead of "I." He would say, "My am going out to play," until he weaned at three-and-a-half, when for the first time he called himself "I." Evolutionary psychologists (who propose that infants have an innate need—social and biological—to attach to their primary caretaker) would notice the difference between Levin's secure attachment and my dissociated one as a child.

When I first got Laska, she was only seven weeks old. But, whereas Levin had been prelinguistic as an infant, Laska was *alinguistic,* a term that denotes those forever outside the community of human speech. I knew little about my puppy's world despite having lived with several cats and my first Labrador, Sarah. Sarah had been a simple, loving dog and our relationship had unfolded without much scrutiny. Such unexamined living was not possible with Laska. Although extremely distressing, our lack of attunement gave birth for me to unprecedented self-knowledge as well as to a new intellectual passion. I read memoirs; historical, anthropological and sociological accounts of the human/animal relationship; debates about animal rights; studies in applied ethology, a field that now researches domesticated as well as wild animals; and more. Only some readings found their way into my journal, but all together they changed the direction of my teaching. After my sabbatical, I designed a course called Sociology of Animals and Society and incorporated a segment on companion animals into my already established curriculum. The research inspired by Laska also found its way into my original sabbatical project.

If Laska altered my intellectual life just as Levin had, her most dramatic influence was upon my emotions. Romans of antiquity designated some dogs as healers or "cynotherapists," believing that they could minister to the sick with soft, healing licks. Laska's sharp white teeth turned out to be more effective than the healing modalities I was using to uncover my past. She chewed right through the cellar door where my childhood self was still locked up.

REMEMBRANCE

Last week's breakthrough with Laska, when she curled in the crook of my legs on the orange futon, makes me want to celebrate our new happiness by reading my puppy journal from two years ago. I even have the idea of attempting to publish it. Yet I find myself hesitating. Why remember the bitter feelings I had over our misconnections, the self-hatred that arose whenever my far past crowded into the present, the daily defeats as a steward of her care? A three-and-a-half-year estrangement from my parents amplified the disharmony of Laska's puppyhood. It is no coincidence that my relationship with her improved around the same time that I reconciled with my mother and father. Why would I want now to evoke not just one, but two stories of family unhappiness?

Whenever I am puzzled by something substantial—remembrance, for example—I seek guidance from stories told by great writers of the past. This advice seeking may come from teaching courses on the classics of Western literature for eleven years. Over the years I have found the medieval poet Dante's *Divine Comedy* a virtual guidebook to the soul. I place my story of Laska and me next to Dante's tale the way the smallest circling moon is drawn to vast Jupiter. As a teacher, I discovered that his gravitational field affects my students too, though they often forget the Greek, Latin, and even biblical classics they have read. When I ask who has heard of Dante's *Inferno,* many raise their hands. Hell is memorable. It is the place where, utterly solitary even in the company of others, the eternally damned tell their stories with the compulsive repetition trauma causes. Having suffered a crisis of the soul that we moderns would recognize, Dante descends to the dreadful, unchanging world of hell with the Roman poet Virgil as his guide. Then, as now, guides are necessary for explorations of the soul. For the second part of his journey, Dante passes through Purgatorio—the place most like earth because there, spurred by hope and right action, souls can change. Lastly, to become fully restored to himself, Dante ascends to Paradiso, the unchanging realm of eternal joy and peace, guided by his beloved Beatrice. The *Inferno* often is taught without *Purgatorio* and *Paradiso,* a pedagogical decision that gives greater weight to vengeance and violence than to hope and joy. During my first year with Laska, I shared this partial view. Hell seemed everything—it was hard to see the good. Wisely Dante states: "But to give account of the good which I found there [on the whole journey] I will tell of the other things I noted there [in hell]."[5] I learn from him that you can't go up without first going down to the place of the "other things." If I am to tell Laska's and my story, I must include all of it.

THIS afternoon the past returns of its own accord as if demanding attention, and the upset it provokes makes me even more reluctant to read the journal. An encounter between Laska and a former dog trainer brings her puppyhood back with a jolt.

I come outside to meet Joyce, the thirty-year-old wife of one of the men who are reclapboarding portions of my house. Her flaxen skin is almost the same color as her hair and her eyebrows, all of which draws attention to her dark eyes. At this moment she is looking down at Maggie, a young Australian sheepdog tied up under a tree who belongs to another of the workers. The force of Joyce's stare arrests Maggie, who was about to jump. Instead, as if to make herself very small, Maggie tucks herself tidily right on Joyce's feet.

"She's a submissive dog," I say, comparing her to Laska.

"A submissive dog wouldn't try to jump up," Joyce corrects me, still standing straight-backed, staring at Maggie.

"You speak with authority," I say.

"I've had five years' experience training dogs," she replies.

The dog now turns her multicolored face up to Joyce, regarding her adoringly with yellow eyes. Though Joyce stares at Maggie, not at me, I feel my own spirit, against my will, bend to Joyce's.

Because she seems so competent, I decide to let Joyce meet Laska without intervening the way I usually do with guests. I learned from a trainer to keep

Laska's focus on me. When visitors come, I hold treats in my hand as I ask Laska to lie down and "relax," a command she learned after one utterance. "Relax!" means that she shifts her weight from the New York Forty-second Street library lion's crouch to a more casual position, extending her back leg on the floor. From this position she watches me with full attention and I reward her with treats while a visitor gets settled. Then I ask, "Would you like some cheese?" which keeps her interest on me. I stuff the end of a bone with cheese and Laska happily takes off to her fleecy blanket by the kitchen radiator. By the time she's finished licking the cheese out of the bone she's forgotten to accost my guest and wanders around the house amiably.

I bring Laska out on the deck with a leash to let Joyce meet her. She comes up to Joyce and sits when asked, allowing Joyce to pat her head. Soon, however, she gets nippy, turning her head rapidly from side to side, trying to grab Joyce's hand. Then she begins to jump. Joyce grabs her by the scruff of the neck and forces her to sit. Laska looks up at Joyce in surprise, quiets for a moment, then jumps at her face with open mouth. This time Joyce pushes her right down to the deck floor with her hand on her throat. Laska thrashes vigorously, showing her teeth as well as the whites of her eyes. She struggles free and lunges at Joyce, who forces her down again. Their contest seems to be happening in slow motion in front of me while a memory floods me in orange.

▼▼▼

I leave the door to the studio open by accident. Twelve-week-old Laska prances into the studio from the kitchen, tail held gaily, spots a ficus plant in a pot on the floor, and heads for it, just like a child would. I stamp in after her small, swiftly trotting figure; she already has a ficus leaf in her mouth. Not even knowing if the plant is harmful I "take her down." She thrashes wildly, whites of her eyes showing. Then she curls her lips so that her nose wrinkles and bares her needle-sharp teeth to the max. Shocked, I succeed in shutting Laska's mouth with my hand and yell, "No! Bad girl! Leave it!" Shaking with a scared rage, I pick my puppy up, my hand around her mouth. I feel Laska's teeth crunch together and don't even care if her tongue is between them. She still struggles, though much subdued, as I carry her out of the room and shut the door behind us. I am still shaking as I drop her rather rudely in her pen, which is in the living room, and sit down at the kitchen table.

▲▲▲

Rousing myself from the memory that transfixes me, I realize that Laska might feel betrayed by me *right now.*

"Let me take care of her," I say to Joyce and take Laska's leash, making her lie down by stepping on it near her collar.

Laska crouches there, looking up at me, her eyes still bright with challenge. Panting lightly, she keeps her ears half-forward and half-back, a visual sign of refusal to yield.

Joyce gazes at her, somewhat out of breath herself. Having heard Joyce say that as a trainer she "rewarded the good and ignored the bad," I am surprised when she offers, "If Laska had been my dog, I would have broken her will."

"I tried," I say, "but I wasn't able to." Relieved to have taken charge of Laska, I lead her into the house.

PRIMORDIAL ORANGE

Back inside I take Laska off her leash. She becomes the dog I am newly accustomed to, spirited and friendly. I fill her water dish, pour myself a drink of iced herbal tea, and sit down at the kitchen table. My chair faces the door to the studio, which is open. Rainbow flecks refracted from a prism that hangs in the studio window glide across the white wall like vivid memory fragments.

Joyce and Laska's tussle prompted a flashback about the ficus leaf episode. In a similar manner, flashbacks sometimes had followed moments of conflict between Laska and me during our first year. I would "remember" a childhood incident (from between eighteen months and age five) or one from when I was older.

These flashbacks did not begin with Laska. A year before she came along, I had been talking about my dreams and looking at cracked, yellowed photographs (many of them from infancy) in psychotherapy. I found these exercises upsetting, even though they had been my choice. I also had been meditating daily—as a novice, I frequently fell sleep. However, one July morning as I focused on breathing in and out, I noticed how I paused deeply between breaths, so much so that I could feel my heart beat against my ribs. Over the next few weeks I noticed other bodily states. They exuded from my breathing, the sound of my heart, positions in sleep, the silence of objects around me, or fear of my own hands on my thighs, as if they were someone else's hands. When I felt stuck (in line at the post office, for example), electric jolts streaked down my legs and weakened them. At times there was a hush inside me that waited for someone coming. Scene fragments of unaccountable lucidity seeded my dreams. Unlike the images that Laska had provoked, these bodily sensations (or images, in the case of dreams) seemed related to infancy, somewhere between six months and a year.

Research has shown that "memories," especially from the remote past, may not be real; additionally, such memories would not present themselves in narrative form. For example, beginning at around eighteen months, someone might be able to remember a very brief episode or fact, but not a sequence of events. Also, the present continually alters memories throughout a person's lifetime. Hence, memories rarely reproduce the past accurately.

The following narrative and several others in the journal that also come from my infancy or early childhood clearly are reconstructed memories. As such, they may well be creations of my mind and not accurate portrayals; I do not recount them for their truth. The flashbacks matter because the bodily states they describe greatly influenced my state of mind when Laska came along. Whether the flashbacks are accurate or not, I have come to believe that their essence (if not the details) reflects some emotional truth, however altered and rearranged by the complexities of the mind. I include them not as faithful accounts of literal truth, but as images that deeply affected my early relationship with Laska and forced me to confront myself.[6]

▼▼▼

I am an infant alone in a room. The wood lamp in the shape of a brown and white spotted dog crouches on its haunches. Its ears droop and its tongue protrudes. When you lift its extended paw, the light turns on. A wooden teaching clock with a pink round face, cheerful cheeks, and twinkling eyes sits beside it. Hands that extend from its snub nose tell the time if someone moves them. The lamp and the clock keep watch, but their wooden expressiveness is terrifyingly inert. Window curtains give off a fresh, laundered scent. When they blow lightly against the walls, the bright red apples, yellow lemons, and green leaves printed on their borders curve and fold. Their vivid hues warm my eyes and dance in my head. Whenever I breathe out, I pause, with only the thump of my heart to interfere, so that I can listen for someone coming. When I have to breathe in again, it feels sad to have to go on living all alone. The same breeze that moves the curtains touches my skin like the breath of someone near. But the muscles of my arms and legs yearn to be folded against my body as they were inside my mother. The pores on my skin open like the mouths of a million baby birds. Nourishing touch does not come.

What does come is ice and fire. This is what I know about love. The person I later call Mommy picks me up out of my crib, sits down in a chair, and sticks a rubber nipple into my mouth. The nipple is too long and the lukewarm milk comes too fast as I suck. I thrust my tongue against the nipple to keep from choking. She holds me on her knees, not close, and I stare at the white ceiling as I drink. When the bottle is empty, she puts me over her shoulder to burp me. I like the smell of her hair. Then she places me on the changing table across from my crib. She lays her hand on my belly to make sure I lie still. Her fingers are closed away from me in a loose fist.

"You stink," she says, and I can tell from her voice that this is bad.

As she changes my dirty diaper, she yanks my baby arms and legs. I look at her face for reassurance but it holds an absent expression. When she finishes she stands quietly for a moment, her closed hand on my belly. I'm full of milk and she seems more peaceful so I smile at her. Her face remains immobile, her eyes cast down. The sight alarms me so I look away to calm myself. I try again but her face hasn't changed. Now I'm so tense that I begin to hiccup. After a moment I spit up. I turn my face away from hers, whimper, and fall into a listless stare.

The person I later call Daddy comes into the room. "How's the kid?" he asks in a friendly voice.

"She ate and now she's spit up," a soft voice above me answers, annoyed.

"Here, I'll wipe her face off," he says.

He takes a clean diaper cloth and gently rubs it across my cheek. She leaves the room. I hear the door close behind her. The friendly sound of his voice and his gentle touch make me turn my head toward him. Unlike her pale, lashless eyes, his prominent eyes are dark, moist, and full of life. My belly softens, my whole body relaxes, and I smile at him. He picks me up, holds me against his chest, enfolds me in his arms, drawing my arms and legs up close against my body. I listen to the slow thud of his heart, feel him breathe in and out, and his breaths seem to pass through me. I nestle closer as if to embed myself in his chest forever. Too soon he puts me back on the changing table.

"What should we do now?" he asks.

I wriggle my stomach happily and he responds by tickling my ribs and knees until my body flies apart from terrifying surges of laughter. Because I am too worked up and don't know how to soothe myself, bubbly pains arise in my belly. My whole body stiffens, and I begin to cry.

"Would you like me to be Bippi, the sad-eyed clown? He knows how to get you to stop crying."

Even though my diaper is dry he undoes the safety pins in each corner. As he takes my diaper off he seems different from himself and I stop crying, out of alarm.

"Would you like me to sing you the ice cream song?" he asks. Bippi's voice cracks a little as he sings:

Bippi, Bippi, how nice it would seem,
The tip comes off in a smoosh of cream.

First he strokes my sides with two warm hands and runs them down my bowed baby legs. While he does this, he looks at me urgently with pleading eyes, so vivid they seem shiny wet. Then he reaches between my legs with large fingers and fumbles with my soft underparts, rubbing them over and over and touching a little bump with his finger tip until the fleshy V of me swells outward and my heartbeat and breath become riotous. Electric jolts streak down the insides of my legs and the inside of my lower body becomes heavy and drops down throbbing, pulling heart and lungs with it. Before my whole body empties through the swollen opening, I disappear up to the ceiling. I watch from there as he grips my thighs, extends his arms rigidly, screws his eyes shut, and purses his lips. When his eyes open again, he looks scared. I fear his large warm hands, his moist Bippi eyes. I crave them. I come back down from the ceiling onto the changing table. He doesn't notice that I've been gone. Bippi puts my diaper back on. He doesn't look at me while he brings the soft white cloth up between my legs and pins it on both sides. He puts me in my crib and leaves the room.

Even if I cry, I know that no one will come for a time longer than long. But I'm not sure I want anyone to. Frightening things happen when I am noticed. I begin to like the time between breaths, but I can't stop breathing. I am weary. I curl up on my side and enjoy the friendly warmth of my white wool blanket against my cheek. I draw my knees up to my chin. The arch of one foot locks into the arch of the other, as perfectly as pieces of a puzzle, and I sleep.

▲▲▲

A CHILD OF HER TIME

Ever since it came to me a year ago, I have attempted to place this first flashback in a social psychological context. Because of my recently acquired knowledge about memory, I am forced to concede that the correspondence between the flashback and the outside world, while compelling, must remain speculative.

My maiden great-aunt Len taught French at Hunter College. She adored my father, whom she'd helped through dental school, and when I, his firstborn, came along she devoted herself to reading advice books about babies. A small, stout woman, Aunt Len told my parents what to do with me, and because her unsolicited advice filled an interest gap, it did not go unheeded. At twenty-nine, my father was preoccupied with setting up his dental practice. My mother was profoundly depressed and enraged over a traumatic childbirth that left her with an unwanted child. I don't mean to single her out—other women of her generation and circumstance (middle-class with little opportunity for a life outside the home) have told me, "I wish I'd never had children." I was an accident conceived on the floor of my father's office, since my grandparents' house where my parents first lived after getting married offered little privacy.

In the 1940s, fathers were not allowed in the delivery room and while my mother labored, my father enjoyed dinner and a few Lucky Strikes at his brother's house. A second cultural norm compounded my mother's misery—physicians routinely used high forceps to pull babies out. The clumsy metal spoons that scarred my face lightly, tore and stretched my mother's pelvic floor muscles. Equally serious, it left "'a tear in her psyche.'" Naturalist and author Sally Carrighar quotes this phrase in her book *Home to the Wilderness* to describe the effect on her own mother of a high forceps birth. She explains that such deliveries can forever distort a woman's perception of her child. Though helpless infants, Sally Carrighar and I were regarded as menaces. Both of us were "difficult" babies, which exaggerated the misperception. I suffered from colic and may have shared Sally's oversensitivity to stimuli. When a temporary lack of oxygen occurs during a complicated birth, it can cause minimal nerve damage. Sally was injured in this way and as a baby suffered from stress and was not easy to soothe.

The 1940s weren't a good time to be a baby in need of comfort. Advice books instructed parents to feed babies on a strict four-hour schedule and never to pick them up when they cried. This method of child rearing perfectly mirrored my mother's need to keep me at a distance. Few people, including researchers, understood that a dissociated mother can disturb a baby greatly. In the 1970s, evolutionary psychologist John Bowlby argued that a baby's attachment to its mother is vital to healthy development. In order to thrive, all young mammals need secure attachment to their caretakers. In their book *Ghosts from the Nursery: Tracing the Roots of Violence,* Robin Karr-Morse and Meredith S. Wiley explain the effect of a depressed mother on a baby:

> Through tiny subtle exchanges like normal eye contact, and the timing of vocalizations and touch, mothers and caregivers teach their infants a series of coordinated interactive behaviors that shape the babies' efforts to regulate their own feelings. The baby of a depressed mother learns, as all babies learn. In this case, however, the baby learns a series of miscoordinated interactive failures in which the reciprocal and synchronous aspect of normal interactions is missing or greatly reduced. The result is often withdrawal by the baby, as well as diminished expectations of attention and comfort from others. Babies generalize the behavior mirrored from the depressed mother to strangers.[7]

Karr-Morse and Wiley go on to describe the effects on a baby of a parent like my father, who was soothing one moment and frightening the next:

> A totally different pattern exists when the parent is abusive. Here the caregiver's behavior may be even more unpredictable. The parent not only fails to respond positively to a baby's signals but also erratically inflicts pain when the baby signals for comfort. In this situation, children learn that they can't make the world work to meet their needs effectively and that they need to be vigilant for signs of coming assaults.[8]

A baby in distress needs someone to calm it, not to excite it. Unfortunately, my father delighted in "getting a rise" out of me and if terror was an ingredient, he liked it even more. I once watched him tickle six-month-old Levin, who was propped up in a baby seat. My father made my son laugh until the laughter became hysterical, and I became anxious as Levin's cohesion, fragile enough at his age, disintegrated. I remember his small face in profile, blurred from the frantic laughing, yet my father wouldn't stop. I strode over and sharply lifted Levin out of reach.

I gained some insight into this wild-card side of my father only when I was in my fifties and my father in his eighties. It happened over the phone. I had called to ask that he reconsider his and my mother's decision to cut off financial help for my psychotherapy. The timing was especially bad because I was just beginning to have hazy recollections of sexual abuse. This was a year before the Bippi memory arose.

"It's no one in the family," I assured him, although I did not know if that were true. Then I continued, "But it is so important that I keep on with my therapy work. The memories are very upsetting."

Silence. Then my father said, "I was sexually abused."

Now *I* was the silent one. My father rarely spoke of his childhood and I had little experience asking him questions about it.

"What happened?" I asked as I peered down the phone line as if trying to see his face.

"On my way home from school some boys chased me . . . into a stable," he answered matter-of-factly, but then cleared his throat as if it had tightened.

I wanted to hear the whole story more than I had ever wanted to hear anything in my life, but all that came out was, "So how did you get over it?"

"I don't know," he replied, with a shrug in his voice. "I just did." I knew he intended his words to be a lesson to me.

Oh no, Dad, I thought to myself. You have acted out the spirit of those moments over and over in an attempt to shake off the terror and helplessness you felt. My heart constricted as I imagined him at, say, age nine. His breath was fire in his lungs from running hard and his thin legs shook as a gang of boys forced him down in the straw with the mocking words "Jew boy." The horses that pulled trolleys paced nervously in their stalls, their eyes, so much like his, mirrored his fear but not the horror, which he suffered alone.

His disclosure shifted the focus from my trauma to his, a dynamic that characterized my relationship with him. I knew that the conversation was over and that I had lost. I hung up the phone obsessed not about the loss of therapy money, but about how I had missed an opportunity to learn more about my father. Was his confession related to the brief disclosure he once made years ago—that a gang of boys in the Jersey City of his childhood had chased after him, calling out, "Jew boy"? It was typical of my whole life with my father that there never was a satisfying completion to anything. He would slip away and I would be left with traces of moments to extract love or understanding from. It reminded me of a hike I once took in my twenties up Mt. Katahdin in Maine. I had run out of water so I dipped a bandanna into fresh rain pooled shallowly in a rock. I sucked eagerly on the cloth but the water was scant and though I twisted and twisted the bandanna, no more drops came.

Aunt Len's tutelage, my father's childhood trauma, and my mother's absent attention were fatal ingredients as a recipe for infant care. Yet, behaviorist James B. Watson, whose ideas shaped child rearing in the 1940s, would have found only one thing amiss in my family. He regarded the sexual stimulation of babies, which apparently was a common practice throughout the culture, as a form of "coddling." As Christina Hardyment explains in *Dream Babies: Three Centuries of Good Advice on Child Care:* "Watson felt that the key to success in bringing up a better baby was not to over-stimulate the love-response by too much stroking. 'There are rocks ahead for the over-kissed child.' Mothers and nurses had discovered by trial and error the efficacy of caressing the child's lips, ears, back of neck and sex organs in order to quiet it."[9]

In my family Aunt Len might have encouraged the Bippi side of my father. As I learned from my sister Karen when we were adults, Aunt Len's self-soothing habit was so strong that she masturbated in front of Karen when my sister was about thirteen years old. My sister and I had shared a room before I went off to college. After, Len sometimes slept over in my old bed when she came to my parents' house for dinner; that way, she wouldn't have to travel uptown alone at night. Karen said that she could hear Len masturbating in my bed, which was just across from hers. While Aunt Len approved of the restrictions on feeding and holding babies, she was unlikely to have agreed with Watson's warning against masturbating them.

Watson himself aroused babies, but under the safe cover of research. In her article "It's All in the Upbringing," Joanne Cavanaugh Simpson states that Watson "dropped (and caught) infants to generate fear and suggested that stimulation of the genital area would create feelings of love." What he meant by love I can only guess at; to me, masturbating a baby administers a deadly potion that mixes love with chaos. Few people in the field criticized Watson's "chilling project" or the ethics of his research, at least publicly.[10]

Newborn care in U.S. hospitals also eerily legitimated my parents' behavior toward me. Most mothers in the 1940s gave birth in a hospital, and all across the country, hospitals contained central nurseries with plastic bassinets (aptly called "isolettes") set in military rows. In the isolettes the babies cried, their eyes screwed shut. To quiet them, nurses often rubbed the infants' sex organs because it took less time than rocking them and because every one thought that babies didn't remember. Even the most respected minds of the day thought that the world was just a booming, buzzing confusion to the very young. From feeding a baby only every four hours, to letting it cry without comfort, to masturbating it as a form of silencing, the culture controlled a baby's body and sanctioned what seem to have been the unfortunate psychological needs of my parents. At the same time their ignorance and unhappiness caused me suffering. Neither disrespect nor blame motivates me to write; simply, I am the sole participant observer of my childhood—there is no one else to tell the story.

It is a story I wouldn't have remembered fully if it weren't for the ministrations of Laska's rude, innocent ways.

SKUNK CABBAGE

I open the door to the woodshed and discover that a skunk has been living inside. It dug entrance and exit holes in the dirt floor and chewed on bags of cocoa mulch, cow manure, and several cardboard boxes. It ruined my snow tires by chewing on the rims, still covered with rock salt from the winter roads. I've known a skunk was around because I smelled it in the yard and twice on Laska when she got "skunked" at night. I washed her down with douche solution, which I find works better than tomato juice or even official skunk-smell removers.

Laska follows me inside and sniffs around the dirt floor indented with delicate skunk pawprints. To my human nose there is no scent of skunk in the shed.

I come out first; Laska follows and throws herself down on the grass. Creeping along on her belly she pushes her muzzle into the grass, first on the left side then on the right. She used exactly this motion when trying to rid herself of skunk scent that thickly clung to her fur. Yet, Laska wasn't skunked just now. The faint smell of the animal in the shed arouses a memory that causes her to react to the present as if it were the past. Watching her crawl across the grass in alligator fashion, I feel a new kinship. We *both* struggle with flashbacks.

"It's OK, darlink," I say, using a recently adopted term of affection that came from my Russian grandparents.

Laska raises her head and begins to pant lightly. Her eyes lose the vacant look they held a moment ago when she was lost in a memory.

"You weren't skunked," I add gently.

Still lying in the grass she thumps her tail, and as she looks fully into my face, her eyes brighten. My recognition of her seems to draw her out of herself.

This moment of communion makes me reluctant, once again, to revisit our past, which could disrupt our hard-won accord. I remember Mary Oliver's poem "Skunk Cabbage," a title that, according to the dictionary, refers to "an ill-smelling, eastern North American swamp plant having minute flowers enclosed in a mottled greenish or purplish spathe" (which, to paraphrase the dictionary, is a leaflike plant part that encloses a flower). Oliver describes the plant in spring:

Skunk Cabbage
And now as the iron rinds over
the ponds start dissolving,
you come, dreaming of ferns and flowers
and new leaves unfolding,
upon the brash
turnip-hearted skunk cabbage
slinging its bunched leaves up
through the chilly mud.
You kneel beside it. The smell
is lurid and flows out in the most
unabashed way, attracting
into itself a continual spattering
of protein. Appalling its rough
green caves, and the thought
of the thick root nested below, stubborn
and powerful as instinct!

But these are the woods you love,
where the secret name
of every death is life again — a miracle
wrought surely not of mere turning
but of dense and scalding reenactment. Not
tenderness, not longing, but daring and brawn
pull down the frozen waterfall, the past.
Ferns, leaves, flowers, the last subtle
refinements, elegant and easeful, wait
to rise and flourish.
What blazes the trail is not necessarily pretty.[11]

The skunk cabbage precedes the finer, delicate plants, for rude force is needed to "pull down the frozen waterfall, the past."

Dante encouraged me to look at the depths as well as the heights of human experience, an approach Brian Swimme and Thomas Berry echoed when they said that humans "give voice" to "exalted and terrible feelings." In a similar manner, Mary Oliver emboldens me to look at what is "not necessarily pretty"; in particular, her poem clarifies the true reason I resist looking back. What wasn't pretty was *myself.*

In the childhood flashbacks I experienced in meditation, I was more sinned against than sinning. But when conflicts with Laska provoked additional flashbacks and caused me to mistreat her, I lost my innocence. Some dog owners and trainers might consider acceptable such corrections as yanking a dog's leash to get her to mind, hitting her over the head with an empty plastic Coke bottle, swatting her on top of her muzzle, spraying her with a water bottle, or even making her eat her own stool sprinkled with Tabasco sauce to discourage coprophagia (eating of feces). Perhaps the intention behind the action makes a difference. My reactions were full of rage and fear. What made my behavior even more repugnant to me was that I don't believe in corporal punishment and had never resorted to it in raising my son.

Because Laska's and my relationship was alinguistic, it aroused *prelinguistic,* or primordial, responses in me that had their origins in the attachment disorders I developed during my early childhood. (I say "disorders" in the plural because, as Karr-Morse and Wiley explain, mothers and fathers can pose different attachment problems for babies.) A small, toothy puppy became a source of alarm. Many unhappy human/canine relationships have similar roots. Frank Ascione's and Phil Arkow's groundbreaking book *Child Abuse, Domestic Abuse, and Ani-*

mal Abuse: Linking the Circles of Compassion for Prevention and Intervention reveals the connection between violence toward animals and human domestic violence. Both acts usually originate in the childhood mistreatment suffered by the perpetrator. A double vision oscillates throughout my journal of Laska's first year that reminds me of the wild animal images on a ruler I keep on my desk. It belonged to Levin as a child and in moments between working at my laptop I play with it. The long narrow scene holds elephant, lion, and giraffe parents and offspring. You can animate the figures by tilting the ruler toward or away from you. The lioness, for example, either beams at her cub or roars at it fiercesomely. Laska's and my situation was more complex. Often I saw *her* as the lioness and myself as the cub.

Perhaps our predicament is not that uncommon. The growing number of advice books and the unhappy statistics from animal shelters suggest that raising and training a dog isn't easy. Currently, 38 percent of U.S. households keep canine companions, which roughly amounts to 50 million dogs. In *Between Pets and People: The Importance of Animal Companionship,* Alan Beck and Aaron Katcher explain that more than 70 percent of people considered their pets to be members of their family. Yet so many families abandon or give their dogs up before the age of eighteen months. The national adoption rate is only 50 percent; and five to ten million dogs are killed each year. A friend of mine who volunteers for Labrador Retriever Rescue, an organization that places orphaned Labradors, said that most of the problems were "situational"; family dynamics rather than the dog's disposition caused the relationship to fail. Memoirs by dog owners do not tend to recount these difficult relationships; rather, they tend to feature the dog-as-therapist theme. Parts of my journal share this self-serving perspective—Laska as guide to the vagaries of my psyche. I use the term "self-serving" because I don't want my needs to determine the meaning and worth of Laska's life.

Laska's and my situational disturbance cleared up once I trained *myself* to maintain a calm and steady manner with her. When my behavior quieted, she became more willing to accommodate my requests regarding her behavior (she still tests me, but I've come to enjoy her independence). I don't know if Laska loves me unconditionally; we expect this emotion from our dogs, perhaps unfairly, and the absence of it may cause us to reject or turn against them. If Laska has affection for me now, the sentiment is based on respect, an attachment that was impossible until I treated *her* with respect and developed a healthy self-regard by achieving insight into my own past.

The poem "Skunk Cabbage" encourages me to consider our troubled first year (the "appalling . . . rough green caves" and "thick root" that pushed up out of the "chilly mud") as necessary to the "subtle refinements" of the happy relationship that has come after for both me *and* Laska.

I believe that our story has a necessary place in the literature on companion animals.

BEGINNINGS

Besides seeking advice from the great writers in Western tradition, I reread them for a childlike reason. I have developed a love of customary lines and scenes. In much the same way, Levin knew where the little gray mouse hid on every page of *Goodnight Moon,* a bedtime favorite. He loved to point the creature out with his small index finger when I read the story to him.

If I were to ask, When does my story with Laska begin? I would think of the opening to Homer's *Iliad,* from around 750 BCE (before the common era). "Begin it when," Homer sings, plunging the reader into an argument between King Agamemnon, brother of Menelaos, and his great warrior, Achilles, over rights to a beautiful slave girl, Briseis, a spoil of war. When I first read the *Iliad* in midlife as a teaching assistant in a humanities course, having returned to graduate school, I had no idea what was happening for pages and pages of the epic. I decided to just keep on reading in the hope that eventually I'd find the story intelligible. Scholars surmise that Homer's audience knew exactly how to place this beginning moment of the story, being familiar with the common store of cultural tales.

Without tradition as a guide, I must create my own entry point for my and Laska's story. Let's say it begins at the start of the monthly journal I kept of Laska's and my first year.

Yet does it? For the story extends backward to the estrangement from my parents three-and-a-half years before Laska arrived. It goes back even further to the cultural and familial world of my childhood and infancy (hidden inside the crumbling building from the dream I recounted in *Bearing Meaning*). Or does it begin with my parents' parents and the historical time in which they raised children? Wherever the beginning point of any story may be, the living and the dead shape our lives.

This web of causality causes me to rethink an idea Caroline Knapp proposed in her memoir about herself and her dog, *Pack of Two: The Intricate Bond between People and Dogs.* Like me, Knapp lived on her own. At first, her supposition that she and her canine companion, Lucille, constitute a "pack of two" appealed to me. I liked the way she played on ethological research that explains dog behavior based on dogs being pack animals. Knapp goes on to argue that there is nothing pathological about a human and a nonhuman animal making community with one another.

Though we lived alone, during that first year with Laska I felt the influence of my family and, importantly, what social psychologist George Herbert Mead calls the "generalized other"—the commonly held beliefs and practices, past and present, of the society I belong to. The pack of many also included the influence of Laska's lineage—her family of origin, her Labrador retriever breed (Labradors actually originate from Newfoundland), and the ten-thousand-year history of dogs living alongside humans. These numerous presences enlarge our story considerably.

Yet, like Homer, I choose the invocation, "Begin it when . . . ," open my journal about the first year of Laska's life, and read.

Journal

JANUARY 1997 — JANUARY 1998

January 1997

Meeting

JANUARY 9

TODAY I imagine that Sarah, our Labrador retriever who died in 1995 at age eleven, begins her life over again. Holding an unknown puppy up to my face just the way I held Sarah twelve years ago, I think it is she.

My son, Levin, then twelve, had wanted a female puppy. We traveled to the north shore of Massachusetts to look at a litter in a breeder's home. There were two female pups, each with fat bellies, tapered tails that stood straight up, and sturdy but unsteady legs. I picked one up and held it to my face. She looked away. I put her down and caught the other one. I brought her face close. Her eyes stayed on mine only for a moment, yet a sweet liquor of yearning streamed out toward me. To my happiness Levin chose that second puppy.

This time the search for a dog sends me from Burlington on icy roads south instead of north, to Stacey Anderson, a breeder in Springfield, Vermont. The Green Mountains have changed since I drove through them last summer. Then they swelled softly under the cover of leafy trees. Now the view is more severe. The naked tree trunks look like dark lines etched into the gray, creased rock of the upper slopes. Several horses stand stiffly in a winter pasture. Ice hangs off their shaggy unkempt coats and their breath sends white puffs of steam into the air. These chilly sights mirror a certain cold that has lingered around my heart since Sarah's death.

I arrive at Stacey's modest ranch-style house. Waiting for her to come out of the rescue shelter she built behind her house, I stop at one of the outdoor cages.

A tall, rangy, black dog with ears that stand up and then flop over (a Labrador-Doberman mix, I am later told) looks at me with Sarah's eyes from behind the metal grating. His look beseeches me to take *him.*

A short while later I sit on a metal chair in Stacey's kitchen. Yellow and black Labrador puppies surround me, shouldering each other, grabbing at ears or muzzles with sharp little teeth, bringing one another down with a mouth to the throat. Because of Sarah I want a black female. Once again, there are two black females to choose from. First I pick up the smaller puppy, the one with a thin red string around her neck, who prances gaily. With the Labrador-Doberman still on my mind, I try to focus on the puppy I hold. She squints as if she doesn't want to look at me. I put her down and pick up the larger puppy. This one stares right into my eyes with a fuzzy but confident look. An impossible hope rising, my heart asks, "Sarah, is that you?" I cannot see her clearly through my glasses so I push them up on top of my head. I am aware of the strain to my hands, weakened by arthritis, from the weight of her. The changes in my body counsel me that this moment is not the one of long ago. I bring the puppy close to lick my nose, but she will not and turns her face. Putting her down on the floor I again take up the one with the red string. She squints as before but licks my face with a "Hey, why not?" air. I release her to the floor, remembering that the newest books on puppies advocate much more sophisticated methods of choosing a puppy than the look-you-in-the-eyes and lick-you-on-the-nose test. You can judge their personalities by a series of behavioral tests. Though I carefully read this advice before looking for a new puppy, I decided that since Sarah had been such a great dog I would follow the same approach we had used with her.

I pick up the puppy who looked at me without squinting and hold her on my lap. She sits quite still, her back to me, looking with interest at the floor. One littermate has another by the neck. When the downed puppy yelps, the other one releases his grip and immediately ends up in the same predicament. The puppy I am holding braces her sturdy legs against my thighs and I notice a quiet concentration that I like. Observing her equanimity I am angry at myself for soliciting that lick on the nose. Out of my loneliness for Sarah I asked for a speeded-up intimacy. Despite this insight I hold my hand up to her face and she licks it.

How do I choose? Perhaps because of her squint, the puppy with the red string collar produces a negative magnetic pull in me. The sensation reminds me of the black and white Scotch terrier magnets you could buy from a machine at Howard Johnson's when I was a kid; they repelled at one pole and attracted at the other. Toward the puppy on my lap I feel a positive tug. Though she has given me a confident rather than a yearning look, I like her for it. I like, too, her small refusal, when she would not lick my nose, of my large need for love. As she sits with composure, I look at her small, perfectly formed shoulder blades. I run my fingers over the soft whorl of fur on her chest. She is the one. I set her down among her brothers and sisters, whom she can't leave until she is seven weeks old. I write out a check for the deposit, put my coat on, and leave. As I make my way to the car over the icy snow I feel the shelter dog follow me with his eyes. I keep looking straight ahead.

JANUARY 11

SINCE picking out a puppy I catch myself daydreaming about having back the two things I have missed most, living without a dog: their loving eyes and companionship outdoors. I say, "catch myself" because I feel disloyal to Sarah. From the first moment I held her as a pup, Sarah had a yearning look. As she matured, she kept that trait. Toward the end of her life she developed a habit of ducking under my legs when I sat at the round living-room table where I worked. With just her shoulders sticking out, she would turn her head up to look at me, pulling her ears back and flattening them so that the skin smoothed away from her expressive eyes, bringing them into a prominence that verged on nakedness. Her short, black, dense eyelashes did not shelter her look so much as make it feminine. The small hollows above her eyes, which deepened with age, carried time inside them. Looking up at me with her brown liquid eyes, even with their milky cast, Sarah radiated a sweetness like translucent golden honey when it catches the light. Her look was so truthful and deep (as if I could see straight into her soul) that I became emboldened to trust what could be trusted in the world. And time slowed down like a quieted heart.

Our walks together were no less a communion. Sarah's and my favorite place was a beach on Martha's Vineyard, where I have spent several weeks each summer, ever since my son's father and I broke up over twenty years ago. The beach lies at the foot of a cliff that was a gently sloping meadow before the ocean washed half the meadow away. Just under its summit the cliff is pitted with Cappadocian cavelike dwellings where swallows have bored into the ruddy sand. They flit in and out of the dark square holes as if they are souls on retreat from the world. The base of the cliff is clay, cracked in the sun's heat or slick when wet. The colors are rich and varied—shades of gray, red, yellow, and white. An unkempt layer of topsoil hangs over the top of the cliff. Despite their exposed roots, the meadow grasses keep growing right up to where the ocean takes them. Eroding several feet per year, the cliff never looks the same from summer to summer.

Whenever I return after winter and see the changes, I am reminded of the poet Wallace Stevens's words—there is no "imperishable bliss." What's more, impermanence (he uses the harsher word "death") is "the mother of beauty." [1]

Sarah and I used to walk at dawn, heading south along the expanse of dun-colored sand, the cliff on our left and the booming ocean on our right. Where the cliff ends, a low, continuous ridge of dune begins, with fresh green grass poking up in clumps. Behind the ridge is a brackish pond, in front a ragged, dark edge of sea debris—seaweed, sharks' eggs, and broken shells, including those of tiny crabs.

If I close my eyes, I can picture Sarah on one of the walks we took together during our last vacation just a few weeks before she died. A black, compact shape, she trotted along slightly ahead of me. Her haunches, moving in a less springy motion than they had the summer before, looked tired, and her panting exposed her worn-down teeth. Yet she tilted her head up in a jaunty way, glancing back at me with her expressive eyes. Sarah's look told me of her pleasure despite the diminished power of her body. She no longer chased the tide cast onto the sand in frothy loops, delicate as lace, but she still crossed over the dunes to the pond, looking for Canada geese and long-necked swans, then reappeared, her head up, looking for me as I looked for her.

Sarah's animal joy drew me out of myself. Entirely free of fear, I became continuous with the booming ocean, gray-green with fresh white crests like horses' manes blown back, with the numberless grains of sand, with the pink-blue morning sky stretching every which way without end.

I can feel myself resist accepting that the perishable bliss I had with Sarah is over; at the same time I marvel at the stubborn nature of the heart. I saw Sarah die a natural death. Decreed by nature, her death couldn't have been more final. Yet my heart refuses what my eyes saw. Frustrated with myself, I come to see that standing stock-still against change is a form of love, though not as evolved, perhaps, as letting go. I must be patient. Life has a way of taking care of itself. This new puppy surely will nip my heels into the present.

JANUARY 13

EVER since I was a child, animals have been my solace. At first, horses. Their large, liquid eyes and unpredictability mixed them up with my father, who "played horses" with me, as I called it, bucking me off his back. My father took me for my first real horseback rides in Texas, where we lived during the war. I preferred Zan Zac, the brown trotting pony, to Pokey, the white walking pony. My spine bent pliantly and I laughed with pleasure as I bounced up and down on Zan Zac's back.

I drew horses from the time I could hold a pencil. As I traced the satisfying curve of the creature's neck and back, my body hummed. The line felt like an invocation, as if the drawing would become a live animal. Apparently, Paleolithic peoples, famous for their beautiful cave paintings of animals, imagined that the forms they traced on the walls summoned animals to them, assuring a good hunt. I think of my horse drawings as belonging to the Paleolithic days of early childhood, when a wish can come true.

I conjured a long-faced horse with a mournful expression who looked just like my father, and a square-faced horse—my father's creation—with a strong jaw and a line down the side of his cheek that made him look grave. My parents saved my childhood drawings, even dated them, and I now have them. I was about four years old when my father and I made the first image in the collection. He drew a horse with firm, straight lines, and I added the rider in a child's hand. My father's horse became a template for my favorite of the two types. I often depicted him looking with kindly attention at a young girl seated on his back, her hair in pigtails. In an effort to understand my past better, I recently looked at the drawings along with photographs from my childhood. I discovered that the square-faced horse resembled my grandfather. Insecure about his own looks, my father more than once had told me, "Mike, was he *handsome.*" I also discovered something about my own unconscious desires when I looked at the pictures. After my son's father and I divorced, I fell in love with a man with a strong jaw and a grave line down his cheek. At age forty I found and then lost the square-faced horse that my child's imagination had conjured.

Besides drawing horses, my main connection to animals came through books. I stared at the illustrations so intently that, like the drawings, they came alive. Slender-legged deer in *Bambi* (the original version by Felix Salten) leapt one after the other behind a stand of fir trees, dark shapes against the deep snow. The albino stallion Thunderhead, in a book by the same name, fought with his father; with his yellow teeth bared, the whites of his eyes showing, his large ragged hoof started up a line of blood on the older stallion's shoulder. Then there was the black horse in *Chinky Joins the Circus* who stood perched on a box, his four hooves close together as he bent his proud neck down to receive a treat reward. Though too young to read the words, I knew the stories because my father read them to me as I sat beside him. While he read, he often absently brushed a stray lock of hair behind my ear or rubbed my forehead with his large warm hand. What I liked most of all was that the stories always were the same. No surprises ever happened. Even the sad or scary things, you knew about ahead of time.

Perhaps I loved my father *through* horses. His ungovernable feelings frightened me, despite the sweeter moments I enjoyed with him. The square-faced horse with his calm, dignified attentiveness must have represented a dream of how I wanted my father to be. Yet I loved horses for their wild side, for the promise of freedom and defiance they offered. The muscles under their shiny coats pulsed with life, their explosive energy filling me with joy. I loved their eyes, gentle as a doe's, as well as the naked expression when they flattened their ears and extended their heads in anger. I loved it when, as a newborn foal, Thunderhead struggled to reach his mother's teat and, "finding the bone of the thigh, instead, . . . gave a savage bite at it and kicked out in anger."[2] His unbridled rage enlivened me.

I trusted animals more than humans. You knew where you stood with them. I even preferred storybooks in which animals did not talk. In the world of my family, talk often wasn't kind, got you into trouble, or wore you out. My mother would call me "stinky" if I smelled bad or "pesky" if I bothered her or "little Miss Know-It-All" if I opposed her.

My limited popularity with my mother depended upon my speaking precociously at social gatherings. I once told her party guests that our car, stopped at a traffic light, "had died but its heart was still beating." On another occasion I told another crowd that the moon "had broke"—it was in its quarter phase. My mother liked me on those nights.

My father favored me when I was "animated," as he put it. The trouble was that I was Pinocchio to his Geppetto: he took an interest only when he was the source of my aliveness. On the lighter side, he liked to catch my face on film in a moment of surprise, as when my mother brought out the seven-layer ice cream cake with frozen sweet cream frosting they ordered each year for my birthday. On the darker side, he enjoyed my reactions when he imitated a gorilla. At bedtime he might appear in the doorway and shuffle toward me, somehow elongating his arms, which he swung back and forth. By walking on the outer soles of his feet, he made his legs look bowed. He hunched his head into his shoulders, growled menacingly, and thumped his chest as he closed in on me. No screams of protest helped. The more terrified I became, the more he liked it.

Worn out from having to earn my parents' love and from feeling that human relating was hazardous, I longed for the animal silence of my companions in books. I fell in love with dogs when I discovered Albert Payson Terhune's classics about collies. By then I was in early grade school. I shared with my cousin Judy, six months older, a love of these books almost as great as our love of giggling. We read Terhune in the years we spent summer vacations on Cape Cod. Each week Judy's father drove us to Hyannis for another book—*Lad a Dog, Treve, Wolf.* They were hardcovers with colorful portraits of the collies on the jacket. Before starting each book I opened it and buried my nose in the pages, loving the scent of the fresh white paper. I loved the courage of Terhune's dogs. As he described them, "A collie down is not a collie beaten"; and he wrote of their steadfast loyalty, "Perfect love casteth out all fear." [3] I wanted a collie of my own right then, or at least some day.

Live animals didn't come until later. One early attempt to bring an animal into the family ended abruptly. When I was three, my parents brought a kitten home. "It's wild and it's going back," they said that same morning. I remember their fear as they pulled the dusty kitten out from where it had lodged itself in the refrigerator motor.

The next family pet came many years later—a canary. It lived in a cage. In seventh grade, when the assignment was to write about my best friend, I had written an essay on Charky, our neighbor's dog at Candlewood Lake in Danbury, Connecticut, where we spent summers and weekends in winter. He was a mix of Labrador and some kind of spaniel. Charky had silky black fur and brown points on his legs and eyebrows. I remember his expression as direct, simple, and loyal. Like me, Charky adopted a family to get what he could not find at home. I had attached myself to a commercial artist's family who lived year-round in our summer community. The Rolands and their three children seemed full of love for one another and, like Carson McCullers's lonely girl in *The Member of the Wedding,* I thought of them as the "we of me."

Whenever we were in Connecticut, Charky came to our home and he and I spent long hours together outdoors; my mother did not allow him in the house. An excerpt from my first poem, written at age fourteen, described a moment Charky and I often shared:

> The dog and I would race down the wild section
> of gray-brown land.
> I would be proud because I knew every rock and every
> rise of ground
> The whole way down, never having to look once as I strove
> to match the dog's pace.
> Then we would reach the bottom, my hair tangled
> and smelling of wind and last year's leaves.
> I'd stand there panting for air and watch the dog as he
> listened quietly.
> We'd both be trembling a little, at being warm and alive
> in the dead season around us.

Charky and I frequently walked down to Candlewood Lake at night. He was as dark as the unlit macadam, but I could feel him return to my side after he explored a tantalizing scent in the grass that flanked the road. When we reached the water, I lay down on the pier and looked up at the night sky embedded with stars. I could smell his fur, damp from lake water, as he rested beside me.

When we left for the city, Charky chased after our car for as much as two miles. Watching through the rear window, I felt anguish for him as his tongue swelled large and pink to cool his body down from his exertions.

During the last year of high school I stayed in New York on weekends, enjoying the chance to be alone. One day, after graduation, I was sitting in the family car. We were about to leave for a weekend in Connecticut, the first time since the fall that I would join the family. I was in the car with my father waiting for my mother and sister, who were delayed upstairs. My father looked at me with his sad eyes and said abruptly, "Charky died of distemper this spring. We didn't want to tell you until you were done with school, so as not to upset you." I stared at the rearview mirror in which I would never again see Charky's devoted chase of our retreating car. I wept bitterly for his death and for having forgotten him in the tumult of my own life.

When I entered high school, our family got a Siamese cat. He had rich chocolate markings, a broad head, wide-set blue eyes, and a strong build. Though my parents, my sister, and I often were not on speaking terms with one another, all of our lips left kisses between Suki's ears. The top of his head seemed the only place where harmony existed. Suki shared my affections with Charky, but ours was an indoor relationship. Choosing me as his favorite, Suki sat on my books when I tried to study and at night slept crowded up against me, using my behind as a pillow. When I left for college, Suki transferred his loyalty to my mother. He lived to be sixteen, and the night he died Suki crawled painfully up onto my mother's bed to say goodbye. Then he left her and lay down in his litter box, as if to merge with what must be discarded. My mother found him curled on his side there in the morning.

In 1978, when Levin was six years old, we returned from summer vacation to find a calico kitten inside the chain-link fence that surrounded our tiny yard. She was quite wild and had made a lair for herself in the tall grass that I hadn't cut for lack of a mower. Anytime we approached her, she hid there, only her fresh young face peeking out. We put out a bowl of milk for her each day. One morning she came up to Levin, who was standing beside the dish, and brushed against his leg. The next day we put the bowl inside and left the door open. Gingerly she came up the stairs and walked into the house. Levin named the kitten Snowy, after Tintin's dog in his favorite comic book. Snowy gave birth to a litter of kittens well before she was a year old. I called it a teenage pregnancy. We kept one calico, which Levin named Zorro because she had a Z-shaped black marking on her forehead.

Sarah came along in 1984 because Levin, age twelve, wanted a dog. Her arrival created a new situation for our two cats. Snowy had no fear of the lively puppy, but Zorro was terrorized. Sarah sensed the difference and pursued Zorro anytime she was on the floor, so Zorro spent most of her day on top of an upright piano in the living room, staring balefully down at Sarah. After Levin left home, the three animals remained with me. In 1994, when Snowy was fifteen, she suddenly lost weight and her coat looked dry and unkempt, yet the vet could find nothing wrong with her. One morning after a thunderstorm she disappeared, departing as mysteriously from our life as she had arrived. Zorro outlived Sarah so that at least in her golden years she had the freedom to hang out anywhere she wanted. I gave her to a student in preparation for bringing a rambunctious puppy into the house.

The puppy I chose a few days ago is the first animal of my very own. In a strange way it feels as if I've bought her in part for the small girl I once was who longed for a creature to breathe beside her.

JANUARY 15

IT wasn't until the week before Levin was born that I found a name for him in my favorite book, *Anna Karenin,* which his father, Eric, gladly accepted. We both had read Tolstoy when we were fellow students in college. So there is no point in getting anxious that, as yet, I have no name for the puppy. Actually, I'm thinking of taking a second name from *Anna Karenin.* Levin, a central character in the book based on Tolstoy himself, has a dog. I remember a scene with this dog, a female, when the character Levin returns home to his estate in the country after a disappointment in love. Tolstoy writes:

> Laska kept poking her head under his hand. He stroked her and she curled up at his feet, her head on her outstretched hind-paw. And in token that everything was well and all right now, she opened her mouth a little, smacked her flabby lips, and settling them more comfortably over her old teeth she subsided into blissful repose. Levin watched these last movements of hers attentively.
>
> 'I shall go and do likewise!' he said to himself. 'I shall go and do likewise! Nothing's amiss . . . all is well.'[4]

Oh, how I remember that sense of well-being Sarah used to arouse in me.

Laska.

JANUARY 18

I HAVE made a setup in the living room for the puppy. A former student, James, helped me out. He took a wrench and pried apart two segments of a low, round metal pen. He attached each side of the pen to the entrance of a metal crate, the door of which remains open. The pen has a door, too, so that when I leave it ajar Laska can come out of the pen. Underneath the pen and the crate and extending in either direction, I placed an inexpensive piece of linoleum in the pattern of a parquet floor. The old pine floorboards have big spaces between them that would be hard to clean. The setup replaces my round living-room table and the dark red Oriental rug that lay under it. But I don't mind the change. I want the puppy to be able to see me when I'm in the kitchen. I've also laid down a big square of linoleum in the kitchen so that I won't worry about the pine floorboards before she's housebroken.

I got the idea of this setup from Sarah's breeder, Rachel Parker, who, like Stacey, raises her pups in her home. On top of the crate, as she did, I put a pile of newspapers torn in half at the fold. Inside, at the back of the crate, I placed a cardboard box to make the space smaller and cozier until the pup gets bigger. Just inside the entrance to the crate I made a bed for her with a fleecy blanket I bought from a catalogue. I don't remember such things being on the market in Sarah's early years.

The puppy will sleep in the crate but have the pen to play in. She'll use the paper in one corner for going to the bathroom during the hours I'm away teaching. She'll also have her food and water dishes in the crate, two plain stainless-steel dishes with angled rims that protect against clumsy puppy paws. At night she'll sleep upstairs in my room in another crate. Sarah used to sleep right in my bed or under it when I wasn't sleeping alone. When I developed arthritis, my naturopath advised me sternly to remove Sarah from my bed. My lovable pet suddenly became a transmitter of microorganisms.

I had found it painful to force Sarah out of my bed. I missed her compact, warm body curled up in the hollow of my stomach. Even worse, I could not explain my reason for the sudden unkindness. I couldn't say, "I want to stay active so we can take walks together and because of this, Sweet Pea, we'll have to sleep separately."

Sarah spurned the L. L. Bean cedar bed I placed next to mine until I put a duck-down sleeping bag on top of it. This she burrowed into each night with just her nose sticking out. When she awakened in the morning, she often stood up shrouded in the bag. She would walk some distance before it slid off. This used to remind me of Dante's description of Adam in *The Divine Comedy.* Adam, having been created right after the animals, shared a likeness with them. Dante compares Adam, who is shrouded in light, to the way an animal under covers looks as it stirs, the covers following its movement. Being near Sarah always made me feel included in that blanketing light.

With my new puppy, we'll have separate beds right from the start and, though I wish it were otherwise, at least it will be just the way things are.

JANUARY 21

MY new friend Merle Auguste offered to drive me to pick up Laska the day after tomorrow. This way I can hold Laska on the way home, a two-hour drive. I don't feel ready and want to wait until the weekend but Merle says Thursday is the only day this week when there won't be a danger of black ice on the roads.

I met Merle through a foster German shepherd named Steely whom I took care of the summer after Sarah died. The doggie day-care center that rescued Steely gave him to me for a few months. After that, one of the day-care workers planned to adopt him. Steely had intelligent, only partly domesticated eyes, a long coat with coppery highlights, and a loping gait. I later learned the nature of his abuse. His owner, Jake, had kept him inside with the family until he was four months old. Then he put Steely outside on a chain close to the house, where the puppy remained right through the winter. Except for giving him food and water, Jake never paid Steely any further attention. In the spring, Jake chained Steely one hundred yards from the house. A caring couple in the neighborhood knew, because it had happened with previous dogs, that Jake's next action would be to shoot Steely. One day, when Jake was away, the couple rescued the young dog. But Steely never forgot the treatment he received. He lunged unexpectedly on the leash at people whom he considered threatening, taking their arms in his teeth. I got desperate when he nipped a garbageman and one of my son's friends, both of whom he considered trespassers.

If the doggie day-care center I obtained Steely from took him back, he would be put down. Several German shepherd rescue hotlines also advised destroying him. "He's a legal liability," one man warned. My last call was to Merle. One of the rescue centers suggested that she had the ability to evaluate Steely. I was delighted at this narrow chance for him. He was only eighteen months old and it seemed unthinkable that he should have to die.

Merle, in her forties, was a shepherd breeder until a back injury forced her to give up her profession. When I explained that Steely faced euthanasia, Merle immediately offered to come to my house. She spent about an hour with us and told me she was sure that, in the right hands, Steely could learn not to display what dog handlers call fear aggression. She said it would take at least a year of concentrated effort. Through her contacts she found a home for Steely, and I've heard that the young man who adopted the dog has brought him around to being a fine companion. Our mutual concern for Steely drew Merle and me together across class differences. Merle never went to college, while I taught at one, yet our friendship flourished, and I more often received wisdom from her than the other way around.

"Why didn't Sarah look at me while she was dying?" I asked Merle over the phone, weeping, a few weeks after turning Steely over to her.

"It would have distracted her. She was practicing a kind of autohypnosis by panting that helped her with the pain. She needed to concentrate on that," Merle replied gently.

Because she helped me save Steely's life, I'd like Merle to be godmother to my as yet unacquired puppy.

JANUARY 23

MERLE sits on the floor while the puppy with the red string around its neck clambers all over her. The makeshift collar is considerably frayed since two weeks ago, no doubt from puppy roughhousing. This second visit, Stacey has brought out just the two black females. When she puts Laska down, the puppy begins exploring, trotting along the edges of the room and sniffing the floor. I sit alone on a metal chair.

"You should take this one," Merle says, as the puppy with the red string covers her face with licks. "She's more people oriented."

Confused, I pick her up again and she squints at me. "But I like the other one better," I say, though I do wonder why Laska shows little interest in us.

I also think, "Yeah, but Merle, *you* are the one the squinty-eyed puppy is crawling over."

Merle has a way with animals, a gift she acknowledges with some modesty. During the four months that Steely lived with me, I could not have any people in my house without putting Steely in his crate. After a while, he accepted the presence of my son, who was living with me just then while finishing up at the University of Vermont. He greeted anyone else with savage barking and lunging. I had spoken with such fear of this side of him that Merle brought her own shepherd as a decoy the day she came to evaluate him. Distracted by Melody, whose nose he pressed his own against as soon as she came through the door, Steely seemed not to notice Merle. About a half hour later, when Merle put Melody in the car and came back alone, Steely accepted her completely. Most poignantly, toward the end of her visit he went up to her and put his large, fearful head into the shelter of her arms as she rested her elbows on her knees.

"This is a gesture of trust," Merle explained to me, "because in such a position he is defenseless."

Her evaluation over, Merle got up and went to the door. Steely sat down beside her, wanting to go too. "This often happens to me with people's dogs," she had said quietly, possibly to offset jealousy in me.

I do not begrudge the attention the squinty-eyed puppy showered on Merle. But I do notice that even with Merle's charisma, Laska prefers to explore the room.

Stacey reenters the kitchen holding one of the male puppies on her wide hip with the ease of a midwife. She overheard our conversation about which puppy to take. She looks at me, her friendly eyes large behind reading glasses, and says, "It's best to stick with your original choice."

Relieved, I agree with her, give her a check for the full amount, and accept Laska on the end of a bright, multicolored leash.

As we drive home, Laska curls up in my lap. I am so glad that Merle has given me this chance to be with her in the first moments of her life with me. She drapes her head over my arm or tucks it into the crook of my elbow and seems to sleep.

I remember how Sarah had whimpered and even howled as we took her home. Levin joined her in the back of the station wagon and though he held her against his chest, he could not console her. That first night she had cried so much he got no sleep, since her pen was in his room. For a week after that, she woke up crying several times a night. Only I heard her, my mother's ear attuned to a youngster's distress in the night, even though my room was at the other end of the apartment from Levin's. I would make my way into his room, where he, apparently adjusted to the noise, lay fast asleep. I would hold Sarah on my lap in the dark until she quieted, then return to my bed. Sarah also lost interest in eating unless I fed her by hand, pellet by pellet. Gradually she found comfort in her new home as her yearning nature transferred from her mother and littermates to us.

After Merle drops us off, I walk into the house with Laska in my arms. Laska half-awakens but doesn't look around. I sit down on the staircase to the second floor, which is near her crate setup. My bookbag falls off my arm and coins spill onto the floor. I can't imagine how to pick them up without disturbing Laska, who has fallen asleep again on my lap. I leave my down jacket on, though

I quietly unzip it. I sit there for a long time, irrationally worrying about the coins she could swallow if I don't remove them.

Then, with one arm around Laska, I reach for the phone, which rests on the floor almost out of range, and call Merle. "I'm sitting on the stairs and she's asleep on my lap. What should I do?" I ask. It is a silly question, prompted by the need not to feel completely alone with the responsibility of this new life.

"Puppies always sleep for a reason," she replies, though she doesn't explicitly tell me what to do.

I thank Merle and put the phone down. Laska could be very tired from the trip or perhaps she isn't ready to face the total change in her life just yet. The quiet of the house closes in around me. Years ago, when Sarah came home with us, there had been other arms besides mine to hold her.

I choose to keep sitting on the stairs as night darkens the room and the coins gleam faintly on the floor.

JANUARY 24

"WHY would you want a winter puppy?" some friends have asked me, explaining how much easier it is to house-train a puppy in warm weather.

At ten o'clock tonight it is ten degrees Fahrenheit and the snow is so cold it crunches beneath my bulky felt-lined boots out in the yard. Laska, who is supposed to be pooping, huddles all shivery on top of my boots like a baby penguin sheltered by her parent. The lopped-off moon, remote and severely white, offers us no comfort. I wish Laska would get to work sniffing around for the perfect spot. Then, along with shivering, she begins to whimper, so I pick her up gently and take her back in. Soon after, she poops on the paper in her pen. I am happy about that, but how can I train her to go outside in this weather?

JANUARY 25

WHAT does Laska look like? She's got that perfect all-of-a-piece look, like a young child just past infancy, satisfyingly compact like a nut or berry, full of potential. She has the square Lab muzzle; ears too big for her head because she will grow into them; a soft, thick coat with shiny patches of adult fur coming in; four perfect black paws with little nails visible. There is a bare patch just behind her nose from a scrap with a littermate (Sarah had a scratch at the edge of her upper lip when she came home with us). She holds her gay tail high and wags it wildly when I call her. She comes sometimes in a series of bounces, especially yesterday, a comparatively warm day when the yard was flooded with sun. Her new eyes shine in the midst of this compact perfection, though their focus seems somewhat fuzzy, as if she hasn't fully arrived inside herself yet.

JANUARY 26

I GIVE Laska a bath. Combing her coat before turning her over to me, Stacey had found a flea and kindly apologized for giving her to me unbathed. Laska seems to enjoy being washed. In the downstairs bathroom, I set her down in the deep trough of the utility sink on a rubber bath mat so she won't slip around. She stays quite calm, turning her head to watch the sponge but not protesting. It is one of our first peaceful moments. Since bringing her home, I've been so busy taking care of my life or cleaning up after Laska that I've not had time to tend to my puppy *herself,* as I do now with the bath.

Already after just a few days with Laska I have a whole new view of my life with Levin. I will never again think of myself as having been a single mother. First of all Eric, Levin's father, and I didn't separate until Levin was three and a half. After that we lived only ten minutes from each other, and Levin spent a day and two nights with his dad each week. When Levin was small, I never felt that *all* the responsibility was mine.

JANUARY 27

ONLY four days since I brought Laska home and she's matured so much. This morning she chewed on a Nylabone with some force. Last Thursday, in Merle's car, she just mouthed one tentatively. Tonight, beyond the linoleum, Laska discovers the broad, deep cracks between the pine floor boards, full of a hundred years of debris—minute scraps of dried food, lost screws, dust balls, insect shells, shreds of paper, human and animal hair, pennies. She follows them methodically with her nose and eyes. She explores the living room in much the way she explored the kitchen at Stacey's. She barks at the woodstove handle and plays with the blue pull toy shaped like an infinity symbol. Last night she slept seven and a half hours. Laska knows to pee and poop on the newspaper if she's inside her pen. If she's outside it, she hasn't figured out how to run through the open door in time. Instead she picks a spot as close to the newspaper inside the pen as possible. Merle had the great idea of putting paper in that emergency spot until she's old enough to figure out how to get through the door or, even better, to ask to go outdoors.

I can't believe how often Laska relieves herself. Both her black squatting shape (pee) and humped-over form (poop) look like punctuation marks concluding each short stretch of activity.

This morning she howled and howled, her head straight up like a wolf, when I went upstairs for a bath. Merle explained the reason to me: "She is a pack animal. You need to leave something with your scent on it in her crate so she knows she isn't all alone. She howled so that someone from the pack would know where she was and come for her."

Just now she upset the ashbin and wants to sit on my lap because she scared herself.

February 1997

Cutout Paper Dolls

FEBRUARY 1

ADVICE books don't always help. First of all, there are so many more of them than I remember from Sarah's puppyhood. Can the job of raising a puppy be *that* hard? To not confuse myself, I return to the monks of New Skete's book, *How to Be Your Dog's Best Friend: A Training Manual for Dog Owners,* that was the only book I read when Sarah was little. That was where I learned that dogs are pack animals, like wolves, and need a leader. Despite this new knowledge, I persisted in wanting equality between me and Sarah. I wanted love to determine our bond, not the fact that Sarah was a pack animal. In retrospect, what did I mean by love? To begin with, human and animal love might not be the same. Also, in both species, love surely must be a mixture of nature and culture: instinct, genes, basic needs, and hormones all play a part in whom we love and why. Today I am aware that a dog's natural inclinations are not necessarily symmetrical to mine. I might prefer equality in our relationship, while my dog might need hierarchy. It seems respectful to shape my behavior to the dog's requirements, since I'm asking the dog to do the same with me.

Wanting to learn more, I buy the monks' second book, *The Art of Raising a Puppy.* I come upon bewildering advice. The monks tell me that the socialization period for a puppy occurs during the first twelve weeks. It is crucial that my pup meet as many dogs as possible. At the same time, I'm told that the puppy is vulnerable to illness, especially the deadly parvovirus, until it is fully immunized at six months. How am I to see that Laska becomes properly sociable yet doesn't perish from exposure to other dogs? She also needs to meet lots of people during the first twelve weeks. If she does not, she may become people shy. From the monks' advice, I begin to think that I need to join the Rainbow family commune if I want a well-adjusted dog.

FEBRUARY 2

UNTIL today only my student James, who helped me set up the pen and crate, has seen Laska and me together. I ask James if he'll take pictures of us and he gladly obliges. I sit on a chair in the living room, dressed in a red plaid flannel hunting shirt and jeans, with Laska on my lap. Looking at the pictures later, I see the typical expression of a new mother, circles under the eyes from lack of sleep, a shy pride over the small being in my arms.

FEBRUARY 3

SINCE the time Laska howled when I left her alone downstairs, I make sure she has a shirt with my scent on it for company. But she shouldn't be left alone too long, Merle said, because she's very young. I've tried carrying her around in a human baby sling but she's too active. Unlike a baby, she has good use of her legs. She follows me everywhere I go in the house and curls up between my feet with her head on my green felt slippers. Sometimes she goes to my red plaid flannel shirt that I leave hanging on the doorknob in the kitchen and sits or lies down under it. This morning she stood on her hind legs with her paws on the shirt asking to be picked up. It made me sad to see her do that. I realized I've been so busy working, cooking, and washing up after myself and her that I haven't been holding her enough.

Also, to my dismay, I discover I've been feeding her only a quarter of a cup of food instead of a half cup. She was getting thin and straggly looking. I wonder why I made that mistake. I know that my mother tried to nurse me but it "didn't work out." There probably is a terrible story in those three words, though that was all she ever told me. I've seen babies with tense mothers get convulsed with hunger and cry so much that they can't take the breast. And then the breast gets so engorged the baby can't latch on. Many mothers blame the failure of breastfeeding on their babies, seeing them as rejecting. Some babies fall asleep at the breast, which can also make a new mother lose confidence. How strange that this *puppy* takes me back to my mother, which never happened with Levin. Levin's and my life began as if the world started over anew. Breastfeeding him came as easily as if it had been family custom for generations.

FEBRUARY 4

LASKA slept from eleven last night until five this morning. She peed and pooped, then slept again until seven thirty. Despite the good night's sleep I'm tense today. I come downstairs barefoot and as soon as I let Laska out of her pen she goes for my toes. Her bites feel like bee stings. Though it makes no sense, her assault seems pitiless. How can she call attention to my toes, which were once shapely and are now crumpled from arthritis? I get my green felt clogs and cover my feet, but I remain angry at her.

I developed rheumatoid arthritis eight years ago. It began quite suddenly in one finger and one toe, a hot tenderness that didn't go away. The rheumatologist had written in his report that the ball of my foot was "remarkably tender to the touch." The word "remarkable" seemed strange to me, as if it were a compliment. The condition worsened over the next two years, spreading to most of my joints. I couldn't get out of a chair without grasping a tabletop or doorknob with my hands. Then I found a naturopath who suggested radical changes in my diet. Within a month the arthritis retreated to my hands and feet.

The "temporarily able-bodied" (everyone without a disability) grow up expecting to get better after being sick. Activists in the disability rights movement invented that phrase (also known as TABs) to indicate that eventually—for example, in the aging process—everyone acquires a disability. I keep a positive outlook and take good care of myself as best I can (giving up ice cream wasn't easy), but a degenerative condition can elicit fear and despair.

Right now Laska is pouncing on a tattered diaper I saved from Levin's childhood because diapers make great rags. She grabs the cloth and shakes it between her teeth until she loses her balance. For a moment I see an innocent puppy learning about the world through a joyful, all-out assault.

FEBRUARY 5

TODAY my closest Burlington friend, Crow, comes over to meet Laska. Though Jewish, Crow did not turn to the tradition when she renamed herself. One of her favorite spots is a pine grove that belongs to a convent located a few blocks from my house. One day, as she lay there on a bed of pine needles, she saw a flock of sleek, black crows fly overhead. As she heard them call raucously to each other, she decided to name herself Crow. Her choice suits the jet-black hair that stands up vigorously from her head, the bright, observant and slightly rascally look in her dark eyes, and her warm, brusque manner.

Crow enjoys arguing, though she does it good-naturedly. For instance, from time to time she chides me that I ought to consider a lesbian relationship. I reply, "I am a heterosexual in self-imposed exile. Just because I need a break from trying to get along with a man doesn't mean I'm on my way to becoming a lesbian." Crow counters with, "Your feminist consciousness is too high to be able to stand the patriarchy." I tell her that I like the word "exile" because it implies that I was driven away. As if, after the divorce from Levin's father and a brief second marriage, a judge extended his arm, pointed his finger at the distant hills, and decreed: "Since you clearly cannot get along with men, you must leave the land of patriarchy."

I met Crow a year after coming to Burlington, in 1990. Someone brought her to a discussion group I offered at my house on Yom Kippur, the Jewish Day of Atonement. When I met Crow, she eyed me in a canny crowlike way. I felt that she was a woman to be reckoned with and was drawn to her.

When Crow comes through the door from the mudroom to the living room and looks down at Laska, who is sitting at my feet, she clearly scares my puppy, who cowers back as Crow bends to pat her. I pick Laska up and she puts her head inside my flannel shirt as if to say, "You are the one I trust." Her gesture reminds me of the way Steely, six months ago, buried his head in Merle's arms the day she came over to evaluate him.

Crow looks a bit hurt at Laska's fear. Despite the awkward greeting, Crow accepts my invitation to stay for a cup of tea. I put Laska in her pen and we go into the kitchen. "So how are ya, honey?" Crow asks in her usual rough, affectionate manner.

"Oh, I don't know," I say. "I'm tired, and unsure of myself with Laska. I seem to need more hands than two. In short, I'm a new mother."

"You don't sound like yourself," Crow says, accustomed to my happy descriptions of Levin's childhood.

"I know," I reply. "With Levin, being a mother came so easily. I'll tell you one thing, I have new respect for your honesty about your shortcomings as a mother when your daughters were young."

Slouched casually in the Breuer chair across the table from me, Crow throws her head back and laughs appreciatively over my newfound compassion. She often chides me about my high standards for mothers. I take the time, as a dentist's daughter, to admire her strong, white teeth. They mirror her physical vitality. Crow spends a lot of time exploring nature, accompanied only by her dog, Sabra, a German shepherd mix. Neither Crow nor Sabra is young, but they both are extremely fit.

"So what should I do?" I continue.

Pleased to be asked for advice on mothering, Crow draws on her familiarity with Twelve Step wisdom. "These are the three most important things you should do," she says. "Reach out for help, don't isolate (these come from AA), and here's one of my own—be gentle with yourself."

Though I have the uncommendable habit of dismissing formulaic phrases, whatever their source, I cling to what Crow has just said.

"Speaking of mothers," Crow continues, "I'm going down to Florida to visit mine. You know she's in her nineties now, and still going about everywhere on her own."

"Will I be able to call you there, if I need to?" I ask, mindful of her advice to reach out.

"Only in the first part of the week. I'm going to camp in the Everglades for part of the time."

"What about snakes and alligators?" I ask. Since moving to Vermont I sometimes think about camping; but experience suggests that I would lapse into sullenness over the inconveniences.

"They are around, but that's the point, to see some wildlife."

"Oh, Crow, you are my inspiration."

"Well, honey," Crow says, getting up from her chair, "I have to go pack and take care of a million things."

"Who will look after Sabra?" I ask.

"A friend from AA is going to housesit."

"That was a great photo of you and Sabra in the paper the other day," I say as we head for the door. A quarter-page image featured Crow riding in the rain on the bike path that flanks Lake Champlain. Sabra loped along on a loose leash beside Crow's bicycle.

"Yeah, that was sweet to see, but the photo doesn't show me going flying when Sabra stops to poop." Crow says.

"Maybe I'll be able to bike with Laska some day."

"One day at a time," Crow says, as a sensible reminder.

"Good point," I reply, as we hug goodbye.

FEBRUARY 6

MY office at school is right next to a professor of gerontology's. Taped to his door is a portrait of an old man with flowing hair and beard, drawn by Leonardo da Vinci; taped to mine is a flyer inviting people to become labor assistants to women in childbirth. About once a year, perhaps noticing my ever more graying hair, John Strand asks me, "When are you going to take up the subject of aging?"

Today, John comes out his door just as I'm about to enter mine, and I bring the subject up myself. "Guess what, John?" I say playfully. "The beginnings of life continue to be my subject—I just got a new puppy."

"Well, that should whiten a few hairs," he replies. John is several years younger than I. He looks at me with a mild expression and an air of reserve that I believe comes from his Ivy League background. This new development in my life seems to draw John out of himself; he is a devoted dog owner. "What's the puppy's name?" he asks.

"Laska, which comes from Tolstoy's *Anna Karenin,* the same book I got my son Levin's name from."

"Alaska without the A," John says, smiling.

"True, well, Alaska *is* near Russia," I reply, enjoying the collegial banter.

When Sarah died a few years ago, John was one of the few people who didn't immediately say, "So when are you getting a new puppy?" In fact, he invited me into his office, took a large, framed picture of his two Springer spaniels off a bookshelf, and told me how sad he'd been when one of them died.

"It takes a while to get over the death of a pet," he said, gazing at the portrait.

Perhaps John's research on death and dying gives him special insight into two subjects *and* experiences that many people in our culture seek to avoid. As my mother once put it, with characteristic urban wit, "In New York, death is just an option." She meant that, for the affluent few, modern medicine could prolong life almost indefinitely.

Right now, John and I are standing in the basement hallway of the small clapboard building that houses the Sociology Department. Both of us enjoy privacy and chose out-of-the-way offices on account of it. I put my key in the lock of my door, balancing the mail I collected in the crook of my arm.

"I have a new respect for women faculty with young children," I say to John. "I don't know how I could manage a job like this one with a baby; it's hard enough with a puppy."

John kindly tucks a letter that has escaped my grip back under my arm and says, "I'll let you get on with your day." He turns away and heads upstairs.

Once through the door, I drop the mail on my desk, turn the computer on to check my e-mail, and sit down in front of it. My office is a corner room and ample light comes through the two walls of windows. Just now, the sun plays on the image of a sprightly red hen that strides across the surface of a dishtowel I converted into a wall hanging. When Levin first saw my office a few years ago, he said cryptically, "Chickens." This code word referred to my habit of decorating spaces with maternal subjects or reminders of my early years as a mother. Draped across two chairs are brightly colored baby blankets I'd crocheted when pregnant. A stuffed chicken made of felt sits on top of one of my file cabinets; her bright eyes keep track of the two chicks at her feet. A painted ceramic ashtray Levin made in kindergarten sits on a bookshelf alongside a box he made out of Popsicle sticks.

As I read my e-mails, I have the same feeling that afflicted me when I returned to work after Levin was born. From the age of two and a half months, Levin attended a child-care center that his dad, Eric, and I cofounded along with several other families. We were just a group of parents, many of us with full-time jobs, but we succeeded in organizing and administering what became the Oxford Street Daycare Cooperative. Harvard University provided space for the center, and we parents interviewed and hired teachers. Oxford Street still exists more than twenty years later; when Eric and his second wife had a baby a few years ago, they placed him at Oxford Street too. As a newborn, Levin spent every morning at day-care, five days a week, while I worked as a graphic designer for a government-funded organization that assisted community groups in the Boston area. After I dropped Levin off at the center, I arrived at work with the nagging feeling that I'd lost something. "I've got to find it," I thought, as if I'd left my pocketbook in a restaurant; then I realized that it was Levin I'd left behind, and that all was well with him.

This time around I'm a more seasoned mother and know exactly what I'm missing. I want Laska in my office with me, but what would become of the wall-to-wall carpeting?

FEBRUARY 7

TODAY I come home from class and take the mail out of the antique iron mailbox. I look absently at the envelopes and notice a gray one whose return address says ASA Governance. I almost throw it away but something about the envelope catches my eye. It looks fancy. Dropping my bookbag to the floor, taking off my down jacket, and checking Laska who lies in her crate attentively watching me, I open the letter. It begins: "Dear Dr. Pfeufer Kahn: I am very pleased to inform you that you have been selected as a 1997 recipient of the ASA Jessie Bernard Award." Jesse Bernard was the Margaret Mead of sociology, and ASA is the American Sociological Association, which developed a national award in her honor. The award is given for a scholarly work that "has enlarged the horizons of sociology to encompass fully the role of women in society." As I write this news in my journal, that I won an award for my book *Bearing Meaning: The Language of Birth,* it feels as if I'm writing to someone who knows nothing about it. But the unknowing person is myself.

I sit down heavily as tears spring hotly from my eyes. "Laska," I say, "I won the Jesse Bernard Award for my book."

I go over and take Laska out of her pen. She always hops as I scoop up her back legs, as if trying to help me lift her. Returning to the chair, I can't stop crying. The sobs coming out of me, deep and hoarse, sound more like grief than joy. Laska, having never seen me cry before, begins nipping my hands. I put her back in her pen so she won't keep biting me or pee on the floor.

I take another look at the letter. There will be a ceremony at the ASA convention in Toronto this coming summer. The tears and hoarse crying continue as I reread the letter every five minutes, expecting it to change. I begin to see that the grief comes from being *seen*. The many stories about my life in the book brought respect rather than belittlement. My parents often shamed me when I spoke my mind as a child. Like some kind woman entering a closed-up room and with swift, competent movements stripping off the cloths that shroud the furniture, the letter brings the whole of my life freshly into view and into renewed inhabitance.

Having learned from Sarah's death the benefit of crying, I let the feelings rise up through me until, after a half hour, I gradually quiet. I go over to the stairs, sit down, and call two friends in Boston, both of whom are worried at the shaky sound of my voice when I say hello. Then their happiness over the news helps me become happy, too. I call Levin and leave a message on his pager. All the while Laska watches me in what has become a habitual manner, curled up with one front paw tucked back, her head and neck held high and very alert, her eyes following me carefully.

FEBRUARY 8

JUST now, I sit on the living room floor and Laska goes wild nipping me, not mouthing but real little bites to my ankles and hands; she even nips my face. I close her mouth with my hand and put her on her back, but I can't subdue her. I retreat to the stairs, where I conduct my life these days, and call her breeder, Stacey.

"Hi," I begin, "this is Robbie Kahn. I bought a puppy from you a few weeks ago."

"Oh, hello there," Stacey replies in a friendly voice. "How are you doing?"

"Well, we're all right, but Laska is pretty nippy and putting her on her back doesn't help."

"This is typical puppy behavior," Stacey says reassuringly. "You should put Laska's lips under her teeth so that she bites herself. You'll see how quickly she'll stop biting you."

"Well," I reply, uncertainly, "if you think that won't hurt her."

"Oh no," Stacey says spiritedly, "it is a harmless way to get a puppy to stop biting."

I thank Stacey for her help, but, unconvinced, I decide to call Vivian Marsh, a dog trainer I first heard of from Sarah's vet. I'd wanted to teach Sarah not to pull on the leash but never pursued my plan to reform her bad habit.

"Rather than correct Laska," Vivian says cheerfully, after I explain the problem, "distract her with Gummabones, those soft Nylabones. Carry them with you everywhere and put them right in her mouth so she chews on them, not you."

"My first dog, Sarah, loved Gummabones," I say. Since this advice sounds so helpful, I decide to tell Vivian more about me and my puppy. "Another thing," I continue, "is that Laska doesn't ever lick me on the face or let me hold her on her back without biting at me."

"Try to see it from the puppy's point of view," Vivian replies. "It's scary to be on your back."

Her advice makes me feel foolish because *Bearing Meaning* is all about seeing things from the baby's point of view.

Laska napped while I talked to Vivian. Now she wakes up and I lift her out of her pen. I sit down on the stair, so that I'm not at the same level with her, and place her gently on the floor. As if she heard my complaints in her sleep, Laska lets me rub her tummy. She then licks my face when I take her out into the yard. On the way to buy Gummabones, she looks at me shyly from where she lies curled up right behind the gearshift. When we get to Pet Food Warehouse, I carry her inside tucked under my arm. It feels cozy. I pick out several of the puppy-size translucent bones wrapped in gaily colored packages, full of hope about Vivian's plan. As soon as we are home, I try to give Laska one of the Gummabones. She keeps her eye on my hand and goes for that instead.

I fear that Laska has a behavioral problem because she wasn't nursed long enough. Stacey weaned the litter at three weeks, which is customary, though in my opinion too soon. At the same time, the people who co-own Laska's mother with Stacey took her back to their home. Thus, the pups didn't have the benefit of their mother's discipline, the way Sarah did with her mother, Lady Jasmine. The day we picked Sarah out, I watched Lady Jasmine chasten the other black female pup for jumping up and biting her mother's ears. Growling sternly, Jasmine seized the unruly puppy in her jaws by the neck, and the pup instantly became meek and seemingly contrite. Sarah sat pitched back on her hindquarters, watching as if astonished.

In our phone conversation, Vivian agreed with me that it's better to let the mothers wean their puppies. But, she added: "Unless we breed the dogs ourselves, we don't have full control over the puppies available. We can't shape it just as we like."

During my search for a suitable puppy, I spoke to many breeders and I noticed that they all had a preoccupation with the *mother's* imagined well-being. They'd say, "Those sharp little teeth! By three weeks the mother is not going to want the pups around her." They didn't mean that the mother should be taken away altogether, as Laska's had been. Just that the pups should be weaned. Yet, why were the breeders concerned about those sharp teeth on the mother's flesh rather than the pups' need for comfort from her? And what if the mother *wanted* to keep nursing her puppies? Feeding them solids would cause the pups to lose interest in their mother's milk, just as it does with human babies.

In my opinion, the breeders I spoke to had transferred infant-feeding ideas from human to nonhuman animals. Despite the known emotional and physical benefits of breastfeeding, we are a bottlefeeding culture. Nursing longer than three weeks surely must have a quieting effect on a puppy. Also, when the mother weans the pups, she teaches them to lick her mouth, which sets off a reflex in her so she will regurgitate food for them. Maybe Laska, deprived of her mother too soon, never learned how to lick as a way of relating. On the other hand, her littermate sister did lick my nose; that makes me wonder if, along with maternal influence, temperament shapes a puppy's behavior.

Despite her fiery toothiness, Laska still looks newly arrived and even a little scared when she shows the whites underneath her eyes. Though I've bought fleecy toys and Gummabones for her, she likes best the toys she finds for herself. She plays most with a rubber guard you put under a couch leg to protect it from the floor and with a plastic cover for one of the screws that holds the toilet to the floor. Her choice of toys reminds me of how Levin preferred to play with kitchen serving spoons, a strainer, pots, or my keys.

FEBRUARY 9

LASKA grows so fast, almost between naps. She was six and a half pounds last week, nine pounds this week. Today, when I come home, she for the first time greets me with an object in her mouth; it is the fleecy "pot holder" I bought her. A retriever.

FEBRUARY 11

MY young German friend, Sigrid, who is married to one of my colleagues, visits us. Sigrid is an accomplished masseuse and my monthly sessions with her never fail to smooth away tension. Today she comes just to meet my new puppy.

As soon as she enters the kitchen from the mudroom Sigrid squats on the floor, allowing Laska to clamber excitedly all over her. They look all of a piece: black Laska and Sigrid wearing black jeans, turtleneck, and fanny pack. Sigrid looks up at me with her strong-featured yet soft face, set off by a new, rakishly short haircut. She exclaims with an accent, "Laska's so sweet." I notice the familiar melancholy tone of Sigrid's voice, which I associate with Europeans' long history compared to Anglo-Americans'.

I watch as Sigrid plays with Laska in a pen formed by the crook of her legs. My puppy puts her paws on my friend's chest and looks up, wild-eyed, at Sigrid's face. She grabs the sleeve of Sigrid's shirt with her teeth and shakes her head back and forth. Sigrid laughs at these antics; then with her masseuse's hands she guides Laska onto the floor. The pup immediately turns upside down and Sigrid rubs her belly gently. At first Laska pushes Sigrid's hands away with her back legs, but then they flop apart, in that pliant-bodied puppy way, as she relaxes to Sigrid's touch. After a few minutes of these caresses, Laska becomes restless and squirms around. Knowing when to stop, Sigrid lifts Laska up for me to hold while she gets off the floor. I keep Laska with me as Sigrid and I sit down at the kitchen table. Laska curls up peacefully in my lap. Clearly, my friend's presence has soothed both her *and* me. Sigrid's influence comes not from didactic advice, but from modeling behavior with Laska. I say appreciatively, "You are like a *doula*."

"What's that?" Sigrid asks in her world-weary voice, right out of a movie.

"It's a Greek word for a woman who takes care of a new mother."

"Oh, you mean she mothers the mother?"

"Exactly," I say. "For some reason Laska makes me tense. It calmed me so much to watch you play with her, you were so relaxed, and now look how quietly she rests in my lap. This is an unusual moment for us, and it is thanks to you."

"I guess a *doula* can even help a woman whose youngster happens to be a puppy," Sigrid says, smiling. We sit quietly for a few minutes; then Sigrid gets up from her chair and says, "I'll let myself out the door," adding, "you two stay where you are."

I sit alone at the kitchen table with Laska in my lap; even though Sigrid has gone, it feels as if she keeps a steadying hand on my shoulder.

FEBRUARY 13

I HAVEN'T told my parents about my new puppy. It is almost three years since I became estranged from them, though a persistent low-level estrangement has been normal in our family. When I was young, I didn't understand the sources of this condition. I could see that my father was very busy because he worked on his dentistry even at home, making wax castings over a Bunsen burner at the dining-room table. My mother seemed to want to be by herself. I don't know what she did when we were away; I suspect that she slept a lot of the time. When my father took my younger sister, Karen, and me ice skating at Rockefeller Center or sledding in Riverside Drive Park on Sundays, my mother never came along.

Besides these once-a-week activities, and the occasional party with guests or outings to a Broadway play, most of the time our family lived in a kind of inanimate suspension. In this uncomfortable atmosphere, my father made me his confidant almost as soon as I could talk. "What is the matter with your mother?" he would say to me over dinner, and we both would look in her direction. My mother's face seemed shut down, the way a baby's would if you tried to force-feed it. Since he said "your mother" instead of "my wife," I figured that I was the cause and, potentially, the cure for their unhappiness.

There were times when my father suddenly broke the lifeless atmosphere. His unpredictable eruptions remain so vivid that I recall them exactly. They jolted me the way a jack-in-the-box can affect an unsuspecting baby.

▼▼▼

I am ten years old; my sister, Karen, is five, and our family is at dinner. We sit almost on top of one another in our cramped New York kitchen. A Formica table with metal legs is pushed up against one wall. My father sits at the head of table, next to the back door. My mother is at the other end, the stove behind her chair. I am seated next to my father, with my sister beside my mother. To get to the sink behind us you have to squeeze past our chairs. Not just the kitchen, but the whole apartment, is too small for a family of four, given that my father, a dentist, can afford a bigger home. We eat as usual in a stiff silence, forks and knives scraping our plates. Without warning my father explodes into his well-known, yet always startling, imitation of Xavier Cugat's one-man band. We had seen the gimmicky musician perform on the Ed Sullivan Show *on our brand new TV console. "Chink-a-chink-a-boom-boom," my father cries out, bouncing up and down vigorously in his chair, moving his long arms in every direction to strike drumsticks on the invisible percussion instruments arranged all around him. His prominent, pained eyes are very large and shining, and he seems startled by his own antics. "Let's make your mother laugh until the tears come," he interrupts breathlessly. And the tears do come, but my sister and I are not sure that they are just tears of happiness. Sometimes our mother seems to need an excuse to cry. We laugh, too, somewhat wildly, over this common ritual between our parents that we do not understand, though we sense that a loss of control is the aim. My father often says that he likes to "get a charge" or "a rise" out of us. My father's one-man band is the funniest thing that's happened all day, but it causes my sister and me a certain unease. We could be the next to lose control; our father might start tickling or scaring us or being too affectionate. This evening we are lucky.*

▲▲▲

Looking back, I understand why *Brigadoon* was my favorite Broadway play as a child. It is a story about an enchanting village that appears on earth once every hundred years. The play matched my sense that an orderly brightness and happiness were as far from my day-to-day life as a brightly lit-up Broadway stage.

In my teenage years, my parents gained access to a social world that gave them some relief from the seeming cul-de-sac of their private life. My father published several influential articles on restorative dentistry and an eminent dentist who was retiring offered him his practice. The dentist's patients were movie and stage personalities or came from high society. In the 1960s after I left for college, my parents began acquiring contemporary sculptures, paintings, drawings, and prints. Their discerning choices brought them a fine collection as well as the acquaintance and respect of many patrons of the arts. These advances in status dazzled my parents, children of Russian Jewish immigrants. They both grew up poor in Jersey City; my mother's father peddled dry goods, and my father's dad owned a candy store. When he died, my father said, "Mike only had enough money saved to pay for his funeral."

Despite their improved economic circumstances, my parents continued to live in the small, rent-controlled apartment my sister and I grew up in.

It never was easy, even after we left home, for Karen and me to see the dramatic transformation that came over my parents in the company of their new acquaintances. My father's eyes shone with an untutored excess of feeling, and my mother looked as freshly enchanted as a girl on her first date. It was even harder to see what happened to my parents when they were alone with us again. Their faces seemed to go slack, as if they had just heard unwelcome news. As I grew older, I was struck by how little these friendships or my parents' material success seemed to alter their inner lives. My sister and I felt unable to make them happy, which baffled and saddened us.

Through the years my mother claimed that her children didn't give her *nachas.* Reverting to Yiddish, her mother tongue, my mother meant that Karen and

I hadn't brought prosperity to her life or caused it to shine. Then three years ago my parents suddenly withdrew critical financial help for the care of my health and my home. Their decision shocked me because I thought I had just gotten the *nachas* knack. I was on the verge of receiving tenure and of having a book published. I had been a gracious host to my parents and to my sister's family in Vermont. These gatherings, unusual in their happiness, had seemed to promise a new family story.

After my parents cut off support, I felt that I had no choice but to distance myself from them to protect myself against further harm. Since then I haven't seen or spoken to my mother or father, although I observe holidays and birthdays by sending cards. This sad estrangement keeps me from calling them now about Laska. My puppy's fresh young life stirs a longing in me to resume relations with my parents. At the same time, I hesitate. What if they unwittingly disrupt me again, the way they did three years ago? I am an adult. How odd that I still find myself afraid of them. I do think it best, however, to keep Laska a secret.

Journal writing about my mother and father may be a wiser idea than breaking the estrangement. I've kept a journal for more than ten years, but I never write about them. The words "journal" and "journey" both come from the Latin *"diurnus,"* which means "daily," or "of a day." Unlike Hansel and Gretel's crumbs that showed them the way home, my journal allows me to trace a daily path away from my mother and father. Perhaps now I can use it to gain more understanding about my life as their daughter.

FEBRUARY 14

LAST night Laska slept through the night—eight and a half hours. What a Valentine's Day present! This morning she sees a kitty in the yard and, though immensely excited by it, manages to pee and poop outside rather than on the newspaper inside.

Outdoors in the yard Laska runs, black shape against the white snow like moving calligraphy. She holds her otter tail aloft and her hind legs, spaced well apart, pound like a racehorse's and move in unison. They splay apart as they overtake her front legs, and her ears flap out from her head as she runs. I give Laska her first furry yellow tennis ball, one of the half dozen Sarah gathered just before she died, stealing one each day from a yard where a dog lived that we passed on our last walks together. Laska barks at the foreign ball and then sits smartly for me to give it to her. Her motion is so abrupt that her ears swing out from her head. She shows no interest in retrieving the ball.

Today she grabs a sock that is lying on the bathroom floor and makes off with it when I call her, apparently aware that I don't want her to have it.

FEBRUARY 15

FOR two days I've tried Stacey's technique of pinching Laska's lips under her teeth so that she bites herself instead of me. The worst moment was the first time I did it. She let out a howl that sounded almost human. There was a pristine innocence to it as if it voiced the first pain experienced by a living being since the world began. The sound made me feel as if I were ruining both our souls.

I talked to Levin about Laska after this episode. "I don't remember Sarah biting this way."

"Are you kidding, those sharp little teeth?"

"Really?"

"You don't remember because she was in my room with me."

This morning Laska licks my ankles, giving just an occasional bite. Merle said Laska has been treating me as if I were a littermate. Perhaps this means that she regards me as her equal. I was getting the feeling that she wanted to dominate me. Nonetheless, Merle said, if she gets rowdy I should simply put her in her pen, saying, "No bite, bad girl." I like this approach; pinching her lips is too harsh.

At lunchtime, Laska whines at the door. She goes out to pee. In the afternoon, she whines to go out for a poop. Ten weeks old and almost house-trained!

FEBRUARY 16

EVEN when Laska *is* house-trained, I oughtn't bring her to school; dogs aren't allowed in UVM buildings, except for guide dogs.

I didn't know this rule when I arrived in 1990, and so I regularly brought Sarah to my office. One student, Greg, particularly seemed to like Sarah. He'd had a brain tumor and the intensive chemotherapy he endured stunted his growth and made him slow at his studies. Despite his handicap, Greg was a dedicated student and I admired him greatly. The first time he met Sarah, he sat right down on the floor and put his arm around her. In response, Sarah tilted her head up in a characteristic gesture, flattened her ears, and opened her mouth, as she enjoyed his scratches on her chest.

"The nice thing about dogs," Greg said, "is that they like you just for who you are."

"That's true," I replied from behind my desk. "You don't have to win her over with good grades."

"Yah," Greg said emphatically, and put his head right against Sarah's.

About a month later, I left Sarah in my office as I usually did when I went off to teach. I returned to find a Day-Glo flyer pinned to my door; large, angry-looking type informed me that if I brought my dog to the building again, it would be *arrested*. I am sorry for my students' sake and my own that I can't keep a dog in my office. Like them, I do better in the company of animals.

FEBRUARY 17

I ROUND the corner of the house to find Laska, whom I let out into the yard, under the woodshed, a place frequented by neighborhood cats. She looks up at me, her mouth open and full of pasty brown cat shit. I pull her away by the scruff of her neck. How do you clean a puppy's mouth? Later, she poops in the house after being out of her pen for twenty minutes, near but not on the newspaper. I yell so loud and pull her by her neck so hard she runs away. Now she'll probably never poop on that paper again.

I'm trying to teach her to lick, not bite. Yet, given my concern about my health, how can I let her lick me with her mouth full of shit?

FEBRUARY 18

LASKA and I spend time in the yard and walk around the neighborhood, but we've never gone downtown. Today, I lift my puppy into the hatch of my rusted Volvo station wagon because she's already too big to curl up behind the stick shift. We drive to the post office. I get out to mail a letter and leave Laska in the car. There, right by the blue mailboxes, I see Abbie. She sits casually on the post office's tubular metal fence with her dog beside her. Abbie is a young woman whose tanned face, even in winter, well-worn clothes, and competent hands remind me of homesteading Vermonters who chop their own firewood and can their homegrown vegetables. I have run into Abbie and her dog before.

Two summers ago, only twelve hours before Sarah died, we came upon them at Red Rocks, a conservation woods on the shore of Lake Champlain. Sarah and I had taken a walk in the late afternoon just after a thunderstorm. Sarah waded in the woods' pools and lapped at the water, which was filled with matted leaves, branches, and whole limbs of trees. She made her way through a murky puddle at the base of a large fallen tree, its roots pulled out by the storm. As we traveled up an incline, we noticed a tall black dog. It sat on the crest of the hill and watched us approach. Sarah wriggled up to him, acting like a puppy, as he bent his head regally to touch noses with her.

"What is his name?" I asked his owner routinely. I only thought to ask Abbie's name a year later, the next time we met, close to the first anniversary of Sarah's death.

"Buddha," she replied.

Maybe it was the chill air after the thunderstorm, but the name and the way he sat so still, as if preparing us for something somber that Sarah's wriggling form denied, seemed an omen. Although he was an enlightened being, Buddha taught that impermanence and suffering are inevitable. The greeting over, Sarah and I continued on our walk.

Now, outside the post office I take another look at Buddha. His black, long-legged body, tapered rectangular face, wolfish impersonal eyes, and tail that curls over his back make him seem a hodgepodge of dogs of all kinds. Maybe this time he brings another message. I suddenly see him representing the collective dog soul (if one believes there is such a thing) to which Sarah returned and from which she sends a blessing. As if fulfilling my fantasy, Abbie smiles and looks at Laska's fresh young face peering at us from the car window. "You've got a cute one there," she says.

Next I drive to leave off a roll of film. I park the car, take Laska out of the hatch, and set her down on the sidewalk, thinking we'll go for a little walk. Remembering the advice books' warning about keeping a puppy protected until it is fully immunized, I look down at the sidewalk. It looks grimier than my neighborhood; I see bird droppings, sharp fragments of a plastic cup she might eat, cigarette butts. Nonetheless I walk along with her. At first she trots smartly by my side, but then she shrinks away from the fumes of passing cars, which are right at her level, and sits down, refusing to go any farther. Relieved, because I don't feel comfortable having her so exposed to the world, I pick her up, take her to the car, and drive us back to the refuge of my house and yard.

FEBRUARY 19

I STAND at the kitchen sink, cracking a boiled egg. My green felt clogs and brand-new silk long johns underneath a flannel nightshirt keep me warm. As I look out the window into the yard, the February sun seems watery, as if diluted, which matches my weak sense of comfort. Sunday. A whole day for just me and my pup. I long to curl up on the couch with a book, and Laska on my lap.

Suddenly I feel hot needles all around my unclad heels; they sting as if I had stumbled over a nettle branch. No matter how often they happen, Laska's assaults startle me. I thought she was playing with her fleecy duck. I push her away with one foot and my clog flies off. She scrambles for the shoe but then, seeing better prey, attacks my crumpled toes. "*No, Laska,*" I yell, dropping the egg into the sink. I bend down to push her away and try to get my clog at the same time, which she has scooted some distance from me. Now she goes for my hands and jumps up, mouth open, at my face. I stumble over to my shoe, keeping her away from me with one hand, and as I put it on I grab her by the neck. Her head swirls side to side like a screech owl's. "Bad girl, no bite!" I say, forgetting to put her in her pen, as Merle suggested I do at such moments. She flips onto her back, eyes wild, mouth open in what looks to me like a snarl. I put my hand on her chest but she manages to get her mouth on my wrist. I pull away. Instantly she's on her feet and leaps at me, her eyetooth snagging a hole in the silk long johns. "That's *it,* I've had it," I yell between gritted teeth, as a scared rage heats my winter cheeks. I swat her on the side of her face, not even caring if I hit her eye. This stays her for a moment, and afraid of myself, I grab her and almost toss her in her pen. Though it's only 9:00 am on a Sunday, I call Stacey, Laska's breeder.

"Hi," I say, "this is Robbie Kahn."

"How are you and your puppy doing?" Stacey asks warmly.

"Oh, we're fine," I say thinly.

"But . . ." Stacey says.

"Well, Laska just ripped a pair of silk long johns. I tried your advice but she bites me all the time." I look over at Laska in her pen. She rests curled up in a tidy ball, her head up, ears pricked forward, and watches me carefully. "Nothing I do stops her," I add, feeling the way I used to when Levin was sick as a little boy. I'd call the doctor about a symptom he had, and just then it would seem to vanish. Laska looks so peaceful: am I making this up? I cast my eyes down at my torn long johns—*evidence.*

"I've heard this before about Nancy's puppies," Stacey says unexpectedly.

"Really?" I reply eagerly, as if I just found out that a toothache I thought was psychosomatic had a physiological basis. It's Laska's genes! But how does this tantalizing piece of information help me? "I can't even have her sit on my lap and pat her. What should I do?" I continue.

"She'll grow out of it at about five months," Stacey says in a seasoned tone of voice.

Though this ought to have been the end of the conversation, I ask the question that haunts me the most. "Do you think she loves me?"

"That will come later," Stacey says. "Now is the time of exploration and play. Her father, Shak, didn't settle down until he was two. I used to flick him away from me with a towel. These days he sleeps by my side on the couch when I watch TV."

What a gene pool, I think to myself.

"It's a comfort to learn about her family," I reply. "Thanks so much." After a brief pause I add, "Is it OK if I call from time to time?" I am afraid to be left alone with Laska.

"Yes, of course," Stacey replies.

I put the phone down slowly and head toward the stairs to get dressed for whatever kind of day I can put together. As I pass Laska's pen, I say, "Hi, puppy," hoping for a fresh start. She regards me with bright eyes, mouth slightly open.

FEBRUARY 20

DURING the years Sarah was alive, my scholarly research centered on childbearing. In fact, *Bearing Meaning* was published in 1995, the year she died. Now that Laska has come along, I find myself turning a sociological lens on animals and society. In one course, Self and Social Interaction, the students and I examine notions of self and other.

"Self and other" is academic jargon, but useful. It signifies that life is a web of relationships made up of the "self" (that's me), and the "other" (that's anyone who is not me). "Not me" could be one person, groups of people, animals, trees, rocks; it could even be parts of myself that I do not understand, or that I consciously or unconsciously reject.

Spiritual traditions foster an awareness that each small self belongs to a larger Self. In Judaism, for example, God instills the breath of life into Adam's nostrils, and the Hebrew word for breath, *ruah,* also means soul or spirit. This biblical story describes a larger Self that is not merely transcendent, removed from the world, for the breath that originates with God dwells within each of us.

Sociologists usually study the "self and other" in a secular context. What concerns them is the tendency of social groups to see "others" in a distorted way, out of ignorance or fear. Men once believed that women should not use their minds because it would cause their reproductive organs to go awry; white people once considered people of color not deserving of human rights; grownups once denied the emotions and intelligence of the very young; humans still regard animals as inferior creatures on the evolutionary scale. All these judgments about the "other" demonstrate inequality; and since most sociologists share the democratic impulse that characterizes modernity, they study inequalities with an eye toward social change.

For some reason since Laska's arrival, I notice how writers we read in my Self and Social Interaction course describe the human/animal relationship. Our semester begins with Karl Marx. Sociology arose in the nineteenth century as a child of twin revolutions—the industrial and the French. Marx is the great analyst of industrial transformation and of social revolution. However, my students seem to find the name "Marx" radioactive, as if it gives off hazardous energy. Marx himself famously said, "I am no Marxist"; and I have found many of his writings surprisingly unlike the social orders that claim his ideas for their own. I try to help my students cultivate an appreciation of him apart from his historical legacy.

I particularly love the *Economic and Philosophical Manuscripts,* written in 1844 when Marx was only twenty-five years old. Marx proposes a human essence, which he calls "species-being." This term seems to link us to nature—we are one species among others. It also seems to connect us to a state of being—we are not defined by our busyness of mind and action. With my new sociology-of-animals lens, I see how badly I have misread Marx. He actually takes pains to show that species-being sets us *apart* from animals because, unlike them, we engage in "conscious life activity." He states: "It is true that animals also produce. They build nests and dwellings, like the bee, the beaver, the ant, etc. But they produce only their own immediate needs or those of their young; they produce one-sidedly, while man produces universally; they produce only when immediate physical need compels them to do so, while man produces even when he is free from physical need and *truly produces only in freedom from such need*" (my emphasis).[1]

Marx bases his definition of humans upon their superiority to animals. He assumes that animals do not have true consciousness—they do not engage in "conscious life activity." To be fair, Marx did not have access to recent research on animals. Ethologists are discovering that animals *do* have conscious life activity: they can form abstract concepts, act altruistically, and have an awareness of self. Primatologist Jane Goodall even believes that primates have a capacity for awe or spiritual awareness.

Marx is the first of a sequence of writers that we will be reading in my Self and Social Interaction class. Their work spans the mid-nineteenth to the late twentieth century. It will be interesting to see what, if anything, each of them says about the human/animal relationship.

FEBRUARY 21

I BEGIN to see that Laska's biting rouses far deeper fears in me than the reminder of a physical disability. I feel abused by her lack of gentleness toward me, as if I've been pitched back into my family of origin. What's worse, I feel like an abuser, reacting toward her as my parents reacted toward me.

I hear my mother in me say her usual, "That's *it.* I've *had* it," yanking my baby arm and shutting me up in my room for far longer than a young child should be left alone. One day I poke Laska coldly with my finger to get her to pay attention, just the way my mother used to do with me.

I see my father in me when I am shaking with rage at Laska. I remember one time as a teenager I was cornered in the bathroom. My father faced me, his hand on his chest, and choked out the words, "You are going to give me a *heart* attack."

I have been so unnerved by my uncontrollable reactions to Laska that yesterday I wanted to return the Jesse Bernard Award to the American Sociological Association. It's embarrassing to have a national award when I cannot live up to the book's message to treat the very young with kindness and respect.

FEBRUARY 22

CROW is bent over a big cast-iron frying pan filled with vegetable and rice stir-fry. She usually makes this dish when I come for dinner because it fits my arthritis diet. She pushes the food around with a wooden spoon a few last times, and then says, "OK, honey, that should do it."

"Great," I answer, "I'm starved." As Crow sets the table, I note with affection her pepper tin. Crow is a militant antimaterialist. I don't consider myself much of a consumer—for instance, I don't like the act of shopping—but I am a slave to beautiful objects. I've never forgotten what a mentor of mine once said about yuppies: "The only thing worse than bad taste is good taste." True, I keep my peppercorns in a thirty-five-year-old barrel-shaped grinder, and the wood knob on the turning handle is so worn from use that it falls off into my supper. But I would never think of putting a battered Durkee pepper tin on the table. The container has words printed on its plain metal sides (I don't allow items that "speak" on my kitchen table) and is so twisted that the plastic top won't close down.

"Shall we light the candles?" Crow asks. We often have dinner together on Shabbat, sometimes with her girlfriend, Val, and sometimes, like tonight, by ourselves.

Crow takes her place before the two Shabbat candles, removes her glasses, and sighs. I feel her leave the week behind and sigh too. In Jewish tradition,

Shabbat is a day of rest that allows you to enter a kind of time that partakes of the sacred. Reminded that you are more than the sum of a week's activities, your soul is refreshed. Crow lights each candle and then, closing her eyes, reaches her arms out wide and sweeps her hands toward her eyes three times, to gather the light of Shabbat into herself. We recite the blessing over the candles together; I've learned Crow's version, which replaces male-gendered words with female ones. For example, the male term for God, Adonai, becomes Shekinah, which means to dwell within. In the Hebrew Bible, Shekinah is the feminine aspect of God. Next, Crow lifts a cup of grape juice, substitute wine, for us to bless. This is a long prayer and I know only the first line of it in Hebrew or in English, so I mumble and fake my way through the rest. I know that Val, who isn't even Jewish, can recite the long prayer over the wine by heart. Last, Crow uncovers the braided challah bread and the rice cakes I brought along. We place our fingers on them and recite a blessing.

All the prayers done, I say eagerly, "Let's *eat.*" Crow laughs, returns to the stove for the big frying pan, and places it right on the table. We heap our plates full. Tonight, Crow and I talk about feminism, as we often do.

"Guess what?" I say, chewing on a mouthful of food. I don't have to worry about manners around Crow, which I enjoy. "Thanks to you, I'm using the book *Radically Speaking: Feminism Reclaimed* in my feminist theory seminar."

"No kidding," Crow replies, also chewing.

"Yeah," I continue, "it was great to find a book by feminists who believe that patriarchy still exists. At the beginning of term, my students thought a radical feminist was a bra-burning, man-hating lesbian."

"Right *on,*" Crow says, but then changes her mind. "I gave up bras years ago, and I'm lesbian, but I don't hate men anymore."

"How come?" I ask.

"I used to be a separatist. On a trip to Egypt I refused to enter the pyramids because they were too patriarchal." She smiles at this memory. "Today I'm sorry I missed out on the pyramids and I'm no longer a separatist. AA changed my consciousness. It's full of men, and their stories of recovery impressed the hell out of me."

"Crow, your ability to change impresses the hell out of *me.*"

"Thanks, honey," Crow says. "So what do you tell your students a radical feminist is?"

"I tell them that the idea they have about a radical feminist comes from the media. In reality, a radical feminist is someone who believes that our societal problems stem from patriarchy. I give the example of what feminist theologian

Mary Daly said about the connection between a patriarchal religious tradition and the family: 'If God is the father, then the father is God.' I tell them about the former wife batterer I heard interviewed on National Public Radio; he said that he used to think it was OK to beat his wife because Genesis told him to rule over her. These examples help me explain to the students that patriarchy is a social institution. At least that's my definition of it—I don't think that patriarchy equals men."

"I don't disagree," Crow says. "That Genesis story is heavy," she adds. "You can see why I struggle with Judaism the way Jacob wrestled with the angel."

We fall silent for a while as we eat plentifully, each of us taking seconds and thirds out of the frying pan. Sabra, Crow's old German shepherd mix, comes up to the table and pokes her nose into my lap. Her eyes have grown very expressive, something I noticed in Sarah when she aged. But Sabra has outlived Sarah by several years and still is sprightly. A touch of envy comes over me until I remember Laska.

"I think Sabra is reminding me that I shouldn't leave my puppy alone too long," I say to Crow.

"Well, I don't have any room for dessert, anyhow," Crow replies. She clutches at her stomach and says, "Ooh, I overate."

"You always say that when we eat together. Remember what I advise?"

"It's OK to feast at a feast."

"Right."

I help Crow clear the table and bend down to hug her because I'm so much taller.

"Thanks for dinner, my good friend, and for recommending the book to me. It is the backbone of my women's studies course," I say as I bundle up in my down jacket, hat, and mittens.

"Tell your students there are plenty of radical feminists out there," Crow says as I walk out the door, "and that patriarchy is alive and well."

FEBRUARY 23

TODAY I leave Laska in her pen; I need time-out from her biting. She lies curled in a tidy circle, her head held high, and her ears pricked forward as she looks at me, the whites of her eyes showing. My resolve wavers. Am I my mother, who so often kept me apart from herself? Or am I Laska, for whom the fleecy blanket, fleecy duck that squeaks, and bleached beef bone do not replace a loving relationship? Suddenly the sight of her doubles, as if I looked through a lens that had gone out of focus, and the second image slowly transmutes into myself as a small girl.

▼▼▼

My room seems like a house of my own. For Christmas, my parents gave me a toy stove, doll's bed, teacups and saucers, little table and chairs. We are Jewish but we had a Christmas tree in the big picture window because Daddy said that Texas is not like New York, where we used to live. We have to make believe that we are Christian until we can go back home. For now we have to stay in Texas so that my father can fix pilots' teeth at the air force base because our country is at war. Sometimes I wonder if my parents want me to cook for myself, even though I'm only three years old. The bed even has a miniature You-you on it as if I am supposed to put myself to sleep. The real You-you is a white wool blanket with satin edging. I named it "You" to keep my "I" company. I used to drag the blanket around so much it got dirty. One night when I was sleeping, my mother cut the blanket in two so she could wash one half at a time. She didn't expect me to notice, but I did. I made such a fuss she had to sew it back together. To keep it clean my mother rolled the You-you up and tied a ribbon around it. Then my mother's mother, who is a seamstress, made a tube-shaped cover. She embroidered the words "You-you" on it. To me, her kind handiwork carried a sad message, for instead of people, the You-you was to be my companion.

▲▲▲

This memory seems like cutout clothes from an old paper-doll book. Possessing a life of their own, the images loop tabs over me and Laska so that I cannot recognize us for ourselves.

FEBRUARY 25

I COME into the living room to find Laska perched on top of a cardboard box inside her large wire crate. She sits quite erect and looks at me. As I return her gaze, she shifts her weight from one front paw to another, as if to plant herself more firmly. Laska is a confident youngster. Originally I put the box in her crate to make the space smaller; that way she would feel cozy when she slept. Merle, whose idea the box was, told me that Laska might chew it to pieces. I never imagined that the pup might use it as a lookout. She resembles a black bear seated on a high rock at the zoo. Laska is wild—it runs in her family—but her genes also carry ten thousand years of domestication, and that influence should prevail. I call my puppy and she scrambles off the box, landing on her chin. I step forward, worried that she hurt herself. Laska gets to her feet, shakes her coat out as if to make a fresh start; then, with her tail wagging gaily, she trots up to the edge of her pen. "Hi, my little black bear," I say.

FEBRUARY 26

TODAY I walk with Laska past Ohavi Zedek synagogue, right around the corner from my house. The neighborhood I live in used to be a Jewish community with the original Ohavi Zedek building at its center. Congregants lived close enough to observe Shabbat, the day of rest, by walking to services. In the 1950s, Ohavi Zedek moved to a newly constructed building not too far from the old one. Today many, if not most, members live in other Burlington neighborhoods or outside the city, and they drive to services. But the rabbi emeritus lives up the block from me, and the rabbi lives across the street from the synagogue.

Laska and I approach the modern-looking long brick building with windows installed high in the walls. Grass, shrubs, and trees surround the structure, and a wide walkway leads up to the entrance. As I approach the carved wooden front doors, Laska strains on her leash to reach the shrubs growing alongside the building; new surroundings excite her curiosity. I keep her by my side as I peer into one of the full-length glass windows that flank the door. The large antechamber with its stone floor leads to the sanctuaries. Their doors are shut, but I can see into the room that serves, by turn, as a basketball court for the community, playroom for the Hebrew school, and dining room for festivities.

I stop by today because, busy with Laska, I haven't been coming to the synagogue. To my surprise I miss it. My proximity to the synagogue stirred a fatalistic sentiment—it was meant to be. Ohavi Zedek is a Conservative congregation. Conservative Judaism is less secular than the Reform but less traditional than the Orthodox. Just as Goldilocks found the right bear's porridge bowl for herself, Conservative Judaism suited me—holding neither too much nor too little of the tradition.

I don't see anyone inside the synagogue, and I move away from the window. I am relieved that I don't have to explain my absence to anyone; at the same time I'm disappointed because I want to show off Laska. I guide my puppy back along the walkway; it doesn't seem respectful to let her sniff at the bushes. As we head down the block to pick up our customary route, I promise myself that I will resume attending services next month.

FEBRUARY 27

I SIT across from my therapist, Daniel Sutherland, on a plump couch with big arms, a little pillow tucked in the small of my back for support. Embroidered on the white cover is an elephant. A tall man with black wavy hair, Daniel sits across from me in an armchair kin to the couch in appearance. Even behind glasses his eyes show such compassion whenever I express deep feeling that they become a mirror in which I can look more kindly upon myself.

"I'm worried that the journal I started about my parents will lead to obsessional writing. I'll examine what went wrong from twenty-five directions, just the way my sister says I do, and still not figure anything out. I feel that I've been their indentured servant long enough." I pause to see if he gets the pun based on the fact that my father is a dentist. He smiles, and I continue, "I've hardly ever written about them, why should I now?"

Daniel looks off to one side, as if receiving counsel from unseen presences—he channels energy by laying on hands during every session—and replies, "Whenever you write about something, you become more clear. That is why you've kept journals over the years. I think your idea makes a lot of sense."

When I get home from Daniel's, I turn to Natalie Goldberg's book *Writing Down The Bones* for further assurance. Years ago her advice freed me from a stubborn writer's block that prevented me from completing *Bearing Meaning.* In the table of contents I find a chapter called "Obsessions." I turn to it and read: "Writers end up writing about their obsessions. Things that haunt them; things they can't forget; stories they carry in their bodies waiting to be released."[2] Her words give me confidence to continue.

I still intend this to be Laska's journal. Yet, as with babies, there is never just a puppy, but a puppy and someone. Laska's and my story is unintelligible unless I understand better my history with my parents.

FEBRUARY 28

WE play "down." First Laska sits smartly, which she learned several weeks ago. Then I draw her down by putting my hands in front of her nose and lowering them to the floor. Once she's there, I praise her extravagantly, saying "Good girl, wonderful." She looks up at me, aware that she's done something commendable. Then she gets a treat. I'm also teaching her how to lick my hand for a treat, which I hope will help her stop biting. Merle explained that I shouldn't pull my hands away abruptly when she grabs for me, because I am triggering her chase instinct, which in some dogs is very strong. Now I try to move them slowly, but it is as hard as languidly withdrawing your hands from a fire.

Laska's look isn't fuzzy anymore. When she's wondering what I want during training, her eyes look discerning, the whites showing a little as she scans my eyes. Laska always looks more at me than at the treat.

Peace in the house. Because I'm writing I turned off the radio, which has been on almost all the time. Merle told me it would comfort Laska whenever I'm gone, but I've kept it on even when I'm home. I recently admitted to myself that *I* needed the radio too.

March 1997

Blue Sky

MARCH 1

A CAR door slams and I listen expectantly. Levin said he would arrive by two o'clock this afternoon; he usually is punctual. This is my son's first trip to Burlington since he graduated from UVM last spring. At present he lives in Cambridge, Massachusetts, where he grew up. Soon I hear a key turn in the lock, and Levin's tall figure appears dimly visible through the glass panes of a wooden door that leads from the mudroom to the living room. Sandra, the lead singer in a band Levin cofounded during his student days, follows him into the house.

"Hey, Mom," Levin says, as he opens the mudroom door. Now twenty-five, Levin wears a short down jacket shaped like the Michelin tire man, rumpled cargo pants, and high-tops. I can't tell what state his hair is in because it is hidden under a knit cap. The clear regard of Levin's gray-green eyes and the smile folds of his lower lids are not diminished. These two familiar aspects of him, known to me ever since he was a youngster, enrich my inner landscape. It is as if, before his arrival today, I stood in a garden planted with immature annuals that represented my new life—marigolds, basil, morning glories, and nasturtium. Now abundant perennials cultivated during the years I lived with my son surround me in a dense tangle—poppies, coreopsis, fescue, lavender, and columbine. I move toward Levin, and as we hug, each of us bends forward so that our two bodies form an A shape; then we kiss each other on the cheek.

Sandra enters the room and greets me with, "Awright! It's been a while." Her dark, round face is full of light, a quality that I attribute to her gospel-singing days. I take Sandra in my arms and hold her solid shape closer than I allowed myself to hold Levin. Since his adolescence, Levin and I have an unspoken rule about our embraces. Last summer I watched with a certain envy as a friend of mine, married with three children, received a hug from her son, who is only slightly younger than Levin. He took his mother in his arms, held her for a long time, his body against her body; then he tilted his head back and gazed at her face affectionately. Without the buffer of a husband/father and siblings, I can't imagine Levin and me hugging the way my friend and her son did, although we love each other no less than they. Maybe there *is* something to Freud's oedipal theory.

As I pull away from Sandra, Levin gives me a customary in-transit look, in which his eyes appear to take in a horizon wider than his mother's world. He has returned, but I am not his destination. "We have to bring in the instruments," Levin says, and he and Sandra go back out to the car. Maybe I imagined their arrival—but his small duffel bag on the floor reassures me. This evening Levin and Sandra will join the other band members of Baby's Nickel Bag, who still live in Burlington, for a performance. With reference to the phrase "Nickel Bag," their CD cover reassures, "It's a natural high."

Laska, who was napping, is now awake. She stands on her hind legs, her front paws up on the metal bars of her pen, and yips excitedly. After they bring everything in from the car, Sandra goes off to meet one of her Burlington friends. Levin removes his coat and hat, walks up to Laska's pen, lifts her, and tucks her in the crook of his arm. Suddenly I see him as a twelve-year-old, skateboarding, while holding his new puppy, Sarah, in exactly the same way. Levin used to practice skateboarding in a tennis court surrounded by trees across the street from our Cambridge apartment. Harvard University owned the land, and I regarded our trespass as an unconventional form of alimony from my first husband, Eric, who was a graduate of the architecture school. I see Levin back then as he rode toward me on the board, standing sideways. The skateboard wheels made an abrasive sound as they passed over the rough pavement. Levin's hair was spiked but not dyed (that came later), and his camouflage jacket flapped in the wind. He had decorated it with studs, safety pins, and a painted skull, underneath which he had written, "Let the kids have their say." Levin's face looked a great deal kinder than his frown, set jaw, and accouterments suggested. As he rolled by me without looking, Sarah, her front legs hanging down in a relaxed position, often turned her young face in my direction, giving me a friendly glance.

Now, as Levin walks from the living room into the kitchen, Laska turns *her* head toward me, just the way Sarah did. Despite how much my puppy resembles Sarah in Levin's arms, I am aware that thirteen years have passed since he was twelve. Laska is my dog, not his or ours. In a few days, I will be alone again with her.

We sit down at the round kitchen table, where we've had so many conversations over the years. As Levin holds Laska on his lap, he strokes her head with his large, shapely hand and his calm energy soothes her, as it does everyone. Eventually, though, she bites him and I am almost happy. I'd been afraid that her toothiness was my fault and that if *Levin* had raised Laska, she would be just as loving as Sarah. Levin doesn't seem to mind that her teeth leave little indents in his fingers. He puts her down on the floor and then laughs and laughs when she chases her tail, a big project these last few days. She catches it in her mouth, turning into a joined circle like one of the fantastical beasts whose bodies twist back on themselves, contortedly, in the shape of alphabet letters in the medieval manuscript *The Lindisfarne Gospels.* Then Laska falls over. Still grasping her tail, she pulls her rear end right off the floor.

After a few minutes I say, "She isn't house-trained yet," and Levin puts Laska back in her pen. He returns to the table. Despite his earlier indication that I am a way station, Levin takes time to ask about my new life with Laska. "One morning," I say, "she ate three quarters of a plastic measuring-spoon handle. I watched her poops for the white handle. She threw some of it up in the middle of the night. A few days later she jumped up on snowdrifts by the fence to get at the bittersweet berries. She ate lots of them and got diarrhea." Diarrhea is a dangerous condition in a young puppy, I tell Levin. The vet said she could "succumb" from it, and that I would have to guard against "a puppy's tendency to do itself in." Both bad things happened when I was trying to get a little time to myself. Noticing my use of the word "bad," I add, "'Bad' in the sense that she was a 'bad girl,' and 'bad' because the things she ate were dangerous."

The day I brought Laska home, her breeder, Stacey, had shown me a picture on her computer screen. A beautiful five-month-old yellow Lab curled up in an oversized half-shell looked at me sweetly. The picture was a memorial to the puppy, who died from eating plastic wire that got tangled in her intestines.

I tell Levin, "Laska isn't really trying to commit suicide, she is just exploring, and she puts everything in her mouth, just like a human baby. When she had the diarrhea she even had to drink Pedialyte, an electrolytically balanced fluid for human babies with upset tummies."

When I finish my story, I gaze at Levin wearily and say, "Eight months seems like a long time. It's weird, but I'm longing for her puppyhood to be over. It's not turning out to be the cuddly, fun time I thought it would be." With this last remark I remember all the mothers I've heard who wanted children to grow out of toddlerhood quickly because it was just too hard. I had little patience for their impatience. Now I feel ashamed of my lack of compassion.

Levin listens to all these stories. I see on his face an understanding that Laska is a more complex puppy to raise than Sarah had been. She did not get into mischief the way Laska does. I see, too, as the stories tumble out of me, how much I've missed someone to share these ups and downs with.

MARCH 6

A LITTLE while ago, I started taking Laska for long walks in the hope that if she had more exercise, she'd bite me less. Anger spurred me to walk with military precision, making her stay right by my side. If she surged ahead of me, I turned and walked rapidly in the opposite direction, snapping her at the neck. I'd read that this technique teaches a dog to heel, but my use of it lacked kindness. No dope, she developed a habit of scratching herself at one particular street corner when I commanded her to sit. I yanked her across the street, unable to control my fury with her, which mounted against my will. It was poignant to watch Laska's small, compact shape as she trotted briskly by my side. Head up, very alert, she seemed determined to take care of herself. Since I was so unreliable, why would she want to depend on me?

I knew enough to call Merle for help. She said that Laska was much too young to be taken for long walks or taught to heel. So now we go for "puppy walks" of no more than ten minutes with no lessons. Merle tells me what I already know but have not been abiding: "The most important thing is that she have a happy childhood."

I try to see things from Laska's point of view. She wants to sit on the sidewalk pitched back on her haunches and look at the red cardinal eating orange and red bittersweet berries off the tangled mass of vines that in summer makes my yard look like Circe's island. Or watch a student trudge by with a plastic coffee mug dangling enticingly from her bookbag. Or follow the course of a cottony cloud borne by the wind or a slightly darkened stream of smoke as it rises out of a chimney. All these sights are brand-new to her.

Today's walk takes us to a pale yellow field a few blocks from our house, where there is lots to explore. Laska seems happier to be walking on her leash here than on the cement pavement. Enticing smells and sights distract her from the unnatural restriction. The grasses weave over each other like an etching, and frost has stiffened the stalks so they crunch when I step on them. We go to the pinewoods just next to the field where Crow had lain down and found her name. Despite being on a leash, Laska "loses it," as Levin used to say about Sarah, who did the same thing. She spins around in crazy circles, her tail curved down close to her haunches, perhaps for speed's sake. On the way home I notice that long crisscrossing ice crystals have formed in puddles on the sidewalk; crystals take on intricate leaf shapes. The first formation takes the side of winter, the second of spring. They mirror perfectly my state of hope yet hopelessness about how Laska and I are getting on.

MARCH 7

I SIT on a low stool in an examining room at Richmond Animal Hospital. The rangy clapboard building has a homey feeling about it that lessens the medical atmosphere. Richmond is a rural town twenty minutes from Burlington and not far from Camel's Hump Mountain, where I look forward to walking with Laska. For some reason after Sarah died I didn't want to go back to her vet; Merle recommended Richmond so highly that I decided it was worth the trip.

Laska and I are here for her second routine puppy checkup. Our vet, Juliana Moore, leans against the examining table as we talk. A tall slender woman in her forties, Juliana is doctorly without being distant. Laska sits at Juliana's feet; she is quite still for a pup, but her whole body shimmers with pent-up energy. "How are things going with Laska?" Juliana asks.

I gaze up at Juliana from the stool, and my shoulders slump with discouragement. "Biting is our big problem. I try to stop Laska, but the more I do, the more she bites me."

Juliana pushes her wire-rim glasses back into place and says, "Some people enjoy controlling animals and others don't. I don't particularly myself."

I am relieved to hear that, like me, Juliana doesn't enjoy confrontations. My back straightens a bit.

"Why don't you not handle Laska too much for now?" Juliana continues. "She will eventually stop biting. Just give her a quick pat on the back," and she demonstrates by sweeping her hand lightly over Laska's compact shape; Laska immediately springs to her feet. "That way you avoid her biting your hands."

Juliana's advice turns the disturbing dynamic between Laska and me into something almost ho-hum, and I drive home reassured.

MARCH 8

WHEN I come home between classes to visit Laska, I change my clothes; in pursuit of respect, I now wear suits for teaching. All over the country, professors complain about lack of respect from students, and UVM is no exception.

I chide colleagues my age with the reminder: "We were the sixties generation that advised our comrades to question authority, so we have no one to blame but ourselves."

My favorite story about respect comes from an incident in one of my upper-level seminars. I'd instructed students to consult *The Chicago Manual of Style* if they had questions about the proper way to cite books and articles in their term papers. The following week a student raised her hand and announced to the class, and possibly the known universe, "*The Chicago Manual of Style* just doesn't *do* it for me."

In an instant, I became a waitress who had just found out that the wine I recommended to my client sucked. "That isn't a reason not to use it," I replied.

"I'm just being honest," she said, with an edge of hurt feelings.

The classroom full of students became electric.

"Well, honesty isn't always the most important attribute," I answered, but I knew it was a lame reply, and so did everyone else. It would have been better to acknowledge her feelings and then summon a credible defense of *The Chicago Manual of Style.* But what would I have said? I find the book tedious and confusing myself, yet I want my students to learn and to follow the established customs of writing. Perhaps I have to go back to the wine cellar for a vintage more suited to my students' palates.

MARCH 9

THERE'S a particular blue to the winter sky in Vermont I never witnessed in New York City, where I grew up. The blue is concentrated, the way you see it in photos taken from space ships circling the earth, and most saturated just above the tree line opposite the sun. It bewitches me. Seeing the blue this morning, almost gaudy in comparison to winter's usual gray, I decide that Laska and I will go up to Camel's Hump Mountain. A friend graciously allows me to walk or snowshoe on her land, a Nordic ski area much too hilly for me to ski. "Just we us two," I say to Laska, borrowing Levin's childhood phrase.

I take a spray bottle, which I learned to use with Steely to deter him from lunging at people, to keep Laska off my snowshoes and poles. I wear jeans so I don't have to worry about her ruining my ski pants. It's a good thing I do. As soon as we enter the woods, hundreds of acres filled with rabbits, moose, black bears, and deer, Laska gets a predatory gleam in her eye and heads straight for me. She leaps high, as if on springs, aiming for any part of my down jacket. I grab the spray bottle from my fanny pack and shoot it at her. Right away, my mood begins to darken. But the blue sky rebukes me and I make an effort to recover. The spray bottle works, and so as not to sink into the soft snow, Laska settles down to walking in the ski ruts machines have made for the cross-country skiers. As peace returns to my heart, I become aware of my surroundings. The woods are so quiet that I can hear snow falling off the trees. Elsewhere it lies draped on branches in heavy, sagging folds like the robes of Demeter. Camel's Hump is vividly clear; the topmost ridges resemble muscles under gray-white skin, the trees sticking out like stiff black hairs.

On the way back Laska chases a tall young woman whose shapely legs are sheathed in shiny purple tights. She skies past us and then turns onto an uphill path, with Laska in scrambling pursuit. I am transfixed as I watch the woman scoop Laska up in her arms effortlessly and carry her back to me, gliding down the hill without any fear of losing her balance. "I wish I could ski like that," I say, planted on my solid but stolid snowshoes.

After snowshoeing I run into my friend Kyra, the owner of the land, a vibrantly healthy woman in her early forties. She reminds me of Buddha's Abbie, a real Vermonter. Kyra has strong arms and legs, her face is tanned from the time she spends outdoors, and there is a flush to her cheeks as if she just got back from cross-country skiing. Admiring her beauty, fresh as the smell of the snow, I am surprised when she says, "You look so beautiful and healthy and outdoorsy. So strong, not needing anyone to define you. And I admire your courage going out into the deep woods. You're so motherly to your puppy. Reading your *Bearing Meaning* helps me see your maternal side." I drive back down the hill affixing her words like a Post-it to my sense of myself. Motherly to my puppy! That remark more than anything is one I want to keep.

MARCH 10

THE toilet tank leaked water into cracks between the floorboards. As I pay the plumber for his time, I notice that my checking account is low. Expenses are piling up lately: my printer at home needed a repair; I had orthotics made for my shoes; and in a few days I'm taking my car in to be fixed. Whenever my finances worry me, the events that led up to my parents' cutoff of assistance crowd like unwelcome guests into my mind. The year before their first visit to Vermont, I sat across from my mother at the card table they had set up in the bedroom of their New York apartment. This surface served as a place to pay bills and eat meals, though they had a dining room and study. It was as if they had recreated in Manhattan the cramped, familiar quarters of their childhood homes in Jersey City.

My mother handed me a check, averting her face. I asked, "Mom, as long as you *are* giving me the money, couldn't you do it graciously?"

Without a trace of humor she said, "You can't have everything."

My father's reluctance to help me financially was harder to make out. It seemed mixed up with shame, as if I were a welfare case. I often felt that he confused me with less affluent family members who over the years had asked him for money.

Though my parents had helped me at times during my adult life, when I became a single mother and entered graduate school in 1976, I became dependent upon them in a way I never had before. As a student and mother of a young child, I wished to work part-time. This decision reduced my income and made it impossible for me to seek psychotherapy without asking my parents for help. They acquiesced to that request and also were willing to replace my fifteen-year-old rusted-out car. They even offered to modestly supplement my rent so that I could move to a neighborhood with a good public school for Levin. But with each transaction over money, my parents gave me the sense that my needs burdened them and brought shame on me.

After I got a tenure-track job at UVM, my parents kept their promise to help me buy a house when I had acquired, as they put it, "a real job." I never realized how peaceful it could be to have my own home; and I felt grateful to my parents and as if their relationship to me had turned a corner.

Three years after I moved in, my parents drove up from New York for their first visit. Karen, her three-year-old son, Matty, and her husband, Bill, flew in from California. Levin and his then-girlfriend, Alexandra, were in Burlington, as he was attending school at UVM. Sarah was still alive. I had invited everyone in August so that we could celebrate my father's eighty-third birthday.

Ever since he turned seventy, my father had celebrated his birthday with an annual party at my parents' summer home in Connecticut. Each year they readied for these festivities tensely. My sister and I and our families helped out beforehand, but we dreaded the joyless preparations and felt hurt over the way my parents became full of smiles only when the guests arrived.

When I invited my mother and father to Vermont, I hoped that this time we could celebrate my father's birthday as a *family.* The high wooden stockade fence that surrounds my yard seemed to protect us from outsiders. In the hours before the meal, we sat out on the deck in the sun. The fresh blue Vermont sky seemed to signal new beginnings. All the same, I felt as if I were in a pointillist painting by the French Impressionist Seurat, a tranquil scene of three generations and a family dog enjoying a summer day. When you look closely at Seurat's paintings, you see an ocean of little dots, and none of the forms make any sense. Because of our chaotic family history, I felt that same double possibility—the orderly shape of our day could disintegrate at any moment.

As we sat together, my sister took notes on what my father and mother remembered of their genealogy to create a family tree. As my father spoke, the upward tilt of his eyebrows exaggerated the sad look in his eyes. Watching him, I thought he might be scanning faces of departed relatives in his memory. Karen listened intently to my father, leaning forward in her chair. Her soft face, young looking for a forty-six-year-old, held an expression of compassionate concentration. I often felt that she worried too much about our parents. I don't remember a lot about what anyone wore that day except for Karen. She dressed in a similar manner whenever she wasn't at work—an oversized T-shirt, Spandex knee-length tights, cotton sports socks, and jogging shoes. To me, her attire signaled a readiness to run, to escape the New York apartment of our childhood with its gray wall-to-wall carpeting. When my father got to the part in the genealogy about how he was the first professional in his family, my mother said, "Your name should appear in movie credits for your patients' teeth." She meant Paul Newman's beatific smile at the end of *Cool Hand Luke* and Danny Glover's self-satisfied grin in *The Color Purple.* Sarah, who was then nine years old but still mischievous, stealthily pulled Kleenex tissues from the pocket of my mother's stylish long black skirt. When my mother became aware of Sarah's transgression, she clapped her hand over her pocket. I waited for recriminations. To my amazement, instead of expressing annoyance, she laughed, seeming to enjoy the tug and pull of wills.

Then there were the other family members. Levin gave an impromptu performance of himself as a model. Earlier, he had showed us a newspaper ad with his picture in it. "Yes, that's *it,* hold it right there, that's perfect, darling," he crooned, providing a voice-over as he stretched his long body into exaggerated postures. Alexandra gave him her full attention as she sat on the topmost deck step. Her beautiful melancholy face was temporarily lit with a smile.

Matty was playing with colored wood blocks from my own childhood that I'd lent him. His dark, shoe-button eyes revealed less about him than did his wide, mobile mouth, which just then looked lonesome. After my sister stopped taking notes, he settled on her lap, took her left thumb in both small hands and rubbed it the way he used to when he still nursed, a far away look in his eyes. Was this four-generation habit of thumb-rubbing (my father soothes himself by rubbing his own thumb, as did his father, and as do I) a genetic trait or did we acquire it through imitation?

Karen's husband, Bill, also a lawyer but with training in philosophy, stood apart from us, as usual. A tall man in his early fifties, with a full head of wavy gray hair and bright eyes behind glasses, he leaned against the house as he told us how he got a discussion group going on the Internet about Aristotle. "I pretended to be several people in conversation with each other," he said. We laughed because Bill often held forth on a variety of subjects, so that it was easy to imagine him dividing into multiple speakers, like the sorcerer's apprentice's brooms.

There was nothing remarkable about the afternoon, except that it was just *us* and that seemed sufficient. As we walked to the table set up in the cool of the trees, my father, whose eyes shone with a pleading joy, said, "I want to do this every year." Then to Bill, whose arm he had taken, he added in wonderment, "We are all getting along."

"Do you think it will last?" Bill asked.

"Yes," said my father, affecting a deeper voice than he possessed. He seemed to assume this more "manly" tone whenever he wanted to appear sure of himself.

After we took our places at the table, my father turned a video camera on each of us for birthday remarks. Rising from her chair, my sister began to weep as she said, "This is the first time we have felt like a family."

I stood up to comfort her, tears starting from my own eyes. We hugged, forming a triangle over my mother who sat between us. The momentary tableau, with us joined together and positioned above our mother, seemed to indicate that we had transcended the old family story. When everyone left a week later, I foolishly thought that I had fulfilled a lifelong dream. *I* had created a Brigadoon where my mother and father could feel happy and at ease just in the presence of their family.

Yet, exactly one week after their visit, my parents wrote a letter withdrawing their financial support. My letters in defense of the good that therapy had done me in my professional life, and in relation to them, and the need for help with my house and my health, only drove my parents to a therapist of their own. Their decision to seek professional help was highly ironic, because they always had scorned therapy whenever I praised it. Never before (and our relationship had been far less happy in the past) had they cut me off. With a crazy logic, their withdrawal of support seemed directly related to how *well* we were getting on and to the positive developments in my life. I was on the verge of publishing my first book and receiving tenure—didn't these accomplishments qualify as *nachas?* Then the final verdict came: their therapist agreed that I should receive no further help from my parents. I wrote once more to my father, asking him to reconsider, and he replied by saying that he was too busy to answer my letter.

Why did the cutoff happen? On the one hand, my parents' decision seemed driven by a fear that I would move ahead in my life. Perhaps they were afraid I would forget them or no longer need them. On the other hand, they didn't seem to *want* family happiness, as if our close moments scared them. Whatever else money stood for, it was a tool for my parents to curtail my independence—both by giving it and by taking it away.

The withdrawal of support and my father's seemingly indifferent letter snapped a bond in me that had remained, though considerably frayed, over the years. I decided neither to visit my parents nor to call, but I did observe their birthdays and holidays by sending cards.

MARCH 11

ON my way home from the Ma'ariv (evening) service at the synagogue, the first I've attended since acquiring Laska, I see a neighbor out on the sidewalk, looking through a telescope. I stop and inquire about what he is studying. He invites me to look at Mars. The planet is a reddish-white sharply distinct round of light. "Where is the Hale-Bopp comet?" I ask, thinking that's what he's been looking at. "There," he says, pointing north. He gives me binoculars and there indeed is the Hale-Bopp comet, streaking from right to left low across the horizon, a long gray white tail flowing behind. How do I reconcile the awe I feel over such sights with how I feel standing in an institutional room praying to a closed green cabinet, with a worn-out book of weekday prayers in my hands?

The cabinet, called the ark, holds the sacred texts of Judaism, the Torah, which consists of the first five books of the Hebrew Bible. Tonight, the streaking comet is what brings the sacred close, and I long for God in nature and among the animals rather than in a synagogue.

MARCH 13

LASKA'S top incisors, the milk teeth, are gone and the permanent second teeth are coming in. Shed over a stick or bone, they fell out when I wasn't looking. The rapidity of this change reminds me how short a dog's life is. Maybe that awareness caused me to become frightened yesterday when Laska got trounced by my car mechanic's big homely chocolate Lab, Max. Last week when I had made an appointment for my car, I bragged to Theresa Smith, the owner's wife, that I had a new puppy. Theresa and her husband, Frank, love dogs. The collar that belonged to their previous Labrador retriever still dangles from a file-cabinet handle in the office, even though they've had a new dog for two years. Theresa encouraged me to bring Laska along, assuring me that Max was friendly to other dogs.

I parked my car outside the Swedish Pit's big, unadorned garage, took Laska out of the hatch, and set her down on the ground. She pranced confidently on her leash up to the glass door. Max must have seen us coming because as soon as I opened the door, he threw his heavy body on top of Laska and clamped his mouth on her neck, getting his saliva all over her coat. Laska sank down to the soiled rug and lay still. Theresa rushed in from the office, pulled Max off my puppy, and explained, "Max is never like this. He is in a bad mood. He was so sick yesterday that he had to be hospitalized. They even stuck tubes in him." I stared at Theresa's sharp-featured face; when Theresa explains an expensive repair bill to me, I tend to find her expression shrewd. In this case, there was no reason to doubt her story. Max lay at her feet, panting as if exhausted. I ought to have felt concern for them; instead all I could think about was Laska. What if Max's saliva passed an illness on to her?

"May I call you tomorrow," I asked, "to find out the test results about Max's sickness?"

"Sure," Theresa said.

I added, "Do you think that Frank can work on the car with Laska in the hatch?"

"That might be a first for him, but I don't see why not," Theresa said.

I put my puppy back in the car and left the windows open for air. A metal grate divides the hatch from the rest of the car to prevent Laska from jumping out an open window. During the next hour or so I visited the work area to find Laska sitting, very alert, high above me in the car elevated on lifts.

I call today and Theresa tells me that Max's sickness wasn't caused by a bacteria or a virus. "He might have been poisoned or he might have had a delayed reaction to being hit by a car a few days ago, luckily only lightly," she says.

Theresa's explanation relieves me, but the incident raises an awareness of impermanence. Anxious, I call Laska's vet for reassurance. My puppy hasn't completed all of her vaccinations, and I want to know if the encounter with Max put Laska at risk. "Not if he's had all his shots," Juliana says. "I'm sure he has," I reply, "his owners are not careless about him." Suddenly, I blurt out, "It's all so fragile." "It *is* fragile," Juliana replies, not even waiting for me to explain what I mean by "it." As a vet she deals with sickness and death of pets every day. I appreciate that Juliana acknowledges my distress rather than giving me a pep talk. But after we get off the phone, my anxiety continues. Here is Laska, her life streaming unstoppably alongside mine as Sarah's used to, now sprouting the teeth she'll take to her death, the teeth that will be ground up with her ashes. I can't help thinking these things. Just so, when I put a collar on Laska for the first time, it reminded me of removing Sarah's collar for the last time after she died. She had rested on her side in the back of the station wagon with one ear flung back, as she used to lie when she was a puppy. Death and life take one another by the hand. This image sounds poetic, but it hurts.

MARCH
15

MY friend Sigrid joins Laska and me for a walk at Camel's Hump. I know Sigrid's distaste of the strict animal-training techniques in Germany and I decide to leave the spray bottle at home.

"She's gotten so big," Sigrid says in her soft world-weary voice when she comes through the door. She reaches down to pat Laska, who wiggles eagerly in response. I manage to get the collar around Laska's neck without much trouble because my friend's presence distracts her. No one has accompanied us on a walk before, and I look forward to Sigrid appreciating what a fine puppy Laska is. Just as with a child, it is gratifying to receive such praise.

Our walk starts out well. As soon as I see that predatory gleam in Laska's eye, I take a handful of treats from the fanny pack and throw them ahead of us. Laska searches for the spots where they've disappeared into the snow. This is a great distraction. Then she gets interested in dog tracks along the ski ruts and follows them, head down, ears dropped forward, her big paws clumsy in the deep snow. Pretty soon she forgets about us.

"Look how independent she is," Sigrid says, and my heart swells with motherly pride. Sigrid's praise helps me see that I like the very trait that causes me aggravation.

"She's been like that from the beginning. The day I went to pick Laska up, she chose to explore the breeder's kitchen rather than greet me. The down side is that she's hard to train."

"In Germany we have very well trained dogs and horses," Sigrid replies. "Too well trained." She doesn't elaborate, and I don't want to ask her meaning since I am uncomfortably reminded of Hitler's obsession with precision and perfection.

"That's probably why you have some of the world's best horse-show competitors."

"Yes, but why would a horse want to round his neck and tuck his head in the way dressage horses have to? Wouldn't he rather be walking along, completely relaxed?" I am relieved that Sigrid's reason for saying "too well trained" doesn't appear to be a reference to German history.

"Supposedly, dressage builds upon the natural movements of a horse," I reply a little defensively, since I love the discipline.

"It's a question of choice. The horse isn't the one deciding how he will carry himself."

I look at Laska's small black shape as she trots ahead, her hindquarters wobbling because of the uneven snow on the trail. "What about my situation with Laska?" I ask. "If I don't train her, she will be impossible to live with."

"Maybe your standards are too high," Sigrid answers, kindly.

"I *know* that I'm too exacting," I say. "I judge myself, too, for not being a better dog owner."

"I think that you and Laska are doing fine. She's just a puppy, and a very nice, spirited one; she'll settle down."

We continue in silence. Our short conversation reminds me that I prefer coming to the mountains alone with Laska. Talking breaks the silence and distracts me from the woods. Now I am able to notice that the fresh snow, scattered lightly with brown pine needles and tiny dried berries, resembles rice paper.

Toward the end of the walk, Laska is moving in an even more wobbly way than before. I realize that our walk probably has been too long for a puppy her age. The vet and Merle warned that a puppy's tendons are not yet strong and shouldn't be overexercised. For instance, jogging with a pup isn't a good idea. Like an overtired kid, Laska proceeds to fall apart, becoming hyperactive. She starts jumping at Sigrid's rust-colored nylon shell, hoping to get a good grip on it with her teeth. Springing high, she comes back and back at her, like a large black gnat. Finally, I grab her and manage to get her leash on. This quiets her down some and we head down a sloping field toward the car. Beyond this field are many others, all of them ringed by the Green Mountains. Dusky at day's end, the mountains rise in gentle overlapping peaks; to the west, across Lake Champlain, the more severe Adirondack Mountains are faintly visible. The spacious beauty contrasts with the narrow places inside myself, and I take a deep breath of air that holds the scent of snow and fir trees to bring home with me.

MARCH 16

"IT'S her way of connection," Merle says, "to hold you with her teeth." On occasion, Laska will lick me, for which I praise her profusely. Today she is being very demonstrative. When I came up to her pen this morning, she greeted me, wriggling, her tail moving like a windshield wiper in a big storm. I lifted her up and she eagerly licked my face. This afternoon, still sleepy from a nap, she tenderly mouths my arm. As I feel her warm tongue on my skin, a long ago moment with my sister emerges into consciousness.

▼▼▼

Snap, Crackle, and Pop dance impishly on the Rice Krispies box. Behind me, dishes clatter in the kitchen sink. Our mother is washing up after breakfast. She wears a housecoat made by my grandmother. Her father will call soon from across the river in Jersey City. My mother will like that. I still feel my father's wet coffee kiss on the top of my head. He has gone away to his dental office.

My baby sister and I sit at the red Formica table with metal fluting around the edges. I trace the table border with two fingers; they are a horse's front legs prancing. A soggy Rice Crispy that escaped my mother's dishrag gets in the way. My finger spiritedly kicks it to the floor. Far below our apartment I hear the roar of traffic on the West Side Highway. Cars honk like geese calling, and the sound makes me lonely. The morning drifts, not held steady by a grownup's presence.

My baby sister, Karen, looks without interest at the narrow side of the cereal box. Only words there. We fought over who would get to look at the picture. I won. Karen brings her bottle with the rubber nipple to her soft full face, closes her eyes, and drinks. I am seven and she is two, but I like milk almost as much as she does. I pick up my half-full glass. As I drink I reach for Karen's free hand, small and plump, where it rests on the table. I stroke her skin, soft and pliant as a mother's breast. By turns she strokes mine. My body suffuses with warmth. I relax against the vinyl-covered chair cushion. We could be the two orphaned polar bears I would see half a century later on the public television program, Nova. *A doubled image, each mouthed the other's craggy shoulder covered with white fur. Comfort.*

▲▲▲

MARCH 17

EACH year I teach, I notice that young people have successively more difficulty understanding abstract thought. I attribute this problem to their overexposure to electronic media, and underexposure to books. Seven years ago it was easier to teach Marx, Weber, and Freud than it is today. Many teachers share my awareness of a decline in literacy. I find myself wanting to assign easier books. Yet, as I tell my students in the first class, I know that my passion as a teacher is to help them learn how to read and write. Why teach books they could easily understand on their own?

For instance, the Jewish philosopher Martin Buber would be an excellent writer to include in my Self and Social Interaction class. The course lacks a full discussion of the self/other couplet that takes the sacred into account. Buber's famous book *I and Thou* is all about a relation of self to other that includes divinity. Buber describes two kinds of self/other relationships. An I-It relationship is one where the "other" (human being, animal, or nature) is seen as an object or a thing. An I-Thou relationship is one where the "other" counts as much as the "self" and is one where mutuality and reciprocity abide. Buber believed that an I-Thou relationship connects us to the eternal Thou, which dwells in each of us. When I ask students to raise their hands if they believe in something larger than themselves, whether it be God or nature or—in AA language—a "higher power," most do. Buber's abstract style of writing might get in the way, but his subject matter is one students would like.

Buber is on my mind today because I'm reading *The Souls of Animals* by Reverend Gary Kowalski. Kowalski's book makes an important contribution to recent debates about the human/animal boundary. Judaism and Christianity deny that animals possess souls, even though the root of "animal" is *anima,* the Latin word for soul. Kowalski cites Buber as one of the few theologians who did believe in an animal soul. He describes Buber's experience of an I-Thou relationship with a horse; the encounter gave the philosopher his first intimation of the sacred:

> It was through his [Buber's] rapport with a horse he befriended on a visit to his grandfather's country estate when he was eleven years old that the Jewish thinker first awakened to "the immense otherness of the Other."
>
> The barn, filled with the warmth and closeness of other living beings, became a temple for the young boy, where he sensed the presence of the ineffable. When he stroked the horse's "mighty mane" and felt the life beneath his hand "it was as though the element of vitality itself" bordered on his skin. There was a bond of understanding between him and the mare, as if they both, without saying, knew that the other had glimpsed the same wonderful secret, or heard the same murmuring currents of being.[1]

Most, if not all, of my students would find the phrase "murmuring currents of being" an understandable metaphor because it is nature based and not restricted to any particular religion. I am moved by Buber's description of how the mare communicated "the element of vitality itself." This phrase describes a quality that Laska possesses in abundance. With her, *I* become the student, and I have little excuse for not understanding the "text" Laska teaches because it is anything but abstract.

MARCH 19

WHEN young lady Laska looks at me with her deferential "I'm paying attention to you" look, the whites of her eyes show on the bottom. I've noticed this before but today for the first time I see that they look like crescent moons.

MARCH 20

FREUD is an easy target. When my students take a shot at him, it is hard not to hand them a prize, as if they had played a target game at the Champlain Valley Fair and won an oversized stuffed dog. Though few have ever read Freud (many of his writings are rather impenetrable), they know some version of his penis-envy theory and that it has fallen into disrepute. As we discuss him today, the sentiment in the room gets heated.

"It's ridiculous," Lesley says. She's an athletic young woman dressed in jeans and a loose wool sweater, with a baseball cap backward on her head. "I've never felt penis envy in my life. I like being a girl and I play baseball and soccer."

"I'm insulted that Freud defines me by my sex organs," adds Joel, a tall, thin young man slouched casually in his chair. "That's not what makes me who I am. I *earn* my respect in the world."

The portions from Freud I give them to read in *General Psychological Theory* mention penis envy only briefly. But, like Marx's, Freud's name is radioactive and provokes strong, protective responses.

"Why don't we keep our attention on the chapter about the unconscious," I say, in an attempt to turn the discussion in a different direction. "I certainly don't disagree with you, though it's important to remember that Freud might be talking about the *symbolic* importance of the penis."

"I can tell you a story," I continue. "A former landlady of mine, who was also a fellow graduate student, told me about the day she quit her psychiatrist. You see, generations of women have suffered at the hands of therapists who took the penis-envy theory literally. She walked up to her therapist's desk, sat on it, took his pen from his hand, and, looking down at him, said, 'I don't have penis envy,

I have *power* envy.' She walked out of the office and never came back." Everyone laughs, and it seems I can continue with the topic for the day.

"Let me say in defense of Freud that I appreciate him for three reasons." I pick up a piece of chalk and write on the board as I speak.

"First, there is the unconscious," I say, beginning my list with that word. "Freud brought the unconscious to our attention. He helped us see that it is active, yet hidden from our conscious minds. It is like magma, the molten interior of the earth. Full of censored memories and impulses, the unconscious erupts unexpectedly and disrupts the smooth crust of everyday life." I love the classroom because I can speak as elaborately as I wish to my captive audience.

Jane, an older woman with grown children, often asks for more information. "Can you give an example?" she says.

"Sure," I answer. "Slips of the tongue. My favorite story about that is an incident I saw on TV."

Right away, the room grows quiet. No shuffled papers or changes of position; students are very fond of examples from the media. "Many years ago in Cambridge, Massachusetts," I begin, "I used to watch *The Ten O'Clock News,* a public television program with commentator Christopher Lydon. He was a tall, lean very proper Bostonian who always wore a bowtie. One night, giving the financial report, he said, 'The stock market was erotic . . . I mean erratic today.'" Laughter from the students. "Christopher Lydon smiled, but you could tell he was embarrassed. If it had been color TV, I'm sure I could have seen him blush. That is an example of the unconscious at work."

"Besides the unconscious," I say, adding the word "infant" to my list, "Freud brought the infant onto the world historical stage. Society really hadn't noticed infants before he came along. Even though I don't agree with everything he said about babies, I am grateful to him for noticing them.

"Third, sexuality. Freud made it possible to talk about sex. True, he overdid it; I mean, I don't think that I am teaching and you are learning just because of our sublimated sexual desires. But sex had been a taboo subject before Freud."

I pause and ask if anyone has a question. No one does, so I continue. "Let's look more closely at how the unconscious works. Freud helped us understand that we have deep resistances to change, because of unconscious voices inside of us. Another way the unconscious affects us is through transference. Have you ever noticed that a girlfriend, boyfriend, or roommate reminds you of one of your parents?" Heads nod. I don't ask for examples, because in a class of forty it is hard to be that open. "Well, those misperceptions would be examples of transference. Poor Oedipus," I add. "We might imagine that we married our mother and killed our father, but he actually *did.*" Laughter. I'm just warming up, but a few minutes later a restless stirring in the room announces that my time is up. "We'll continue with the unconscious next time," I say abruptly, adding to no one in particular, "it's not a part of the mind that allows itself to be forgotten."

MARCH 21

I LEARNED from one of our local newspapers that Reverend Kowalski, who wrote about Buber, is right here in Burlington, and that he is finishing a new book called *Goodbye, Friend: Healing Wisdom for Anyone Who Has Ever Lost a Pet.* In a small city—Burlington has a population of thirty-nine thousand—it feels easy to contact someone you don't know. They seem more accessible than an unknown person does in New York City or Cambridge, the two other cities I know best. When I phoned Reverend Kowalski a few days ago, he was most willing to meet me for lunch.

At Brueggers Bagel Bakery, I content myself with a cup of tea because there isn't anything I can eat that is on the diet I follow for arthritis. With vicarious delight I watch Reverend Kowalski raise the yeasty bagel, bulging with cream cheese, to his lips. He is the cleric, yet I am the ascetic.

"I was so happy to learn about your book," I begin. "When my Labrador retriever Sarah died, I couldn't find much to read for comfort. Plus, many people I talked to didn't seem to realize that her death was a real loss to me. They'd urge me to get another puppy right away."

Reverend Kowalski looks at me sympathetically from behind his wire-rim glasses. He is a tall man of fair complexion with reddish hair and craggy features. I expect him to say something, but perhaps because he is eating a bagel and cream cheese, he remains silent.

"I was interested in what you said in the newspaper article," I continue, "about how no one has ever asked you to preside over the burial of a companion animal."

"Yes," Reverend Kowalski answers, "I find it interesting too. It shows me that our society lacks rituals for the death of a pet."

"I wonder if I haven't buried Sarah's ashes yet because of that." I pause, and then ask, "When I do, would you be willing to conduct a service for her?"

"I'd be happy to," he says, with a smile.

"I did have one kind of ceremony; it happened unexpectedly. Last summer I gave a paper about Sarah's death at the American Sociological Association's annual meeting. It wasn't a traditional academic paper, in fact it pretty much just told the story of her death."

"How did you get it accepted?" Reverend Kowalski asks.

"There is a new subspecialty in sociology called sociology of emotions, and it fit in with their interests."

"You said that the presentation was a kind of ritual?"

"Yes, it was the strangest thing. I read the paper to a small group of people seated at a round table. I expected the usual scholarly response at the end where someone raises his hand and says, 'If I may object to the point you made in your paper . . .' Instead, no one spoke. I looked up from the page I'd just finished reading to find everyone weeping. At the sight, I began to cry too, and we just sat in a circle and cried. It felt like a lamentation ritual. When I got home I realized that I had given the paper on August 13, the anniversary of Sarah's death."

"That's a moving story," Reverend Kowalski says with quiet emotion. "May I see the paper sometime?"

"I'd be happy to send it to you," I answer.

We talk a while longer, and then Reverend Kowalski looks at his watch. I know it is time to end our lunch, so I tactfully say, "Well, I'd better go now. I have a new Labrador puppy, and I try not to stay away from her for too long."

"I'm glad that you have brought another dog into your life," he says, as we rise from the table and walk toward the door.

I hurry home to find Laska looking sleepy and friendly. She stretches, extending her front legs, and drops her belly on the floor. Then she yawns, showing her rather slender, pink tongue, the tip of which curves in a heart shape, and her tail waves slowly back and forth. I scoop her up and take her outside. I look at the yard and try to imagine where I will place a tree that Sarah's ashes will nourish.

MARCH 22

LASKA'S coat is getting rich and wavy as if turned by the sea. How she'll love the ocean! Her paws are big and blunt, and one top tooth is coming in though the old one hasn't fallen out yet. Today we walk at Camel's Hump in the rain. The snow is soft and slushy. Off to our left, a woods stream runs swiftly with the melting snow. The pale yellow field at the edge of the woods is wet, the long grasses matted down. Laska chases a bevy of birds, so much in her element as a retriever, and comes tumbling-running down the hill when I call, her ears flapping.

Time for Laska's supper. Her stomach is growling so loudly in her sleep that it sounds like the gurgle of a radiator.

MARCH
23

I ATTEND a Sunday brunch at the synagogue. The subject is same-sex marriage and several lesbians speak in favor of its being legalized. I ask Rabbi Noah Rubin, "Would you marry a same-sex couple?" The rabbi is a short, slender man with long red hair in a ponytail and a red beard. His eyes, which assume a beseeching expression when he seeks agreement for his opinions, remind me of my father's.

"Yes," he replies, a florid cast rising in his face and an imploring look in his eyes, though he speaks with conviction, "as long as they both are Jewish." I assume he would consider a convert acceptable.

I admire the rabbi's courage, but I also find what he said hilarious. Turning to Crow I quip, "I suppose he'd marry two *ETs* as long as they were Jewish."

MARCH
25

ONE of my former students, Jessica, shows up at my door. Jessica was a student in a graduate humanities course I taught in the English department at UVM. I was a literature major as an undergraduate and treasure the chance, every few years, to teach some of the classic texts of Western tradition. As a first-year student, Jessica was very unsure of herself, though I always thought that she spoke and wrote intelligently. Since graduating, she has given a paper abroad at a prestigious conference. Jessica's academic success seems to have influenced her self-respect, as evidenced by the changes in her looks. Her red, curly hair is pulled back from her face (it used to go every which way), her skin is clear (it used to be full of eruptions), her eyes are accented with eyeliner, and her lips are colored a reddish black (I don't remember her wearing makeup). When Jessica takes off her long black coat, I see that she's dressed in a stylish tight-fitted black sweater and velour pants. I'm often struck by the transformation my students undergo as they mature. They return, newly dressed and coifed, with an independent air that comes from their encounters in the world beyond school. And there I am, if at home, still clumping around in my jeans and Birkenstocks.

We hug, and then Jessica notices Laska in her pen. "Oh, what a cute puppy!" she exclaims, as her whole demeanor changes from a chicly dressed woman of letters to that of a young girl. "Can I pick her up?"

"You'd be better off giving her a pat where she is; she's teething and could tear your nice clothes. Her name is Laska, a name I picked out from *Anna Karenin.*" I figure Jessica will appreciate the literary allusion, but she is too absorbed looking at Laska to pay attention.

As Jessica reaches the pen, Laska hops on her hind legs, eager to meet her too. "Hi, Laska," Jessica says, and gives my puppy a few pats. I can tell that Jessica would like to spend more time with Laska, but ours is a business meeting and so she heads into the kitchen.

We sit down at the table.

"Jess, you look so well," I say. "Confident and happy."

"You can tell?" she asks, with a coy edge to her question.

"I certainly can. But I called you for a different reason. I am going on sabbatical next year and have a book project that I'd like research help with."

Jessica's face lights up with interest. I realize I forgot to put the teakettle on, so I get up from the table.

"What is it about?" she asks. "Babies?"

"Believe it or not, no," I reply, laughing. My students are well acquainted with my favorite topic, and sometimes tease me about it. "I'm calling it *Creatural Lessons: An Archaeological Memoir of the Body.* My plan is to question sociology's conviction that culture, not nature, shapes us. You know that jargon phrase—'social construction.' To most sociologists, the world is socially constructed, just one big Leggo game. Only kidding. I think, and this is in my first book too, that our bodies teach us many lessons, simply as bodies. The way childbirth can."

I pour the tea, hand a mug to Jessica, sit down, and continue. "I plan to address the theoretical questions about culture versus nature, but I also intend to weave in stories about how certain body experiences in adult life, like birth, sexuality, disability, and attending the natural death of my old dog, Sarah, helped me overcome damaging experiences in my childhood." As I say this, I wonder how much I *have* overcome the past.

"That sounds fascinating," Jessica says, sipping her tea.

"There is so much I need to read for the book, and if my grant comes through, I'll have enough money for a research assistant, if you are interested."

"I am, for sure," Jessica says.

"I've also been keeping a journal about Laska and me. But that is a side project at the moment."

We talk for a while more. When Jessica gets up to leave, I notice her black suede boots with three-inch soles.

"How do you get about in winter in those boots?"

"They are OK," Jessica replies, "as long as it doesn't snow."

"Well, I hope you have another pair for when it does."

"I do, Mom," she chides. And then, "Bye Laska, you literary puppy."

So she did hear what I said.

MARCH 27

I JUST got back from the Ma'ariv service that I attend several evenings a week. It lasts just half an hour and I feel civilized by it. Laska lies on her left side in the pen, her pink tongue sticking out. She doesn't get up when I call her. The shaky fear I've been having since Max, the chocolate Lab, attacked her at the garage floods me and I begin to weep. Like a river, my tears carry me back to 1995, the evening before Sarah died.

After our walk in Red Woods Park, where we met Buddha, Sarah and I returned home. I made supper, dropping lettuce leavings and blueberries on the floor, giving Sarah whatever I didn't use. As darkness closed around the house, I heard the radio announcer say, in his warm, husky voice, "Everything's going to be all right." The Celtic program *Thistle and Shamrock* came on, and one tune was so lilting and cheery that I got up and invited Sarah to dance. Dance meant that she stood on her hind legs, letting me hold her front paws, and she would look at me shyly, her ears flattened as if unsure of herself on two legs. I found Sarah lying on her side behind my chair, and when she didn't respond to my invitation I thought she was just tired from our walk.

I went upstairs to shower and then into the studio, where I slept in the summer to escape the heat of my bedroom. I didn't see Sarah until she was standing directly in front of me, where I sat on the couch bed. Her head was lowered parallel to her hunched, tense body. She looked at me sideways without raising her head, with an expression I'd never seen before. It was a clouded, solemn look, verging on severe. I began to say, "Pooch," in a routine greeting, but as her look entered my awareness, fear flooded my body and the word came out in surprise. Then she walked with effort across the room and lay down heavily, her head up, looking at me. My hands shaking, I dialed her vet, only to be told that there was another vet on call for the weekend. When I reached Dr. Osher, he said that I should look inside Sarah's mouth and tell him what I saw. I went over to where Sarah lay and opened her mouth. Afterward I felt that, in my anxiety, I hadn't been gentle enough. Her tongue was gray, small and creased looking, receded inside her mouth, and her lips were gray. I told him what I saw. He said I should bring her in (I later learned gray is the color of shock). Finding no friends home, I called my contractor, Marc Wells, who lived with his wife and child nearby. Though it was ten-thirty at night, he kindly agreed to carry Sarah to the car and accompany us to the hospital.

In the brightly lit examining room, Sarah grabbed nervously at the metal table with her black claws. Then she settled on her haunches and even wagged her tail at Dr. Osher, weakly swishing it across the metal table. He looked at her tongue, her gums, listened to her lungs, took her temperature, listened to her heart, performed an electrocardiogram, which was normal, and speculated that she might have a ruptured spleen tumor, which is a hereditary trait in Labradors. Though nothing had changed, the careful examination reassured me. After he finished, Dr. Osher said, "What do you notice?"

"She's breathing rapidly," Marc answered.

With his words, I noticed for the first time that Sarah was preoccupied with breathing. Poised on her haunches, she held her graceful, compact shape tidily and looked straight ahead with her ears slightly back, listening to us. I was aware of how separate we were from her, not because she was a dog but because of her urgent breathing, so unlike ours. Dr. Osher said, "I think you should go home and come back in the morning so that I can test her blood levels again."

We drove back to my house separately. Marc came in to put Sarah carefully on two blankets by my bed, and then he left. Alone with Sarah, the night felt large outside the studio windows. I decided to call Levin's girlfriend, Alexandra, to see if she might come over. On my way home I had passed their apartment, and I noticed Alexandra's car in the driveway and a light on in the house. Levin was in New York for the weekend. To my relief, when I said, "Sarah is very sick," Alexandra replied, "I'll be right over." Soon the doorbell rang. I let Alexandra into the house and brought her into the studio. Both of us sat down on the bed near Sarah. She was faced away from us, still breathing rapidly with her mouth closed. It was the way she breathed on a hot summer day when she lay on her side and wanted to sleep. I thought of this comparison, but it didn't comfort me. Every time Alexandra and I stopped talking, fear of the unfamiliar processes I saw in Sarah, and fear of how much I needed her, engulfed me. At about two in the morning, I noticed Alexandra yawn. Our conversation was flagging. Checking inside myself, I found that I was steady enough to be alone with Sarah. I suggested that Alexandra could go to sleep in the living room.

I lay on the couch next to where Sarah rested, breathing quickly. I put my hand down frequently to touch her back or shoulders. Though I couldn't sleep, it felt more peaceful and natural to be in the darkness. Also the darkness prevented me from looking at Sarah and worrying over every slight change in her condition. With the light off, I could avoid my tendency to become obsessively observant when I think something is wrong. In the past, if I saw a dry nose or an imagined bump in Sarah's side, I would scrutinize her or palpate her body. Made anxious by me, Sarah would avert her head and move away. I worried, though, that I was being too reserved toward her. Later I saw that by protecting Sarah from my own shock (and grief), I provided a comforting space in which she could attend to her death.

At around 3:30 AM, just after I heard her begin to pant with her mouth open, I smelled a poop. Turning the light on, I saw that she had passed a small normal-looking poop. "Good for you, Pooch," I said, wanting to reassure her. I figured she was panting because she was upset to poop in the house. I cleaned up and put a sheet under her rump. I said, "Good for you, Pooch, and you just poop as much as you please." Sarah went back to panting with her mouth closed.

About fifteen minutes later, I smelled another poop and turned on the light to find Sarah gagging as if she wanted to bring up something huge. All that came out was a little clear-looking stomach juice or saliva, and two small pieces of a green apple she had greedily eaten off the ground just before our walk. This time the poop had little bright red beads of blood in it. I called Dr. Osher to ask about this development but, again, he didn't think it was cause to come in. The thing to do was to repeat the blood test in the morning.

Around 4:00 AM, Sarah again started panting with her mouth open. Hearing her, I turned the light on. The sound of her panting this way was so ordinary seeming that for a moment I thought she was getting better. Later, I understood that she needed more oxygen than the closed-mouth panting provided. I even thought I saw her tongue pink up. Then, beside me on the blankets, unable to find a comfortable position, Sarah began to shift her body bit by bit, as if measuring off angles in a 360-degree circle. She moved to a new position, stayed there for a few minutes, and then moved again, always crouched on her haunches. Although her movements were so precise that she seemed in possession of herself, they were too symmetrical to be normal. I kept listening for quieter breathing. So often, Sarah's regular breathing and deep contented sighs had comforted me. I became aware of how easily and lightly I was breathing, even when I sighed deep slow sighs, while her breathing was labored, without any pause or rest. We were right next to each other, both breathing. Yet, my slow breathing was powerless to give peace to her.

At around 4:30 AM I heard Sarah lurch to her feet in the dark and wobble strangely over to the west wall under the window, where she collapsed and resumed panting. Fooled by her rising to her feet, I said, "Good girl, Pooch," praising what I took to be a turn for the better. "I think you're going to make it," I said to her from time to time, quietly. With the bitter difference of knowledge that is irony, my encouragement of her was accurate. For Sarah was doing a fine job of letting go of her life. Maybe around 4:45 AM, I smelled another poop. I put the light on, aware as I had been each time I did it of the unnatural-sounding click and the bright interruption of the reassuring darkness. I saw a third poop, normal in consistency but again beaded with small bright drops of blood. Although I wished the red were from Sarah eating beets, I knew deep down it wasn't. I cleaned up the poop, putting it in plastic for Dr. Osher to inspect. I was half-aware of the futility of such rational behavior, yet couldn't leave off doing it.

When I returned from the bathroom, I found Sarah gravely transformed. As if unstrung, her front legs were splayed out in a V shape, her head extended on the floor. Her eyes looked blasted, black as the night outside. She no longer was panting but breathing shallow, watery breaths every fifteen seconds or so. Bringing the phone over to where I could be beside her, I somehow got myself down on the floor, despite trouble with my knees. I called Dr. Osher at home. It sounded as if he wasn't asleep.

"Dr. Osher," I said, keeping my eyes on Sarah's face and listening for her breathing, "I think she's dying." I said the word "dying" deliberately, trying not to avoid what was before me. "Her breaths are far apart and watery."

"The prognosis wasn't good," he replied, for the first time letting me know that all along he'd had a hunch that she was terribly ill.

"Is there any point in my bringing her in?" I asked, already picturing how difficult it would be—to wake Alexandra up and tell her, feel her panic or concern, move Sarah, have Sarah bump up and down in the car, then the bright room, the metal table.

"It's hard to say," he offered. "It's really up to you."

I felt utterly alone with my decision. I could sense the friendly and patient doctor at the other end of the line; I saw myself on the floor, Sarah lying splayed out beside me.

"I think I'll just stay here with her," I said slowly and put down the phone.

Sarah and I were alone together, with the night outside the window. Just we us two. I put my head down close to Sarah's, looking at her. A year or so ago I had become aware of Sarah's aging. It was then I had decided that when she died I didn't want to communicate my need of her but simply to let her know that I loved her. My certainty that these were Sarah's final moments gave me the strength to fulfill my resolve. My head down near hers, I said softly and slowly simple, familiar phrases that I had always spoken to her, "You're a good girl, Sarah Pooch, Little Sweet Pea. I love you very, very much and I'm so thankful for all you've given me for so long." I saw her back legs stretch and straighten with ever so slight a tremor. And then, as if waiting until I had finished what I wanted to say, she just stopped breathing.

Quiet in the room. It was perhaps 5:00 AM. First dawn was coming on, slightly gray. I waited for more breaths, although I knew no more were coming. I lay Sarah on her left side, carefully putting her splayed out front legs alongside each other. I tried to put her tongue, which protruded from between her worn-down teeth, back in her mouth. I brought over the blanket she rested on, slipped it under her body, and shrouded her in it. As I lifted Sarah's upper body, her head flopped loosely to the floor, a motion I had never seen before, and I knew that such slackness didn't belong to the living. Later, I remembered that moment and wondered, as I still wonder: where could she have gone so suddenly, how could she be so suddenly gone?

I interrupt my sorrowful reveries and stare at Laska, who lies on *her* left side with her tongue hanging out. I still see no sign of life, but I do become aware of the reason for my anxiety. Now that I begin to care about Laska, I fear losing her. She's worked her way into my heart with her crescent moon–eyed look, her ripply coat and tight otter tail, big blunt paws, and the way she peeks around the corner of the kitchen cupboards to tell me she wants to go out. I call her name anxiously, with an emphasis on the second syllable, "La*ska*." She starts up and I feel guilty for rousing her out of a deep sleep. I need to remind myself that I have no authority over her life. Writing about her in a journal, which I regret not having done enough of with Sarah, won't keep her with me permanently either. Sarah died on Sunday morning; "Sunday Morning" is the title of Wallace Stevens's poem in which he talks about "perishable bliss." The last lines of Stevens's poem encourage the reader to live fully, even though life's trajectory leads to death:

> At evening, casual flocks of pigeons make
> Ambiguous undulations as they sink,
> Downward to darkness, on extended wings.[2]

April 1997

"Puppy Book"

APRIL 1

APRIL Fools' Day is the perfect time for a late snow. Delighted to be alive, Laska pulls on bittersweet vines that sag under the weight of the heavy snow, with the result that she shakes snow down on herself. She drags torn-off vines around the yard leaving a zigzag trail behind her. When bored with one scrap, she gets another. Eventually she gambols over to low tree branches and chews on one of them until the pale wood shows under the dark, wet bark. Like a metronome, her tail waves back and forth, keeping time with her happiness. I watch out that she doesn't eat berries.

This afternoon we go to Camel's Hump, where two feet of snow fell. I snowshoe and Laska bounds in and out of the drifts that are higher than her belly. She stops to inspect a decomposing log, sniffing at the gray fungus that ripples out from it. I continue on ahead, knowing she'll catch up with me. Soon Laska comes running, passes me on the left, and without interrupting her forward motion makes a high bound, turns her head, and rips my woolen glove with her teeth. I wore an old pair for just this reason. Though she hasn't harmed anything valuable, I resent Laska for startling me. I long for the walks Sarah and I used to take up here. Sarah usually trotted ahead of me and would look back frequently, as if we were joined by an invisible tether. But the sky is that intense concentrated blue and its beauty forestalls an unhappy mood. I resolve not to let this porcupine of a puppy ruin my afternoon. I clump along on my snowshoes, pretending to be alone. Streams run between snow-covered rocks; the sun is high and warms my face. I see only deer prints and hear nothing but birds, snow dripping off trees, and the swiftly moving stream, much of which is meltwater. Despite the snowfall, it is clear that spring has come.

APRIL 5

I SIT next to the cantor on one of the green velvet–covered pews in the small sanctuary. Tonight is Havdallah, a service held every Saturday at sundown to mark the end of Shabbat. Not that many people attend, but if a minyan exists (ten or more people) the cantor reads the next week's Torah portion. I enjoy the ritual of this service. After the cantor darkens the small sanctuary, he lights a long braided candle and hands it to one of us. The candle alone illuminates the prayer book he sings from. After the short service the cantor extinguishes the candle in a cup of wine. I am early enough to be able to chitchat with Rabbi Noah Rubin, Cantor Aaron Solomon, and the rabbi emeritus, Ben Abraham. Rabbi Abraham is a short, compact man, strong in appearance despite his years. During World War II he fought in the Battle of the Bulge, and his habit of ready wit seems forged in what must have been a horrific experience.

"So how goes it?" the cantor asks, turning his head toward me, his hands tucked behind colorful suspenders. I enjoy the amusement in his eyes and the way his full lips hint at something hilarious. Cantor Aaron's easygoing manner and his habit of telling really corny jokes emboldens me to talk about my puppy. The rabbis might overhear, but I am sure they are inured to human failings.

"Well, not so good and not so bad. I have a new puppy. That's good, *tov,*" I say, eager to show off my Hebrew. "But she bites me all the time." I don't know the Hebrew word for "bad."

"Sure you're feeding her enough?" he quips. "Our poodle Eli did the same thing when he was a pup." He pauses and appears to survey a scene I can't see. "He's still a rascal. His latest thing is to drag toilet rolls through the house, leaving a paper trail from upstairs to downstairs." From his merry eyes, I can see the cantor is about to tell a joke. "Must have been a lawyer in a past lifetime." He waits for a laugh and is not disappointed.

"Actually he jumps and bites even now," the cantor continues. "We've been getting help from a trainer and, boy, is Eli a different dog with her, *sooo* eager to please," he says, drawing out the word for emphasis.

"What's the name of the trainer?" I ask.

"Vivian Marsh, she's very nice and very good."

"Oh, I've talked to her briefly over the phone."

"Cass and I needed help in a big way. Our first poodle was gentle and loving and we went back to his breeder hoping to get a dog just like him. Eli is the complete opposite. He's been such a handful that at one point we thought of giving him up."

"Our experiences are almost identical," I say eagerly. But before I have a chance to tell the cantor more about Laska and me, it is time to begin the service. When the sun goes down, all kinds of meaningful conversations stop abruptly in the small sanctuary. The interruption is fun because you take whatever is left unexpressed and put it into your praying. Devotional words are part of a conversation, too, held with the sacred.

APRIL 6

LASKA chews vigorously on an oversized rawhide bone. Knotted at both ends, it is almost as long as she is. I bought a big one so she wouldn't be able to break off little pieces that she could choke on. She turns her head sideways to get a better grip on it and the whites of her eyes show. Sunlight streams onto her and onto the parquet linoleum in the kitchen, the pattern of which is an optical illusion, imitating elegant, intricately laid wood. Illusion: I am more and more aware of how I *transfer* feelings to Laska and then act as if she is their source. For instance, I often expect Laska to reject her name. In the patriarchal story of Genesis, God granted Adam the right to name the animals *and* Eve. Who gave me the power to determine Laska's name? Consciously, I don't believe that I have imposed my will on my dog, but unconsciously I do. I get up from my chair to break the reverie, but the insistent sound of a fly buzzing carries me back to Texas during World War II.

▼▼▼

I have a cold and, though I've been told not to, I go to the door when the postman comes. He stands in front of me, but I still see the bright Texas day behind him and I long to be outside. As soon as my mother takes the mail and the postman turns his back, she grabs my wrist. She says, tightly: "That's it. I've had it," and though I scuff my heels on the floor, she drags me off to my room, where I will stay until my father comes home.

Today I don't want my You-you but the brown stuffed horse, Zan Zac, with a yellow mane and tail and a rascally eye, which my parents gave me a few months ago on my fourth birthday. He is named after the real trotting pony I love so much. I sit on Zan Zac pretending to ride him right out of the house. I like my stuffed animals much more than my dishes, teacups, and stove, which remind me of my mother, who seems as trapped in her house as I am in my room. Still sitting on Zan Zac, I pick up Rudyard Kipling's Just So Stories. *My favorite is* The Elephant's Child. *When the crocodile tugs on the baby elephant's nose, the little elephant pulls back, yelling, "This is too butch for be." He says "butch" for "much" and "be" for "me" because his nose is closed shut by the crocodile. Mine is stuffed up by a cold. My mother tells me I should blow it in the handkerchief she gave me, embroidered with tiny daisies, but I usually forget to.*

I love that sentence in the book for another reason. Right now I feel "too butch" because my father was angry at me last night. When he came home from work, he picked me up and said, "Kiss." I stuck out my lower lip and turned my head. I didn't want one of his big wet kisses just then. "Kiss," he repeated. I screwed my eyes shut and pushed at his shoulders with my hands. My father put me down and walked out onto the screened-in porch. He sat down to read the newspaper. The next morning my father didn't pay attention to me. He ate his breakfast absently. I tried to get his attention, but a hurt-tickle went through me when I put my hand on his knee, like when you bang your funny bone. He got up from his chair without seeming to notice me and soon went off to work. I didn't give in and kiss my father, but how could I be without him? He is the one who loves me.

I hear the front door slam. I hear my father say, "Where's the kid?" Maybe he's forgiven me. But then my mother replies, "She went to the door with that cold of hers when the postman came and got a draft. I can't take it anymore." She bursts into tears. Since my father asked where I was, I open my bedroom door. Maybe he won't mind if I come out. I see my mother run into their bedroom and throw herself on the bed, sobbing. My father goes in after her. I return to my room and look again at The Elephant's Child. *I can't read yet, but I remember the words from when my father reads to me. One of my favorite moments is when the baby elephant treads on "what he thought was a log of wood at the very edge of the gray-green, greasy Limpopo River, all set about with fever-trees." The log turns out to be the crocodile. I let the words swarm around me like brightly colored tropical birds.*

▲▲▲

APRIL 7

I MAKE my way down the auditorium aisle of my Sex, Marriage, and the Family class and smile at Amber as I pass. Though she's a '90s activist in environmental issues and animal rights, she dresses like a '60s hippie. Today she wears pantaloons with a floral design and her hair is tied back in a colorful scarf.

"I'm psyched about today's talk," Amber says, leaning forward in her seat as if to get a better view, though the speaker isn't here yet.

"Me too," I reply. At Amber's suggestion I have invited a representative from People for the Ethical Treatment of Animals. Normally PETA does not lecture on companion animals, but when I described our class to Kate Allen, their representative, she agreed to gather data on the subject. Amber's recommendation couldn't have come at a better time. My difficulties with Laska have made me aware that a course about families ought to include a lecture on the animals who share our lives.

I continue down the aisle to the front of the auditorium. Attendance looks good today, and I don't fool myself that the speaker has nothing to do with it. I've often thought that I ought to wear shoes with high soles and a dramatic papier-mâché mask, as the ancient Greek actors did, to teach a class of 150 students effectively. Without them, I'm just that speck at the bottom of a canyon, even with a clip-on microphone.

A short, wiry woman of about thirty appears at the back of the auditorium and I wave to her, figuring it's Kate. She wears a black pants suit, a white shirt, and a red scarf tied in a careful knot around her neck. Her black-and-white color scheme suits the polemical stance of PETA and the red scarf metaphorically signals the organization's militant activism.

"It's a pleasure to have you with us," I say, taking Kate's hand. She gives me a friendly glance but does not smile.

I let Kate's hand go and she brushes her straight black hair behind each ear as if getting ready for action. Then she says, "I'm very glad to be giving this talk; I've found material about the history of the humane movement and about companion animals."

"Well, let's get the microphone on your lapel," I reply, "so that everyone will be able to hear what you say."

"Oh, I don't think I need it," Kate says and she is right. Her voice carries just fine. She begins with a rhetorical question: "Do you know the cuddly puppy or cute kitten someone gives as a Christmas or birthday present? Well, that little pet usually doesn't last long in our homes. In fact, more than 70 percent of people who acquire animals give them away, abandon them, or leave them with shelters, which house twenty-seven million unwanted animals a year, seventeen million of which are killed, most of them under eighteen months old and in perfect health."

Kate pauses for a moment. I can't tell what the students are thinking, but I'm as shocked as I think she would like me to be. She continues: "A hundred years ago animals were considered to be personal property, not much different from a plow, shovel, or other useful or valuable object. I'm not sure how far we've come. The statistics I just presented show that we give our pets up so easily, as if they *were* just objects.

"But first some background. At the beginning of the nineteenth century several influential thinkers proposed that even if animals couldn't reason or speak—by the way, animals can do both—they *could* suffer and deserved humane treatment. You might be interested to know that Maine passed the first anticruelty law in 1821, but it wasn't enforced. Britain followed with the first effective law in 1822, although the penalties weren't very harsh. The law protected animals who had commercial value, not family pets or wild animals. In addition, an organization formed that became the Royal Society for the Protection of Animals."

Amber raises her hand and asks, "Why did animal suffering become an issue at that time?"

"That's an interesting question," Kate replies. "Maybe because in those days more and more people lived in cities, where dogs and horses pulled carts through the streets. Every day people saw animals burdened down and suffering from exhaustion, dehydration, or malnutrition. If an animal fell in its traces, the owner might beat it or even leave it to die. Did you ever read the story *Black Beauty* when you were a child? That book describes the kinds of cruelty horses suffered in cities."

I raise my hand and add, "Perhaps the movements toward democracy in England and France during the seventeenth, eighteenth, and nineteenth centuries created an atmosphere where equality was in the air. Also, with the rise of the middle class, an awareness grew that one's place in society wasn't fixed, the way it had been when there were only two social classes—aristocrats and peasants or serfs."

"Maybe," Kate answers, "but nineteenth-century animal advocates used words like 'inferior animals,' 'lower animals,' and even 'dumb brutes.'" She adds, heatedly, "We at PETA don't believe that humans are superior to animals, and we don't rate mammals higher than other creatures who also feel pain and deserve our protection. Did you know that silkworm cocoons, with the silkworm inside, are boiled to obtain the fibers? There are many alternatives to silk nowadays. PETA recommends what we call 'compassionate clothing,' clothing that doesn't come from harming animals of any kind. What we wear—that is a family issue."

Kate stops; she seems to realize that she's gotten onto a more customary PETA topic—animal exploitation and actions the public can take to oppose it. She continues, "Getting back to my story, the U.S. followed Britain's lead by creating, thanks to animal advocate Henry Bergh, the American Society for the Prevention of Cruelty to Animals. The New York State Legislature chartered that organization in 1866. Gradually other states adopted similar charters and the provisions grew broader. They included all, and I quote, 'brute creatures,' and required that the animals receive adequate food, water, shelter and so on. However, the penalties for violating the law were weak and not easy to enforce. Other than those legislative moves, I'm sorry to say that the legal protection of animals hasn't progressed all that much in the last one hundred years. By comparison, what would we think if women still were their husbands' property or if children still worked in factories? That was the legal standing of women and children a century ago; the legal standing of animals today is that backward."

"What about the animal rights movement?" Amber asks, not even waiting to be recognized. This class is becoming something of a dialogue between my student and Kate.

"You bring up an important point," Kate says, smiling for the first time. "The earlier movements were concerned with animal welfare, compassionate treatment of animals. The animal rights movement that began in 1975 with Peter Singer's book *Animal Liberation* takes a more radical approach. Typically the movement advocates freedom for animals from any human interference, vegetarianism, acknowledgment that animals are sentient beings, and insistence that we act as their stewards, not as their dominators. Some animal rights advocates seek legal standing for animals."

I raise my hand. "I imagine that the animal rights movement arose in the 1970s because other social movements were afoot—the civil rights movement, the women's liberation movement, the gay and lesbian movement, and the antiwar movement against the Vietnamese conflict."

"I'm sure that is true," Kate says.

Amber returns to the question of legal protection. "The Endangered Species Act of 1969 is one law that protects animals. And even where there aren't laws, consumer pressure has had an effect." She adds, sounding rather like Kate, "Have you ever seen a rabbit's eye burnt from some cosmetic liquid dripped into it? Thanks to consumer pressure we now have cruelty-free cosmetics that aren't tested on animals, that is, if you care to wear makeup."

Kate says, "Amber is right, there are some legal advances. Besides the Endangered Species Act in the U.S., we also have the Animal Welfare Law of 1966, the Marine Mammal Protection Act of 1972, plus other federal and state laws. But these statutes are limited, they have many exclusions, and they don't protect animals as a whole. For example, the U.S. Constitution offers no protection of animals. I invite you to think about laboratory animals used in medical research; think about animals raised or hunted for their fur; think about factory farm animals—pigs, cattle, chickens (I assume you know something about these); think about thoroughbred horses exploited by the racing industry and beaten so that they will run faster, in full view of cheering crowds; think about Doberman pinschers whose tails are cut off and ears sliced to match the so-called breed standard; think about puppy mills. Female dogs—I won't use the word 'bitch'—are forced to produce litter after litter. Their puppies are confined to wire cages stacked in a high pile so that the puppies end up eliminating on each other. Never buy a puppy from a pet shop; people who run puppy mills sell to them."

Kate pauses and looks around the room, her eyes bright with challenge. She continues, "I want to say more, specifically about companion animals and families, although what I've said so far has implications for our pets. Much of the nineteenth century legislation against animal cruelty really had humans in mind. The idea was that if you mistreated animals, you were likely to mistreat people. Here is what a judge in Mississippi said in 1887." Kate bends her head and reads from a sheet of paper:

> Animals whose lives are devoted to our use and pleasure, and which are capable, perhaps, of feeling as great physical pain or pleasure as ourselves, deserve, for these considerations alone, kindly treatment. The dominion of man over them, if not a moral trust, has a better significance than the development of malignant passions and cruel instincts. Often their beauty, gentleness and fidelity suggest the reflection that it may have been one of the purposes of their creation and subordination to enlarge the sympathies and expand the better feelings of our race. But, however this may be, human beings should be kind and just to dumb brutes; if for no other reason than to learn how to be kind and just to each other.[1]

"Do you see? The judge emphasizes human moral improvement rather than animal well-being. But he is also right; there *is* a connection between cruelty toward animals and violence in human relationships. At the beginning of my talk I told you about the huge number of pets abandoned or given up for adoption. What about the companion animals we *do* keep? How are they treated? The answer is, not all that well. For example, many dog owners chain their pets outside; some leave them there day and night, season after season. PETA has a saying: 'A chained dog can only watch and want as life goes by.' Pet abuse is so widespread that, besides animal shelters, there are national networks of rescue centers for purebred dogs; the centers take in traumatized animals and locate homes for them."

I raise my hand and ask, "What relationship is there between pet abuse and family life?"

"They are deeply connected," Kate replies, and her face becomes tense. "We spank our children, so why should we refrain from hitting the family dog? PETA has another saying: 'People who are violent to animals rarely stop there.' One study done in New Jersey found that 88 percent of families with abused animals also abuse their children. Children, often the very ones who were abused by their parents, may be cruel to animals. I'm sorry to say that there also is sexual abuse of companion animals. For example, an abusive husband may force his wife to have sex with the family dog. Animal abuse is not just a *symptom* of a problem amongst family members; animal abuse *itself* is a problem, one that we must do something about.

"I am not a family psychologist so I can't tell you how family abuse can be stopped. But as a PETA representative I can make some recommendations that would protect companion animals from abuse. You should only bring a pet into your life if you can act responsibly toward it; the responsibility is ongoing and involves commitments of time and money. Your pet requires good medical care, adequate exercise, obedience classes (for dogs, of course, not cats), the right not to be left alone too long, and most importantly your patience, understanding, and love. Additionally, you must spay or neuter your pet to avoid the euthanizing of unwanted animals. These may seem like small recommendations, but they would go a long way toward improving the lives of our companion animals."

Kate pauses, looks at her watch, and says, "Are there any questions or comments?" Perhaps because the subject of animal abuse hits close to home—How many in my class were spanked as kids and may have witnessed or committed unkind behavior toward their family pets?—the students remain silent. I suppress a desire to say that we need to understand the role of the human unconscious in the abuse of our pets, but I can't bring myself to speak, afraid that somehow, like an untidy slip under a skirt, my relationship with Laska will show.

Kate continues, "Before our time is up, I want to tell you a little bit about PETA. We are the largest animal rights organization in the world, with a membership of over five hundred thousand. PETA was founded in 1980 and is dedicated to establishing and defending the rights of all animals. We operate under the simple principle that animals are not ours to eat, wear, experiment on, or use for entertainment. PETA enjoys the support of celebrities like Paul McCartney and Cindy Crawford, and the organization works hard to get its message into elementary schools, as well as colleges and universities. That is why I am here today."

Students begin stuffing their notebooks into bookbags. I applaud our speaker, and the class follows suit. I tell Kate, "That was an impressive presentation." Amber tells her, "Wow, you *rocked*!"

APRIL 11

LEVIN is asleep on a futon in my workroom. He and Sandra, lead singer of Baby's Nickel Bag, arrived late last night after I'd gone to bed. They are here for a concert celebrating the release of their band's CD. Since returning to Burlington Levin chooses not to spend the night in his old room because, as he put it on his last visit, "there's nothing in there." During some of the time he studied at UVM, Levin lived in a five-hundred-square-foot room that is part of a shed addition to the main house. It has a woodstove, all kinds of windows—skylight, picture window, small octagon shaped—and a trapdoor to the storage room below. For privacy, Levin often came and went through that makeshift entrance. His band, which practiced in the room, schlepped their equipment up the back stairs, and once a week the main house thrummed with the sounds of Levin's flute, Jay's bass, Chris's guitar, Phil's drums, Twa's percussion, and Stephanie's keyboard. When Levin moved to Boston last summer, he left many of his paintings and possessions behind. Still, the big room is just bare enough to make a person melancholy. I would like to store some of my own things in there, but I still think of the space as his.

The door to my workroom is shut so that Laska won't disturb Levin. I come downstairs to find Sandra asleep on the couch. Laska follows me down the stairs hippity-hoppity like a rabbit, large ears flapping around her face, and her tail wagging. She's gotten big, twenty-five pounds now, her coat shining and richly wavy on her back and tail. Laska climbs on Sandra, awakening her. Sandra good-naturedly greets the wriggly puppy and then goes back to sleep.

In the afternoon Levin is standing by the TV looking at a local newspaper. Sandra is putting on boots with three-inch soles; I say to her, "I've been singing." My announcement surprises me and strikes me as plucky, because Sandra has a rich, contralto voice imbued with gospel spirit.

Not looking up from his paper, and with a certain bemused embarrassment, Levin says, "Mom's going to sing."

I haven't actually planned to, but Sandra says, "Oh, do, I want to hear." So I sing the Hebrew prayers that Cantor Aaron helped me learn. I've been attending more and more services at the synagogue. Often I am called to the bimah (altar) on Shabbat morning. Since the time of Moses, *kohanim* (the name Kahn is one variation) have been regarded as a priestly class descended from Moses' brother, Aaron. As one of the few *kohanim* regularly at Shabbat service, I frequently receive the first aliyah—the privilege of singing a ritual prayer before and after the cantor or a congregant reads the first Torah portion of the morning. In Judaism, the Torah is read throughout the year and begun over again in the fall. Though it isn't democratic to be honored as a *kohayn,* this unearned privilege has given me an odd form of self-respect. I am a valuable member of the tribe, or family—a sense that I missed growing up.

When I finish, I tell Sandra, "That's the best I've ever sung."

Sandra's face is alight with enjoyment. "I like the gritty sound to your voice," she says. "It gives the songs strength."

"Maybe I inherited sand in my throat from my Jewish ancestors who escaped to the desert from Egypt," I say, playfully. At the end of this month Jews around the world gather to celebrate Passover by telling the story of the exodus.

"Let my people go," Sandra sings in her deep, clear voice.

Levin keeps his head down, reading; he is seemingly uninterested in our conversation. He might prefer that I didn't sing, but his knowledge that the synagogue gives me a community to belong to may make *his* exodus easier. Levin plans to move from Boston to New York—two hundred miles farther from here.

APRIL 12

THIS morning, after last night's concert, Levin and Sandra sleep late. After we eat soy cheese omelets with broccoli that I make for brunch, they ready themselves for the trip back to Boston. This has been something of a whistle stop, since they arrived only yesterday. As Levin packs the car, I follow him outside and say, "Well, the next time I see you, you'll be a New Yorker."

"I plan to come up every five to six weeks," he responds. Then his face clouds as he imagines the difficulty of following up on his offer. "It might be unrealistic, but if we could split the expense it would help," he adds.

"I'm sure I can split it with you," I say, as my mind moves quickly, wondering if he wants to come for my sake or for his or both. His words carry the poignancy of an epic journeyer who promises to himself and those he leaves behind a return. But the journey may take him on paths that foreclose keeping the promise.

When Levin already is in his car, our eyes meet. I lift my eyebrows, adding a little smile. The expression mimics that of the cartoon character Snoopy when he is in the doldrums. For years, Levin and I have exchanged that look to acknowledge life's pathos. His eyes catch the sentiment and instantly reflect it. So I bend down to the low Saab and tell him through the open window what is also true: "Just remember, I'm fine." His eyes lighten with relief.

A mentor of mine, ten years older, once said about his kids, "You think they are done separating and then they separate some more." On this trip, Levin took the VCR tapes of his concerts and performance art, another sign that his life departs from mine. The members of the mobile middle class expect their children to live far away; yet whenever Levin takes more of his history with him, I need time to adjust. Over the years Levin has shown me these videos, and now memories of him in them return to me. It is as if a whole bunch of Levins, representing his most playful and outrageous sides, escape the tapes and crowd round to comfort me. There is Levin at sixteen, dressed in rumpled clothes, who strums a guitar atonally as he plays industrial noise music in his high school to lyrics so scandalous that the director turns off the microphone; Levin at nineteen, wearing long dreadlocks, who folds and extends his long limbs in jetés and pliés as he imitates the ballet dancer Mikhail Baryshnikov in a narrow hallway of a San Francisco apartment building; Levin at twenty, hair cropped close, who wraps and unwraps himself in a muslin winding cloth as part of a performance piece about birth, death, and regeneration; Levin at twenty one, who is onstage with BNB and—as Sandra sings, "We've got to bring it all together/We've got to love one another"—adds in a falsetto voice, "It's a new *styahle,*" as he raises one hand in a 1930s truckin' motion; Levin at twenty-three, who gives a slide presentation at UVM, dressed in a white suit that is too short at the arms and legs, and who gestures at the slides with a gold-painted hand at the end of a stick while speaking in an elaborate academic style intended to make no sense, though he wins a prize for his project.[2] All these beloved Levins cavort around the rooms of my house and then fade away, leaving an unnatural quiet. The cessation of movement reminds me of how the sand stirs up when you walk in a shallow pond and afterward the water clears as the grains settle. Soon the quiet of my new life will seem full again. Funny how, as Levin's mother, I will always represent the past to him even though I move beyond it, just as he does.

APRIL 13

DOCTORS have been criticized for taking only a negative history of a patient. Remembering this, I take out a journal book a student once gave me, the cloth binding decorated with golden retrievers and ducks. From front to back I write the bad and from back to front, as if in Hebrew, I write the good (*tov*) about Laska and me. Here's what it says:

❖

What's Wrong
Jumps—comes from behind or in front and grabs at clothes; grabs at hands or clothing of people in street; jumps up when I'm sitting in chair. *Mouths*—makes passes at hands when bringing ball to me, when putting on or taking off collar, if I try to pat her head, neck, or ears; grabs at treat even after waiting for me to give it to her; mouths at my face instead of licking, at my hand if I try to take stick away, at the leash at times on walk, at my hand which is now mouth level when I walk by. *Watching*—keeps an eye on me with whites showing underneath, as if strategically, as she goes about yard; when making eye contact whites show underneath, as if she is strategically submissive. *Come*—sometimes does, but not all the time, squeaker helps; brings ball but may then run off with it or grab at hand when I reach for it. *Expression*—hardly ever flattens ears against head submissively, never pees submissively; hackles raised when I go upstairs to fetch her and she knows she shouldn't have gone upstairs.

What's Right
Physical contact—likes me bathing her, lets me wash her neck and face; likes being rubbed on inside of thighs, lets me rub her chest, likes belly rubbed but often keeps her mouth open, teeth showing, if asleep lets me rub her all over; will sit with my arm over her shoulder and hand on chest. *Habits*—sleeps seven to eight hours; asks to go out to pee and poop, has regular poop schedule five times a day (before and after breakfast, 12–1, 5–6, 9–10); doesn't chew on furniture; if sprayer and treats are near, licks my hand instead of biting; little fuss over collar if sprayer is near. *Obedience*—walks on leash pretty well (half her body ahead of me); comes most of time; sits, lies down, gives paw, learning how to stand, learns *very* fast; will focus on treats on leash as distraction from jumping on person or another dog; will "be quiet and go lie down" in pen if I tell her to; usually drops objects she shouldn't have taken if I ask her to. *Bonding*—follows me everywhere; sits and leans against my legs when I'm at the kitchen sink; very excited to see me in morning (jumps up and down on hind legs in pen, ears flattened, wriggles all over) but then tends to mouth instead of lick unless I have spray bottle and treats; however, does lie across my lap if I sit on stairs and lets me rub inside of thigh and chest and settles down *some.*

THESE lists describe the outside of things, which doesn't seem so bad. Missing are the feelings the "wrong" behaviors provoke in me, which are far more unruly than Laska. I am reminded of a diary I kept in second grade, where there was also a missing account—"Puppy Book." The journal records a week in the life of three make-believe dogs—Licorice, Taffy, and Caramel. Like the lists I just made about Laska and me, my "Puppy Book" hints at but does not reveal the feelings that shape the story. Since the past influences my life with Laska so much, I decide to compare the two accounts. From a cardboard file box that holds my childhood drawings, I take out several yellowed composition-book pages held together by a rusted paper clip. I am surprised to discover that the "Puppy Book" takes place in the month of April. Penciled in my large childish hand is a day-by-day account of small canine calamities—a delayed picnic, a canceled visit to a friend, sickness, injury to an ear or tail, broken puppy beds, a lost dime. One mishap after another "ruins" any chance that Licorice, Taffy, and Caramel can have a satisfying time. The puppies also fight and bite a lot, and the humans (unnamed) whip them when they misbehave. Candy treats for good behavior are the only evidence of kindness. A therapist reading the story back then would have noticed my child's inability to imagine family equanimity or happiness. The "Puppy Book" seems to be a prologue to my account of Laska and me, fifty years later.

APRIL 14

SINCE I made the lists yesterday and reread the "Puppy Book," I am convinced that I should seek formal training help. The problems of Taffy, Licorice, and Caramel can't be changed, but there is no need for Laska to suffer their fate. So far I've relied on telephone consultations and an occasional visit from Merle. I don't like asking her to come over because I know she has trouble with her back, and she refuses to let me pay her for her time. I make an appointment with the dog trainer Vivian Marsh instead, whom I'd spoken to on the phone about Laska's biting, for a private lesson.

At our first meeting with Vivian, held in a large attic space of her ranch-style house, I watch as she works with my puppy. If Laska bites her, Vivian presses her thumb down on Laska's tongue, holding Laska's lower jaw in the rest of her hand. At the same time Vivian speaks to Laska so cheerfully, saying, "*Oops,* something got stuck," that Laska doesn't associate Vivian with her discomfort. Indeed, Vivian seems to be on Laska's side. The pup's only concern is that her tongue not be held that way again.

Vivian moves her short sturdy body with quick confidence as she trains Laska. I admire her competence, especially the way she manages to discipline Laska without taking the rap for it. It makes sense that her broad face, with its pointed chin and slanted eyes that crinkle in the corners with amusement when she recounts a dog's wily tactics or her own, resembles a fox's.

When Laska behaves well, Vivian rewards her with treats, which she keeps in canisters all around the room. Instead of saying, "Good girl," she repeats the original command as praise. She says, "Good leave it," or "Good off."

"Too often dogs are rebuked but not praised," she tells me. "Buy a carpenter's apron," she advises, "so you can carry treats around the house with you." If I sense Laska about to jump on me and rip my clothes, I should ask her to sit and immediately reward her with a treat.

If Laska jumps on Vivian, Vivian bonks her on the head with an empty quart-size plastic Coke bottle or sprays her from a bottle filled with water. I use a spray bottle at home with Laska, but my puppy knows I'm behind it. Vivian wields the spray bottle (or the Coke bottle) so deftly that Laska doesn't associate them with her.

"You want the corrections to come out of the blue," Vivian says. "The old way of using force has been replaced by the use of treat rewards and corrections like the spray or Coke bottle."

Within a short time Laska can't seem to please Vivian enough. I leave Vivian's house encouraged that in time I will be able to elicit similar responses from my puppy.

APRIL 15

IT is late afternoon as my feminist theory seminar students and I sit around a table in the Women's Center. The small brick building houses the Women's Studies Program and other women's organizations on campus. Our seminar room is newly decorated in light pink, purple, and mauve hues; the soft colors appear on the comfortable upholstered chairs, floral Roman shades, and even in the paintings by UVM women students on the walls.

Today we discuss an essay from the book Crow recommended to me, *Radically Speaking: Feminism Reclaimed.* In "Light Bulbs, Radishes, and the Politics of the Twenty-first Century," well-known feminist Robin Morgan describes the beast-of-burden status of women worldwide. I often read to my students, which draws their attention to the printed page:

> Women are more than one-third of the world's formal labor force, but receive only one-tenth of world income and own less than one per cent of world property. Outside the formal labor force—whether as homemaker, nun, farmer, or domestic servant—women's work is regarded as unskilled, marginal, transient, or simply "natural," and is invisible in the

> Gross Domestic Product accounting of virtually all nations. Nowhere does the work of reproduction of the species count as "productive activity." The environment is a "woman's issue" because women are the fuel gatherers, water haulers, and fodder collectors of the world, as well as most of its farmers (eighty per cent of farmers on the African continent alone are women).[3]

I stop reading and look around the room; the feminine decor tempers Robin Morgan's words. "What do you make of these unhappy facts?" I ask.

Deandra, a tall young woman, runs slender fingers through her waist-long black hair. She always sits directly opposite me at the other head of the table; sometimes I get confused as to which of us is the teacher. "For one thing," she says, "they make me aware of my privilege as a white Western woman."

Avra, a student activist who works on issues of race, leans forward in her seat and pushes a batik scarf tied around her hair back off her brow. "Most of the women Robin Morgan wrote about are women of color. In a literature class, we read Zora Neale Hurston's novel *Their Eyes Were Watching God.* Janie, the main character, describes the black woman as the 'mule of the world,' because of the labor she has to perform."

Avra's comment reminds me that all of us in the room are white. Few women of color at UVM (and elsewhere) take women's studies courses; they consider feminism to be a white women's movement, and there is truth to the perception. "Hurston's quote amplifies what Morgan said," I reply. "The image of the 'mule of the world' shows a connection between women and animals; under patriarchy they share a common fate as beasts of burden. There is a whole vein of feminist scholarship that explores the woman/animal relationship but, unlike Hurston, many women of color writers do not explore this subject. For too long black women have been considered more animal than human. Given that patriarchy ranks animals lower than humans, quite understandably women of color have little interest in pointing out their connection to animals."

"I like the way Robin Morgan uses a radical feminist lens," Deandra interjects, shifting the discussion to a theoretical level, as she often does.

"And what is that lens?" I inquire, adding for fun, "Aren't radical feminists bra burning, man-hating lesbians?"

"No way," Ross replies with a smile. He is a slender young man with a mild face, the only male in our class. As if fate's tease, Ross is the brightest of a group of bright students. "Radical feminists believe that there is a web of societal forces that directly or indirectly oppose the loss of male dominance."

"Here is the way Morgan defines radical feminism," Deandra continues, taking charge of the class from her end of the table. She bends her head to read and her long hair falls around her face:

"'The word 'radical' . . . refers to 'going to the root' (as in radish) of an issue or subject.'"[4] She lifts her eyes from the page and looks directly at me. "Morgan is saying that a radical feminist lens reveals the root of social problems."

"What is that root?" I ask.

Kerri, a young woman with heavy-lidded eyes that appear full of slumber, even though she pays keen attention, replies, "Patriarchy."

"Yes," I respond, "male domination used to be a taken-for-granted organization of human relations. Radical feminism has made us aware that both men and women live under the social institution of patriarchy."

"As a feminist man," Ross offers, "I want to say that the men's movement is proof of how influential the feminist critique of patriarchy is. Men are feeling that their power is threatened and they want to speak out loudly enough to drown the feminist voice out."

Noting that some of the quieter students look bored or tired, I say, "Let's break for our snack." At the beginning of the semester I asked students to bring something in to eat and drink each week. Sometimes the menu is traditional junk food—soda pop and chips, cookies or pretzels. Tonight Deandra brought apple cider and Sandy contributed homemade oatmeal raisin cookies. I use snack time, which is fifteen minutes long, to dash home and let Laska out for a pee or poop. Luckily I live just four blocks from school.

As I drive to my house, my mind is full of excitement from the lively discussion in class and I am eager to get back for the second half. I open the front door and enter the living room to find Laska curled in a tight ball with her nose stuck under the tip of her tail. Being rather sleepy, she is reluctant to go outside, so I accompany her. As I stand in the yard, I look up to see the constellation Orion. In winter the great hunter strides directly overhead; now I find him low on the horizon. "Patriarchy displaced," I say out loud, and Laska looks up at me to catch my meaning. I return her to her pen and hurry back to the class to tell my students that the night sky augurs well for the feminist impulse.

APRIL 16

I'VE changed Laska's feeding schedule; Stacey, her breeder, said that at four months Laska should eat just two times a day. I find the transition hard because she looks at me expectantly when it's her old lunchtime.

Dusk in the studio. We have just returned from our after-supper walk. I go to take off Laska's leash. She sits obediently as usual, but as soon as I approach to take off her leash she pursues my hands with her mouth, white teeth gleaming. When I try to calm her with a pat, she moves after my hands in double time. "Damn it," I say, "why don't you let me *pat* you?" I yank the leash in a short, sharp motion, the same one I used when I tried to get her to heel. Besides being used to train a dog to walk by your side, this technique serves to break the habit of mouthing. Surprised, Laska looks at me. I try to pat her again. She bites. I snap the leash three or four times, feeling that scared rage begin to swell. Again I try to touch her head. More bites. I back off and look at her in the fading light. Laska sits very erect, her eyes bright with challenge and her pricked-up ears held tense against her head, as if for protection. "Why don't you ever flatten your ears submissively with me," I say between gritted teeth. I yank her over and over until she sinks to the floor crouched on her haunches and gags repeatedly. I reach down and she allows me to pat her head without protest. Sure that I've hurt her neck, I feel despair and then revulsion. Closeness should never be coerced.

I set Laska down in her pen and put my coat back on for a walk on my own. Street lamps, the heads of which bend over as if scrutinizing me, slowly suffuse with orange light as they come on, and a memory carries me back to early adolescence. I was twelve years old when my mother went to Europe for the spring and summer. Our downstairs neighbor, a cultured gentleman in his seventies, needed a traveling companion. Why did my father let her go? Perhaps he hoped that the trip would bring her back in a happier state than when she left. My mother and father hired a housekeeper, gave my bed to her, and gave my mother's to me. My parents slept in twin beds (each with its own sheets) placed next to each other. I had never found them in the same bed together, but the arrangement brought me too close to my father. The day my mother's first letter arrived, he sat on his bed and I sat on hers. When he read the line, "I needed this like I needed to live," he cried. I wasn't sure that I wanted to know his feelings, especially since his tears didn't seem to be happy ones. Also I had my own troubles. Wasn't I the cause of my mother's misery? Feminists nowadays tend to side with the unhappy housewife; perhaps they give too little thought to what it feels like to a child if her mother dislikes being with her.

When summer came, my sleeping arrangements worsened. My father moved my sister, the housekeeper, and me to our Connecticut home. My mother's parents came from Jersey City as they did every summer to share the house with us. As was true in New York, there were no extra bedrooms, nor was sharing my sister's bed a possibility. So the housekeeper took my bed and I shared a small Castro convertible with my father. We slept in a downstairs room with its own bathroom, isolated from the rest of the family. The Castro convertible mattress sagged at the middle and during the night my father's long, hot body rolled up against mine. I usually awakened at such moments, filled with a kind of nauseated dread. When we were adults, my cousin Judy told me, "We were scandalized that your parents put you beside your father." But no one in her family intervened.

In the scene I remember today, we are still in New York.

▼▼▼

My mother has been gone only a few weeks and school is not yet out, but already I feel lost and angry. In hygiene class I learned about periods and even though I am a bit young I peer into the toilet bowl every day for a sign of it. How will I be able to ask my father for help if I start to bleed? Perhaps because I feel abandoned by my mother, my relationships with my girlfriends deteriorate. One night my father notices my glum demeanor. He sits down on his twin bed and makes me get on his lap. "Tell me what is the matter," he demands.

"I don't want to," I say, uncomfortable with the feeling of his thighs under mine. Lights on the George Washington Bridge are strung across the dark water from New York to Jersey like a dream of escape.

"Tell me."

"It's about my friends."

"Well, what happened?"

"Daddy, I don't want to talk about it," I say, my voice rising. I get off his lap and go over to my mother's bed. He suddenly gets to his feet, his pained, prominent eyes staring at me. "If you don't tell me, I am going to a hotel," he says in an agitated voice.

"I don't want to tell you," I repeat, bursting into tears. He goes to his closet and tears clothes out of it. Then he goes into the storage space in the hall to get a suitcase to throw them into.

"No," I scream, "don't leave!" He gives me no reply, his eyes full of a frightened anger. He strides out of the bedroom through the dining room and then the foyer. He is almost at the apartment door. I run after him, barring the front door with my body, my arms outstretched, and shriek, "No, no!"

"Well, then," he hisses from holding his chest muscles so tight. I follow him into the bedroom, sit on his lap, and tell my story.

▲▲▲

APRIL 17

I CALL Merle to ask her if she thinks I hurt Laska's neck. She assures me that Labs have tough necks and, with rheumatoid arthritis, I couldn't have yanked her as hard as I thought I had. She reminds me to put my puppy in her pen if she gets wild, to avoid confrontations.

Laska no longer accompanies me into the bathroom when I put water in her food dish. She goes right to her pen and waits, sitting, for me to bring her "supper" (all her meals go by that name, even if it's breakfast). Nor does she follow me to the large bottles of spring water every time I fill the teapot. She doesn't waste action (going into the bathroom doesn't bring the food any faster), nor does she investigate as much, as if everything were brand-new. The world has aged some for her.

APRIL 18

IN my Self and Social Interaction class, we have moved on from Marx and Freud to social psychologist George Herbert Mead. Like Marx, he elevates humans above animals. Mead's book *Mind, Self, and Society* was published in the 1930s, and so he lacked access to the ethological research on animals that we have available to us today. Writers may think ahead of their historical time, but it isn't fair to require them to. Marx and Mead *were* ahead of their contemporaries when it came to understanding human development. They both recognized that we are social beings through and through. Having been left alone too much as a youngster, I appreciate their insight. Our cultural tradition holds that we begin life as separate individuals and go on from there to form social affiliations. Even Freud, astute though he was about the human psyche, believed in individualism. To him, need forces us to seek the other; left to our own devices we would remain as self-contained as an egg. Recent research on infants reveals a radically different trajectory, one that supports the insights of Marx and Mead. The findings show that we become persons *in relationship to* others, not separate from them. Sociability is a need in its own right. In any culture, if born healthy and undrugged, a newborn will wriggle up her mother's body to reach the breast and begin suckling; a newborn will focus his eyes best at ten inches, which is the distance from his position at the breast to the mother's eyes; a newborn will prefer the sound of its mother's voice, her face, and her scent to all others; a breastfeeding newborn will have the same REM patterns of sleep as its mother; a baby will begin smiling at around two to three months (unsighted babies begin smiling slightly later).

Marx and Mead were ahead of their time when they wrote about humans' fundamental sociability, but they shared the Western assumption that we are superior to other species. For Marx, our "conscious life activity" sets us apart from other creatures; unlike the bee, he says, the architect creates a structure first in his imagination. For Mead, humans' capacity for language is unique to our species. Animals, Mead says, speak through a "conversation of gestures," whereas humans communicate through "vocal gestures" that depend upon the use of "significant symbols." He gives the example of a dogfight. When dogs confront each other, Mead says, they adjust their physical positions relative to one another, more or less instinctively. Mead does not deny that emotions lie behind the dogs' conversation of gestures—in a fight they may be angry or afraid. But he does not believe that animals *intend* to express an emotion; rather they release a feeling that, in turn, releases one in the other animal.

Mead was aware that humans also engage in a conversation of gestures. When people walk in a crowd, Mead says, they unconsciously shift their positions relative to those around them so that, for example, they don't bump into each other. But for Mead, genuine language arises only when there is an exchange of significant symbols through vocal gestures, where the "self" can "take in the attitude of the other."

By "taking in the attitude of the other" Mead means that the "self" consciously imagines the effect of her words or actions on the "other," which may cause her to modify her behavior. For instance, when I explain Mead's ideas to my students, I try to make him accessible to them. If I notice incomprehension or boredom on their faces, I ask them to question what they don't understand. Their vocal responses help me adjust my presentation of Mead in order to achieve greater clarity.

In this exchange, the students and I depend on significant symbols that hold a common meaning; we know what the abstract terms "self" and "other" refer to. And in communicating, we are influenced by what Mead calls the "generalized other," whose attitudes we have taken in. By "generalized other" he means that we share certain ideas given to us by our society and historical tradition. For example, as Americans, the students and I have been taught to favor equality over hierarchy, democracy over authoritarian rule.

A good example of the "generalized other" operating in Mead's work is his arrogant attitude toward animals, which mirrors Western tradition. He says: "We . . . tend to endow our domestic animals with personality, but as we get insight into their conditions we see there is no place for this sort of importation of the social process into the conduct of the individual [animal]. They do not have the mechanism for it—language."[5] Since animals have no personality, Mead claims that they have no rights; hence, we may take their lives. Viewpoints like his, which predominate even today, have sparked the animal rights movement. I can just see the PETA representative, Kate, push her hair back behind both ears as she prepares a refutation of Mead's diminished view of animals.

Even today most social scientists believe that we fall prey to anthropomorphism (projecting human traits onto nonhuman others) when we find common ground with animals. In *Why Elephants Weep: The Emotional Lives of Animals,* Jeffrey Moussaieff Masson asserts that the real problem is not anthropomorphism but "anthropocentrism," which "reflects a passionate wish to differentiate ourselves from animals, to make animals other, presumably in order to maintain humans at the top of the evolutionary hierarchy and the food chain. The notion that animals are wholly other from humans, despite our common ancestry, is more irrational than the notion that they are like us."[6]

A strong example of anthropocentrism can be found in Mead's use of the term "lower animals." Though he does not address himself to Mead, Masson challenges the idea that the vocal gesture defines true language:

> Nonverbal communication among humans has sparked increasing interest among academics and therapists in the last few years. Many complex mental states are conveyed more conveniently by gestures than by sentences, while others appear to escape verbal language entirely. . . .
>
> There is little doubt that humans communicate thoughts and feelings *without* words; indeed, there is growing evidence that a great part of communication with others takes place outside verbal speech. Just as humans communicate through body language, gestures, and expressive acts, formalized through mime and dance, consideration should be given to the nonverbal statements about feelings that animals make.
>
> Animals communicate information through posture, vocalizations, gestures, and actions, both to other animals and to humans who are attentive.[7]

In other words, a conversation of gestures isn't inferior to one of vocal gestures, and gestures themselves can act as significant symbols. (Perhaps Masson should have added that we now know that animals are capable of sophisticated vocal gestures.) Were Mead alive today, I believe that he would share Masson's perspective, because we extend and deepen the human capacity for sociability when we acknowledge the intelligence of animals.

APRIL 21

IF I say "Laska" brightly, she looks at me expectantly, and then if I say, "I'm getting to love you," she jumps up on me, wagging her tail, her face open and happy (though she's not supposed to jump on me). Right now she is asleep in her pen, without the cardboard box that used to make it smaller. I am reluctant to get up and give her supper because of the commotion of her eagerness.

JEFFREY Moussaieff Masson's defense of nonverbal language, which I quoted a few days ago, reminds me of Sarah's behavior whenever she got into the garbage can in my absence. Instead of greeting me enthusiastically as I came through the front door, she would be lying down in the living room or even upstairs out of sight, ears flattened against her head, a guilty look in her eyes. Hadn't she taken in the attitude of the "other" by anticipating my disapproval of her garbage eating, and wasn't she showing me, through a conversation of gestures, that she felt contrite?

Even at the level of spoken human language, animals are far more competent than we give them credit for. Laska understands what I say to her, even if she can't answer back with words. She knows the difference between a "treat" and a "special treat" (a rawhide chew); and if I say, "Would you like a special treat?" she will go over to where I keep them, point with her nose, and look at me expectantly. Sarah got so excited whenever the word "run" was mentioned that if I needed to tell anyone my plans, I would say, "I'm going for an 'r-u' today," so as not to get her hopes up. Very quickly, Sarah learned what "r-u" meant and the ruse no longer worked.

Like me, Laska possesses a notion of George Herbert Mead's "generalized other"; the trouble is that hers differs from mine, which causes communication problems. I believe in equality (thanks to the social revolutions over several centuries in England, France, and the United States), and Laska believes in hierarchy. If I don't act like the leader of our pack, then she will. Perhaps, too, my body carriage, tone of voice, and smell convince Laska that I'm not leader material. There are all kinds of significant *gestural* symbols that can convey my greater authority, such as eating before she does, going through doors ahead of her, or asking her to sit before I feed her.

Philosopher and animal trainer Vicki Hearne shares Masson's defense of nonverbal communication. In her book *Adam's Task: Calling Animals by Name,* she explains that horses speak through "kinesthetic language." She states that it takes courage to forfeit the grammars of human speech:

> The reason the rider must be brave hasn't a lot to do with the danger of getting dumped, run away with or scraped off under a tree, although such fears may present themselves as emblems of the harder-to-articulate fear which usually goes: "But how do I know what s/he's going to do?" (Since s/he won't talk to me.) The horse will have the same fear—"This rider isn't talking to me!"—because the one thing they know for sure about the other is that each is a creature with an independent existence, an independent consciousness and thus the ability to think and take action in

> a way that may not be welcome (meaningful or creature-enhancing) to the other.[8]

Masson and Hearne both express the view that animals and humans are cocreatures rather than higher and lower animals; each possesses the ability to "think and take action." The idea of our common ground as creatures attracts me and is at the heart of *Creatural Lessons,* the book I plan to write during my upcoming sabbatical.

However, I must remember Masson's warning that it is a mistake to see animals as just like us. First, he explains, animals have their own form of anthropomorphizing, which he calls zoomorphism. They ascribe *their* attributes to humans. He quotes Elizabeth Marshall Thomas: "When a dog with a bone menaces a human observer, the dog actually assumes that the person wants the slimy, dirt-laden object, and is applying dog values, or cynomorphizing."[9]

Second, Masson cautions, humans must not assume that we know how animals feel. He describes elephants that display what seems to be a moment of joy: "All the elephants performed similar greetings, spinning around, leaning on each other, rubbing each other, clasping trunks and trumpeting, rumbling and screaming. So much fluid streamed from their temporal glands that it ran down their chins."[10] (The temporal glands are located a short distance behind an elephant's eyes and they secrete fluid that looks like tears.) We recognize joy in an elephant because it resembles human joy. But Masson warns that we should not assume that our feelings are identical. "After all, we have no idea how one feels when one's temporal glands are streaming fluid. There may be forms of joy in elephant society different from any joy that humans experience."[11]

His two lessons pertain to my life with Laska. She treats me as if I were a dog, and I attribute dark motivations to her "lack of kindness." Can book learning provide a shield against unreason?

APRIL 24

I LOVE going to Pet Food Warehouse, because there I see other people looking for objects to keep dogs amused and out of mischief. Today I run into Molly Powell, who writes for a local newspaper. She has blondish wavy hair and that rushed air of a reporter. When I tell her I have a bitey new puppy, she responds, "Oh, God, it was so bad with my puppy that I had to buy gloves. My hands were all lacerated from his bites."

"So what did you do?" I ask.

"I called up my mother and said, 'This is supposed to be a loving relationship and it feels like torture.'"

"Did he stop biting?"

"Yeah," she says, gathering several rawhide bones to take to the register, "but it took about a year."

The salespersons at Pet Food Warehouse are unusually friendly and helpful. One of them, overhearing our conversation, says, "Here's a trick that keeps dogs happy." She takes up a hollow bleached beef bone and continues, "You stuff cheese down this hole and your dog will be busy with it for hours."

I buy two of them.

On the way home with the magic bone, I stop at a supermarket to get some fat-free cheese. As soon as I get to the house, I stuff the cheese into one of the bones. I make Laska sit and ask her, "Would you like some cheese?" She looks into my eyes with perfect concentration, learning the new word instantly. I put the bone in her open mouth and at first it seems too heavy. Then she grips it tightly in her teeth, trots briskly over to one of her fleecy blankets, and settles down with her treasure. Not a dog to be fooled, Laska wearies of this new treat as soon as her tongue can't reach the cheese; she is done with it in a mere twenty minutes. So much for my having hours of time to myself in which she is happily busy. This much is clear—she's very intelligent. Why waste time licking at unreachable cheese, when she could amuse herself by vexing me?

APRIL 26

LAST night was the Shabbat service that occurs during the Passover week; it is traditional to read from the great love poem *The Song of Songs.* Just a few people were present—Gloria, an elderly woman who looks blandly at you with a dentured smile; Sanford, a good-looking businessman who is the vice president of the synagogue; Jack, a short, stout, choleric man with a florid face and a black cowboy-style hat who looks as if he will burst from inner rage; Courtney from Brandeis, a gifted student of Judaism, dark-haired, pale and solidly built, her eyes large behind far-sighted glasses; her tall mother, who walks bent slightly forward as if perpetually solicitous; her short, stout father, who limps due to a foreshortened leg; myself, missing my second husband whose favorite poem this had been; and the rabbi, wearing a yarmulke and a green vest as if he were celebrating St. Patrick's Day. I was glad Courtney's parents were present. They seem to have genuine affection for each other, a trait that I thought suited a reading of *The Song of Songs.* We went around the room reading a chapter each.

Gloria read right on down from the verses to the editor's commentary without noticing that the font sizes were radically different, to say nothing of the content; Jack used an affectless voice as if he were reading a grocery list—your two breasts, your eyes, your thighs, your neck. Courtney read studiously; Sanford, as if the poem were a business brief; Courtney's parents, in plain tones (I'd hoped for more passion from them); and Rabbi Noah, as if he were giving a sermon. I was struck by how unaccustomed most of the people seemed to be to reading aloud. I believe this unease is due to a flaw in our culture, addicted as it is to electronic media. Was it lack of experience, or did people feel the need to distance themselves from the aromatic sexuality of the verses? I gave my chapter all I could as a person used to reading out loud to my students and as a woman who had not always been a heterosexual in exile. My second husband, Ishmael, had loved to quote the poem. One of his favorite phrases had to do with not pressuring him to make love—I used to be that eager: "I adjure you, O daughters of Jerusalem,/By the gazelles, and by the hinds of the field,/That ye awaken not, nor stir up love,/until it please."[12]

When I saw Crow a few days later, I said, "In itself the poem is a *turn on.* But the way people read it, you'd think they were trying to renounce sex forever."

APRIL 29

TODAY, by feeding Laska one treat after another and keeping the spray bottle by my side, I am able to get her to sit quietly and let me put her leash on without her biting in ten directions at once, like the Blue Meanies in the *Yellow Submarine.* When I praise her enthusiastically, in a bubbly, perky tone as if she just won ten thousand dollars on a quiz show, I see it register in her face that this behavior will give her rewards. A while later she rests her muzzle on a kitchen chair and looks at me. It is such a peaceful moment, the way she rests her head and the look she gives me. I feel all kinds of hope for the future.

May 1997

Hackles and Strategies

MAY 1

I STUFF old nylon stockings with cedar chips that I bought at Pet Food Warehouse. A large bag costs only five dollars, and although intended for gerbils and hamsters, the chips are as effective against moths as an expensive sachet. When I put my woolens away, I notice the damage inflicted on them by my puppy. I now have several ripped sweaters, a torn woolen glove, and the snagged brand-new silk underwear. The sight of my clothes harms my recent optimism about my relationship with Laska. Our situation reminds me of my arthritis. Sometimes I feel no pain in the balls of my feet when I walk, or my hands feel strong rather than weak and the knuckles look less swollen. At such moments hope arises that I can overcome a degenerative condition. When the symptoms return, I feel as powerless as the child I once was, shut away in my room.

A few years ago after a particularly bad flare-up, I told Crow that I didn't know which healer was my best guide. Should I follow the advice of the naturopath, the energy healer, the osteopath, or my allopathic physician? Their approaches were all different. Crow said, "You confuse yourself by working with too many providers. In AA we learn to listen to one person." Perhaps I seek multiple opinions because my problems seem complex, or perhaps out of a scholarly thoroughness. Whatever the reason, I never follow Crow's advice. As far as Laska is concerned, I turn to Merle, Vivian, Laska's breeder, books, friends, and even people whom I hardly know at all, like Molly Powell at Pet Food Warehouse.

Today I decide to call Laska's breeder, Stacey. I catch her at a good time and she is happy to advise me; she suggests an approach based on the old-fashioned style of correction. When Laska jumps at me, I should punch her on top of the head or kick her in the chest with my knee.

I once witnessed punching at a Labrador retriever dog meet. New and enthusiastic Labrador retriever owners, Levin and I had decided to attend a show when Sarah was six months old. The competition took place outdoors in a big green field. After watching the ring for a while, I wandered over to where the retrievers sat or lay in their crates. Sarah's breeder, Rachel. had brought some of Sarah's mother's new pups to the meet, and I thought it would be fun to look at them. I soon was distracted from the puppies by the sight of a heavy-set woman engaged in obedience training her equally bulky black Lab. I walked over to watch. The Lab was standing some distance from her on a dirt road. "Come," she called. Owing to his weight, he waddled rather than trotted up to her and stood looking at her. To my astonishment, the woman punched him hard on the top of his heavy head, which caused him to complete the exercise by sitting down. Perhaps noting my shock, she said, "I breed them with hard heads on purpose." At the time we attended the meet, I was well acquainted with Sarah's stubbornness. For all her sweetness I never could train her to walk properly on a leash; she pulled so hard on her leash that she choked herself. But I didn't yet associate Sarah's willfulness with her breed. Even so, the dog handler's method seemed inhumane to me.

After I get off the phone with Stacey, I try out my new tactics; the sun is warm and the grass vividly green after a soft rain. I step off the deck into the yard with the intention of *this* time teaching Laska how to retrieve. Sarah brought a ball back as many times as you threw it. On hot days even after her tongue swelled with blood and hung way out of her mouth to release heat from her body, she never stopped fetching. I used to worry that she would get heatstroke and to her disappointment I would put the ball away; I never knew Sarah to quit on her own. When I throw a ball for Laska, she just runs away with it. I bend down to pick one up and Laska springs at me. As she rises in the air, I manage to punch the top of her head with my fist. Dropping back to the ground Laska looks at me with surprise, an expression that gratifies but also disturbs me. The warm sunlight and bright green grass seem to reproach me for creating an ugly moment on such a fine day. I turn and go back into the house, leaving her outside.

A little later I return outside and again Laska leaps at me. This time when I punch her she sits down and tilts her head skyward at an angle away from me. Fixing me with her one visible eye, she purses her lips and commences to bark.

The drawn-out complaining sounds seem to say that I should not treat her this way. I agree. But when I try to walk past her into the yard, she jumps at me again. I kick her in the chest with my knee. I am afraid I've hurt her, but she springs at me again, this time with her hackles raised. Shaken, I say, "No, Laska, off!" and return to the house. I believe that her new reaction signals an increase in aggressive behavior; at the same time I feel cruel and abusive.

In my dial-for-help style I now call Vivian; I find her at home cooking food for her schnauzers. Vivian says that Laska's raised hackles are not necessarily a sign of aggression. Laska might be aroused in an excited way or she might not be sure she can trust me. In keeping with her training methods, Vivian suggests I not use force; rather I should praise Laska by saying, "Good off"—which links the command "off" with praise—the times she *isn't* jumping on me. As it has in the past, Vivian's advice soothes me, and I vow to follow it.

MAY 3

DOG owners all across Vermont give their Labs (the most popular breed in the state) ordinary pats, while I have to *train* my dog to be patted. I put the carpenter's apron that Vivian suggested I buy around my waist and fill the easy-to-get-to-pockets with treats. Then I ask Laska to sit in front of me. She is, and always has been, a punctilious sitter. It isn't a cinch to get her to come close though. But as the treats pour out from my hand to her mouth, she scoots along the floor on her bottom until her head is near my knees. I reach down with my other hand and stroke the sides of her face and the top of her head. She never lets me touch her in these places. Maybe treat rewards will transform Laska into a pattable dog. When I tell Merle, who isn't in favor of liberal treat rewards, about my plan, she suggests a different approach. She says to pat Laska where she *does* like it (on the inside of her thighs) and leave her head alone.

MAY 4

ACCORDING to dog-breeding lore, puppies get 75 percent of their traits from the mother. Is this resemblance due to genes or to the fact that she raises them? Whatever the reason, when I met Laska's mother, Nancy, I never could have guessed she'd whelp feisty pups. The day Merle and I went to pick Laska up, Nancy's owners brought her by. Crowded into Stacey's small kitchen were five large people (some tall, some wide), eight pups, and their mother. The only puppy I was able to identify was the one with the red string. The others, Laska among them, turned into a blur of plump little bodies, clumsy paws, wagging tails, and eager faces. I sat down on a chair right in the midst of everything and turned my attention to Nancy.

She was the most beautiful Labrador I'd ever seen. Even after whelping, the lines of her body were graceful yet strong, and a thought furrow that ran vertically the length of her brow marked her intelligent face. Despite the crowd and confusion she kept a calm demeanor, and when she looked into my eyes I sensed her quality of attention. Nancy remembered her pups and it was touching to see how she nosed each one affectionately. At six, Nancy had reached the upper limit of her breeding years and this was her last litter. Because of her age, it had taken her all day to give birth. For their part, the puppies knew exactly who Nancy was, crowding around avidly to lick her face. They even tried to nurse. But having been taken away from her offspring at three weeks, Nancy made no effort to take charge of them.

After twenty minutes or so, Stacey brought in Shak, the father, from the kennel so that I could meet him as well. Shak was a young chocolate Lab with a wavy coat. He had a compact body, bulkier than Nancy's, and the annoying habit of springing up and down around you in a circle as if he were on a pogo stick. As soon as Shak entered the room, paying no attention to the pups, he headed greedily for Nancy, head thrust forward on his thick neck, amber eyes glowing. Stacey quickly took Nancy into the living room and put up a gate to keep him out. In an instant, Shak scrambled over it, grazing his large shiny balls against the topmost rail. Not surprisingly, Nancy's owners soon took her home.

I can easily see Shak's 25 percent contribution to Laska's temperament—she's as airborne as he. And I can fully understand, too, why Stacey flicked him with a towel to keep him away from her when he was a puppy. Laska probably got a good deal of the remaining 75 percent that ought to have come from her mother from her father as well; according to Stacey, the older dogs in the kennel disciplined Nancy's litter. As a high-ranking member of the pack, Shak would have had a decisive influence. Adding what I think of as the "Shak effect" to Nancy's history of whelping upstart pups makes for quite a puppy brew.

MAY 6

THE grant has come through for my sabbatical book projects and Jessica is now my official research assistant. I've been storing scraps of paper with book or subject titles written on them in an earth-brown pinch pot. Over the last few weeks, Jessica has met with me at my kitchen table and we looked through the contents stuffed into the small plump pot. Though no more than six inches high and wide, it held enough titles to keep Jessica occupied at the library for quite a while. Today Jessica turns up at the front door bent over a high stack of books that she holds tightly against her chest. I let her in, expressing motherly concern about her back—does she have to carry so many at once, and can I help? But she dismisses my worry the same way she dismissed my concern over whether her boots, with their three-inch soles, were suitable for the snow. Jessica carries the books into the studio and stacks them on the floor, because I long ago ran out of room on my bookshelves. Later in the day when Laska is out of her pen, she runs into the studio and sniffs the pile eagerly, the whites of her eyes showing. "My little scholar," I say, "please don't literally devour the knowledge."

MAY 7

PERHAPS if I understand more about Laska's breed, I will become a better caretaker. In particular, I want to know what characteristics are usual in Labradors. Intrigued by origins (whether the very first stories of Western tradition as told by Homer and the Hebrew Bible or my own past), I begin with Labrador history. Unlike hounds and spaniels, who are ancient, retrievers are a more recent breed. In 1621, Gervaise Markham made first mention of "Water dogges," though the specific breed, Labrador, came later. Unlike the oldest breeds—and this pleases me as a sociologist concerned about class privilege—Labradors originally did not belong to the aristocracy. They were fishers' dogs who worked up and down the rugged coast of Newfoundland and St. John's Island and were thought to be a variant of the large, shaggy Newfoundland, a woolly-mammoth sort of a dog. Small and compact, usually black, with short, thick water-repellent coats, webbed feet, and otter tails, they were called St. John's breed.

The British encountered these dogs through the fishing trade. Some St. John's dogs jumped off cod-fishing boats and swam to the English shore; others were purchased from the fishers either in British harbors or in Newfoundland or St. John's. Eventually the English renamed the dogs Labradors and they passed into the hands of lords, counts, earls, colonels, captains, and other notable people, including the royal family, which keeps a kennel to this day. I remember a TV clip of Lady Diana and Prince Charles walking with their heads down, as they picked their way carefully along the rocky edge of a stream. They were dressed like country gentlefolk, in tweeds and knickers, and several Labs milled around them, plunging in and out of the water. "Move faster," the energetic dogs seemed to say. Like the original St. John's breed, the British Labrador has a powerful but more graceful shape than the bulkier American Lab.

In the cold, choppy waters off Newfoundland the breed once hauled wood, dragged fishing nets ashore, and retrieved fish and an occasional fishing cap; but in England the Labrador retrieved game birds during a hunt. Helen Warwick, author of *The New Complete Labrador Retriever,* credits British colonel Peter Hawker with giving the first written account of Labradors in 1814. He illustrated his book with a drawing based on one of his females, which he purchased in St. John's. Colonel Hawker entitled the sketch "Commencement of a cripple-chace, after firing 2 lbs. of shot into a Skein of Brent Geese and Two Wild Swans."[1] The scene takes place just offshore, with several large-masted sailboats in the distance. Closer in, we see two men sitting in a long narrow rowboat. One is at the oars and the other sits hunched over, taking aim with a long shotgun at an elegant swan that floats dangerously close by. The air is thick with geese, and in the water a few of them float, upside down. In the immediate foreground we see a compact, yet graceful black dog, immersed up to her shoulders in water, tail held straight out from her body, head up, ears pitched forward as she pursues a "crippled" goose. Drawn almost two hundred years ago, the black dog could have been Laska's mom, Nancy.

Despite my enjoyment of the charmingly rendered illustration, I'm more interested in the Newfoundland part of Labrador history than the British. I suspect that the earlier history holds a key to the high energy of the breed and possibly Labradors' stubbornness. I've been only as far north as Nova Scotia, but in her Pulitzer Prize–winning book *The Shipping News,* Vermont author E. Annie Proulx describes Newfoundland vividly through the eyes of a character returning after fifty years:

> This place, she thought, this rock, six thousand miles of coast blind-wrapped in fog. Sunkers under wrinkled water, boats threading tickles between ice-scabbed cliffs. Tundra and barrens, a land of stunted spruce men cut and drew away.
>
> How many had come here, leaning on the rail as she leaned now. Staring at the rock in the sea. Vikings, the Basques, the French, English, Spanish, Portuguese. Drawn by the cod, from the days when massed fish slowed ships on the drift for the passage to the Spice Isles, expecting cities of gold. . . .
>
> Shore parties returned to ship blood-crusted with insect bites. Wet, wet, the interior of the island, they said, bog and marsh, rivers and chains

> of ponds alive with metal-throated birds. The ships scraped on around the points. And the lookout saw shapes of caribou folding into fog.
>
> Later, some knew it as a place that bred malefic spirits. Spring starvation showed skully heads, knobbed joints beneath flesh. What desperate work to stay alive, to scrob and claw through hard times.[2]

This forbidding place is where Labradors began. It is fortunate that the British took a fancy to the breed, because in 1885 Newfoundland passed a law calling for the destruction of all Labradors as a protection policy in order to promote sheep breeding. Although Labradors originated in Newfoundland, British landowners of the nineteenth century were the ones who preserved and developed the breed. At the turn of the century sports lovers brought a few Labradors to the United States, but the first registered Labrador, Brocklehirst Nell, arrived in 1917. The 1920s and 1930s saw a great influx of Labradors into the United States, at first in the East but later across the country.

These historical stories about dogs remind me of my childhood favorites, Albert Payson Terhune's collie stories. I dreamt back then that when I grew up I would own a collie. Thanks to Levin's desire at age twelve to own a "short-haired golden retriever," I've become attached to Labradors. (Levin didn't realize that the dog he'd seen somewhere and taken a liking to was a yellow Lab; he settled for a black Lab because the yellows had all been sold.) As I learn about Labradors' early days in Newfoundland, I have newfound respect for Laska's willful ways.

MAY 8

I STAND in a gift shop looking at Mother's Day cards. One says, "A mother's love is like the sun that warms the earth"; another, "Mom, you are my guardian angel without wings." I come upon a card that shows a mother bent tenderly over her daughter as she ties a ribbon in the little girl's hair. I stare at it for a long time, as if to torment myself. I read all of the cards on display, but they are emotionally unintelligible to me. Only one will do. It is illustrated with a fluffy brown tabby cat curled up in a windowseat. My mother loves cats. The message says, "Sorry I can't be with you on this special day." The words ring true. Even if I were sitting at the card table in my parents' bedroom with my mother, we still wouldn't be "with" each other. When I get home, I write down a flashback that the picture of the mother and daughter evoked. A metaphor of invisible ink describes the movement of a recollection from my unconscious to conscious mind. It is as if I recorded the memory long ago in invisible ink; now as I seem to remember it, the ink darkens on the page and the words come into view. As is often the case, the flashback returns me to the war years in Texas.

▼▼▼

Every morning I eat breakfast in my pajamas so as not to dirty my clothes. My father already has left to fix pilots' teeth at the air force base near where we live. After I finish, my mother dresses me. I like it when she pays attention to me and I get to feel her soft hands, though she yanks my arms as she pulls them through the sleeves. The day I am writing about, she puts on my red plaid dress with puffs at the shoulders. Then she puts a necklace of large red wooden beads with smaller, darker ones around my neck. She pulls my hand away when I start to feel the beads because she likes me to stay absolutely still.

She pushes my feet into white socks with scalloped edges and laces up my ankle-high white leather shoes.

"Too tight," I say.

She makes me sit down in the red leather rocking chair that looks like a grownup's plump armchair, with a book on my lap. I am to stay in the dining room while she goes into the kitchen to bake.

I look forward to the warm smell of cake in the oven. But all dressed up, I feel like a doll and I don't like dolls. I only play with stuffed horses and dogs, because they run free. On this day, my mother hands me "Chinky Joins the Circus," *which is my best book. In the story, a shiny black pony called Chinky runs away from his kind owners, Paula and Peter. He feels cooped up and bored and misses the salt marshes of Virginia where he grew up. A mean ragman catches Chinky and makes him pull a wagon full of junk with noisy bells strung around a wood frame; the bells let people in the town know the ragman is coming. Though kids, Paula and Peter have taught Chinky tricks. One day the ragman sees how Chinky can stand on a box and "shake hands," so he sells him to a medicine show. Two beautiful young performers, Steve and Marie, adopt him. They are dressed in tights and spangly tops and they love each other and their baby boy. They put him up on Chinky's back, but they have to hold on to him so that he doesn't slip off. I am three years old and would fit much better on Chinky's back than he does. Steve and Marie teach Chinky how to stand on a very little box, all four feet together, and pick sugarcoated prize-winning tickets out of a basket. When Chinky bends his beautiful neck for his treat reward (which I imagine to be licorice because Chinky is black), I can taste it in my own mouth. But, however kind Chinky finds his new owners, he misses Peter and Paula. The medicine show is not doing well and so Chinky is sold to a big circus.*

One day the show comes to Peter and Paula's town. When Chinky sees his dear owners in the audience, he jumps right out of the circus ring and runs over to them. Peter and Paula's uncle buys Chinky back. Home he goes with a festive plume, souvenir of his circus days, still on the crest of his head. I rock back and forth looking at the pictures. I love the bright sheen on Chinky's black flanks. It feels good to run my fingers up and down the bumpy brass upholstery tacks on the arms of the chair.

After looking at the book several times, I get bored. Sometimes my mother allows me in the kitchen and she even lets me lick the cake-batter spoon, but today she wants to be alone. I get up out of the rocker and go into the kitchen. A large rock holds the kitchen door open and my potty seat is right next to it. I can make believe that I've come into the kitchen to pee. Maybe I'm mad at my mother because I lift up my skirt, don't pull down my pants, and sit on the rock. When my mother turns from the kitchen sink and sees me there, she drags me away and shuts me up in my room. I wasn't going to pee on the rock but she doesn't know that. I hear her go into her bedroom and start to cry.

There are two kinds of days when I am alone with my mother—baking and dressing-up days and weeping and sleeping days. On the first kind of day we seem to be expecting guests, but no one ever comes. We don't have friends in Texas and I'm not allowed to play with the neighborhood kids that often. My parents make fun of their Southern accents and say that their parents don't like Jews.

On the weeping and sleeping days sometimes my mother doesn't even get out of her housecoat. She dresses me in a plain T-shirt and overalls, clothes that I like better than fancy dresses, but then she sticks me in my room. Because of me, baking and dressing-up days often turn into weeping and sleeping days.

▲▲▲

MAY 12

I FOLLOW country roads to Underhill, a rural valley at the base of Mt. Mansfield, the highest mountain in Vermont. Unlike Camel's Hump with its one knobby crest, Mt. Mansfield has a long irregular ridgeline. Of the two mountains, Mansfield is more imposing but is also more forbidding looking. I'm on my way to Vivian's house after a trip to Boston to celebrate Mother's Day with Levin. In addition to training dogs, Vivian boards them right in her living room. I left Laska with her, figuring she would be less lonely there than in a kennel; it was our first extended time apart. I called Vivian to say that I was on my way. Vivian told me that she would put Laska's leash on before she answered the doorbell; that way she could make sure that Laska wouldn't jump on me.

I drive up to Vivian's ranch house, get out of the car eagerly, ring the bell, and wait. "Hi," Vivian says with her fox's smile as she opens the door, Laska by her side.

"Hi, Vivian, it's nice to be back," I reply, smiling at her and then turning my hungry eyes on my puppy. Instead of straining hysterically at the leash, Laska sits right beside Vivian, looking up at her before she turns her attention to me. Laska's obedience makes me wonder if she even missed me. We go into the kitchen so that I can collect her food, fleecy blanket, fleecy duck, bone, and cheese.

"So how was she?" I ask.

"Well, she was a good girl," Vivian says, ever smiling, while Laska gazes up at her, "but it took some doing. She certainly has a mind of her own. I had to put my thumb on her tongue at first to get her to stop biting. But she learns quickly."

Vivian pats Laska's head, then gives her a treat reward out of her pocket and says, "Good sit." When Vivian says this to Laska, I am reminded that she praises a dog for doing something right, even if she hasn't commanded it.

"I'm very grateful that you worked with her," I reply. "You provide boarding and training all in one." We chat some more and I write her a check. As if sensing a transition is about to happen, Laska gets restless, and Vivian immediately puts her foot on the leash near the collar, which forces Laska to lie down. Her voice full of praise, Vivian says, "Good down, Laska," and pops another treat in the puppy's mouth.

"I guess I'd better take her home now," I say, "before she contradicts the good things you said about her."

I let Vivian hand me the leash and walk into the hall with Laska, but then remember that I have to pee; it is a long trip home. I call to Vivian, who is still in the kitchen. She says that I can let Laska go and she will hold her.

"Laska, come," Vivian says in her perky voice. I watch Laska trot expectantly into the kitchen, head and tail up, ears pricked forward. It is unbearable to see just the puppy I want who is some other puppy with me.

I drive home full of self-loathing, convinced that I am impossible to live with. I review how judgmental I am and how Laska must feel when I look at her. "You are a watcher," Levin once said when quite young, tired of being under my scrutiny. And it's true. I've been watching Laska the way she now watches me. I blame myself for the frightened anger I can't control, which arises as soon as we get home.

I bring Laska into the house and try to take off her leash. I ask her to sit, and she complies. I bend over her. This is the first time we have been apart for any length of time and, despite my doubts at Vivian's about whether Laska missed me, I hope for a happy reunion. I put my hands behind Laska's neck to remove the choke collar. Instantly her teeth are on my hand from the left side and then the right. Feeling the anger flare up I try putting my thumb on her tongue as Vivian does and Laska goes wild, a blur of sharp white teeth, the whites of her eyes showing. I call Vivian in tears, hardly bothering to say hello.

"I know it works with you," I sob, "but I can't discipline her with my hands in her mouth because she resists, and it triggers a kind of frightened anger in me and I think it makes her aggressive out of fear." My insight, perhaps produced by my time away from Laska, surprises me. Now I am appalled at how my fear must transmit itself to her, maybe even through my hands, like an electric-shock, making it hard for *her* to have equanimity.

"You don't have to press on her tongue," Vivian says kindly. "Why don't you use treat rewards to get her collar off, the way you have been doing when you pat her?"

"That's a great idea," I respond and follow her advice. But maybe because I am tired from the long drive back to Vermont, my thoughts take a dark turn. Why do I have a dog at all? For the first time I consider giving Laska back to Stacey. Vermont has a puppy lemon law that allows you, within the first year, to return a puppy who is deemed unfit. Maybe I could prove that Laska is one sour fruit. Suddenly the pen, crate, leash, collar, and dog restraints featured in mail-order catalogs (prong collars, electric-shock collars to prevent barking or pulling, anti-jump harnesses, muzzles, electric-shock pads to keep dogs off furniture) make me wonder why people have companion animals. In my present mood it seems strange and unnatural for humans and animals to live together. I silently accuse Laska of changing the whole story line of my life. I used to have a way with animals. So much did our elder calico cat Snowy trust me that she broke her waters right beside me as I sat on my bed typing a graduate school paper; she would have stayed there to give birth if I hadn't put her gently in the maternity basket I'd prepared. A few years later Snowy's daughter Zorro became pregnant. I awoke in the night to a puddle of amniotic fluid around my knees. When I lifted the covers there was Zorro in labor, several wet kittens squirming around her. I've been told it's most unusual for cats not to go off to a secluded place when they give birth. Dogs often go off by themselves when they know they are dying; instead, Sarah had solicited my company in her last hours. Even Steely, whose trust of people was impaired, bonded with me and protected me, if anything, too zealously.

I go to bed resolved that in the morning I will consider whether Laska and I should stay together. During the night I get dreadfully sick with a stomach flu, and the next day I hurt my back cleaning the house. My body claims my attention, and the need to make a decision about Laska recedes.

MAY 14

TODAY I go to the supermarket looking for some tasty snacks to stuff in the carpenter's apron that I wear when I'm in the house. To keep Laska's interest, Vivian advised me to vary what I feed her. I browse up and down the cracker aisle, a section I haven't visited since Levin was a kid. I buy Cheese-Its and Hannaford's zesty Italian and vegetable crackers. When I get home, I mix the crackers with regular dog biscuits and break all of them into small pieces.

Today when Laska gets ready to jump on me, I think fast enough to say, "Laska, sit!" and reward her with a treat. Later I sit in a Breuer chair (they are so comfortable that I have several around the house) and feed treats to her in a stream, all the while stroking her head. We take a walk and I use a technique that Vivian taught me. I let Laska amble along on a loose leash. She forges ahead of me and I jiggle her leash just over her back. When she stops, slightly surprised, and turns around to look at me, I praise her, catch up to where she stands and reward her with treats. Vivian said that if I keep getting her attention this way, Laska eventually will walk by my side. After a while I see people on the street coming our way. I make Laska sit down for a treat so that she won't jump on them. Above all, I give *myself* the treat of believing that we will have a happy homelife some day.

MAY 20

I DECIDE to impose a benevolent authority around the house with bonker bottles. They can be my stand-ins with Laska. I go to the supermarket and wheel a shopping cart up to the recycle window. A stocky young man who looks as if he lifts weights comes to help me. He looks at my empty basket and then at me, a question in his eyes.

"I've come to buy empty bottles," I say, embarrassed to explain my purpose.

"We don't usually sell them," he replies, settling his baseball cap more securely on his head.

"How about if I give you a quarter for each one?" I say, adding, "I'd like six please—two-liter Coke bottles."

"OK," he responds, still puzzled, and turns to rummage through the piles of bottles. He finds six; I pay him and head for the car with the bulky-looking bottles in the shopping cart. When I was a child, Coca-Cola came in feminine-shaped glass bottles with the name written in a graceful white script; today, those bottles are collectors' items.

When I get home I put the bottles on tables and counters all around the house so that I can bonk Laska lightly but noisily on the top of the head if she misbehaves. A little later we are in the kitchen and I try to put Laska's collar on for a midday walk. She busies herself with biting one of my hands, at the same time keeping an eye on the other. As soon as I reach for the Coke bottle, she stops chewing me and acts contrite. I notice that she glances up at them sometimes, as she wanders around the house. Tall, stout, and commanding, they seem to be a moral code in physical form that reads, "NO BITE." I would prefer not to be surrounded by their beamy Americanism, but I need them.

MAY 21

TODAY Laska and I hear a strong wind roar through the mountains at Camel's Hump long before we see the trees bend to it. As it reaches us, the tops of the poplars, maples, and birches lean, showing their leaves' pale undersides. Finally the wind eddies about us, causing last year's leaves to spin in crazy circles, very much the way Laska moves when she "loses it."

I sit on a mossy bank from which I can see Camel's Hump Mountain. I coax Laska up beside me. She sits, then lies down, biting young sapling shoots past the green layer under the bark, until the yellow-white wood shows. The sapling looks like a deer shedding its antler velvet, shreds of gray bark hanging off the graceful trunk. Laska chews because her second teeth are forcing their way up through her gums the way green, spearlike shoots of new growth push through the dead dry leaves, lifting them right off the ground. Her incisors are all in and her fresh white molars are jagged as young mountains. When Laska sits up again, I put my arm around her shoulders; to my surprise she keeps those new teeth to herself. We sit side by side and the heavy stone mountain seems to float before us in the blue sky. For the moment, we are at peace.

MAY 22

SINCE I finished teaching for the year and turned in my grades, I don't have to hold myself on a short tether, every minute accounted for between school and Laska. Wednesdays had been the worst—up at six, took care of Laska, got ready for school, ate breakfast, walked Laska (time permitting), taught, came home and hung out with Laska, taught, held office hours two-thirty to four, read and prepared for classes every spare minute, came home to Laska, fed her and let her out, taught from five to eight, came home to dinner, let Laska out, bed. Maybe more time with my puppy will bind us together.

Another excitement is that I am now free to begin my sabbatical research and writing in earnest. The only dampener is that I won't receive a full salary next year and don't know how I will support myself. So today I decide to visit my bank, which recently advertised free financial counseling. When I arrive, the receptionist introduces me to Tom Brooks, a young man with a smooth, bland face and pale hair. He invites me to sit down in a chair on the other side of his desk. I feel like a housewife in a 1940s movie, faced with financial ruin because her husband died. I see myself on the cinema screen: I sit very erect to conceal my vulnerability; my feet, clad in pumps, are placed primly side by side. I wear a flowered dress with a wide white collar that buttons down the front and a hat that tilts down toward my eyes; and I hold my pocketbook, which is perched on my lap, with both hands, though it contains nothing in the way of assets.

"I'm not sure why I've come, because I don't really have any savings for you to advise me about," I begin. "I'm here because this year I'm going on sabbatical without a full salary, and I don't know how I'll manage. I have received a research grant from the university and have applied for two others outside UVM, but I don't know if they will come through. Grants these days are highly competitive. At the moment, I live from salary check to salary check." Then I add, "I do have an equity loan with the bank, which I use for special expenses, like a summer vacation, and for emergencies."

Tom looks at me without judgment and says, "Your situation is not at all unusual. There are many women your age in exactly the same predicament."

Suddenly I feel less solitary and my straight back softens a bit. I am part of a sociological picture, one that I know about as a sociologist but forgot to apply to my own situation.

I continue, "I'm feeling somewhat crazy, having decided to take a sabbatical without financial security. As far as the grants go, a mentor of mine once said, 'The money never comes when you need it.' So all in all, next year feels pretty scary."

Tom looks at me thoughtfully, and then in a slow, deliberate voice says, "You know, a sabbatical is a precious time of creativity and rejuvenation; I would hate to see you waste it worrying about money."

Though it's been short, I realize that our meeting is over. I rise from the chair, shake Tom's hand, and remark gratefully, "This is the best advice about the uncertainty of next year anyone has given me, and who would have thought I would receive it in a *bank*."

I'M back on the job with my Labrador retriever research project. From Annie Proulx's description in *The Shipping News,* it is clear that the Newfoundland coast requires the St. John's water dog to be hardy. Carol Goode, author of *Labrador Retrievers Today,* gives me a closer look at what that life might have been like. She speculates that the fishers fed their dogs through the winter when they hauled wood from the interior down to the shore. In the summer they left the St. John's dogs to fend for themselves. The dogs survived on fish offal and fish heads or even hunted fish themselves. They had to "scrob and claw through hard times," as Annie Proulx put it. I once watched a lively young black Lab swim off the shore of Lake Champlain. He repeatedly dove, disappearing for long periods of time before reemerging, a great spray of water spouting up around his head. I asked his owners what he was doing and they said that he was looking for fish. On occasion he even caught one.

Carol Goode believes that Labradors' struggle to find their own food may explain their insatiable appetites and account for why they will eat just about anything. My sister, Karen, had a large black Labrador, Cannonball, who wore a red bandanna around his neck in memory of having been teargassed in the Berkeley student demonstrations of the 1960s. He used to attend classes at the Berkeley campus quite on his own (my sister lived in Berkeley but wasn't a student at the school) and became something of a campus mascot. Cannonball once got into his dog food bag and ate until he passed out on the kitchen floor. He lay there unconscious, food dribbling from his mouth and gas passing from his rear end. Vivian told me about another Lab who ate three pounds of dry dog food. They had to keep her away from water because, if she drank it, the food would swell and burst her stomach. This gross habit (or is it a survival trait gone awry?) has a training advantage. Focused on food, Labradors respond well to commands accompanied by treats.

The Labradors' foraging summers and their harsh life as ocean-going dogs would have endowed them with other traits besides overeating. They would have had to be highly energetic and stubborn, just to survive. Like Carol Goode I am surmising, because I have no fishers' stories to read for descriptions of temperament. History rarely is written by the less-privileged classes, who had neither the time nor the ability and were often illiterate. Nowadays, social historians would go to Newfoundland and record oral histories told by the fishers about their dogs. But in the eighteenth and nineteenth centuries there were only the words of the favored classes to go by, at least to my knowledge. Here is a hint at the hardiness of Labs from an available source. Helen Warwick recounts a mid-nineteenth-century story about the Fifth Earl of Buccleugh's dog, Brandy. On a trip across the Atlantic in a small craft, the dog jumped overboard into a rough sea to retrieve a crewman's cap. He was in the cold waters for two hours before he could be rescued. The Labrador was so exhausted that he had to be revived with brandy, hence his name. Only a dog of great energy and purpose would have set himself such a mission, and only a dog of great endurance could have survived it. I'll bet Brandy hung onto that cap the whole time he was in the ocean. When Sarah was five months old, I threw a stick for her into a pond. She dashed in after it and grabbed hold with her teeth, but in her enthusiasm looped one of her front legs over the stick. The weight of her body was dragging her and the stick underwater, but she would not let go. I had to rush into the pond to rescue her, because her stubborn will to retrieve that soggy piece of wood might have caused her to drown.

Tolstoy's *Anna Karenin* offers a glimpse of Labradors' life as hunting dogs of the aristocracy. The character Levin and his dog Laska are out for a morning shoot and, in his typical protean fashion, Tolstoy puts himself into the mind of Laska herself:

> Running into the marsh, Laska at once detected all over the place, mingled with the familiar smells of roots, marsh grass, slime, and the extraneous odour of horse dung, the scent of birds—of that strong-smelling bird that always excited her more than any other. Here and there among the moss and the swamp-sage this scent was very strong, but it was impossible to be sure in which direction it grew stronger or fainter. To find this out it was necessary to get farther to the lee of the wind. Scarcely aware of her legs under her, Laska bounded on with a stiff gallop, so that at each bound she could stop short, going to the right, away from the morning breeze blowing from the east, and turned to face the wind. Sniffing in the air with dilated nostrils, she knew at once that not their scent only but they themselves were here before her, and not only one but a great many of them.[3]

What a feast for the senses, Laska's hunt in the marsh, compared to my puppy's outing this morning. The grass that flanked the sidewalk looked exhausted from car fumes and the murky puddle Laska deliberately skirted held nothing of interest besides a discarded Starburst candy wrapper and a squashed cigarette butt.

In their more recent history, Labradors have become service dogs for the unsighted and for people with other disabilities. The trainers deliberately choose dogs with an independent streak because they have to be able to make judgments on their own. For instance, an owner may ask her seeing-eye dog to cross the street when it would be dangerous to do so, and the dog must be able to refuse the command. With Laska's independence and intelligence, she would have made an excellent guide dog. But when I think of her wild side, I wish that she could have an adventurous life off the briny coast of Newfoundland or be out at dawn hunting game, as the dog Laska does in Tolstoy's novel. We *have* been on adventures, but I fear they have swept our little craft down the fiery orange magma of the unconscious.

MAY 24

LASKA and I are back for our second lesson with Vivian. It's been a little more than a month since the first one. Once we are up in her attic training room, I put the carpenter's apron around my waist and stuff the pockets with a potpourri of treats. I walk Laska up and down the length of the large space to show Vivian how much better she walks on the leash. I sit in a chair and ask Laska to take her place in front of me. I show Vivian how I am able to pat Laska's head so long as I give her one treat after another in a veritable cascade. Laska eats the small pieces greedily; they are gone in an instant. Vivian pretends to be a pedestrian coming toward us, and I ask Laska to sit at my side and reward her with treats for not jumping up.

The first time we came to see Vivian, I had watched on the sidelines, but this time *I* am Laska's trainer. Like one of the green shoots I saw at Camel's Hump, a small confidence begins to grow inside me. At the end of the lesson, which is more like a demonstration, Vivian says, "It's amazing what you've done in a few weeks."

"I think we're going to have a nice life together," I reply. Deep down I know that my rapport with Laska is fragile and easily subject to disruptions. All the same, change can happen quickly, so why shouldn't I be hopeful? I show a public television documentary in my Sex, Marriage, and the Family course called *When the Bough Breaks.* It shows early therapeutic interventions in the lives of three families whose young children suffer from severe sleep or eating disturbances. Within a very short time, two of the families resolve their problems. It turns out that the difficulty lay not in the children but in the unconscious behavior of the grownups toward them.

One story resembles Laska's and mine. A mother comes to consult about her second child, whom she finds difficult and claims not to understand. Her relationship with Callum is particularly frustrating because it contrasts so sharply with the one she has with her first child. A turning point in the therapy work comes when Callum, just over a year old, flops back on a beanbag chair, his belly showing between his shirt and pants, and looks at his mother, an expectant expression on his broad face. At first she interprets his gesture as a game of power: he's got the chair, not she. Later, she realizes that he simply is asking, through a language of his body, if she would hang out with him. Psychologist Donald Winnicott stresses the importance of allowing a baby to "lie back and float." Parents often neglect these moments of *being,* just as significant as ones of mastery and striving. Callum wants to lie back and float in the quiet presence of his mother. Her eventual understanding of this simple, touching request transforms their entire relationship. When we last see them she is holding Callum upside down over her knees; her and his upside down faces mirror the same smile, the kind that smoothes the muscles completely, reminiscent of Buddha.

Anthropologist Margaret Mead once said that some parents and kids just flow, while others have to work at it. A good relationship between Callum and his mom didn't come naturally. Though Laska and I can't hang out yet the way Callum and his mother learned to, or the way Sarah and I used to when she was a puppy, we sometimes get along. Perhaps with the help of bonker bottles, treats, and my resolve to forget about acting democratically, Laska and I too will have smoothed-looking faces.

MAY 25

I AM walking from the back of the yard to the deck. I hear Laska at a full gallop, pounding the grass like a racehorse as she overtakes me. Why did I forget to come out with the carpenter's apron on? My body stiffens in anticipation of an attack and I yell out, "Laska, *off*!" To my left, I see her soar through the air in a high arc and miss me. "Good off," I say, and take her into the house for an immediate reward. I've noticed lately that she leaps at me but doesn't make contact. Could it be that these "misses" are deliberate?

Nicknames are a sign of affection; a few weeks ago I realized that I lacked any for Laska. In honor of my silk underwear I first tried out Longjohn Laska. Then, when I read Helen Warwick, who bred the old Lockerbie line, I called my puppy Lockerbie Lady Laska. One of her ancestors from the 1960s is Champion Lockerbie Kismet and, like him, Laska is slender and graceful, though strong of build. Next I tried Pupcake. But, so far, none of them have stuck.

TODAY, Shabbat, a tall swarthy man comes up North Street dressed in a suit and a baseball cap with a plastic coffee mug in his hand. I make Laska sit by feeding her treats as he approaches. "Good training," he says, flashing a smile as he goes by. Later I am surprised to see him at the Shabbat service. Afterward I run into him in the coatroom and thank him for his compliment. We fall into conversation. He asks a lot of questions about dog training. One is, "When do you train?"

"All the time," I reply. "When we walk, when I put on the leash and take it off. There isn't a moment of the day when I'm not training her."

"Spoken like a teacher," he says.

"Well, as a matter of fact, I teach at UVM," I reply. "What do you do?" I ask, surprising myself by my directness.

"I teach at Keene State, in the law school," he says.

I invite him to walk back down North Street with me, completely forgetting that I have driven to the synagogue because I was running late this morning. It is a sunny, fresh day and he puts his sunglasses on; as a result I can't see his eyes. He tells me that he is in Burlington for the annual marathon. We stop outside my house.

"Training my puppy has been interesting," I say, "because she has changed the whole story line of my self-image." I add.

"Wha . . . wha . . . wha . . . what do you mean?" he asks, stuttering for the first time. I am touched by what I imagine to be an unconscious disclosure. Has my vulnerability brought his to the surface? This feels like an oddly intimate moment.

"Well, I used to think I had a way with animals, and now I'm not so sure," I answer.

"Ob . . . ob . . . ob . . . obviously you still do," he says, coming to my defense, "Ju . . . ju . . . ju . . . just look how well your dog was behaving this morning."

Not accepting his praise, I continue, "But it's good to have the whole story line changed."

"Sign of an intellectual," he responds, without a trace of a stutter, as if the role of intellectual is as much of a refuge for him as it is for me. Then he smiles down at me. Looking up at him, all I can see is my own face in his glasses, alternately smiling and frowning at the sun.

"Well, I have to be off now and get ready for the marathon," he says. "I enjoyed our conversation—and good luck with your puppy."

"It was a pleasure meeting you," I reply.

Then he is gone. Maybe he is an angel, I think, drawing on my patchwork spirituality for some explanation. My energy healer believes in "guides" and the Hebrew Bible speaks of angels. This stranger was so appreciative, and even though I was with him such a short time I felt valued—by a *man.* Since I am a heterosexual in exile, this hasn't happened for a while.

An hour later I look out the window at the empty limestone driveway and think, "Where on earth is my car?"

MAY

31

AS I step outside the house at dawn, the smell of fresh bread fills the air. I used to think that the sisters in the convent a few blocks from my house baked bread. Bread has sacred meaning in many religious traditions, and I loved to picture the women laying out rows of still-warm, fragrant loaves on a long wooden table. But Crow told me that the true producer is Bouyea-Fassetts, a commercial bakery located next to my local gas station, a bakery known for its doughnuts. Laska and I head toward the stand of pine trees behind the convent. I am hoping that the dog owned by one of the sisters isn't in the gazebo at the center of the grove. When Sarah was still alive, I met the sister and her dog, Noah. He had a coat of bristly gray and black fur, a sharply pointed face, and a tail that curled stiffly over his back. The sister was just putting Noah inside the screened-in gazebo; she apologized for his ferocious barking. I thought to myself that he seemed to be guarding the biblical ark from intruders, consigning us to the coming deluge. Noah's temperament surprised me; for some reason I imagined that a convent dog would be peaceful and loving. Today, I pause at the entry to the woods. The gazebo is empty, so I continue on with Laska.

The crisscrossed mat of pine needles feels soft under my soles. Laska picks up a shaggy pinecone and shakes her head violently until she loses her balance. I notice a cracked sky-blue robin's egg on the ground and, looking up, see a nest perched among the branches. I listen but don't hear any hatchlings calling for their mother. We walk the length of the pinewood and on our way back I suddenly see a dog standing regally at the top of a slope of a hill. A shaft of light that streams into the woods from the rising sun lights his shiny coat. A large dog with a handsome face, he has thick reddish brown fur tipped with black, a white blaze down his chest, and ears that stand up and then flop over. As he looks at us intently from about four yards away, I realize that he is not on a leash. Laska sees him, too, and strains at hers as she paws the air.

"Arlo, come." A man follows him. Instantly the dog turns and bounds to his master's side and they walk in our direction.

"What a fine-looking dog! Where did you get him?" I ask as we meet. Laska leaps on her hind legs and bestows quicksilver licks around Arlo's face while Arlo regards her with dignity.

"From a pound in Germany, when my wife and I were abroad," the man replies. Perhaps close to forty, he has a lined face and pale blue eyes. I notice that a few of the creases are sleep marks, which I'm sure my face hold, too, since we recently awakened from a night's sleep.

Where dogs greet by sniffing, their owners make each other's acquaintance by exchanging names. "I'm Seth," he says.

"Robbie," I reply, "and this is Laska." Laska, meanwhile, is nipping Arlo's legs.

"Why don't you let Laska off the leash so that they can play together," Seth asks.

"I'm afraid she'll run away. The street is not that far off."

"Oh, she'll be fine," he reassures me. "She'll stay with Arlo; he is very well trained."

"I can see that," I observe, with a touch of envy.

I bend down and unclip the leash from Laska's choke collar. Instantly, she charges at Arlo, jumping and grabbing his fur. He takes off with her scrambling after him and they tear around the pinewood, their coats dappled by the sun. Arlo seems to tease Laska by staying just far enough in front so that she can't get at him; she pursues pell-mell, her mouth open, tongue hanging out, yipping in frustration, which only wastes energy and slows her down. She doesn't give up, though.

Seth and I stand quietly and watch the exuberant dogs. After not too long I notice that Laska's gait has become wobbly; she is tired. "Maybe that's enough for today," I say. "Laska is still pretty young."

"Arlo, come!" the man calls, and his dog heads straight for him as Laska trails farther and farther behind. Arlo takes his place beside Seth and I look into the dog's wide-set rust-brown eyes, impressed by their intelligence. I manage to snag the exhausted Laska and put her leash back on.

"Well, thank you," I say. "This was fun for my puppy. Perhaps we'll run into you again."

"We come here often," Seth replies. "My wife is expecting a baby soon and I like to let her sleep late."

I didn't know men could be so considerate, I say to myself.

Seth and Arlo leave the pinewood in the opposite direction from ours. Laska and I move past the trees and then the convent, and from deep inside the austere brick building with its narrow windows, I hear Noah bark.

June 1997

Red Heifer

JUNE 3

THERE is a delirium to the days before the summer solstice, an ecstasy of opening and light. Flowering black locust and ivory silk lilac trees, mock orange and rose hip bushes, phlox and columbine plants, even the grass itself—all breathe heavy fragrance into the air. Yellow pollen dust falls like manna, eddying with white winged seeds. Birds announce the end of sleep. At seven in the morning the sun arcs above the trees and at night it is slow to descend.

Laska wakes me at five; I get us out of the house quickly so as not to miss the dawn. We walk several blocks to the convent and enter the pinewood with its wide-spaced stand of trees. A papal red cardinal interrupts its distinctive song to look at us, then flies to a farther tree. Like the birds that celebrate dawn with their songs, many religious traditions honor the moment before the light. This morning I recall a Buddhist lesson Sarah taught me about the dawn. All my life I have avoided daybreak, preferring to get out of bed when the sun is already visible. Left alone as a five-year-old with my newborn sister, Karen, while my mother drove my father to the train in Rockville Center, Long Island, I used to wake up in the empty house feeling as gray and cold as the dawn light.

Then in 1995, three weeks before Sarah's death, I began walking with her at sunrise on Martha's Vineyard. I wrote about our time on the beach earlier in this journal, but not in connection with my aversion to the dawn. Leaving rosette-shaped prints on the sand, Sarah trotted ahead of me, though she looked back frequently, her eyes full of light and her mouth open, as if to take in great draughts of the fresh, salty air. With my old black dog for company, I became part of the vastness all around me, and desolation ebbed like the outgoing tide. These early morning excursions on the beach turned out to be a preparation for the solemn lesson of Sarah's death. Though I knew it was unreasonable, I wanted Sarah never to leave me, and when she died just before sunrise, she put me to the test. Could I tell the difference between loss suffered because of parental neglect and loss endured because of a completed life?

I needed help to make the distinction. Before Sarah died, I had been too scared to read *The Tibetan Book of Living and Dying,* as if it would bring bad luck. A few weeks after she left me, I dared to look at it. Adapted for Westerners from the *Tibetan Book of the Dead,* the book explains that the dissolution of death resembles a sky shrouded in darkness. That is what Sarah's eyes looked like as she took her last breaths. After death, all living things return to the Ground Luminosity from which they arose, for Ground Luminosity is "the fundamental, inherent nature of everything, which underlies our whole experience, and which manifests in its full glory at the moment of death." When we dissolve into this elemental immensity, we become one with daybreak: "The end of the dissolution process and dawning of the Ground Luminosity" is like "the way night turns into day."[1] On our ocean walks Sarah led me as a mother would a child into a reality larger than any I had known before. When she died, she taught me that both of us belong to Ground Luminosity, which the book also calls "Mother Luminosity." And so it seems that I have become a child of the dawn.

As Laska and I walk in the pine grove, the sun appears over the treetops. Droplets of dew hanging off the tips of pine needles return to the air. I pray, in I know not what tradition, to remain as open as this day.

JUNE 5

WHENEVER my former student James visits, I check out his hair. Like my son's when he was a teenager, James's might be shaved or growing out; you never know from one day to the next. I almost can't look at his ears. He has stretched the lobes to accommodate big, round objects or multiple thick rings, and he has pierced his nose and even his tongue.

James took my Sex, Marriage and the Family course a few years ago, and then he worked as a teaching assistant in the class. After he no longer was a student of mine, I hired him to help me every now and then with things around the house I can't manage, due to the arthritis. Right now, James is rolling up the linoleum, because Laska is pretty much housetrained and I don't need her old setup anymore. I'll keep Laska's big wire crate in the house, but the pen attachment will go into the shed, as will the linoleum, and I'll have my nice wood floors back. Worried that Laska could accidentally rip the rings out of James's ears with her claws if she jumped on him, I put her in the crate while he works. As I stand and watch him, I decide to ask a question that has puzzled me ever since I've known him. After all, he seems to be such a reasonable fellow.

"James, do you know why you pierce yourself?" I blurt out.

Bent over the linoleum, his heavy earrings dangling down, James replies readily enough, "It's funny, I've never really thought about it."

"I know this is going to sound heavy-duty psychological," I begin, "but I can't help seeing piercing as an unconscious form of penance. As if you had to pay for something terrible that you did as a child."

Straightening his back, James looks at me with interest and in a characteristic gesture, puts his hand on his chin.

"But," I add, "maybe piercing is really just a matter of fashion." I fall silent.

James still has his hand on his chin, as he gazes introspectively at the newly revealed wood floor. "I've never really put the two together," he begins, "but my dad died when I was little and maybe I feel guilty about that, even though I know it doesn't make sense."

"These things don't make logical sense," I offer, "but they affect us all the same." I can see that, despite his interest in the topic, he is just about done helping me and has to go off to his real job at the local food co-op. "Well, something to think about anyhow," I conclude, "and meanwhile, thanks so much for your help."

After James leaves, I let Laska out of her crate and she eagerly explores an area of the house that had been hidden from her. For my part, I admire the golden brown color of the old pine floor, most of which I haven't seen since January. Linoleum is such a tight, airless substance compared to the porous wood. The difference in the substances reminds me of my own moods, which alternate between feeling closed and inert or open and flowing. Laska makes her way from kitchen to living room and back again, sniffing the wood carefully. I notice the claw marks Sarah left on the floors, a kind of narrative of her life with me. Laska's clumsy puppy paws will now add her story line to Sarah's.

JUNE 6

MONEY has been flowing my way. First, I receive a grant from a Vermont agency, the Lintilhac Foundation, whose founder began the nurse-midwifery program at the UVM hospital. Then, two feminist friends with ample resources give me private funds. Altogether, I now have enough money for my sabbatical year. With school over I can begin research and writing in earnest. My first plan, however, is to resume meditation, which I've found indispensable in avoiding writer's block.

Since 1990, I have meditated daily during the summer when I don't have to teach. I practice Vipassana meditation, which belongs to the Theravadan tradition of Buddhism from Southeast Asia. In the Vipassana method, you close your eyes and bring your attention to your breath as it flows in and out of your body. Whenever thoughts arise (as they continually do, because the mind produces thoughts the way the mouth secretes saliva), you observe them without judgment, let them go, and return your attention to your breath. Now, with a sabbatical, I can meditate every day for an entire year. I do a forty-minute sitting meditation and, over time, my body has learned how to be still. By placing my tongue on the ridge in front of the roof of my mouth, I even can keep myself from swallowing. My body may be disciplined but my mind is as restless as ever, busy with memories of the past, plans for the future, judgments, worries, fears, sorrows, longings, and more.

As a way back into meditation, I decide to reread Vietnamese monk Thich Nhat Hanh's *Being Peace.* I come upon a passage where he urges us to look deeply at anger, without judgment. His insight helps me realize that I tend to condemn my reactions toward Laska:

> If I have a feeling of anger, how would I meditate on that? How would I deal with it, as a Buddhist, or as an intelligent person? I would not look upon anger as something foreign to me that I have to fight, to have surgery in order to remove it. I know that anger is me, and I am anger. Nonduality, not two. I have to deal with my anger with care, with love, with tenderness, with nonviolence. Because anger is me, I have to tend my anger as I would tend a younger brother or sister, with love, with care, because I myself am anger, I am in it, I am it. In Buddhism we do not consider anger, hatred, greed as enemies we have to fight, to destroy, to annihilate. . . . If you cannot be compassionate to yourself, you will not be able to be compassionate to others. When we get angry, we have to produce awareness: " I am angry. Anger is in me. I am anger." That is the first thing to do.

I want the anger to stop or I wish it weren't there. But only what Thich Nhat Hanh calls "deep looking" can help me calm my temper: "Meditation on your anger is first of all to produce awareness of anger, 'I am the anger,' and then to look deeply into the nature of anger. Anger is born from ignorance, and is a strong ally of ignorance."[2] According to Thich Nhat Hanh, as I become less ignorant of the causes of my anger at Laska, it will dissipate.

Thich Nhat Hanh considers detailed remembrance important to the resolution of anger. He describes how two monks resolve a conflict: "Both monks try to remember the whole history of the conflict, every detail of the life having to do with the conflict, while the whole assembly [the *sangha* or community] just sits patiently and listens: 'I remember that that day it was rainy, and I went to the kitchen and you were there . . . ,' telling as much as he can recall." Thich Nhat Hanh explains why recollection is every bit as important as meditation: "To meditate is to be aware of what is going on in yourself, your feelings, your body, your perceptions, your family. This is very important for any kind of life. The second technique is to recall, and the more details which the community has, the easier it is to help."[3]

Thich Nhat Hanh's praise of remembrance encourages me to continue writing about the recent past with my parents and about the flashbacks from my early childhood. But his mention of community makes me realize that I feel ashamed (except in the presence of my therapist) about the flashbacks. To whom can I speak of them safely? In U.S. culture, self-awareness can be mistaken for self-absorption and recollection for an inability to "get on with it." Surely, meditation will help me avoid writer's block; maybe it will give me courage to speak about the strange inner landscape I've been traversing.

JUNE 7

I CONTINUE to discover Laska's natural and cultivated traits. In the heat she sleeps upside down, her back legs apart, as she airs her underbody.

Developmentally it seems that Laska is in adolescence, and she commits mischief that I thought she'd left behind with her earlier puppy days—jumping on the couch, stealing my backrest, my socks, and my shoes. When she takes something, she actually seeks me out. Head up, her body held in a stretched-out stance as if she were in a dog-show competition, she stands with the item hanging from her mouth—a poacher who seeks recognition. I take treats along when I retrieve the object from Laska and today she actually drops my shoe *before* I get to her.

JUNE 11

LASKA and I enter Jericho Town Hall for our first dog-obedience class with Vivian, who gives group as well as private lessons. Rubber mats run around the perimeter of the big, boxy room with metal folding chairs behind them. Five or six puppies already have arrived with their owners. At the sight of the other dogs, Laska strains wildly at her leash, but I manage to get her over to a chair near the door. I sit down and entice her with treats to do the same. She keeps her attention right on me and when Vivian comes over to say hello, she says, "Good job with Laska."

I look out of the corner of my eye at the other puppies. A pale gray husky with brown markings sits calmly in front of a tall, thin unassuming young man. A flustered-looking woman sweet-talks a feisty Dalmatian pup, who pays no attention; he keeps jumping up on her and grabbing the leash in his mouth. A blond woman with a yellow Lab sits across from me. Her puppy is quite young and lies flat out on its side, as if exhausted.

I want to look around more but Vivian says to the group, "Keep your attention at all times on your puppy. That way your puppy will keep its attention on you."

I return my gaze to Laska and find that she has lain down and is still staring at me.

Vivian says, "Now put the treat alongside your face, eye level. You want to train your dog to look at you rather than at the treat when you give commands."

I take a hot-dog morsel from my fanny pack (Vivian advised bringing special treats to the class) and raise it to my right temple; I discover that the exercise is not necessary. Laska already is looking at my eyes, and I now realize that she always has looked at me rather than at the treat. I allow myself a moment of pride.

We practice asking our puppies to sit, lie down, and stay, all for short periods of time. Then each pair, owner and pup, performs a "Come!" exercise. Vivian holds the puppy at one end of the room; the owner goes to the other end, crouches down, and calls her or his dog. Several puppies go ahead of us and I am touched by how they run pell-mell on big clumsy paws to their owners. What will Laska do? I hand her leash over to Vivian, go to the designated spot some distance from them, bend down, and say, "Laska, *come*!" To my surprise, as soon as Vivian releases Laska, my puppy gallops headlong toward me, her body bunching up and then stretching out with each stride. She responds much more enthusiastically, I'd even say desperately, than the other dogs.

Afterward we walk around the room, asking our puppies to heel. I say, "Go slowly!" or "Go briskly!" to Laska because these words seem more respectful of her than the heel command; this preference shows that my democratic inclinations haven't disappeared altogether. Laska follows along on my left side. "Every time your puppy looks up at you, give it a treat," Vivian says. Since Laska looks at me every few steps, she gets a lot of treats. "You and Laska are doing very well," Vivian says, once again singling us out for praise.

On the way home in the car Laska falls into a tired sleep. I drive along wondering why my puppy ran to me so eagerly. Was she anxious because we were in a strange place? Was it because I had hot-dog treats? Was it because of her high-energy temperament? Or might she be more attached to me than I realize?

JUNE 12

THE studio floor has taken on the look of an eccentric construction site, as if I were erecting walls made from the piles of books Jessica brings me. Today, I feel shut out by their sheer numbers and decide, instead of reading one of them, to look through an old journal; it was there I first used the word "creatural."

For a few months at the midpoint of my years with my second husband, Ishmael, he and I kept a lovemaking journal. Ishmael's massive body gave off heat like a burning log (he was the son of a Jewish firefighter). But Ishmael's eyes were cold and wolfish, which spoke not of the sovereignty of the undomesticated but rather of an injury to the soul. It was a fixed, absent stare as familiar to me as my mother's, but more compelling because I could draw from him the loving touch I never could elicit from her.

On Shabbat, the Jewish day of rest celebrating creation, Jewish tradition holds that a man is supposed to give pleasure to his wife. I often balked, fearful of the intensity of our love that deepened over the years. Ishmael would remind me of his and my "conjugal rights." Long ago I had covered myself with an invisible shield. It protected me from the absence of maternal love and from my father's inappropriate behavior; my father had loved to draw me out of myself against my will. Ishmael knew more about my armor than anyone else because he had crafted a shield more durable than mine for similar reasons. Sometimes it was I who persuaded Ishmael to make love to "Sweetheart." Afraid of intimacy, he spoke to me in the third person. But on Shabbat, with God's sanction, Ishmael was fearless. To convince me further, he said that beyond conjugal rights, I needed to respect, as he put it, "canine rights," for Sarah habitually crawled under our low bed to join us as our love cast us into the great stream of creation. Elsewhere in our life I found his legalistic bent overbearing, and eventually it exhausted my ability to respond with trust. But Ishmael's reminder of God's commandment matched my sense exactly that, for us, strong love demanded a discipline of the heart; "pusillanimousness," to use one of Ishmael's words, was unacceptable. We were only too happy to stay together yet apart, like the poster of two penguins he put up in his kitchen, when we first met. Huddled into itself, each penguin eyes the other from a safe distance on the blank white snow.

Ishmael was the first to keep a lovemaking journal, at my suggestion. I wanted him to have *evidence* (in the legal sense, because we lived like lawyers in perpetual dispute) of the truth about us beyond our incessant verbal contention and states of estrangement. I wanted him to remember that touch drew us out of ourselves, fiercely, and incarnated us *into* our bodies. Ever vying for power, Ishmael said, "Well, then, you keep one, too, and maybe some day we'll publish them, yours on one side of the page and mine on the other." We wrote the two journals on three-hole pads of paper, which he bound (together or separately, I can't remember) in a loose-leaf notebook. I wrote on those pads because he did; out of habit, I still use them. Like many women, I had been afraid to have a voice on paper. Ishmael's pads held a magical power for me, as if I were the apprentice in the Walt Disney movie *Fantasia* that I'd seen as a child, who took up the sorcerer's tool.

Here is the entry in which the word "creatural" first appears:

> 8/24/84 Ishmael and I walk along Lucy Vincent Beach in the late afternoon past the clay cliffs to where the grassy dunes begin that divide the ocean from the pond. We hug and Ishmael starts to take off my bra but the clasps won't give as usual and anyway my knees become weak from his touch so we lie down and kiss and hug on the gritty sand. No one is around and Lucy Vincent is a nude beach so Ishmael takes off my clothes and I take off his. We stretch out again on the sand and look at each other. Ishmael's mouth is the way I remember it when we first lay together on my bed back in Cambridge—slightly pursed slightly tense very firm. And the same too is the grave line down his face and the color of his eyes like the sea looking back at me saying I think I am here. My eyes say I am here and you are here and I love you and want to touch you. It isn't easy for me to look at Ishmael this way because elemental reality frightens me especially when it is sexual. The beach gives me courage because we are the color of the sand made of salt water like the ocean part of everything that lies before us. And our consciousness and the love that runs like a current between us binds all that surrounds us into a whole. The ocean is blue green today and very smooth almost like plastic water except when it curls over into a wave and breaks white and lacy over the wavy surface. Debris is scattered along the beach (wood, seaweed, broken shells, rope, sharks' eggs) and Canada geese sit out on the water and a sandpiper runs along on fast legs looking to the left and the right as if it were in a speeded-up movie. Sand fleas bite us and waves slam against the dark

> rocks in the water and against rocks that stick up along the shoreline. We lie on the sand and the waves boom incessantly as if we were outside of time but the cliffs begin to lose color in the deepening dusk. We sit up and I put my legs around Ishmael and hug him with them and then I take him in my arms and kiss him. We rock and rock together and his penis pushes up against me not the color of sand but red like the clay cliffs and shiny. I hold him in my arms as a mother would hold a child. We stand up and go into the water. The waves are not quiet anymore and they march imperiously toward us but I dive in anyway and the salt water is cold and fizzly like wedding champagne. We hug as the strong tide tosses little stones against our ankles and almost drags us off our feet. Ishmael holds me in his arms and smiles at me and asks if I would like to make love. I look down at the salt water thick with plant and animal life and at the waves coming in even bolder than before and I can't do what he wants. The light is going and the waves scare me I say so we walk back along the beach past the cliffs. I'm hardly ever outdoors at dusk and even though I didn't agree to make love smooth or wrinkled sheets on a bed in a stuffy house doesn't seem like the right place anymore. Here by the clay cliffs and the heaving waves I don't worry about whether I am beautiful or ugly or whether I should be this or I should be that. I am the color of sand and I am part of the same water as the sea and Ishmael and I are both part of those elemental realities, both creatural, both water sand and consciousness, beyond women and men and all that particularity.
>
> The lovemaking journal is my idea yet I feel conflict over writing about our experience on the beach. Maybe the moments with Ishmael don't belong in words, maybe words on paper are thieves that steal away the feelings that lie inside of me. Also the writing makes me feel as if I'm being forced against my will to reveal feelings of tenderness toward Ishmael. How can I overcome such a fear?

This journal entry makes me rethink, momentarily, my position as a heterosexual in exile. Why aren't I placing or answering personal ads? The reason is somewhat creatural. Ever since my periods stopped seven years ago, I lost a hormonal motivation to seek out male companionship. Some women, freed from the fear of unwanted pregnancy, feel more sexual after menopause. But with me it was just the opposite. Where was the fertile cervical mucus called spinnbarkeit that signaled ovulation? The fragrant scent of the shiny slippery mucus used to surround me like an aphrodisiacal mist. But sexuality isn't the only avenue to the elemental reality of water, sand, and consciousness. The natural world took Ishmael and me into its sandy, pounding embrace and released us from our fear of being alive. Aliveness—that is the state I long for when I read the journal. For now, my life with Laska provides me with plenty of challenges in the aliveness department.

JUNE 13

TODAY Laska comes over for a pat with her fleecy bear between her jagged white teeth. She appears to have invented a way to stop herself from biting me. I am impressed once again by her intelligence. In *my* efforts at conciliation, I remember to stroke her on the inside of her thigh, because that is a place where she likes to be touched. In the Hebrew Bible, men sealed covenants by holding a person under the thigh, a gesture that today would be considered sexual. In antiquity, touching a man close to the genitals acknowledged his genealogy. When I watch how solemn Laska's face becomes when I put my hand on her thigh, and note how quietly she stands, I feel that we are signing a covenant of mutual trust.

JUNE 21

I CAN'T see much of the sky from my yard or from the routes where Laska and I take our puppy walks. There isn't a broad horizon in the pine grove either, because the trees are so tall. Tonight, because of the solstice, I become impatient for a wider vision and decide that watching television during supper is another form of narrowness. A blue TV screen is a poor stand-in for a June sky. I finish dinner early and take Laska down to Lake Champlain for the first time; that way I can watch the sunset. She can't jump into the back of the station wagon yet but has become too heavy for me to lift. So I make a stepping stool for her out of an upside down recycling bin, and lure her into the car with hot-dog tidbits left over from our dog-obedience class.

I drive down the hill to the lake that is a relatively short distance from my house; someday Laska and I will be able to walk there. I park and with the help of gravity lift her down from the car. We head toward the Boathouse, a two-story shingled building that holds a restaurant and snack bar. It floats huge on the water, like the biblical ark; the sister's grouchy dog, Noah, should come down *here* and take up watch. A pier, where boats dock, flanks the building, which faces the lake. I love to sit on one of the pier's slatted wood benches and look out at the harbor with its stone breakwater, the lake, and the Adirondack Mountains beyond it.

As Laska and I walk along, I try to see everything around us from her point of view; the welter of new sensations seems too much. A dog has 220 million scent receptors compared to our 5 million. What must it be like for her to smell the wet boardwalk to the Boathouse, bare-skinned people, other dogs, discarded paper plates with bits of pizza cheese stuck to them, tossed-away half-eaten sugar cones with melted blobs of vanilla ice cream inside, lakeshore water cluttered with sticks, algae, motor oil, dead fish, ducks, sailboats, and kayaks? Not surprisingly, Laska wants to go everywhere at once; nose down, she pulls hard at her end of the leash and follows one scent after another in a zigzag motion, her tail waving madly. Then her head comes up; she smells a chocolate chip cookie in the hand of a little girl in a pinafore and lunges at her. Next she sees a black-and-white pit bull terrier walking beside a young man whose hair is dyed green. Laska would jump all over the dog if I did not quickly drag her away. I'm sure that pit bulls can be friendly, but once, without any provocation, a pit bull attacked Sarah so viciously that the owner had to lift the pink and white dog off Sarah by its tail. The dog dangled from her hands, wriggling, like a grotesquely large laboratory rat. Since then, I have stayed clear of the breed, especially with an upstart puppy who easily could aggravate a testy dog.

When Laska and I finally make our way down to the pier, I find the sun sunk halfway behind the blue black jagged edge of the Adirondack Mountains. It seems not so much the sun as a presence hidden in the blanketing luminosity of a pink orange mist. Perhaps the vision is one of the souls in Dante's Paradiso, all of whom dwell inside radiant halos of light. The sky is a fresh clear blue that reminds me of paintings by the French artist Poussin, and pink clouds stream across it like unfurled ribbons. There had been a thunderstorm in the late afternoon and I can still smell the invigorating negative ions released into the air by the lightning.

We stay until the pink and blue turns to gray and then return home. Just before bed, I let Laska out in the yard for a last pee, and I see one firefly pulsing, no bigger than a star—an augur of summer.

JUNE 23

AS I wash my teacup, I look out the kitchen window. I see Laska hunched over, pooping. Without changing her posture, she turns around and eats what she just eliminated even as she produces another stool. When she finishes, she eats the remaining poop in quick gulps. Her rapid ingestion seems desperate, as if she were starving and had to feed herself from her own body. I want to run outside and scream "*No!*" but it's too late. A reprimand must follow a misbehavior immediately; otherwise it is ineffective. Instead, I sit down heavily, put my elbows on the kitchen table, and lean my face on my hands as a flashback returns me to my parents' apartment, which overlooked Riverside Drive and the Hudson River in New York City.

▼▼▼

I lie on my back in my crib, listening to the cars stream up the West Side Highway, each one hitting the same fault in the pavement. Bu, bum, bump, they go. Suddenly, my father appears leaning over the railing; his eyes shine so bright that they hurt mine the way the sun can, and I have to blink.

"Well, kiddo," he says, his voice brave and strong like those I hear on the radio, talking about the war, "when I looked outside my office window and saw soldiers marching down West End Avenue, I just knew that I had to join the army."

I gaze up at him and smile because he seems happy. But then he starts to look sad.

"So my little 'I Go Boom,'" (he calls me that because I just learned to walk three months ago and I fall down a lot), "I'm going away for a while and I want you to take good care of your mother."

Now his eyes seem huge, moist and unhappy.

"Aap," I say, and I shake my head from side to side, which means, 'No, don't be sad.'"

"You see," my father says to my mother, who is standing in the doorway to my room, "the kid is saying no; she doesn't want me to go."

He picks me up in his long arms and plants a wet kiss on my lips. "Don't you worry, I'll be sending for you soon. You stay here with your mother for the summer and in September, when you'll be two, I'll send for you. There are lots of cowboys and horses in Texas and . . . " (suddenly my father's face gets his usual "I'm going to get you" look on it and I tense up) "tarantulas, black widow spiders, and scorpions." With these words he runs the fingers of one hand up my belly as if they are the legs of a huge insect and I shriek with fear. This makes him laugh, and my mother too.

He gives me one more kiss, puts me back in my crib, and then he is gone.

After he leaves, the days become as blank as the white walls, the white sheets in my crib, and the white diapers on me. On the wall hangs a wooden clown painted green, blue, red, and yellow with a pointed hat on his head. His arms and legs shoot up and down at crazy angles if you pull on the string. It reminds me of how my arms and legs jerk when my father tickles me too much. No one pulls the clown's string anymore and when my mother's eyes look at me but don't see me, I become as dull as dusk or dawn. But my knocking heart rocks me like a bumpy cradle; my breath billows my lungs; my inner ear sounds with blood whooshing; saliva trickles down my throat and bubbles at my lips; salty wet washes my eyes; sounds vibrate up from my throat. I make them come again and shape them with my jaw, lips, and warm tongue—"Aap," I like to say.

Usually my mother feeds me quickly; then she puts me back in my crib, goes out of my room, and shuts the door. I am unhappy to be alone but my filled stomach feels pleasantly heavy and makes watery noises, and at the bottom of my body warm wetness comes as well as mushy solids. She doesn't change me often. So one day I put my hand inside the soft, thick diaper and feel the warm lumps inside of it. I bring out a brown piece; it looks like dark cookie dough and the strong smell envelops me in place of someone's arms. I squish it in my fingers—this is fun. I take some in my mouth and the texture reminds me of my baby cereal, Pablum. Then I pull myself up until I am standing. I hold onto the crib rail with one hand, and with the other I smear brown marks on the white walls because they look lonely too.

When my mother comes in and finds me painting, she screams, "Yukko, poopoo, what is the matter with you?" The cold anger in her face scares me. She grabs me out of the crib, holding me as far away from herself as she can, and takes me off for a bath.

A while later, all cleaned up, I am back in my crib. The sheets are changed and the walls washed. Everything looks lonely again and the next time the friendly brown stuff comes out of me, I will cheer me and the wall up with it.

▲▲▲

As the long-ago memory fades, I get up from the kitchen table and pour myself a glass of water, as if to clean out my insides. It was part of family lore that I had eaten my own shit and had painted the walls with it. Whenever they told the story, my parents described my behavior with mocking amusement. The flashback fills in narrative details, but there is no question that I had eaten and played with my shit. In the opinion of a psychiatrist I saw in the 1980s, in the case of a baby, "coprophagia [eating of feces] is a sign of severe neglect." Today's flashback relieves rather than shocks me because I now understand the family events that produced such a desperate act. I didn't walk until I was fifteen months old, and three months after that my father left for Texas. He had gone ahead to set up a dental practice at an air force base in Fort Worth and to find a home for us. My mother and I spent the summer alone together in New York and in September we traveled by train to join my father. When babies first learn to walk, they become insecure out of a fear of getting lost. In the flashback, I vividly relive the sudden loss of my father and the days spent alone with a depressed mother whom I already feared. Relatives lived nearby but my mother was too busy packing and making arrangements for our move to spend much time with them. She must have left me alone in my room more than was her usual habit.

Despite the flashback's informational value, it makes me feel desperate about Laska's coprophagia. Is it a sign of severe neglect? Back in February, when Laska ate cat shit, I read about coprophagia in dogs. No one seemed to know for sure why dogs ate their stools, but theories abounded. Vitamin deficiency, boredom, and anxiety are possible causes, or a dog might be copying the behavior of its mother, who routinely cleaned her puppies and the whelping box.

To cheer myself up about both Laska and me, I recall an anecdote about the great artist Picasso (one of my parents' favorites). The story illustrates how emotional or material scarcity can cause a person to do socially unacceptable things. A reporter asked Picasso what he would do if he became a prisoner and was deprived of brushes and paint. With rough exuberance he replied, "I'd paint with my shit!" I admire Picasso's shameless appreciation of his body's wastes and would like to feel as accepting of my own past and Laska's present habit.

JUNE 24

I LOOK up the word "creatural" in the *American Heritage Dictionary.* It isn't there, but "creature" is, and it means: "(1) Something created; (2a) A living being, especially an animal; (2b) A human being; (3) One dependent on or subservient to another: a tool." The term comes from the Indo-European root "ker^{2}" (there also is a ker^{1}) that means to grow. A dictionary definition represents consensus on the meanings of a word, but I feel problematic strings attached to the term "creatural" from every direction. I will need to make clear in my book that it is *not* a synonym for "primitive" versus "civilized"; "nature" versus "culture"; "wild" versus "tame"; "bestial" versus "human." These dualities belong to the colonial imagination of Westerners who fantasized about the indigenous cultures they "discovered." To me, "creatural" means the difference between feeling dead or alive, feeling apart from one's body or inside it, feeling like someone's tool or like a being that breathes and is capable of independent action, feeling that human society is self-created or that we are embedded in a complex reality much larger than the human world alone. That is the intimate starting point of my book project.

I am excited about the theoretical possibilities of *Creatural Lessons.* In our first meeting I told Jessica that I intend to criticize "social constructionism," the conviction that culture or history entirely shapes nature. As soon as they get up at a conference to give a paper, sociologists typically confess to being social constructionists. They declare their loyalty with an almost anxious haste, as if they lived under a repressive regime and have to make their party affiliation clear.

Social constructionism depends on the assumption that whatever human language can't express doesn't count; the borderland of preverbal and nonverbal experiences challenges this supposition. One of the fundamental classifications all creatures make is the difference between being alive and being dead. This distinction depends on "vital signs" that don't rely on language. Social constructionism doesn't account for *this* inescapable categorization. In *Children and Animals: Social Development and Our Connections to Other Species,* human ecologist Gene Myers reports on infant research and his own research on the meaning of animals to children. Myers's and others' findings show that the sense of oneself simply as alive is crucial in human development.

When I requested funds from UVM for a research assistant, I wrote in the grant that I hoped *Creatural Lessons* would cause scholars to rethink social constructionism as an adequate theoretical tool. Social constructionism neglects the importance of our animate life, and therefore it offers an incomplete vision of human experience. I also hope the book will encourage an awareness of the life of the body, of the importance of nonhuman animals to human animals, and of the dependence of human cultures upon the larger natural world. These are ambitious aims, but you have to assert such things if you want to qualify for grants. Beneath these claims, the word "creatural" stirs inside me like a small animal. It waits for my writing to awaken it.

JUNE 25

I READ in the *New York Times* that an unblemished red heifer has been discovered in Israel—one without imperfection, flaw, or defect. Apparently, its color is distinctive—"as red as a barn or rooster," the reporter said. Fundamentalist Jews believe that the animal is a sacred sign. Ancient Jews worshipped at one majestic temple, to which they made pilgrimage, in Jerusalem. The Hebrew Bible states that only priests were allowed to enter the inner sanctuary of the temple, and that the ritual sacrifice they offered had to be red heifers without blemish. In 70 A.D. the Romans destroyed the temple; all that remains of it today is the Wailing Wall in Jerusalem.

To fundamentalists, the discovery of the heifer means that Jews should rebuild the temple on the Dome of the Rock in Jerusalem. They overlook the fact that this ancient site is sacred to three religions—Judaism, Christianity, and Islam. No matter how red or how unblemished the heifer might be, what gives extremist Jews the right to claim this ecumenical place for themselves? Besides this objection, I am not in favor of reinstituting animal sacrifice, a practice that would let out blood even redder than the heifer's coat. I also am distressed to learn that to protect the heifer from acquiring an imperfection, it has been separated even from its mother.

I want to fly down in a helicopter, put a big, broad band around the red heifer's belly, pluck her away, and set her down on a farm in Vermont. There she could ruminate with butterscotch-colored cows and black and white cows, emblems of Ben and Jerry's ice cream, and get herself full of all kinds of blemishes. She could lie in the frozen mud of winter, letting her teats get caked with mud like the cows I see when I pass farms on my way to my therapist, Daniel, in Bristol. Sometimes when I look at the cows' besmirched underbellies, I wonder how the farmers ever get the milk clean enough for people to drink. According to my naturopath, there are twenty thousand parasites on the head of a pin and they aren't angelic in the least. Think of how many there would be in a clump of earth on the red heifer's teat if she were in that muddy field!

My fantasy about rescuing the red heifer shows me that I think of "blemish" as contamination, rather than as flaw or defect. When little, I was shut away too. Instead of keeping me clean, the isolation caused me to soil myself. Oh, I would have been willing to be like the red heifer without blemish if only my parents had seen me as sacred.

JUNE 28

IN an epidemiology class I took in public health school back in 1976, the teacher showed a film about food contamination. You see a man handle raw chicken and then put his hand on a counter. Ping! a bright flash of contamination appears at the site he touched. Then he handles a broom, ping! and an unblemished person who just entered the room to talk to the man becomes a touch away from contamination himself.

My public health school knowledge contributes to my feeling that Laska threatens my well-being. Her behavior may well be inherited and so it is not likely to go away. Eating poops turns out to be a common habit of Labradors. Maybe the early St. John's breed dogs resorted to coprophagia during the summers in

Newfoundland when they had to forage for food. All the same, I feel my mother stir in me when I consider Laska's behavior. My high-forceps birth tore tissues of her body just as it scarred my cheek lightly; I believe that from that first moment my mother feared me and perceived me as a threat. Just so, though for different reasons, Laska seems a cause of harm with her potential to transmit parasites. Should I get rid of my puppy or try to rid her of this unappealing habit? Given my illness, it is understandable that I would want her not to eat shit. Yet, I ought to remember my own lonely enjoyment of the activity long ago and my recent wish to free the red heifer from her isolation and deposit her in a field knee-deep in mud.

JUNE 30

AFTER a fine start, Laska and I end up flunking the dog-obedience class we've been taking with Vivian. We do graduate, technically speaking, but in a most humiliating fashion.

Laska took to barking during the lessons. For the last class, Vivian wanted Laska to be quiet because guests were present to see the dogs "graduate." So she put a head collar on my puppy. It circled Laska's muzzle and went around the back of her head right behind the ears. She could open her mouth, but I could pull it shut if she began to bark. Laska's head collar reminded me of a dunce cap. While the guests looked on, my puppy and I walked toward Vivian to receive our "diploma." To my dismay, Laska tried to rub the collar off with her front paws, first on one side then the other.

As we drove home, I felt like a member of Levin's Bad Club and wished that I had worn his old camouflage jacket with the spikes to the obedience class. An adolescent's defiance of law and order flooded me, and for the moment I was on Laska's side.

July 1997

Ocean and Pond

JULY
4

TONIGHT, the Fourth of July, fireworks crackle, whistle, whine, and boom over Lake Champlain. Laska rests in her crate but keeps her head high and her ears pricked forward; her posture seems to indicate interest rather than fear of the unknown sounds. To my delight I compare her favorably with Sarah on such occasions; Sarah would groan and slink around the house restlessly, tail tucked under her body, ears flattened against her head. I stayed home to keep Laska company in case she got scared. Since I live at the top of a long hill that rises from the lake, I can watch the display from the upstairs windows that face the water. I particularly enjoy the fireworks that snake up into the sky like white comets and explode in overlapping rosettes of red, green, and blue light; afterward, the incandescent particles drift slowly down before they fade into darkness.

The fireworks are a perfect conclusion to this morning's drama with Laska, for whom every day is Independence Day. She and I were out for our customary walk. I watched as she trotted along on the grass that flanks the curb; nose down, ears drooped forward, she searched for the perfect spot to relieve herself. Suddenly she jerked at the leash, and before I could stop her she grabbed a white mushroom in her teeth and ate part of it. I gathered what was left of the plant in one of the plastic bags that I use as pooper-scoopers and peered at it. The fungus had a dome-shaped cap, fluted underbody, and spongy stem ringed by a delicate skirt. I was pretty sure from the mushroom's features (based on a small amount of field observation and book learning) that Laska's stomach was busy digesting the highly poisonous *Amanita verna,* also known as the angel of death. Later I thought that a city ordinance should be filed prohibiting dangerous fungi from growing anywhere they please.

I ran back to the house with Laska scampering playfully beside me. Once inside, I dialed the animal hospital with fingers that trembled in the holes of my old rotary phone.

"Hi," I said, my voice no more steady than my hands, "I have a six-month-old Lab puppy and she just ate a poisonous mushroom."

"You need to make her throw up," the technician answered calmly.

"But how?" I asked. I could not imagine sticking my finger down Laska's throat.

"Give her a quarter of a cup of hydrogen peroxide—it will make her vomit," she explained.

"Hydrogen peroxide?" I repeated, sure that you aren't supposed to take it internally.

"It won't harm her."

"OK, many thanks," I said, in a hurry to get off the phone.

I forgot to ask how I could make her swallow the stuff. Then I remembered a large syringe I once had used to give Steely Pepto-Bismol. I grabbed the syringe from the bathroom, filled it with peroxide, led Laska, who was still on her leash, into the yard, and shot the liquid down her throat. The peroxide foamed at the corners of her mouth and she snaked along on her belly, rubbing her face in the grass, first on one side, then the other. Suddenly she got up and dropped her head as her sides heaved convulsively. I watched carefully as white pieces of mushroom emerged, surrounded by viscous frothy liquid. Then—out came a *bottle cap.* Had she found it in the yard or on one of our walks? Either way, how could I not have noticed? When Laska had eaten the bittersweet a few months ago, the vet had cautioned me to look after her carefully during the first year of her life. I picked up the *Amanita* fragments using a plastic bag and then picked up the metal bottle cap with its serrated edge and wondered how I could keep my puppy, Laska, from doing herself in.

JULY 9

AS Laska and I enter the dark interior of the Martha's Vineyard ferry, I imagine that we've been swallowed by a whale. When we emerge from the boat, having left winter behind on the mainland, it will be a rebirth. Sarah and I used to spend the forty-five-minute trip up on deck where we could watch the Elizabeth Islands slide by and smell the fresh, salty air. Fortunately no one is parked behind my car, so I lure Laska out of the hatch with pieces of hot dog. She hops onto the footstool I brought along and then to the cement floor. As we climb stairs to the upper level, Laska stays right by my side; the same thing happens when we reach the outdoor deck. It is as if she quiets herself against the assault of sensations (saltwater, people, engine noise, boat horn, food scents, other dogs, gulls) by taking advantage of her obedience training. Soon, though, she huddles and whines, moving her haunches nervously, her tail tucked under. I feel the deck floor with my hand and find it uncomfortably hot from the sun. I take her to the plastic bucket chairs, thinking she'll find shade underneath, but she puts her two front paws on the seat next to mine and so I help her up. There she sits for the whole trip. Friendly to people who walk by us, she also watches gulls glide over the boat, begging for food. We pass a buoy rocked by the waves. Hearing its solemn sound she holds her head very high and looks at it with the utmost concentration; she pays little attention to any food dropped on the deck. I'm so taken with watching Laska that I am surprised when the captain announces that we should return to our cars.

Though there is a quicker drive "up island," I take the slow road to West Tisbury so that I can admire the stone fences and hilly pastures of Tashmoo Pond Farm, where Arabian horses graze, and stop at the Scottish Bakehouse, which sells delicious coconut haystacks and chocolate slippers, and at Nip n' Tuck Farm to buy fresh vegetables, eggs, and raw milk. The milk and cookies are for Levin and his new girlfriend, Michelle, who will be arriving on a later boat.

The cabin I rent is located half a mile down a dirt road, in the middle of a large field ringed by trees. The land runs down to a finger of Tisbury Great Pond, a brackish body of water that extends inland from ocean dunes. On a map, Martha's Vineyard resembles an upside-down cow; its back is a ten-mile expanse of beach that faces the Atlantic Ocean. My cabin is two miles from the ocean, but on certain days you can hear the waves pounding against the sand. Directly across the narrow stretch of Tisbury Great Pond is a riding stable. The horses graze right down to the water's edge, and you can hear them snort, squeal, and thunder away as they engage in territorial disputes.

The cabin once was a blacksmith's barn and belongs to a family that lives on the island year round. Buildings as devoid of modern conveniences as the one I rent are rare today on the island; people refer to these primitive places as "camps." The interior space is really one large room with two partitioned bedrooms, a living room and kitchen area with a woodstove, and a tiny bathroom;

there also is a front porch that looks out onto the pond, with large multipaned windows on three sides, and a bed/couch built into the wall, where I sleep. There is no telephone or electrical outlet for a computer. Gas feeds a stove and refrigerator and a hand pump empties into the large kitchen sink. Every morning I fill a big, battered aluminum pot on the stove for dishwater; I also fill a solar bag (a plastic bag with a short hose and shower head) and hang it on the southern camp wall where the sun will warm it during the day; as needed, I flush the toilet with buckets of water; at dusk, I light gas lamps and kerosene lanterns with matches. Over the years, I've devised ways to work around the arthritis; I am still able to perform these necessary tasks by myself.

I drive down the bumpy dirt road, flanked by tall grass and blueberry bushes; after a while the camp appears, small but distinctive in the generous field that surrounds it. I get out of the car, walk up to the crude hand-crafted door above which hangs a set of deer's antlers, turn a small rectangular piece of wood that holds the door shut, and step inside. Wide floorboards painted hunter green, rough-hewn rafters, a view of the horse farm through the east-facing wide windows—all are the same. Levin's metal cutout sculpture of a sheep still rests on a beam over the woodstove. At the sight of these familiar things, the long winter vanishes like morning mist in the field.

Laska acted so mature on the ferry that I let her loose, even though I will be busy unpacking. As I carry in a bag of groceries, I notice Laska prance by with a shiny quarter in her mouth. I grab treats to distract her and she comes over to eat them; I can find no coin. I want to make her throw up but am distracted by getting the camp in order before Levin and Michelle arrive. By the time I finish unpacking, I have to go down to the ferry. I leave Laska in her crate and try to leave my worries behind as well.

This time I take the quick road "down island" and arrive just as the arklike boat pulls into Vineyard Haven. The huge, gray docking logs groan and creak as the boat bumps against them. I can see Levin up on the front deck with a slender woman beside him. Levin and Michelle look pliant, like two graceful plants side by side in the strong sunlight. I watch as they come off the ramp; both are wearing sailor hats with the brims turned down and sunglasses. As Michelle walks toward me, she removes her glasses as if to make herself accessible and, with a hello, embraces me.

"Hey, Mom," Levin says, as he hugs me in turn, a small duffel bag slung over his shoulder.

"You traveled light," I say.

"Yup," he replies with a smile. Like many young people of his generation, Levin has taken trips to India, Europe, Greece, and England, and also crossed the

United States on a bicycle. At twenty-four he prides himself on getting by with little of what most of us deem necessary. "Michelle, too," he adds. "She has been all over the world and takes even less with her than I do."

I make an effort not to size Michelle up as I look at her (a boyfriend's mother can be a formidable person to meet), but I can't help noticing her beauty. Her smooth olive-skinned face has a sophisticated expression without any affectation. For her part, Michelle loops a strand of shiny black hair behind one ear, ducks her head a bit, and says, "Thanks for Levin."

I am astounded by her remark and at first don't respond. Then I reply, "What a kind thing to say. Mothers are supposed to go unnoticed."

We get into the car and on the way home I take the slow, windy road while Levin points out to Michelle all the same places I cherish. When we get to the dirt road, a mother skunk and two babies cross in front of the car. At the sight of us, she draws herself up and arches her back and tail that are striped with white; she looks like a threatened cat. In imitation of their mother, the little ones bunch themselves up, too. Looking into the rearview mirror I address Michelle, who has been watching the family with genuine delight, "I guess the theme for today is mothers and offspring." To myself, I wonder if Michelle's heritage prompted her recognition of me as Levin's mother. Asian families hold elders in respect; by contrast, in mainstream America, parents, and especially mothers, tend to be shed like cornhusks. In my sophomore year of college a friend who looked and acted like Marlon Brando returned from Thanksgiving break with the following story. When he got into the elevator of the apartment building about to return to school, his mom said, "Give your mother a kiss." As the elevator door slid shut, he replied, "Beatniks don't have mothers."

We arrive at the cabin. Eager for Michelle to meet Laska and for Levin to see how well she's grown, I let my puppy out of the crate. She dashes up to them and begins by sniffing their cargo pants; perhaps there is food inside the baggy pockets positioned at thigh level.

"She's beautiful," Michelle says.

My heart fills with pride. But when Levin bends down to pat Laska, she leaps at his face and bangs a tooth against his eyelid. He straightens up; his face, friendly a moment ago, now holds a cold expression. "She tried to bite my eye." "Oh no, Lev," I reply, in a strained voice, "she was just saying hello. The trouble is she's still kind of wild."

"Put that scathing brute in her crate," Levin says, without a trace of humor in his voice over his witty description. "I don't want Michelle to get hurt."

As I comply, I remember Laska's earlier mischief. "I have to call the vet because I think she swallowed a quarter just before you came."

"She is a lot of trouble," he observes.

I ignore his remark because it mirrors my own feeling about Laska just now. I had looked forward to a fun family time together, the four of us. Now it looks as if I'll have to keep Laska apart.

I drive down the road to a nearby phone booth and call the vet, who tells me what I already know. Laska should throw up the coin. Now, instead of being upset with her for jumping on Levin, I am angry at myself for waiting so long to take care of the problem. When I get back to the cabin, I give Laska some of the hydrogen peroxide that I had brought with me on vacation, but it doesn't work. Laska only rubs her face on the grass and lies there, her front paws folded back at a crazy angle, looking sick.

"I told you, she's trouble," Levin repeats. And then, what I least wanted to hear: "Sarah was never like this."

JULY 11

FIRST thing this morning, Laska passes a poop with a flat, round object in it. Like a mad scientist, I inspect it through the side of a plastic bag—it's the quarter. I praise her insides for the wisdom not to hang on to what Martin Luther, who associated money with excrement, called "filthy lucre."

JULY 13

TOMORROW is Bastille Day, the day Levin was born. He will be twenty-five years old. I still joke that giving birth spontaneously on that day was the most political thing I've ever done. Levin's father, Eric, plans to join us for the day; his new wife and young son will stay behind, partly because he will make the trip on a motorcycle he bought in his late forties, a vintage BSA, stylish as a 1950s car.

Eric owned one like it when I first knew him as a student at Brandeis University almost forty years ago. He was six foot three and blond, often had a Galois cigarette hanging from his mouth, and wore *socks* with his sandals, a style of dress I had never seen before. All these traits gave Eric a European air and he won my heart. When my grandparents heard that I was to marry a man I met at Brandeis, my grandmother's friends congratulated her. "How lucky, darlink," they crooned in a Yiddish accent, "a nice Jewish boy." My grandmother never corrected them.

I first visited Eric's parents' home, a town house on the Boston harbor, shortly after we began dating. As I entered the elegant brick building, I became aware of floor-to-ceiling bookcases. On the shelves, I saw well-worn rare editions of James Joyce, T. S. Eliot, and E. E. Cummings. In the living room I admired finely designed Chinese chairs, a lacquered traveling chest, and a three-paneled screen decorated with hand-painted birds perched on delicate flowering branches. A narrow antique oriental rug stretched across a mahogany table, with a Tiffany vase in the center that held yellow and white sweet-smelling freesia. On the walls were Rouault-like paintings by Eric's mother and intricate manuscript illuminations from India. All around the room, thick-leafed, mature houseplants radiated vitality. I exclaimed to Eric, loosely quoting Henry James, whom we'd recently studied, "Your parents' house is like the rich, dark hive of Europe." Their abundant store of books seemed like ripe, succulent fruit to be consumed and replenished. In comparison, my parents' scant collection seemed like porcelain apples and grapes, disturbed only by a dust cloth.

To my surprise, my family held attractions for Eric. Though highly self-educated, his mother and father did not take the same interest in his future that my parents did. Eric's father worked by turns as a graphics and carpentry teacher and a graphic designer. His mother painted and occasionally illustrated children's books. Their income fluctuated radically, but somehow they always had enough money for books, fine objects, and casual clothes in the style of English gentry. My parents had escaped childhood poverty through my father's dental profession. To them, a linear career was fundamental to a meaningful life, especially for someone who planned to marry their daughter. Typical middle-class parents of a girl in the 1950s, their only aspiration for me was that I find a potentially successful husband in college.

In a sense, Eric and I married each other's families. I even worked in his father's office for a number of years and became a graphic designer, my first career. Eventually, I had to leave my in-laws' house the same way I had left my parents', to find my own way in the redolent world of history and culture. Today I regard myself more as Eric's sister than as a former wife, which might explain why we get on as amicably as we do.

Sarah, who came along after Eric and I split up, adored Eric. When he stopped by our house, she would turn upside down, all the while wagging her tail, and even pee, a gesture of submission that she otherwise reserved only for Levin. It will be interesting to see how Laska reacts to Eric. I can't imagine her peeing submissively for anyone and find myself enjoying the thought.

JULY 14

I WAS right. When Eric roars up on his motorcycle in the late afternoon, we all come out of the cabin to greet him. Eric tries to pat Laska and right away she flips upside down, thrashes wildly, and grabs his hand between her teeth. I bring her back inside and put her in her crate. We plan to have dinner in the fishing village of Menemsha and then hang out in the town of Oak Bluffs. Eric will sleep at a friend's house, so he takes his motorcycle, and we follow him in our car. A top-heavy shiny black helmet protects Eric's head, but Birkenstock sandals cover his naked feet, showing his graceful ankles, while his thin shirt and slacks billow in the wind. Despite his strong, well-made form, Eric seems frail and quaint to me, dressed so lightly and hand signaling his turns with a certain stiff righteousness as if to say, "These are legitimate signals, even if out of date."

After we park, we set out for Larsen's fish market. Maybe because I'm often here alone, families on vacation seem to me displays of power. For the moment I have my own. A striking couple, Levin and Michelle attract people's attention. I go unnoticed, having passed into the invisible realm, a change I find not entirely unwelcome; for every wanted gaze in my younger years, there had been unwanted ones. Like other families we order slithery shiny oysters on the half-shell (I don't, because they are not on my diet) and sit on a picnic bench outside to eat them. On the wharf where Levin once stood as a child, young boys drop weighted fishlines from armatures of wood, hoping to catch squid. I watch them and remember what it was like to be a single mother—that pared-down feeling as Levin and I stood, years ago, on the damp, gray wharf where more abundant families also gathered for early night squid fishing.

This evening, because Eric has joined us, I even have what appears to be a husband by my side. After the hors d'oeuvres of oysters, we go to the Homeport restaurant for bluefish, which we order at a takeout window and eat sitting on rocks by the channel that runs from Vineyard Sound to Menemsha Pond. Then we head down to Oak Bluffs. Once there, we become like a family of hunter-gatherers (a heritage that, according to contemporary witch Starhawk, accounts for modern-day consumer browsing) as we wander the narrow sidewalks of the town. Unlike that of hunter-gatherers, on this warm summer evening our browsing seems dazed and aimless—kind of daffy, salt-water taffy daffy. Not even walking in a straight line, we look idly in clothes shops and enter the local fudge store. With a mixture of desire and revulsion, we eye huge, irregular, congealed chunks cut from the recently created lava flow of fudge—strawberry, pistachio, chocolate, and vanilla. I engage in these pursuits though I have no money for clothes and can't eat fudge. I chitchat with Eric about the aging process.

"It's all about hormones," Eric offers. "The impulse to reproduce drives human behavior, and I'm glad to be free of it."

"Me too," I say, privately noting that he recently had a child. Then I add, "When I was about nine, I asked my mother, 'Why are all the songs about love'?"

"What did she tell you?"

"I don't remember. What I do know is that nowadays I enjoy thinking about other things. Despite my accomplishments as an academic and my attentiveness as a mother, I spent my entire fertile years thinking about men."

Eric smiles indulgently and says, "Yes, I remember."

Our mood is so congenial that we almost walk arm in arm.

At Oak Bluffs' Flying Horses, the oldest carousel in the country, the newly restored horses draw my attention; their nostrils flare, their glass eyes gleam with readiness to plunge forward to the music. But no one shares my interest in sitting astride a gaily painted horse and feeling the soft salt air blow against the face as the carousel slowly turns to tinny music. Instead, I allow myself to be guided into a corridor of the building that houses video games; the space is so narrow that I stiffen up.

"It's okay, Mom," Levin says, sensing my anxiety, though unaware of its source—my childhood fear of being shut in. He soothes me, "Nothing bad will happen."

Way at the back of the constricted space is a pinball machine, Twilight Zone. Delighted to learn I've never played pinball, Levin encourages me as I flip the stumpy levers that propel the ball up the board to make lights blink and flash, and to trigger popping and beeping sounds. On my first try I succeed, but then I can't keep my wits about me and the silver ball rolls down the trough between the impotent levers.

At Levin's suggestion, we proceed to a video arcade that reminds me of Dante's Inferno. The large room has black walls and floors and is flanked by brightly lit video machines of every description. They emit violent sounds ranging from shouts and growls to shrieking tires, crashes, explosions, gun salvos, and machine-gun fire. Eric and I watch as Levin and Michelle play a game called Area 51. The title comes from a place in New Mexico, now closed to the public because of a furor over alleged alien sightings. Two-legged scaly beings appear suddenly on the screen and come toward you in a menacing semi-squat posture. The action takes place in what looks like a gutted office building; orange stains splatter the walls like the remains of giant squashed bugs. Levin and Michelle expertly pick off the aliens with pistols that they recharge by shooting them away from the screen; they hold the guns with two hands, the way cops do on television. I am amazed at their accuracy and even more at what fun they are having.

After a round or two, Levin offers me the chance to try the game. I decline, but as I continue to watch them play, I realize why I didn't accept the invitation. What if I begin to shoot and really get into it, as the saying goes? Wouldn't it disrupt the image everyone has of me as disapproving of aggression? The side of myself Laska brings out is one that troubles me, and one that I don't wish to acknowledge. So I go on playing *my* own game—behaving old and momish. I turn to Eric, who had just shot a round and done pretty well, and say, "I can't take it in here much longer." To my surprise, he agrees. We wait until Levin and Michelle finish another set and then we make a plan to all meet at a certain dress shop in about twenty minutes.

As Eric and I walk to the store, I feel less comfortable than I did when we were with Levin and Michelle. "How are Jean and Sacha?" I inquire.

"They are very well and send you their regards," he replies, with a touch of Boston Brahmin grace. "You should have seen Sacha the last time Levin came to visit. When Levin tried to leave, Sacha clasped him around the legs and wouldn't let go."

"Maybe it's easier for brothers to get along when they each have a mother of their own."

"That's an interesting idea," Eric says, and I enjoy this praise.

We arrive at the dress store and I wander off by myself; it feels falsely intimate to look at clothes with Eric. I am relieved when Levin and Michelle arrive; now I can join in their browsing. Michelle tries on a tight beige and black floor-length dress that Levin has picked out for her. Size 4 at the most. I admire her in the dress, wondering what it is like to be petite. I am tall and, though slender, I've always felt out of scale. My generation had to line up in "size places" in grammar school. I had taken no pleasure in each year being taller than almost all the boys in my class. Even today our culture expects women not to take up too much space. Some researchers associate eating disorders with women's attempts to ease their emergence into the public sphere by appearing diminutive.

"I love Michelle's taste in clothes," Levin says, leafing through the dress rack. "She likes simple styles in subtle colors."

Here I am in my faded denim cutaways, baggy tank top, and Birkenstock sandals, feeling like a fifty-five-year-old ten year old. I'm not at home in this world of slinky dresses. I finger a baggy white linen jacket, something I could imagine trying on without humiliation, and check out the earrings, an item I know about.

"Do you like hats?" Michelle asks, trying on a tight-fitting straw one with a little round brim.

"I like my green baseball cap," I say. Besides my winter hats, it's the only kind I wear.

Tired of the clothing store, I offer to buy ice cream for everyone at Mad Martha's, a famous island spot. Levin and Michelle share a small cup of blueberry and

I am struck by his new, frugal manner of eating ice cream. One summer when Levin was six or seven, we arrived early for the ferry that would take us from Oak Bluffs to the mainland. I don't remember who decided that we should pass the time by eating ice cream. We walked up to a take-out window and ordered two large Softies. A plump, older woman turned on a machine that twirled chocolate and vanilla ice cream into first one sugar cone and then another. As Levin and I started back to the ferry I felt the heat rising from the sidewalk, an unpleasant reminder of city life back in Cambridge. We finished our cones at exactly the same moment; like our vacation, the ice cream disappeared too fast. So either Levin or I decided it would be a great idea to get another one. We returned to the take-out window and the woman looked at us with amused surprise. "I've never seen people eat ice cream so fast," she said. Now as Levin, Michelle, Eric, and I leave Mad Martha's, Levin says, "I think I'm done with ice cream." No one reacts to his dramatic statement, so he goes on. "Who would want to drink a pint of half-and-half or cream? That's what eating ice cream is like. Sorbet is good; it is just fruit, sugar, and water. Sometimes I get a mango or coconut ice in my neighborhood on the Upper West Side." Clearly New York, where Levin recently moved, offers opportunities not available in the Cambridge, Massachusetts, of his childhood or in Burlington, Vermont, where I now live. "That sounds great," I say, feeling a part of our life together discarded as casually as an unfinished sugar cone. Over the years, eating ice cream together was a form of communion between Levin and me. The sweet substance seemed to symbolize the primordial milk he once took from me, which I gladly gave. Although the evening is warm, I rub my bare arms, which have suddenly become cold. We head up a long block flanked by one tourist trap after another, and I wonder whether all the dazed, browsing families have similar interior moments. Perhaps some other mother refuses to shoot lizard aliens, imagining it would disrupt the family image of her. Or dare she break free tonight, the way Levin does from ice cream? In the light of streetlamps and shopwindows, the people I see wandering the soft night look simply content, as I'm sure we do, Oak Bluffing like anyone else.

JULY 15

LEVIN and Michelle get up early this morning and before I can put Laska in her crate, she runs past the Indian cloth curtain that acts as a door to their room. A breeze blows the material aside and I see Laska upside down on the floor, thrashing about wildly, teeth showing. In a conciliatory move Levin pats my puppy, but she takes his hand in her mouth roughly. Later over breakfast Levin says, "I don't like the anger she makes me feel," a sentiment I share. Despite Levin's aggravation with Laska, whenever he passes by her crate, where she's mostly been, he says, "Hi Laska."

Yesterday, we three humans spent the afternoon at Lucy Vincent Beach, and I took a walk by myself to survey the area from Laska's point of view. I plan to take her for a walk by the ocean when I am alone with her again. What *enticements*—two dead gulls, sharp spiky crab shells, bottle caps, a douche-bag nozzle, crumbled aluminum foil, soggy plastic bags, and even a fishhook at the end of a weathered line, tangled in seaweed.

JULY 16

TODAY, Levin drives a tomato stake into the ground, to which I attach a long chain. Now, in the mornings before the sun gets too hot, Laska can stay out of our way without having to be cooped up in her crate. Soon after I put her on the chain, she crawls under some low-lying branches of a pine tree that grows beside the house and begins chewing on them. The only hitch is that when I leave her there and later come to release her, she jumps on me and grabs at my clothes; I thought we had left that bad habit behind.

JULY 17

LEVIN and Michelle go off by themselves to explore Chappaquiddick Island at the other end of Martha's Vineyard. I am alone for the first time since they arrived and take the opportunity to read. As usual, I brought more books to Martha's Vineyard than I will have time to read. It is my custom at midday, when it's best not to be out in the sun, to rest in a large hammock woven from multicolored thread in Latin America. I bought the hammock when Levin was a baby and bring it to the camp every year. It hangs inside just where, with the front and back doors of the camp open, a breeze blows through even on the hottest day. When Levin visits, he likes to lie in the hammock and watch me cook dinner. Often we don't speak, and I enjoy the silence and his seeming ability to still allow himself to "lie back and float" in the mother's presence.

I'm in the midst of James Serpell's *In the Company of Animals: A Study of Human-Animal Relationships,* which has become a foundational book in the field of human/nonhuman animal relationships, even though it was published as recently as 1986. As Serpell explains, scholarly interest in this subject is new. Marx and Mead, whom I taught last spring, are two writers in a long lineage of Western thinkers who proclaimed the superiority of humans over animals. This hierarchical ranking precluded any serious discussion of how and why the two groups get on with one another. By 1996, when the second edition of Serpell's book appeared, two scholarly journals, *Anthrozoös* and *Society & Animals,* had been founded, and as the foreword put it, "an exponential growth in the number of books" about animals and people had occurred; there also was increased public awareness of animal-related issues.[1]

According to Serpell, concern about animal welfare is several centuries old, but the subject's popularity today has a lot to do with environmental and ecological crises, the threatened extinction of animal species, and the increased number of pet owners. I would add (as I had when the PETA speaker came to class) that the social revolutions of the 1960s also contributed. The civil rights, anti–Vietnam War, women's liberation, and gay and lesbian movements in the West, and the dissolution of colonial rule in third-world countries—all these social transformations challenged the boundaries that had divided self and other.

In 1986, Serpell noticed that if little was written about people and animals generally, there was even less interest in the specific topic of pet keeping. He provided a social psychological explanation for this neglect. Our hard-line economic exploitation of farm animals is difficult to reconcile with the fact that today more than half of U.S. households live with pets. Logically, the pig that gives us its life, and whose every part is usable, deserves more care and respect than our pet dog, who sacrifices nothing and, indeed, for whom *we* sacrifice. This paradox encourages us to ignore, trivialize, or disparage our bond with companion animals, even though most Americans who live with pets consider them family members. (Serpell states he hasn't revised his book for the second edition because much of what he said ten years earlier still holds true.) The common view of pet keeping in our society remains ambivalent, despite the fact that little empirical evidence exists to suggest that owning pets is either bad for you or silly. Some studies even reveal the opposite, that pets enhance human sociability.

Serpell's book corrects some misconceptions I had acquired in the process of becoming a sociologist. I had learned that, historically, pets belonged to the aristocracy, which kept them for amusement and as displays of privilege; hence, when the middle class arose, it wished to keep pets as a sign of status. For instance, most of the dog breeds we recognize today were created in the nineteenth century; their refinement allowed the middle class, ever unsure of its social lineage, to fixate on pure bloodlines. While all this information is factual, Serpell shows a more complex picture, one that leaves room for affection, rather than mere affectation. First, poor people kept pets too, when the aristocracy and clergy allowed or didn't notice it. Second, anthropological studies show that contemporary indigenous peoples live with pets. Third, prehistoric pet keeping might have paved the way for animal husbandry and livestock farming.

I have more to say about Serpell, but I want to get a swim in, if possible. Yesterday, the surf was huge and so misty from the tumult that it was hard to see past two ridges of waves. Levin was delighted, because his dad taught him long ago how to body surf.

JULY 18

LEVIN and Michelle walk onto the ramp, disappear inside the ferry, and then reappear on the deck. I wait to see them off. This is the awkward time of leave-taking; the distance between the deck and the pier makes it difficult to hear one another, yet the boat remains stationary. Levin resorts to pantomime; he positions his thumb and forefinger as if he were measuring the space between them, and then he narrows the opening to the size of a green pea. I realize that he is showing Michelle how small I am going to become once the ferry leaves. I wipe sweat off my nose and Levin with his finger mimics a tear running down his face. The Snoopy look in his eyes and a shrug of his shoulders mutely inquire, "Are you crying?"

"No," I reply, though I am not sure he can hear me. I wipe my brow to show him that I am just hot. He gestures with his arm that I should step back into the shade and, as I comply, I think, "He's worried about me, and I wish he wouldn't be."

"Spend time with your friends," Levin yells to me from the ferry deck.

"I will," I shout back. On our ride down island, I had told Levin and Michelle that I couldn't decide how much time to spend with people or by myself in the remaining days of my vacation.

The boat horn sounds and the ferry pulls slowly away from the dock. Michelle calls out, "Are you getting ready to shrink?"

Her remark is apt. As Levin recreates the dyad of his childhood in a new form with Michelle, I *am* getting smaller. I nod and then begin to wave goodbye in our habitual manner. I put my arms way up over my head and then crisscross them the way flaggers guide a plane once it has landed, and Levin does the same. As the boat steams away, I stand in the bright hot sun, though I keep on waving until Levin and Michelle become specks in my sight. Then I turn away and walk back to my car with the thought that the shrinking is somewhat reciprocal. I am pleased to notice that I look forward to returning to Laska and the days of solitude ahead.

JULY 19

LASKA and I take our first island walk, which is at Waskosim's Rock, an almost two-hundred-acre wooded area with open fields that is more like Camel's Hump, where we often walk in Vermont, than the beach. I thought we'd begin with the woods and fields. The preserve is hilly and offers views of Vineyard Sound and perched on one of its peaks is Waskosim's Rock, a huge boulder that resembles the face of an open-jawed whale emerging from the earth. In the mid-1600s, the rock marked the beginning of a stone-wall boundary between English and Wampanoag land. The boulder seems a mute reminder of the territorial conflicts between Native and Anglo-Americans that is still going on today. Native Americans recently reclaimed a large portion of the dramatic landmass at the far end of Martha's Vineyard, a place known for its spectacular multicolored clay cliffs. Once called Gay Head, this part of the island has been renamed Aquinnah.

Laska has so much energy stored up from her days in the crate that when I take her off the leash, she "loses it," tearing up and down the dirt path. Almost immediately after arriving, we come to a shallow, winding brook; Laska, who avoids puddles in the city, skitters down the dark humus slope, licks the water once or twice, steps right in, and then splashes madly up and down, watching out for tree roots and fallen logs. There are three or four such places to get down to the brook and she visits each one of them.

At the halfway point of our hour-long walk, she rests from the midday heat and her own exertions under the shade of a large oak tree in one of the open fields fragrant with wildflowers. As I catch up to her, she looks at me as if to say, "Let's take a little break."

I stop under the tree also and reply, "Laska, even though no one but me knows it, you can be a sensible dog."

Our walk off the leash is a success; next we will go to the ocean.

JULY 20

THE water is wild this afternoon, line upon line of white-furled waves crash on top of one another in crisscrossing patterns and then recede, dragging bathers out to sea with them. Perhaps the almost full moon has something to do with this violence.

An envelope of solitude surrounds me again. Tonight, with the soft gaslight illuminating the cabin, I feel cozy. Laska is out of her crate and busy chewing on a bone filled with cheese, as I continue my thoughts about *In the Company of Animals.*

Though James Serpell uses many lenses in his book (historical, anthropological, sociological, ethological, political, and psychological), he does not turn a gender lens on his material. I've noticed this oversight in a number of animal scholars who are men. Had he done so, he might have come up with some interesting speculations about women's role in the domestication of animals. In a chapter entitled "Pets in Tribal Societies," Serpell cites no fewer than five examples of tribes where Western visitors observed or learned about women who suckled baby animals. Native American women nursed bear cubs; Guiana Indians of northern Brazil put young mammals to the breast—"dog, monkey, opposum-rat, labba, acouri, deer"; Barasana women of eastern Colombia, Aboriginal women of Australia, and indigenous women in Hawaii all breastfed puppies. As one visitor noted of the Hawaiian women: "Every woman has a pet animal; and mothers who are nursing their offspring will suckle a puppy." Serpell gives a cross-cultural perspective on this widespread practice of transgressing the human/animal boundary: "If a woman in Britain or the United States were to breast-feed a puppy or a piglet in public (or even in private) she would probably be locked away for indecency. Yet in countless hunting and gathering or simple agricultural societies, the suckling of young animals is considered perfectly normal and natural."[2]

Oddly, although Serpell calls the suckling of young animals "perfectly normal and natural," he doesn't say *why* indigenous women adopted this practice. Was it due to need or fondness or both that they domesticated animals in this manner?

In his defense of suckling Serpell could have added that women nursing human babies in public have been arrested for indecency; only three U.S. states now have laws *allowing* women to breastfeed in public. Advanced industrial society has forgotten that for 99 percent of our history, humans have been hunter-gatherers; human babies have the same embodied needs now as they did then. "Embody" is a social science term that I find extremely useful. According to the dictionary it means: "to give bodily form to; incarnate." Babies incarnate a reminder that we disregard our bodies at a cost; relationally speaking, the only Internet that makes sense to babies is dot.mom.

Breastfeeding human babies, let alone nonhuman animals, has not been a popular cause among feminists. Many, if not most, regard the physical dependence of babies as a threat to women's equality in the public sphere; also, many feminists point out, and quite rightly, that this traditional role has been used to keep women in their place. All the same, I believe that to look deeply at the human condition, we must take the baby's point of view into account. To babies, bodies matter. Their whole understanding of self and other unfolds through sensuous experience.

Laska's puppyhood reminds me of my own early life; she, too, seems "wildly unmothered," to quote poet Adrienne Rich. Perhaps that is why, when she was little, I fantasized about suckling her as a way to solve our problems. After all, she'd been weaned too young, which I'm convinced is one source of her unruly way of connecting. Early on I noticed how she was attracted to buttons on my shirts, which resemble a mother dog's nipples, and how, on occasion, sucking on one of my fingers soothed her. But by the time her biting began, Laska was too old for me to breastfeed her; besides, I had no milk. And, *besides,* those sharp little teeth . . .

But to return to the subject of indigenous women suckling baby animals, I have never read any accounts of this practice, even in books about breastfeeding. Nor did feminist author André Collard mention the subject, though in *Rape of the Wild: Man's Violence toward Animals and the Earth* she argues that a close relationship exists between women and animals and that they share a common oppression under patriarchy. An anthology edited by feminist theologian Carol Adams, *Animals and Women: Feminist Theoretical Explorations,* holds a view similar to Collard's yet leaves the subject out as well. Despite the professed bond with animals, these authors seem reluctant to cross the animal/human boundary *that* far. If women's suckling contributed to the domestication of animals in Paleolithic and Neolithic times, this activity becomes a key force in the evolution of humans' relationship to nature.

JULY 20

I STEP outside the cabin and look up at the stars; the horizon is visible in every direction. Two weeks out of the year at this place, I can feel the vast earth roll toward the sun at dawn, pass under it during the day, and heave away from it at night. Tonight the sky is embedded with stars—matter transformed into needle-sharp, brilliant light. If I stay up for twenty-four hours, I can watch the constellations turn with the earth's motion and the moon rotate in a path of its own. An ancient Sumerian tale from around 2,500 BCE tells of Gilgamesh, the resplendent and powerful king of Uruk, who sought immortality after the death of his dear friend Enkidu. In one test of his worthiness, he had to stay awake for seven days and seven nights. Gilgamesh claimed not to have slept, but small round breads placed by his side each night remained uneaten and became moldy. The loaves' decay provided evidence that Gilgamesh had lied. Sleep is a sign of mortality.

Despite my desire to witness day *and* night, I am content tonight with a glimpse of the filmy scarf of the Milky Way flung across the sky; the faint star cluster, the Pleiades, that you can see best if you don't look straight at it; and a crescent moon that lounges on the horizon, accompanied by Venus, which tags along as the moon rises, like a faithful pet.

JULY 21

I STAND on the platform of a high wooden walkway. The stairs grayed from the ocean air go steeply up and over the dunes that separate South Beach from Chilmark Pond. Laska sits beside me. She looks straight ahead, taking the salt air into her nose and then breathing it out, her jowls puffing slightly with each exhalation. The slender green dune grass lies this way and that down the strip of dunes as far as I can see, blown like a horse's mane by the wind. On my left is the brackish pond Sarah and I knew well. White swans float on the quiet water and their necks undulate as they swim; a blue heron perches improbably on one spindly leg in the shallows; and several brown Canada geese lift into flight, their calls sounding like ancient grievances. On the far side of the pond I see a few large cape-style houses with faded gray shingles and white trim. No one seems to be up yet. On my right, as Homer once described it, lies the whispering, clamorous, tumbling sea.

South Beach extends for ten miles to the eastern tip called Wasque Point, a desolate place where wave currents meet and roil dangerously. As when I walked here with Sarah just before she died, I am aware of my limitations: I cannot look at both the ocean and the pond. That I am unable to see them simultaneously intensifies my sense of how each body of water represents a different aspect of life—the turbulent and the tranquil. Then I remember that once a year the pond and the ocean meet, when conservationists make a "cut" with a tractor or bulldozer to freshen the brackish pond water, a process that preserves the fish and vegetation. Long ago, Levin and I swam in the cut at Tisbury Great Pond. It was like swimming in a fast-moving river that flowed two ways. First the ocean tide rushed into the cut and then, reversing itself, caused the pond water to flow out to sea. It seems that the exchange vivifies.

Laska and I have stayed still long enough for a few geese to float close to the pond shoreline. She starts down the steps toward them, her young body swaying pliantly as she descends. "Laska, come!" I call out; to my surprise she turns around and rushes back. We walk down the steps to the ocean and continue along the beach. Despite my worries, Laska hasn't gotten into any debris, so I haven't needed to keep her on a leash. She trots ahead of me for a while, then dashes at a cluster of sandpipers; they race away along the wet, shiny sand at the water's edge. Next Laska notices the ebbing tide and chases it boldly; when the waves advance toward her she jumps aside, snapping at their frothy edge defiantly. As if proud of her accomplishments, Laska races back to me and sits smartly, one ear flung back, sand on her nose. "You are an intrepid one," I say and give her a treat.

August 1997

Hot Sauce and Book Award

AUGUST 1

ACCORDING to my Lubavitch calendar, which the local ultra-Orthodox congregation in Vermont sends me every year at no cost, the new moon will occur two days from now at eight thirty-nine and one-eighteenth of a second AM (the measurement is precise). Whereas the weekly observance, Shabbat, takes place in solar time, from sundown to sundown, the Jewish month is based on lunar time and spans twenty-eight days. An unillumined moon suits the dark mood I am in since returning from vacation; a poem called "The Recluse" by Allen Grossman puts words to my feelings:

> My life is bountiful, although I dwell
> Absurdly in it. I am a bird disgracing
> This most lovely tree by my poor plumage,
> Half grown and badly worn as if unowned.[1]

Like the poetic speaker's, my customary sense of myself does not match the goodness in my life. Vacations from this underlying malaise can vanish in an instance. To an onlooker there is much I could be happy about upon returning from Martha's Vineyard. Later this month I will fly to Toronto, where Levin will join me, and receive the Jesse Bernard Award at the American Sociological Association's annual meeting. I live in a geographical area that is no less beautiful than the place where I vacation; in September I begin a yearlong sabbatical. Despite these bounties, a sense of unease and foreboding dog me. I am bothered that dusk comes earlier than when I left two weeks ago, that I have rheumatoid arthritis, that my house is run-down, that my houseplants suffered because I forgot to ask the house sitter to water them, that the yard is overgrown, that my sabbatical will come to little. My colleague John Strand comforted me about this concern yesterday. He entered academic life when he was young and so has had several sabbaticals, which come every seventh year. "You never accomplish all that you want to," he said. "What matters is that you have a satisfying time." His advice should reassure me, but it does not. Most terribly I fear that if I do not invite my parents to the ASA ceremony, Levin's plane will crash on his way to it.

Because I'm out of balance, Laska and I are again at odds. Or did I have a false sense on the island of how well we were doing? True, I let Laska off the leash on our walks, a new measure of freedom, and she did not eat her poops—there were so many novel experiences to occupy her attention. But most of the time my puppy had little chance to get into trouble—I kept her crated or on her chain out in the yard so that she wouldn't harm the cabin or get lost (if I left the doors open as a cooling measure). And she resumed jumping up on me when I would release her from confinement and has brought this old habit home with her. Worst of all, she has gone right back to eating her stools. Like Brigadoon, our vacation weeks have vanished.

AUGUST 2

THE air is damp and chilly for summer, but Laska and I go outside to play in the yard. I throw the ball and she runs off with it. Unreasonably disappointed (she has never showed an interest in retrieving balls), I try to return inside and she jumps up, grabs the sleeve of my shirt, and rips it. I know Laska took hold of me to keep me from leaving her alone, but I am furious; I stomp into the house and shut the screen door. She jumps on it with her front paws and her claws tear the mesh.

Later in the day I walk into the studio to get a book and Laska leaps on me again. I grab a bonker bottle, meaning to tap her lightly on the top of her head. I hit her once and then, as anger carries me like an unruly wave, I hit her repeatedly, as hard as I can. She sinks down to the floor, her eyes screwed shut and her ears flattened. When I see her expression, I stop. Then I strike myself over the head with just as much force. The impact is stronger than I thought it would be. Frightened that I might hurt her, or already have, I round up all the bonker bottles, put them in shopping bags, and take them back to the supermarket. The self-administered blows give me a headache for the rest of the day.

AUGUST 3

I TURN to psychoanalyst and author Alice Miller; she will be the moon (suited to illuminating the unconscious) that sheds light on my despondence. Over the years, her groundbreaking work on the hidden injuries of childhood has been a mother to me. In the 1980s, she exposed how normative our mistreatment of children is. "Normative" is a useful sociological term that means a standard, model, or pattern regarded as typical. Out of ignorance, we inflict the same suffering on children that we endured when young. In *For Your Own Good: Hidden Cruelty in Child-rearing and the Roots of Violence,* Miller explains the unfortunate consequences of our child-rearing practices:

> The individual psychological stages in the lives of most people are:
>
> 1. To be hurt as a small child without anyone recognizing the situation as such
> 2. To fail to react to the resulting suffering with anger
> 3. To show gratitude for what are supposed to be good intentions
> 4. To forget everything
> 5. To discharge the stored-up anger onto others in adulthood or to direct it against oneself.
>
> The greatest cruelty that can be inflicted on children is to refuse to let them express their anger and suffering except at the risk of losing their parents' love and affection. The anger stemming from early childhood is stored up in the unconscious, and since it basically represents a healthy, vital source of energy, an equal amount of energy must be expended in order to repress it. An upbringing that succeeds in sparing the parents at the expense of the child's vitality sometimes leads to suicide or extreme drug addiction, which is a form of suicide. If drugs succeed in covering up the emptiness caused by repressed feelings and self-alienation, then the process of withdrawal brings this void back into view. When withdrawal is not accompanied by restoration of vitality, then the cure is sure to be temporary.[2]

One key phrase in this quote is "most people," because it gives Miller's observation a sociological dimension. She speaks of "individual psychological stages," but society shapes these stages, and most of us share the experience of them. Everywhere, at every moment, babies and children learn to deny their own feelings and to comply with their parents' needs. Social scientists have overlooked this destructive social phenomenon. In *The Sociology of Housework,* sociologist Ann Oakley called a disparity of this kind the difference between *social presence* and *sociological visibility.* Her example was housework, which has enormous social presence—all around us, women tend the home. Yet, until Oakley's feminist scholarship in the 1970s, no social scientist had studied this form of human labor; hence, housework had no sociological visibility. Social scientists overlooked housework because most of them were men and did not consider women's labor to be *real* work.

In Oakley's example, the social institution of patriarchy, destructive to both genders, is the culprit. But why do we hide the widespread social presence of adults' mistreatment of children from sociological visibility? Miller finds the reason in our obedience to an "eleventh commandment," which is deeply engraved in our cultural heritage: "Thou shalt not be aware." We "forget everything," as Miller puts it, to avoid the anger that we were not permitted to express as children. Yet, this strong emotion doesn't disappear; it lives on in the unconscious and causes us to do unto our children as we were done to. The biblical Ten Commandments, themselves, give the story away: they instruct us to respect our parents but remain silent on whether we ought to respect our children.

Alice Miller quotes the novelist Mariella Mehr, who describes the difficulty of emerging from her early years intact:

> the god of my childhood wears black robes, has horns
> on his head and carries an ax in his hand. how in the
> world was I still able to slip past him?
> all my life I have been creeping stealthily through
> my landscape, under my arm the little bit of life I keep
> thinking I have stolen.[3]

Her words "creeping stealthily" and "stolen" describe perfectly how many of us feel—that to make off with even a "little bit of life" from the house of our parents seems an act of thievery.

The recognition conferred by the Jesse Bernard Award invites me to stand boldly in "my landscape," but the parents who live on inside me don't approve. The scholarly research that grew out of my dual experiences as daughter and mother drove me to advocate passionately in *Bearing Meaning* for reform of childbirth and infant-feeding practices, work structures, and our cultural stories. I insisted that we honor the maternal body as the matrix of the social order, and recognize the embodied wisdom of the culture of the newly born. Although I dedicated the book to Levin, I wrote it out of a hope that no other women would have to endure a birth like my mother's, nor any child suffer as I did on account of it. (Earlier insults may have warped my mother's life, but my birth seemed to have sealed our fate as mother and daughter.)

When I challenged my parents, I got into trouble: "Don't give me any of your lip," my mother said as recently as a few years ago, resorting to the same belittling phrase she used when I was small. By contrast, my outspokenness in *Bearing Meaning* has not provoked rebuke; instead, I am praised for adding to our understanding of women's role in society.

AUGUST 4

TODAY, despite my rational mind's insistence that I don't need to creep stealthily to the ASA conference, I want to overeat. At age fourteen, I developed an eating disorder. I soothed myself with food, chewed as an outlet for rage, stuffed myself to keep the truth down, punished myself for failing to be silent, tried to grow so big that no one could harm me, and became dull, as if I stared out at the world through wooden-nickel eyes. Following Miller, food, like a drug, covered up "the emptiness caused by repressed feelings and self-alienation."

In 1956, there was no language for my compulsion. I told no one about it and continued to perform well at Hunter College High School and to have a social life with my girlfriends. My parents, the only ones who witnessed my overeating, chose to ignore it. Convinced that I had become unlike other people, I identified with creatures in old horror movies shown on TV, hosted by a vampire named Zacherley. (A friend and I once went to the TV studio, which was in my neighborhood, and met him. In real life Zacherley, whose real name was John K. Zacherle, was a tall, hauntingly handsome man. I still have his autograph, written in a large hand: "To Roberta from her old flame, Zach.") The vampire Zacherley lived in a cave under Central Park with his wife, Isobel. She lay in a crude wood coffin; the lid was tilted open and supported a candelabrum that perched there at a crazy angle—a macabre version of Liberace's piano. If she got too feisty, Zacherley threatened to drive a stake into her heart. He had an unseen son, Gasport, who lived in a dirty, tattered burlap bag that hung from a peg on the wall. Gasport would groan in friendly torment from time to time, which provoked Zacherley to growl, "Shut up, Gasport!" as if his son disturbed the decorum of the place, even though no guests were present.

Zacherley showed horror films like *The Mummy* and cut into them, from time to time, with witticisms that interrupted the buildup of terror. For instance, when the mummy lumbered stiffly along with some of his wrappings trailing on the ground, Zacherley would comment on the scene with the words, "Pick up your rags, you dirty slob." Zacherley's humor, however, did not alleviate the fear I experienced when he showed werewolf films. As I watched a man grope at his face with both hands because the full moon caused his smooth skin to sprout wolf hairs and his teeth to elongate into fangs, I felt that a dehumanizing force seized me just the way it did the werewolf.

Fortunately, in the years I did stuff myself, I never purged (which is very bad for your health); I just ate until my stomach couldn't hold any more. When I became too heavy, I dieted sensibly; but as soon as I lost weight, I began overeating again. For as Miller explains, if withdrawal from an addiction "is not accompanied by restoration of vitality, then the cure is sure to be temporary." Ten years ago, when I developed arthritis, I eliminated foods like ice cream that would aggravate the symptoms. Let's face it, you can't get much of a binge going on sunflower seeds. The eating disorder quieted, though many of the underlying problems remained.

Freud once famously said that if insight into a patient's problems were all that was needed, psychiatrists would be out of work. Insight changes little without a process of "working through." You must confront the unconscious resistances to getting well that are born from fear. By stuffing food down my throat I will suppress myself and appease the parents of my childhood. Quite unconsciously they had not wanted me to become independent of them, much less shine. But if I binge, I will ruin the pleasure I might experience at the conference. How, in these next weeks, will I keep from suppressing the "little bit of life" in me with food and from taking out on Laska my anger at thwarting myself?

AUGUST 5

LAST night I ate thirteen rice cakes slathered with sesame tahini and topped with sliced banana. Although these foods officially are on my diet, consuming too many of them affects my symptoms. This morning my feet and hands are sore and swollen. I can't imagine leaving for Toronto this coming Saturday unless I stop bingeing.

Usually, I take Laska for a walk after her breakfast, but my feet hurt and I am in a bad mood. So when Laska whines at the door, I open it and let her out. Then I reconsider my decision to leave her unsupervised, grab a plastic bag off the studio table where I keep her stuff, and rush out into the yard. She already has swung around to eat her poop; part of it dangles between her teeth. "Laska, *no!*" I yell, as if I'd never seen her do this before. I pick up the remaining pieces with the plastic bag and go inside to call the vet for advice.

A pleasant young technician answers the phone. "Hello," I begin, "I'm calling about my eight-month-old puppy, Laska. I've tried everything to get her to stop eating her stools. I've put Deter pills in her food, which is supposed to make her poops taste awful. Then, on your recommendation, I tried Forbid, which supposedly works the same way. Someone told me to try pineapple juice. She still eats them."

"Try Tabasco sauce," the technician offers crisply, as if *this* will do it.

"To eat?" I ask.

"No, next time she poops, put some Tabasco on it. She'll take a bite and never bother with her stools again."

"Thanks," I reply, "I even have some in the house."

I wait for Laska's next poop, which is sure to come at midday. The sun makes an appearance just as Laska asks to go out. I follow her with a slender bottle of Tabasco sauce in one hand. As soon as she poops, I shake some of the red liquid on it, stand back, and wait. Laska sniffs at the brown mound and disdains it, smacking her lips as if she had taken a bite. Last spring, I sprinkled cayenne pepper over the earth that covered my tulip bulbs; when Laska tried to dig them up, she encountered the spice, which is the ingredient in Tabasco sauce that makes it hot. The familiar frightened anger floods me when I realize that Laska won't eat the Tabascoed poop. I stride into the house, put rubber gloves on my shaking hands, grab a plastic bag, rush outside, pick up some of the poop, take hold of Laska by her collar, and force the stuff into her mouth. She sinks to the ground and attempts to push the fiery mass out with her tongue; her lips curl in a snarl of distaste. Overcome with shame and with fear of my lack of self-control, I run into the house and call Merle. It is as if I'm dialing an 800 number to deter not stool-eating, but abuse. Merle offers to come by that afternoon.

I return outside to see how Laska is doing. I find her lying pressed up against a garbage can. She seems to say, "You made me feel like garbage."

The day passes much too slowly, but, finally, Merle arrives. When she comes through the door from the mudroom into the kitchen, Laska explodes, greeting her with a melee of jumps as if she is on springs, and she grabs at Merle's shirt with her teeth. Merle takes Laska right down to the ground and puts her hand firmly on my puppy's throat. Merle has to repeat this correction several times before she subdues Laska. I notice how, through it all, Merle's manner remains calm and her voice kind. Her authority established, Merle pats Laska on her belly, and even her face, without any resistance from the pup. Then Merle stands up, brushes a hand across her face, as if to clear herself of the tumult, and sits down slowly at the round kitchen table.

I haven't seen Merle for a long time, though I talk to her often on the phone. Merle has a round face with slanted eyes and high cheekbones and she keeps her hair pulled high in a ponytail. Today, she wears a loose pastel-colored shirt and pants. The soft hues of the cloth, her full face, rounded body, and mindful movements and speech, all together make me think: "She's a *Buddha.* No wonder she soothes Laska." Indeed, I have never seen my puppy so relaxed as now—she lies quietly near Merle, belly up. Somewhat calm myself now that Merle is here, I have a moment to reflect on why I called her instead of Vivian, whose advice I also value. Merle is the one who rescued Steely when I thought I would have to end his life. In an extreme situation with a canine, I turn to her.

"I wish I could discipline Laska the way you do," I say. "I can't be forceful or firm without getting angry or scared or startled."

Merle looks at me kindly and replies, "You see, she's confident and you are not."

Amazed at the simplicity of her observation, I reply, "That's true."

"Now, why don't you tell me what happened today and we'll see how I can help you."

As I make some tea for Merle, I go over the incident with the Tabasco sauce.

Merle asks, "Do you have any idea, besides parasites, why Laska gets you so upset?"

I decide to let Merle in on the link to my childhood. "I mix her up with my family. Freud would have called my reaction a 'transference.' I try to see Laska for herself, but a weird distortion happens where she seems to be abusing me; then I turn into my parents and abuse her back."

"I had a feeling something like this was going on. You once told me that you identified with Steely because, like him, you'd been mistreated as a child."

"Yes, but I never got confused about Steely. He was fierce with others but always kind to me. He never brought out the side of me that Laska does."

"I think that you and Laska can get along just as well as you and Steely. It's going to take some work, though. What would you say if I came over once a week to help the two of you out?"

"Oh, Merle," I reply, "that would be so wonderful."

We talk a bit more; I describe the award ceremony coming up this weekend and she encourages me to have a good time in Toronto. I tell her that I plan to leave Laska at Vivian's while I am away. Merle doesn't know of Vivian, but when I describe how she takes the dogs right into her home, Merle looks pleased.

"Laska is too sensitive to be plunked down in any old kennel," she says. Then she adds, "I think it will be good for the two of you to have a break. And when you come back, we'll meet again."

I thank Merle, and as I see her to the door, Laska tries to keep her from leaving by grabbing at Merle's shirt with her teeth. I remember how Steely wanted to go home with Merle—such is her effect on dogs. I shut the door and say to Laska, "I really can't blame you. I'm sorry that Merle is leaving, too."

AUGUST 6

LAST night I dreamt about a young brown and white heifer. I held her by the collar as we traveled on the New York subway to my parents' apartment on West Seventy-second Street. She had bony withers and a round belly; she carried her head level with her shoulders and supported herself on short, spindly, knock-kneed legs. Her face was expressive, with large ears and dark, shiny eyes. I'm often nervous on New York subways, but the heifer's bulky body, and my hand tucked firmly under her collar, reassured me. The stop let us off in the midst of a desolate housing project on Sixty-fifth Street and Twelfth Avenue. As I looked for a way out of the complex, several Doberman pinscher dogs bounded toward us. I called out to their owner, a man who followed along behind them, to make sure that the dogs stayed away from my animal companion. When I awoke, I realized that the heifer is a symbolic mother, whom I am meant to take to Toronto with me. I don't want to turn to Levin for reassurance; he is my son. It is enough that he agreed to join me, especially since he will be my only guest.

The heifer of the dream is so unlike my real-life Laska, who disrupts my childhood habit of seeking solace from animals. Instead, Laska drives me into the human world (for instance, the synagogue) for succor, which is a new experience.

AUGUST 7

ONE day when I was twelve or thirteen, Sybil, a classmate at Hunter College High School, came to my house and looked at my "library"—*The Black Stallion, The Black Stallion Returns, Son of the Black Stallion, Treve, Wolf, Lad a Dog.* She expressed a certain scorn.

"Are animal books *all* you read?"

I flushed with embarrassment and sudden self-awareness, seeing my books through her eyes. I stood before short Sybil (whose breasts had matured early, to such a degree that she needed custom-made brassieres) feeling foolish and gangly, an overgrown tomboy in the presence of a chastising teacher.

"In our family," she continued smugly, "we have *intellectual* discussions at the dinner table."

Our family ate in a dazed preoccupation with the food. My father often became mysteriously withdrawn, his eyes glazed and dull; one night he had absently cut up his paper napkin on his plate, as if it were a piece of lettuce. How was I to become an intellectual like Sybil?

AUGUST 8

I DON'T know what became of Sybil, although I did learn that she graduated from Smith College in three years, rather than the customary four. In high school Sybil and another student competed ferociously for academic recognition. Not only did Sybil's rival graduate from Hunter in three years, she was admitted to Radcliffe College, which took, on average, one Hunter girl a year (Radcliffe admitted many students from private schools, chosen for their economic rather than academic distinction). Perhaps Sybil evened the score with her competitor by graduating early from college.

As for me, for better or for worse, I am an intellectual now. Here I sit, writing in my journal, as I fly to Toronto on account of having written a book of my own. I finished my acceptance speech yesterday; it is neatly typed and I'm happy with how it came out. Once I began writing it, I stopped overeating, and once I stopped that, I focused less on Laska's foibles. I dropped her off at Vivian's this morning and can't say that she looked sad to see me go. Her attention was for Vivian and Danny, the tiny black griffon dog with huge bug eyes and a squashed-looking face, whom Vivian has taken in from a rescue center.

Although I was short on time, I went to Shabbat service last night for pastoral support. As always, there was friendly conversation before the service began. I told Rabbi Noah and Rabbi Emeritus Ben Abraham that I was going to be away this weekend to receive a book award. They are like family now, and I keep them informed of my whereabouts.

"This is a big deal," Rabbi Noah exclaimed.

"I finished my acceptance speech today," I answered. "Right now there is a sentence in it thanking God, but I'm afraid that sociologists, who are notoriously secular, will laugh at me. I brought the speech along in case there was a chance to ask you about it."

"Read it to us," Rabbi Noah said, straightening his yarmulke on his head.

"Here's what I wrote: 'Lastly, I thank the larger forces of being and life for giving me the courage and stamina to translate spoken words into a written language of birth.'"

"That's lovely," Rabbi Abraham offered, with his customary dignity. "Why don't you leave the line in and see what happens. You never know, the crowd might not be as godless as you think."

AUGUST 9

I AWAKE to the peaceful sound of Levin's breathing. He is asleep. Levin did not object to sharing the hotel room UVM paid for, and I was not surprised by his lack of discomfort. When Levin was a teenager and we lived in Cambridge, I used to take him to Stratton Mountain so that he could snowboard; we economized by sharing a room at a guesthouse. At the moment, all I can see of Levin is his short hair, dyed copper, with black M shapes in several places in honor of Michelle. The room is as cold as a "produce refrigerator, you know, where you keep meat." These are Levin's words and they remind me of his first job, when he was fourteen, at an upscale grocery store in Cambridge. I ordered extra blankets last night, which he has pulled right up over his face.

I can't let Levin sleep too long because we plan to go to the beaches on Lake Ontario this morning. An aging hippie recommended them to us last night when we picked up some spring water at a health food store. I don't mind missing conference presentations in the least. I look forward to seeing a different part of Toronto than midtown, where our hotel is located. Here, new high-rise buildings slice the sky with severe, geometric shapes. Many resemble giant wedges of cheese with square air holes; and one, with rounded edges, looks like a gigantic Jell-O mold. Right outside the hotel is a metal sculpture of two portly businessmen clad in overcoats and fedora hats. They stride toward each other, right arms extended for a handshake; at the same time their posture bends backwards and sideways, as if each were pushed by a stiff wind. Their presence seems a perfect symbol of the capitalist interests that shaped the midtown environment.

I use the time until Levin awakes to shower, get my hair just right, and iron the dress I plan to wear later. Levin gets up on his own and regards me with a friendly smile. I keep my back to him as he hastens to dress in the chilly room; then he shaves and washes up. When we emerge from the hotel into the warm summer air, it is a big relief. We catch a bus to the beaches with a plan to have breakfast by the lake. Once we leave the city proper, we enter neighborhoods with one- or two-story buildings, many of which house mom-and-pop stores.

"Look at that one," Levin says, "'Reliable Fish n' Chips.' If they say that, you can just imagine what those fish and chips are like."

I laugh and say, "These neighborhoods remind me of ones you took me to in California, until I think of what they must be like in winter."

"Imagine the wind blowing down from the Arctic," he replies.

"I know," I say. "I've developed a Vermonter's disdain for 'flatland' terrain; when there are no mountains around, I actually feel indignant."

The beaches turn out to be a long stretch of dull-looking sand, with breakers. It is a hazy day and we can't see much of the water. So we cut across a public green to a restaurant that the ex-hippie recommended. The restaurant is crowded and hot. Levin and I order poached eggs with hash-brown potatoes. As we eat, Levin reveals himself to be a lover of New York, a sentiment he knows I don't share.

"In New York the energy that you find at Lucy Vincent Beach or in Vermont lives in people; I find it with my friends," he says.

Characteristically, I immediately question myself; have I become a recluse? I answer defensively, "I need to be in nature to feel connected to something larger than the human sphere."

"If you are going to live in a city," Levin continues, "it should be New York. Who would want to live in Toronto?"

Until his critical assessment, Toronto seemed cosmopolitan compared to the small city of Burlington, where I live. Now the Canadian metropolis appears provincial and again I'm annoyed at how easily his opinion, based on little knowledge of Toronto, changes my own.

We finish our breakfast quickly because we are hungry and because we want to escape the cramped, steamy restaurant. On the bus back to the hotel Levin stretches his long legs out in the aisle and asks, "Do you think there is a place for me in the corporate world?" He has put this question to me before, usually when making a lot of money is on his mind.

"I think that it would be disrespectful of your gifts, of your art, music, and writing," I reply, "to have that kind of job."

Levin absorbs what I say and then states, "I want to take this year, twenty-five, to figure out what I'm going to do. I want to do something like what you've done."

My chest feels so tight with pride, I can hardly breathe.

"Teaching is good," I say, at first assuming he means my job; but then I realize that Levin might have my book in mind. As the bus lumbers along, I think to myself, "Lev, your respect is the biggest award I could ever receive."

AUGUST 10

THE Grand Ballroom of the Sheraton Center glints with artificial light; tiny glass pieces of chandeliers, chairs edged with metal, and fluted glass pitchers of water all refract it. Spotlights illuminate the stage, which holds the speaker's podium, and two huge screens on each side of the stage project the speakers' images to a crowd of about two thousand people. They have come less for the major awards ceremony than to hear the presidential address that customarily precedes it. Perhaps the organizers set the program up this way to assure a full audience. I sit in the front row with the other award recipients; Levin is behind me, across the aisle. I feel comfortable in my calf-length rayon Laura Ashley dress. It has soft lapels, off-white buttons down the front, and a slightly flared skirt; the fabric is delicately patterned with black and cream-colored flowers. Levin laughed when, noticing wrinkles and wanting to save time, I ironed the skirt of the dress without taking it off. I am wearing a handsomely cut black rayon jacket over the dress and have on long cream-colored earrings made from abalone shells. The shell part, clasped at the narrow top by engraved silver, flares out in a graceful ripply shape, like the movement of a wave or a free-flowing skirt. Because of the arthritis I wear plain, black walking shoes. Although two out of the twelve award winners are women, the other woman could not come today. Hence I am surrounded by men, all of whom are more dressed up than usual, in suits and ties. At sociology conferences it is fashionable to dress modestly, as if not to set oneself apart from the ordinary person in the street.

Last week I called my mentor, sociologist Ralph Samuel, to ask what was expected of me at the ceremony. "You have already *done* the work by writing your book; now is the time to receive. You should practice a receiving meditation." When they get to the Jesse Bernard Award, I settle into my chair and take several deep breaths. At first, I am able to follow Ralph's advice as I listen to Rachel Kahn-Hut, past chair of the Selection Committee, speak about my book. But when she gets to the sentence, "This book will be controversial as would any book which so clearly maps out new ground in innovative ways," the woman who oversees our little band of recipients ushers me up to the foot of the stage. Then she leaves me alone; I do not expect this, since she stayed with the previous award recipient until he was summoned. I suddenly become lonely, and then I recall my imaginary heifer. As soon as I do, I feel the animal by my side, brown and white, head level with her shoulders, knobbly-kneed legs. The loneliness goes away. When it comes time to go up on the stage and receive the award, the heifer comes too, climbing awkwardly up the wooden steps. Rachel, a short, dark-haired woman with large glasses, presents the framed award to me, and then it is time for me to speak. I look out at the audience in the hope of seeing Levin's copper-colored hair, but the spotlights blind my eyes. I begin: "When, as a graduate student in the early 1980s, I first held Jesse Bernard's *The Female World* in my hands, it was as if the full-bodied book held me. Her intellectual maternal presence allowed me to hope that in the journey from mother to sociologist, I didn't need to leave the lessons of the milk behind." I go on to thank the award committee, people who have helped me, Levin, and, lastly, God. Then it is over, and everyone applauds.[4]

Afterward, Levin and I attend a cocktail hour held by the ASA section on social theory. A man I do not know comes up to me and says, "I'm glad you talked about spirit. Many of us in the audience probably were glad as well."

With Rabbi Abraham in mind, I reply, "I guess it's good to take the risk."

Over dinner, I tell Levin that a heifer came to keep me company during the award ceremony. "Poor you," I add, "stuck with a mother who has an invisible heifer."

"Well, luckily it's not like Jean's mother," he replies. Jean is his stepmother. "She has knickknacks all over the house."

I take this to mean that at least he can't *see* the heifer.

AUGUST 12

WHEN I pick Laska up at Vivian's after my trip, my puppy runs over and wags her tail but immediately returns to her play in the living room with little Danny, the griffon. Though much smaller than she, Danny bosses Laska around by grabbing her ears with his teeth and hanging on. Vivian puts Laska's leash on and gives her to me while she gets Laska's belongings; instantly my puppy leaps up and grabs at my clothes.

"Remember what to do?" Vivian asks.

"Right," I say, and put my foot on Laska's leash near the collar; she has no choice but to lie down.

"How did things go?" I ask.

"Oh, fine," she replies. I can tell there is a "but."

"I had to put her in her crate a few times; she made a game out of leaping at me when her leash was off. Then she lay in the crate whining to herself, which upset the other dogs. I had to spray her with the water bottle a few times to quiet her down." Vivian gazes down at Laska, who looks up at her with crescent-moon eyes, and adds, "She's hard."

"You have never said anything more helpful," I exclaim. "I'm so glad to know that the problem is not *just* me."

AUGUST 13

TODAY is the second anniversary of Sarah's death. I light a beeswax candle in front of a large, framed picture of Sarah at the cabin on Martha's Vineyard. It was taken the summer before she died. In the photo she rests on her haunches, a tidy black shape on the painted wood floorboards. As is her custom, she positions herself precisely under the multicolored South American hammock. She pants lightly as she regards me with a spirited expression. Her eyes are full of movement and play, and her ears lie neither forward nor back, as if she keeps something for herself alone. The painted floor that surrounds her is green, the color of the heart chakra. Above her, the hammock looks like an upside-down rainbow bent to gravity, a rainbow of the earth.

I peer at the photograph yet have trouble remembering Sarah's eyes; Laska's crescent-moon eyes get in the way. I get my puppy off to bed in her crate and take out the journal I kept after Sarah died. Sometimes words bring the past back more vividly than pictures. Tonight is misty and a foghorn sounds mournfully down at the lake as I turn to the date, 8/31/95:

> I'm disappointed in the writing I've been doing because it hasn't brought Sarah back to life. As a small child who was often alone, I learned to store up comforts in my memory that could be companions to me. My recall became quite active, dogged even, in its retrieval. Yet despite prodigious efforts on the part of my memory, Sarah is not alive again. Crow says that in writing about her, Sarah returns through my words. Her advice doesn't comfort me. I see now the failed effort of the first weeks, writing and writing to keep Sarah from vanishing. Even tonight, I asked Crow, who was visiting me, "Please don't disturb the one last tennis ball of Sarah's that remains on the floor by the living room couch." Left just where Sarah had dropped it. As if she'd be back to grasp it in her mouth with that familiar competence. My retriever, oh that I had your surety. The words I would carry like a ball in my mouth, so round and complete that in passing the prize on to you, you would instantly be real again. Oh my retriever, you

are so much wiser than I. Though it's your heart's passion, you don't take the ball I offer.

I put the journal down and look out the window into the damp, milky night. I begin to cry, not as an obligation to Sarah's memory but in response to the lesson she taught me, which I had forgotten. "You were so right, Sweet Pea," I say. "The present pushes aside the past and that is how it should be."

AUGUST 14

AS promised, Merle comes to help Laska and me out. Today she asks me about Laska's behavior on walks and what equipment I use. When I show Merle the head collar that circles Laska's muzzle (the device that Vivian first put on Laska at the dog-obedience class), Merle suggests that I use the metal prong collar Sarah and Steely wore. Originally I had used a nylon choke collar with Sarah and Laska but it wasn't effective. Sarah had pulled relentlessly and Laska jumped on me and on other people. Vivian said that the head collar would inhibit this annoying habit. The name, pinch collar, sounds worse than the device itself is. The prongs are blunt and do not necessarily restrain by force; rather, they mimic a mother's jaws around a misbehaving puppy's neck. I am relieved to forego using the head collar; the device takes all the joy out of a walk for Laska, who spends most of her time trying to rub it off with her paws or against the ground.

Merle, Laska, and I go for a short walk down the block. The day is warm and breezy. Merle shows me how to create a comfort zone for Laska. I position my puppy by my left leg and hold my hand steady against my hip without any slack on the leash between Laska and me. Soon, Laska regulates her own pace by slowing down whenever she feels the teeth of the collar close around her neck. Our outing is a success.

AUGUST 15

YESTERDAY I wired flowers to my father for his birthday. I have bought flowers at West End Florist on Seventy-second Street many times in the past and can picture the refrigerated display case in the cramped storefront, filled with mums, black-eyed Susans, daisies, roses, other flowers, and greens. Since I became estranged from my parents three years ago, I've often sent flowers for special occasions. This time the florist informed me that my mother no longer allows him to deliver them.

"When I call your mother up, she says that she wants to pick them out herself. She doesn't seem to trust us to bring her fresh flowers. But she hasn't come several times now and a credit is building up. I asked her about it last time you ordered flowers and she told me she'll catch up the next time she has a party."

"But they are not for a party," I wailed. "I mean them to be for their birthdays, or Mother's or Father's Day."

"Well, what can you do," the florist replied, with a New Yorker's resignation over the intractability of people.

AUGUST 16

I SIT quietly in a chair facing the large west window and focus on my breath. My mind quiets, then becomes unusually spacious; suddenly, an image of my father as a young man appears on the threshold to the studio—tall, slender, with wavy black hair. His presence materializes more and now it seems if he were standing there for real. I do not turn my head to look at him but feel myself become a small girl, and I long for him to hold me. I continue to sit. Presently a memory from the past lights up my mind like a strong Texas sun.

▼▼▼

The blades in the mixing bowl whir. My mother is baking a two-layered cake with green icing. It is going to look just like the picture on the Betty Crocker box, the frosting fluted by strokes of a knife. The floor and walls meet in the corner but offer no shelter. A propeller plane drones overhead.

"Daddy home?" I ask my mother's turned back. I like that he comes back from work for lunch.

The flared hem of my mother's flowered dress with white buttons down the front sways as she rubs wax paper smeared with butter around the cake pan. Her back still to me, she brushes a strand of auburn hair up over the rat that holds all the hair around her forehead in a high roll.

With annoyance in her voice she says, "Daddy will be home soon."

I go to the screened-in porch that overlooks a suburban neighborhood of Fort Worth. The warm breeze feels friendly. I climb on my painted brown and white heifer, which is like a rocking horse, and wish I had on my yellow overalls instead of a dress. I hear the heifer say with a merry sideways glance, "Not only did I jump over the moon, I ran away with the dish and the spoon."

That day, except for asking a question, I have been good. Maybe my mother won't fill the slant of light with angry words, dividing me from my father.

The front door slams. He is home. I clamber off the rocker and run to him, my face open and eager. "Daddy."

He crouches down on his coltish legs, gathers me in his arms. Lifts me high. His pained prominent eyes shine as if wet. His full lips plant a kiss on mine. I can smell the pomade he put on his black, wavy hair that morning. He presses me against his scratchy army shirt. I don't mind. I burrow into a fold of cloth, wanting to stay there forever. Then I look back at my mother. Turned now in my direction, her smooth face is impassive, her sensuous lips set one against the other as she regards us with an absent stare. My father looks over my shoulder at my mother. He puts me down and goes over to her. As usual, she turns her face when he kisses her, offering her cheek. She steps back from his hug almost before his arms circle her waist.

She says, "Arthur, you look tired." Though he seemed fine a minute ago, right away my father's face takes on a weary look.

I search my mother's face but cannot read it. This afternoon she will decorate the cake with green icing and we'll have it for dessert at suppertime. My heart unclenches. For the moment I am safe.

▲▲▲

AUGUST 17

I AM sitting at the kitchen table with one foot on Laska's leash near her collar, which forces her to lie down. I have a piece of apple in one hand to keep Laska's attention and a fork in the other hand for my lunch. I learned the leash trick from Vivian and the apple ploy from Merle. The plan is to encourage Laska to lie quietly during my meals, but she rests in a crouched position with her head up as if she might spring to her feet at any moment. First, she rests her head on my foot; then, she tries to bite the nylon part of the leash; next, she stretches out on her side; after that, she extends her head and neck on the floor like a deer run over on the highway; then, she resumes a crouched position and attacks the metal clasp of the leash. When all of these maneuvers have no effect, she looks at me with her crescent-moon eyes; since that produces no response, she looks away and whines piteously to herself. Then she puts one paw on my shoe and, after that, as if she has more important things to think about, sniffs the air. Finally, Laska places her head on her paws and keeps it there. Immediately, I give her the apple slice and praise her mightily, even though, taken up with watching her, I have eaten very little. Merle can get Laska to do a "long down" (in dog trainer's language the phrase means stay down for a long time) while Merle sits at the table with an apple in her hand, but I'm not her. After the fidgety experiment today, I decide to keep Laska in her crate while I eat. Otherwise, she prowls around the house, sniffing at table edges, and jumps up to grab my things (keys, pens, gloves), which makes me so edgy that the food sits like a lump in my stomach.

At our emergency visit Merle said, "Laska goes for your things because she wants to get your attention."

It's true, and I suppose I should be flattered. Laska never tries to get at the treat jars, which are well within reach on the living room and kitchen tables. Only my stuff. Merle's words also explain why Laska runs upstairs if I forget to put up the guardrail but then stands at the top, her ears drooped around her eyes from the pull of gravity as she looks down at me, waiting to see what I'll do.

AUGUST 18

I AM sitting out on the deck, reading more of Vicki Hearne's book, *Adam's Task: Calling Animals by Name.* Laska barks at the far end of the yard. She has chased a black cat up one of the posts of the stockade fence. It sits there gingerly, looking down at her. I call Laska away, but she does not listen. When the cat hears my voice, it turns in the constricted space and leaps off the fence into my neighbor's yard. I am not surprised that Laska ignores me; I am ambivalent about asserting authority over her.

Hearne gives me a new way of thinking: to her, commands are a form of recognition. She interprets the biblical story of Adam and Eve as the origin of our dominion over animals (a privilege granted by God) and of the loss of that entitlement: "When God first created the Earth He gave Adam and Eve 'dominion over the fish of the sea, and over the fowl of the air, and over every living thing that moveth upon earth.' Adam gave names to the creatures, and they all responded to their names without objection, since in this dominion to command and to recognize were one action. There was no gap between the ability to command and the full acknowledgment of the personhood of the being so commanded. Nature came when called, and came the first time, too, without coaxing, nagging or tugging."[5]

I once imagined that Laska would resist the name I gave her, as if I had wielded authority over her unfairly. My personal history shaped this perception, but I am not alone in questioning humans' power over the natural world. Many animal rights activists hold an unfavorable view of the ancient biblical story. To them, it legitimates abuse of animals and nature. Other activists choose to blame us rather than the Bible. In their view God granted us stewardship, not dominion, over nature, a responsibility that we have perverted.

Hearne explains that we lost our authority with the animals when we disobeyed God by eating from the tree of knowledge—for "to fail in obedience is to fail in authority." With the Fall, she asserts, most animals turned wild and refused any longer to recognize human commands: "One may say that before the Fall, all animals were domestic, that nature was domestic. After the Fall, wildness was possible, and most creatures chose it, but a few did not. The dog, the horse, the burro, the elephant, the ox and a few others agreed to go along with humanity anyway, thus giving us a kind of second chance to repair our damaged authority, to do something about our incoherence" (48).

From Hearne's point of view, training promises redemption from the loss of Eden. By "training," Hearne does not mean swatting a dog's rear end with a newspaper, sticking its nose in a "mistake" on the living-room floor, hitting it repeatedly with a bonker bottle, or stuffing a stool covered with Tabasco sauce in its mouth. She does not rule out force, but it is force exerted with the idea that "the dog has the right to the consequences of its actions" (44). Hence a correction, which she distinguishes from punishment, becomes a sign of respect. The examples she provides of corrections are harsher than those I've observed Merle and Vivian use, but I understand Hearne's point when I picture Merle pinning Laska to the ground, or Vivian putting her foot on Laska's leash. The moral meaning in their corrections comes from their *intention;* they are not punishing Laska so much as requiring her to behave well. Hearne explains such moral lessons as the difference between "kindness and cruelty, or perhaps between rightness and cruelty." As she puts it: "A sharp, two-handed, decisive upward jerk on the training lead, performed as impersonally as possible, is a correction. Irritable, nagging, coaxing tugs and jerks are punishments, as beatings are. The self-esteem of the handler gets into them, with the result that, by obeying or failing to obey, the dog takes on responsibility for the handler's emotional wellbeing" (45).

From Hearne's perspective, and I agree, my corrections of Laska have been punishments. My self-esteem has been at stake because I mistake her for my parents. Though Hearne does not discuss the problem of transference (indeed she seems not to respect conventional psychological concepts), she does insist that the "self," meaning the trainer, must not turn the dog into an "other": "One way of understanding training is as a discipline in which one learns more and more about a certain steadiness of gaze, a willingness to keep looking, that dismantles the false figures, grammars, logic and syntax of Outsiderness, or Otherness, in order to build true ones" (79).

To build a true "syntax" or communication with her dog, the trainer must cultivate a "steadiness of gaze" that sees her dog as self in relation to her self.

Because at that point the trainer no longer sees the dog through the tainted lens of "Outsiderness, or Otherness," and conversation becomes possible.

Hearne's observations call to mind Homer's *Odyssey,* which recounts how skilled companion animals are at recognition. Odysseus arrives home disguised as an old man because it would be dangerous to reveal his identity. The goddess Athena, who takes a special interest in this mortal man, transforms not only Odysseus's clothes but his actual body. Yet his old dog Argos, who was a puppy when Odysseus left home, recognizes him in a heartbreaking scene:

> But when he knew he heard
> Odysseus' voice nearby, he did his best
> to wag his tail, nose down, with flattened ears,
> having no strength to move nearer his master.
> And the man looked away
> wiping a salt tear from his cheek;[6]

Old Argos recognizes his master in spite of the disguises. Surely, my task is to uncloak Laska from the disguises I've placed on her, to strip away the Otherness of false identity; only then will I earn the right to give her commands. Canny pup that she is, Laska shows me, through her refusal to be obedient, that she understands Hearne's insights without having read a single word of her book.

AUGUST 19

MERLE and I sit at the kitchen table. The day is hot and so we drink water instead of tea. Laska is over by Merle's side of the table, attentive to her every movement. I am surprised when Merle asks me to tell her more about the phenomenon of transference. "Let's hear some of that book learning," she teases.

"Where has it gotten me?" I say, although I'm excited by her request. It feels so good to have the problem out in the open. I go into the studio, with Laska prancing at my heels, and return with a book. When I sit down, Laska goes back over to Merle.

"I'll read you what psychoanalyst Jeffrey Masson says about transference in his book *Final Analysis: The Making and Unmaking of a Psychoanalyst.* He became famous for his exposé of Freud's ideas about child abuse."

"I'd like to hear about that, too," Merle says.

"It is a story that credits and discredits Freud. Many of his patients said that they had been sexually abused by fathers, brothers, uncles, or friends of the family. At first Freud believed his patients, but when he told his patriarchal colleagues, they were outraged. Rather than risk their disapproval, Freud changed his mind and decided that his patients' stories were *fantasies,* based on unconscious wishes."

"Whoa," Merle says, as if to stop a runaway horse.

"Exactly," I say. "For one hundred years, analysts told women that their abuse stories were incestuous desires, rather than truths. Listen to what Masson says about a therapist like that: 'Interpreting material from a severely traumatized person as fantasies obscures past realities and is felt by the patient as a misunderstanding of the most important events of the past.'"[7]

"That reminds me," Merle says, "of how men often tell women that they are being irrational or emotional, as a way to discount what they say."

"True," I reply. "Patriarchy works on many levels. Actually I'm amazed that Masson, being a man, revealed Freud's cover-up before feminists did."

"And what does he say about transference?" Merle inquires, returning us to the original subject.

"Masson turns it into something positive. Here's the quote," I say, and read to Merle: "'The heart of the transference neurosis is its undoing, its unwinding into the past, carrying along, in its backwash, the compulsion to repeat. These repetitions [are] attempts to seek help and rescue.'"[8] Then, eager to make sure that Merle understands what Masson said, I add, "So transference is an attempt to resolve past trauma."

"That makes so much sense," Merle says.

"Where you come in," I continue, "is that you 'help and rescue' me by showing me who Laska *really* is."

"That's right," Merle says, sympathetically. "Laska is not trying to do you in, she's just a normal, energetic puppy."

Because we mention her name a few times, Laska becomes excited; she puts her paws on Merle's lap and opens her mouth as if she wants to add to the conversation. Merle guides her gently but firmly back onto her four legs, where Laska stands, tail going like an airplane propeller.

"If transference is a desire for rescue," I add, "then Laska is an unusual kind of service dog. She digs me out of the collapsed building of the past with her sharp white teeth."

"There you go," Merle says, with a laugh. "Put that one on your refrigerator door."

AUGUST 20

SINCE I've returned from Toronto, I haven't been able to get going on my sabbatical project. Officially I have until September to begin, but I'd like to start now. I'm jumpy as a flea beetle and as slight, doing nothing more than poking holes in my day the way the tiny insect does to plant leaves.

AUGUST 21

I WAKE up this morning delighted to realize that last night I dreamt about Laska for the first time. I used to dream about Sarah several times a week while she was alive. Often I worried about her in them, or looked after her safety. It bothers me that in the last seven months, since bringing Laska home, I haven't once dreamt about my new puppy. Her absence in my dreams shows the fragile nature, not just of her bond to me, but of mine to her.

In my dream about Laska we wandered off by ourselves and left my parents, as well as Levin and Michelle, behind. On a path that flanked a wood stream, like the one at Waskosim's Rock, we discovered a large segmented ginger root, the skin of which was shiny. Ginger is known to cleanse and invigorate, and perhaps the dream shows that Laska leads me to a fresh reality.

Later in the morning Laska comes over to me. She flattens her ears submissively, right against her head. I've seen her make this gesture with Merle, but never with *me* before. It seems as if she rewards me for opening my heart to her.

AUGUST 22

MERLE and I are sitting on the deck. Her weekly visits are becoming routine and her generosity almost makes me uncomfortable, since she insists on helping us without financial compensation. Laska lies upside down in the grass so that she can sun her belly. Today's subject is bonding.

I begin, "Laska isn't a very pattable dog and so when she does let me caress her, right away I get anxious that somehow the moment will vanish. It's like I'm waiting for the vanishing to happen. I remember having similar feelings with fly-by-night boyfriends."

Merle laughs and says, "Why don't you keep your pats brief and stop before she loses interest or before you get anxious that something will go wrong. I've noticed that you lean over her when she comes to you, which makes her feel trapped."

"Boy, that's observant of you," I exclaim. "I never noticed I did that."

"Another thing," Merle says. "Don't pat her every time she comes to you.

All these tactics will allow a desire to build up in *her* for a pat. It's using reverse psychology."

"That makes so much sense," I reply, and I look over at Laska, eager to try out my new strategies. But she is fast asleep upside down, her ears flared out from her head and her mouth slightly open. Then I continue, "But how will I know if she wants a pat? Sometimes she comes over, but when I try to touch her she moves away."

"Wait until she nuzzles your hand; tilt it so she can get her nose under it and then pass your hand lightly over her head."

We sit a while longer as I tell Merle that I had trouble seeing Sarah's eyes a few weeks ago. "That's because you are letting go of her," she says gently.

I grow sad at her words, though I know forgetting is necessary.

After Merle leaves, I appreciate the tactic she uses with *me:* she gets me to observe my behavior from Laska's point of view. "Think how you would feel if someone leaned over you every time you came up to them," Merle said earlier.

AUGUST 23

I SIT at the kitchen table eating a mashed-up boiled egg, roasted pumpkin seeds, with a flax oil dressing. A healthy breakfast. Even though it's my mealtime, I leave Laska out of her crate so that I can try out Merle's advice. My puppy comes over to me wiggling from front to back, her tail going in circles, ears flattened, and licks my hand. I give her one or two short pats down the top of her head and don't lean over her. She accepts my touch. Afterward, instead of prowling around looking for mischief, she lies down on her fleecy blanket behind my chair. She cups her muzzle in her tucked-back front paw. Her repose fills me with peace, and my breakfast begins to digest just fine.

AUGUST 27

LASKA and I walk to my office so that I can pick up a book I intend to read for *Creatural Lessons.* It is lunchtime and many people (for a city as small as Burlington) pass us on the street. Laska trots along by my left side, just the way she should. A young tanned woman, perhaps a student newly returned from her summer vacation, jogs by us briskly; she moves in time to music on her Walkman and her ponytail bounces up and down with each step. Although she keeps prancing along beside me, Laska turns her head, held high, backward on her neck like an owl to keep the woman in sight. Lately, except for skateboarders, she hasn't been jumping at people on our outings.

When I reach school, I find a sign in my mailbox from the department secretary, Peggy Bard. It says, "Robbie Kahn, Office Hours: Sabbatical." When Laska and I go downstairs, I put it on my door. We run into my colleague John, who advises me to keep myself apart from school activities. "Do as I have done," he says. "Don't come around. If a student calls, say no, unless it's for a recommendation." Laska and I return home, where I find a message on my answering machine from the women's studies secretary. She says, "I didn't want to call too early because I know you are on sabbatical." The respect shown for my time to write and to research contrasts sharply with my parents' reaction whenever I separated myself from them; I feel all kinds of hope about what a good year this will be.

AUGUST 30

TONIGHT after our walk, I take off Laska's collar and she puts her teeth against my hand. I feel her warm breath and then she tenderly licks me instead of biting. Shortly after, on our way upstairs to bed Laska grabs my great aunt Len's wristwatch (an old Hamilton and somewhat valuable) off the living-room table. By the time I reach my puppy, the watch mechanism, which fell out of its case when it hit the floor, is in her mouth. I force Laska's mouth open and remove the saliva-coated rectangular object that was once an heirloom. I tap her firmly three times on top of the muzzle as I've seen Merle do, take her by the scruff of her neck, and drag her into her pen. Luckily, no Coke bottles are around. I look at the watch; though her teeth dented the face of it, the structure seems intact and maybe it can be repaired.

As I drop off to sleep, I have a vision of Laska's teeth breaking apart time past.

September 1997

Regression

SEPTEMBER 1

I CAN'T believe I'm sitting here at home with no one pestering me and it's the first day of school at UVM! The chair of my department told me that on her sabbatical she'd gone to Provincetown when school started to avoid feeling truant. I'm not sure I need to do that, because so many people in my department encourage me to enjoy the time away. My colleague Tom, who just finished his first sabbatical, looked at me wistfully when I met him in the hallway, a syllabus in his hand.

I'm not going out of town but I do plan to celebrate. Today Cantor Aaron's wife, Cass, and their poodle, Eli, are joining Laska and me for a walk at Camel's Hump. We arranged to meet there to avoid traveling with two rambunctious dogs in one car. When I arrive at the parking lot, Cass is standing in front of her car, bent over Eli. She grips his collar while the black poodle, fur cropped close to his body, prances impatiently. I open the hatch a tiny bit and ask Laska to sit; she complies, though she barks in a high-pitched tone. Her leash is on and I grab it as she jumps to the ground. Eli breaks free from Cass and heads for us with Cass running after him. "Please, can you hold onto him one more second so that I can set Laska free?" I call out. I am afraid of getting tangled up in their greeting.

"Sorry," Cass replies, managing to grab hold of her excited dog.

I remove Laska's prong collar to which the leash is attached, while Cass releases Eli. We stand back and watch. Without so much as a sniff of introduction, the two dogs rear up at each other with their paws outstretched, leap like gazelles, and then spin in the air. Cass and I laugh at their riotous black shapes.

Eli is leggy and curly haired with a mop on top of his head; Laska is more muscular and built closer to the ground. Laska's eyes show an almost desperate eagerness. When Eli stops long enough for me to get a glimpse of his eyes, hidden under the mop, they seem to gleam with amusement.

The two dogs appear oblivious of their surroundings—a big, open field and the woods beyond; their attention is fixed on each other.

"Why don't we start up the field?" I suggest. "Maybe they will follow."

"That's a good idea," Cass replies. "Come, Eli!" He ignores her.

I call out, "Laska, come!" To my amazement Laska turns away from Eli and heads in my direction. I reward her with a treat from the fanny pack. Eli follows her and I give him one too.

"That's impressive," Cass offers. "She's even younger than Eli."

"It might just be a fluke," I reply. "Many times I call her and she ignores me. Even with treats." But in my heart I'm proud of Laska.

We start up the steep field; the dogs follow along behind, still obsessed with each other. Cass walks vigorously beside me and I have trouble believing that she is on kidney dialysis several days a week. I learned about her health problem from Cantor Aaron, who told me, when I asked him how Cass copes, "She is a serious meditator." Now, as I turn to look at her small solid shape and placid face, I sense the inner calm of a person devoted to mindful practice. But Cass is also very lively. Once I sat beside her at a Shabbat service and was amazed at her gospel-like singing, accompanied by slapping her hands on her knees in time to the music. When I praised her to Aaron, he said, "That's Cass's Baptist upbringing. Her father was a minister." OZ certainly is a progressive Conservative synagogue, considering that the rabbi and cantor are each married to converted Jews.

"From what Aaron tells me, Eli is a handful, and not what you expected," I say.

"Yes," Cass replies. I listen attentively, happy to know that Laska and I are not unique. "We had a poodle called Baxter who was gentle and loving. We went back to the same breeder thinking that we'd find him all over again. Boy, were we wrong."

"I made that mistake, too," I say.

Cass continues, as if the memories are so compelling that she doesn't hear me. "Eli is nothing like Baxter. Eli's better now, but he used to bite and jump up on us. He was a terrible mischief. At one point we were having such a hard time that we thought of giving him up."

"Yes, Aaron told me," I say. I figure Eli really must have tried her patience, given the equanimity Cass seems to possess. Then I add, "I hope I don't get to that point with Laska."

I look back at the two dogs, who persist in pestering each other even as they explore the woods. Then, noses to the ground, both stop to investigate a clearing under a stand of pine trees. We walk beyond them up the trail.

"Aaron told me Vivian Marsh helps you train Eli and that you board him there sometimes."

"When Eli is with Vivian," Cass says, "he is a different dog. Eager to do whatever she wants."

"Laska, too," I reply. "Does Eli get on with the other dogs there?"

"They get sick of his rowdiness," she says, and shakes her head in mock dismay, so that her brown hair swings across her face.

"Laska affects other dogs the same way," I say, "but she and Eli seem to suit each another just fine."

In the background I hear Laska and Eli pounding along at top speed, like racehorses, to catch up with us. Laska often sprints this way when she's fallen behind on the trail. I keep on walking and she slams square into the back of my legs, knocking me to my knees. I'm so shocked that I just stay there, thankful that I fell into mud and not onto rocks.

"Are you OK?" Cass asks, in a concerned voice. She helps me to my feet.

"Yes," I say, trying to wipe the wet dirt off my pants. "I have to remember to turn around and face her when she runs up to me this way." I try to push away my accustomed mistrust of Laska.

We continue along the path. The two dogs, now in front of us, accost each other, dipping down and rising up, a tangle of legs and heads and flapping ears. Suddenly, worn out, they flop down on their sides at exactly the same moment, facing each other like an old married couple in bed. Cass and I laugh, and I forget about my fall.

We walk around the loop of trail called Echo Woods, pausing to admire a view of Camel's Hump; a cloud covers the summit. Then we return to our cars. The ends of Eli's black ears show wet stringy curls where Laska grabbed at them. In the same way, Laska's face and back are covered with Eli's saliva. Cass and I say goodbye and we vow to repeat this outing another time.

I'll never forget the way Laska and Eli were today. Black against the fading, yellowed grass, the two dogs looked like silhouette figures in violent motion—cut from the same temperamental cloth.

SEPTEMBER 2

WHEN Laska banged into the back of my legs at Camel's Hump, dropping me down into wet, muddy earth, it was symbolic of her general effect on my life. She has brought me to my knees with a shocking abruptness, as one might have in a conversion experience. I can't rely any longer on my old ways of being with a dog, I must learn new ways; and the unmapped journey causes me to revisit my whole life as if I never had known it before.

SEPTEMBER 3

LASKA is to be spayed today. At breakfast I tell her how peaceful it is to not be at the mercy of your hormones. I don't just mean freedom from PMS (if dogs suffer such conditions), but release from the mist of desire that used to settle over me during ovulation. During my fertile years men were almost all I ever talked about with friends—what was working, what went wrong, why, what to do, what not to do. My heterosexual-in-exile stance is easy to maintain as a nonovulating woman. Today love is just one subject among others, many of which call to me with greater urgency.

Despite my reassuring counsel to Laska, I am relieved when our vet calls to postpone the surgery due to Labor Day emergencies. The truth is, I am apprehensive about the operation. I don't like the idea of her being anesthetized, her belly opened, and her uterus and ovaries removed. Sarah at least went into heat once and had an accidental chance to mate. A friend had left the door to our Cambridge apartment open and she slipped out. Sarah had been in heat for a week or more and many suitors waited patiently for her outside the front door. They had grown so well known to us that Levin had named each of the dogs. There was Glow-in-the-Dark Eyes, a black and white long-haired dog with uncanny blue eyes; Whiskers, a black dog with frosty whiskers; Sad-Ears, a basset hound; and Reject, a lean, mean Clint Eastwood dog with a moth-eaten reddish coat and ears frayed from fights, who looked like a coyote. As females have done since time immemorial, Sarah chose the lawless one. I found the two of them across the street in a neighbor's yard and brought her home. She was smiling extravagantly and I am not anthropomorphizing when I say that she looked proud, her back soaking wet from Reject's saliva. We had Sarah spayed a few days later, though it turned out she hadn't gotten pregnant.

SEPTEMBER 4

TODAY'S research entry is the first of my sabbatical year; to celebrate, I've chosen a book that caused me, when I first read it, to go lie down for a while. This reaction occurs when the ideas of another author graze me like a bullet, striking close to my own interests. It usually takes about a week for me to feel gratitude toward her or him for writing from a knowledge base I do not possess, one that enriches my own work.

Cultural studies scholar Marianna Torgovnick's *Primitive Passions: Men, Women, and the Quest for Ecstasy* explores the contemporary cultural impulse (expressed in the New Age movement, for example) to attain what Freud called "the oceanic feeling." (Torgovnick credits Jeffrey Moussaieff Masson with tracking down the likely source of Freud's metaphor. She explains that a French Catholic theologian, Romain Rolland, encouraged Freud to rethink his theory of the origin of religion. Rolland believed that the Hindu saint Ramakrishna gave the best account of the religious sensibility—"being like salt dissolved in the great ocean of the universe.") Torgovnick explains that, historically, Western tradition has suppressed the oceanic desire: "The West has tended to scant some vital human emotions and sensations of relatedness and interdependence—though it has never eliminated them. These sensations include effacement of the self and the intuition of profound connections between humans and land, humans and animals, humans and minerals, of a kind normally found in Europe and the United States only within mystical traditions. The link between such sensations and 'primitive' peoples, while it is not inevitable, is, I will show, neither trivial nor incidental in the Western imagination."[1]

Since its beginnings, Western tradition has defined itself in opposition to "Others," usually indigenous peoples, whom Westerners looked down upon, colonized, or destroyed. Torgovnick explains the reason for Westerners' differentiation from the Other; it is "a rejection of certain 'irrational' or 'mystical' aspects of the Western self, expressed in the attempt to project them either onto groups marginalized in the West (Gypsies and women, for example) or onto primitives abroad" (8). For millennia, organized religion has suppressed manifestations of the oceanic impulse, providing a substitute. (As recently as a few years ago the pope condemned Wicca, a pagan nature religion having its roots in pre-Christian western Europe and undergoing a twentieth-century revival, especially in the United States and Great Britain. The word "pagan" implies nonbeliever or infidel in Judaism, Christianity, and Islam, but the Latin root of the word simply means "country-dweller.") The fateful historical occurrence of Nazism complicated an acceptance of the oceanic impulse in the West; Nazism's rhetoric and rituals played on longings for merger (as in the Nuremberg rallies), "albeit," Torgovnick adds, "in a warped, demonic form" (12).

Torgovnick wishes to recover the "primitive" longing for the oceanic, the desire for a "full and sated sense of the universe" (8). She believes that this impulse is deeper than history and should not be defined by the atrocities committed by Western imperialism and Nazism. She also feels that the oceanic experience need not threaten values central to Western civilization, notably private property and the individuated self, both of which favor separation over merging.

Torgovnick uses a feminist lens in her research; in Western travel writing from the early twentieth century she discovers a link between gender and the oceanic. Faced with the immensity of the natural world, men tend to fear a dissolution of the self, while women find it possible to become a "common component of a landscape" (63). She attributes women's ability to merge less to nature than to culture: "[women] had less of a stake in the norms of their culture and received less reinforcement from them . . . contact with the primitive can provide an 'out' from Western patterns of thought and action felt to be limiting or oppressive, such as nuclear families and their obligations. It can trigger self-transformation and the experience of dissolved hierarchies and boundaries" (16–17).

Torgovnick is not a strict social constructionist, a stance I am grateful she takes. She says: "There is a large and important literature on female differences from males and the controversial question of whether they are biologically based, culturally based, or both, depending on the individual, the specific traits at issue, and context. The latter is my own position" (251). Torgovnick could have tested her dual lens (culture *and* biology) by including in her research the contemporary childbirth and breastfeeding movements. Many childbearing women testify that these embodied events evoke an oceanic sense. I find Freud's theory (and I'm not given to praising him) that the oceanic feeling originates at the mother's breast compelling. As a nursing infant Levin latched onto my breast as if I were his ground of being; for years after, he returned to my maternal body to calm himself. His need enriched my life by connecting me to larger forces of being and life (a phrase I came across in the writing of feminist theologian Carol Christ). To be his earth also humbled me.

Torgovnick appears skeptical about Freud's theory. She says that the "extremely ancient and extremely strong" Western tendency to associate women with the oceanic and the primitive is "not in any sense factual or inevitable—nor do they represent either a proven truth or even consistently arrived at theories. Instead, the links between females, the oceanic, and the primitive are based on myths, fictions, intuitions, individual neuroses, and the wildest forms of speculation" (22). Her thinking might have taken a different direction if she'd considered the oceanic from the infant's point of view, from the culture of the just born.

Torgovnick finds that oceanic representations often go beyond gender. Reversals of sexual identity may occur; for instance, contemporary Western men pierce their genitals (she devotes a chapter to piercings) to imitate "the female menstrual flow, envisioned as a symbol of life force" (17). A state of genderlessness may occur when the line between humans and nature blurs. For example, the iconoclastic artist Georgia O'Keeffe "recorded with pleasure her experiences of the land, such as being covered by dust, unable to perceive clearly the boundaries between her frame and the elements of nature" (128). O'Keeffe's words remind me of my journal entry where Ishmael (as I imagined him) and I transcend gender by becoming part of "elemental realities, both [of us] creatural, both water sand and consciousness, beyond women and men and all that particularity."

Torgovnick's research allows me to place *Creatural Lessons* (and *Bearing Meaning*) in the oceanic genre. The journal entry I just quoted sounds much like the travel writing of Vivienne de Watteville, a young Englishwoman who went on a safari in Africa between 1928 and 1929: "Lying with my heart pressed against the red earth and my forehead upon the stones was not physical nearness only; for as I lay there thinking how I, too, was composed of that same earth I touched and loved, and of the same elements that go to make the rocks and trees and stars as well as the birds and beasts, I felt myself merged into this deep love and unity with the earth, and found that it was at the same time unity with the spirit" (70–71).

Besides studying women's relationship to nature, Torgovnick looks at female relationships that transgress the boundary between human and animal through the work of three primatologists—Dian Fossey, Jane Goodall, and Biruté Galdikas. Torgovnick rejects the idea that biology determined their attraction to ape society but concedes that "at some inner level . . . their dedication to animals depended upon their living apart from the modern human world, in quest of some essential primitive, defined as life force as embodied in apes" (108–109). To me, their longing for the life force comes from culture's frustration of it; perhaps women's "inner level" values culture less than a state of sheer aliveness. In a startling passage Torgovnick interprets Fossey's devotion to a baby gorilla:

> Dian Fossey loved her gorillas so much that when she woke up one morning awash in a sea of warm diarrhetic dung, she was overjoyed. She had expected to find the baby gorilla she had taken to bed, like a sick child, dead of a lingering illness. The warm dung showed that the gorilla was still alive, and likely to recover. Fossey hardly noticed the dung. It was the baby's wellness that counted above all. Psychoanalysis tells us that the abject (often symbolized by excrement) is a displaced symbol of the transcendent. But something more radical was at work without any complex conceptual apparatus in Fossey. Fossey gained access to the joy of

> life through the baby gorilla's diarrhetic dung which signified, for her, renewed health and vigor. (110)

I find this story, perhaps repugnant to many, strangely moving. Torgovnick's interpretation brings to mind my own coprophagia as an infant, an act I committed to restore a feeling of aliveness; just so, her definition of "primitive" as "life force" comes tantalizingly close to my definition of "creatural." When I read that Fossey rejoiced over the baby gorilla's excrement, I felt ashamed of my severe reactions toward Laska for eating her stools.

Torgovnick mentions in a footnote that she had read books about dogs by Elizabeth Marshall Thomas and Jeffrey Moussaieff Masson. It might have profited her to explore human relationships with companion animals. Pet keeping may be one manifestation of the oceanic impulse when we don't anthropomorphize pets by dressing them in human clothes, throwing birthday parties for them, or pushing them around in baby carriages. Companion animals can restore primordial moments that we've lost—of touch, taste, smell, and wordless communication. When Laska stands beside me, tests the night air with minute sniffs, listens to near and distant calls, she mediates a larger reality and draws me out of myself. Torgovnick's omission of domestic animals reminds me of the ecology movement's tendency to advocate for wild animals but not for domestic ones, as if pets were less "primitive" or were even "contaminated" by being associated closely with us.

Today Torgovnick finds the oceanic impulse most vividly expressed in the New Age movement, a cultural phenomenon she feels "passionate ambivalence" about (a sentiment I share). Torgovnick defines the New Age as a "decidedly eclectic collection of phenomena, drawing from a variety of cultural and religious traditions, past and present, Western and Eastern, modern and primitive, familiar and exotically Other" (172–173). Her definition captures my own frustrated oscillation among Jewish, Buddhist, and Pagan (Goddess spirituality) traditions. Although Torgovnick is Catholic, she defines God in a nondenominational way: "I mean the word metaphorically to signify a nonanthropomorphized, genderless entity equivalent to the sum total of matter or energy in the universe." She does not share New Agers' belief that this genderless force is benign; it "acts blindly with regard to individual lives—sometimes helping them, sometimes harming them. I believe that accidents and chance exist, as do unmotivated goodness and gratuitous evil" (175).

Besides disagreeing with their model of a deity, Torgovnick criticizes New Agers for romanticizing or seeking the oceanic through indigenous cultures. She quotes Malidoma Somé (member of the Dagara tribe in Burkina Faso and consultant to the New Age Men's Movement), who says that Westerners "'seek a "shortcut" to their own future . . . through their commitment to learning about indigenous cultures, [and] non-Western spiritualities'" (164). I am attracted to the advice of Vietnamese monk Thich Nhat Hanh, whom I wish Torgovnick had discussed. Hanh has been a major figure in the transplantation of Buddhism to Western soil; he has been nominated for a Nobel Prize, written innumerable books, and lectured worldwide. Hanh advises followers not to forsake their own spiritual traditions but to ground themselves there.

Torgovnick concludes her book with a question and a provisional answer:

> Can we find ways to think about self and nature, human culture and the surrounding cosmos—and ways to act on those thoughts—that honor both strong feelings of interconnectedness and the gains that have been made in the modern era? . . . Buber saw the experience of relatedness not as diminishing the self but as *strengthening* it through recognition of other selfhoods and communion with the eternal. The more one "selves" other beings and other elements, he believed, the more one "selves" oneself. This idea can seem like nonsense in the context of the usual subject-object divisions that structure so much Western thinking. Or it can seem among the greatest and most profound of paradoxes. It may represent an ideal relationship between Western people and the oceanic—a way to acknowledge and accommodate moments of mystical or oceanic consciousness within a modern sense of self and society. It may even approximate the ways in which some traditional peoples understand the nets of Beingness. (218)

I hope to affirm this paradox in my own work when I describe how the oceanic (experienced through nature, animals, and my own body) restored a sense of self and of social connection lost in childhood. Torgovnick quotes Georgia O'Keeffe: "How can we not try to find 'our own sense of balance with the world'?" (199). I am almost grateful that necessity drove me to follow O'Keeffe's advice.

SEPTEMBER 5

MERLE is sitting across from me at my kitchen table. She takes a bite of the fresh, fall apple I gave her, then a sip of water. She cuts a small piece of the fruit and holds it in her free hand. Laska lies right by Merle's side, staring at her eyes, not her hand.

"Many obedience trainers would give a lot to have their dogs look at them this way," Merle says. "They often hold a treat alongside their eyes to teach the dog to focus on their face."

"I know," I reply. "I learned that technique in the obedience class Laska and I took. But I didn't need to use it because she's always looked right at me."

"It is important to see the good in your puppy," Merle replies. "You've got a very trainable dog here."

I peer around the table at Laska and note to myself that Laska might look me in the eye but she doesn't remain in a down stay the way she does for Merle.

Merle asks how our walks are going and takes exception to my answer. "You like to let Laska off the leash in the woods and sniff at things along the curb when she's on the leash. Why?"

"The woods are the only place where she can run free," I say defensively, "and it's fun for her to browse when we walk in the city. She always returns to my side."

Merle takes another bite of her apple, as if the fruit deepened her wisdom, and replies, "Your idea of animal rights is never going to allow Laska to bond with you properly."

Though I try to prevent it, my eyes become mournful, very like my father's, I fear. The expression signals a sense of being fatalistically trapped and is kin to Jewish sorrow.

"Laska is still in training," Merle continues. "You need to keep her right by your side on the leash, the way I showed you."

"OK, I will," I reply truculently.

In defense of Laska's freedom, Merle adds, "And you need to keep her out of the crate when you are somewhere else in the house. I know she gets into things. But you can close off the room you are in so that she'll get used to hanging out with you. You need to do these things so she'll bond with you."

As if to help me regain a sense of competence, Merle changes the subject and asks me about my sabbatical plans. We talk for a while and then Merle says that her back is giving out. She finishes her apple and releases Laska from her down stay with an "OK" that is far more upbeat than the one I just uttered. With surprising gentleness Laska takes the apple piece Merle has been holding all this time. It is gone in one gulp. Merle rises from her chair slowly and deliberately, a sign of the pain she is in.

"Oh, Merle," I say, "you shouldn't have come today. Is your back very sore?"

"It would be if I were at home, too," she replies. "I enjoy helping you and Laska out. It takes my mind off my back."

Laska follows Merle to the door, as she usually does. "She's bonded," I observe, "but to whom?"

SEPTEMBER 6

MY research assistant, Jessica, and I head up the street for a walk with Laska and a talk. In Vermont the seasons unfold vividly. Just now the slant of light almost makes visible the earth's tilt away from the sun; the clouds, which seem to hover close in summer, float remotely in the sky as if in retreat from approaching winter. Why, then, is Jessica wearing what looks like a black camisole for a top, a skimpy skirt, and wedgy sandals? I remember her amusement over my concern about her boots with three-inch soles, so I hold my tongue. Laska pads along between us, as if we were a pack of three.

"This job has got me thinking about my own childhood," Jessica begins, brushing a stray lock of curly red hair behind her ear.

"Is that good or bad?" I ask, worried that she, too, will be afflicted by uncomfortable memories.

"I don't know how to answer your question," Jessica replies. "I guess I'll say that remembering is necessary."

"I've found that to be so," I answer. "Without the flashbacks I've been having, I wouldn't have a chance to improve my relationship with Laska. They light the way."

"I'm supposed to be finding books for you but I can't help reading some of them. One of them, *The History of Childhood,* by a psychohistorian really opened my eyes."

"What's that?" I ask, "A nutty scholar?"

"No," Jessica says, ignoring my bad joke, "someone who studies history from a psychoanalytic perspective. His research convinces me that painful childhoods are a social problem, not just a personal one. So many parents over so many hundreds of years have neglected and abandoned kids, left them with wet-nurses, swaddled and hung them on the wall, beat them, and molested them. Sure, economic hardship and cultural assumptions influenced or even determined the parents' behavior, but the unkindness has to stop, regardless."

We turn our heads to look at each other, and Jessica's eyes flash.

"So many book reviewers sneer at memoirs about childhood," I say. "Isn't it the first time that humanity has heard about life from the *child's* point of view?"

"Alice Miller says that we fear our memories," Jessica replies, "because if we criticize our parents, they will take revenge."

"What have you been remembering about your own childhood?" I ask, recalling how our conversation began.

"I used to think I lived in a happy family, although I felt different from everyone else. No one had my red hair or my facial features. I actually *was* different. When my mother married my father she was carrying another man's baby—me. My younger sister is a beauty; she's the one who resembles my parents."

I suddenly understand Jessica's difficulty fitting into our class as a graduate student. She would come to my office to ask if she belonged. We stop momentarily outside a tattoo store, new to downtown Burlington, downtown being about ten minutes from my house. "The happening place," I quip to myself whenever Laska and I pass by on our daily walks. Inside, a young man with a shaved head, pierced eyebrows and lower lip, and an intricate tattoo covering one arm looks through a book of sample designs.

As if influenced by the fabrication of images, Jessica continues, "My parents tried to make a pretty picture of our family, especially my father. But to me my sister was their *real* daughter. These days whenever I bring up unhappy feelings, my dad tries to cheer me up. Why can't he just listen, without trying to fix anything?"

"What a comfort that would be," I say, careful not to try to fix anything myself. The three of us continue our walk in silence. Laska provides a distraction by breaking ranks to lunge at a skateboarder. He glides by standing sideways on the board and the wheels grate harshly on the pavement.

"I've found it helpful to record childhood memories," I offer. "They almost appear spontaneously, in a kind of automatic writing."

"Writing has always been a refuge for me," Jessica says, "but lately I've just been turning out academic stuff."

"Not to be discounted," I protest. "One paper got you invited to an international conference, where you were the only graduate student. It wasn't a fluke; you *belonged* there."

Jessica ducks her head in shy acknowledgment.

When we return to my house, Jessica bends down to give Laska a pat goodbye. My puppy jumps up and bangs her open mouth against Jessica's chin. To my relief, she giggles and says, "Thanks for the hickey." Jessica gets into her car, tugging at her miniskirt, as if it ever could cover her legs. With a jaunty wave of her hand, she drives off.

SEPTEMBER 7

SINCE Merle's last visit I've been following all her advice about getting Laska to bond with me. With one exception: I'm not sure that I will keep Laska on a leash at Camel's Hump. My puppy definitely is more attentive to me. This morning at breakfast she comes up and bumps my hand with her muzzle. I stroke her head, trace the thought furrow that goes down the middle of her forehead with my finger. To my surprise, she lets me scratch her around the neck and ears. Then, with a solemn look on her face, she swirls in a sitting position and opens her thigh. I stroke it and she flops down on her back so that I can rub her belly. She keeps her mouth closed and doesn't show any alarm in her eyes.

Altogether, she seems more relaxed and lies down in the kitchen, living room, or studio, wherever we are. Now that she seeks my attention, I tell Laska we'll make up for all the lost time with lots of pats. I call her "my baby" (oh, wouldn't the social scientists have a time with that endearment?) to give her back all the puppy time she missed out on, not having a leader she could trust.

SEPTEMBER 10

WHEN I am fortunate to find a book that answers questions for me, I feel as if I am sitting in the room with the author. She or he provides an intense discussion that rivals the chitchat of ordinary conversation, so much so that sometimes I fear I will choose books for companionship. But it doesn't have to be either/or. I don't see why books can't be friends of sorts so long as I don't neglect my real-life affiliations.

Today I'm reading *Beyond Boundaries: Humans and Animals.* Barbara Noske, a sociocultural anthropologist and philosopher, shares my criticism of Karl Marx when he claims that animals have no conscious life activity. Her support will be valuable for my sabbatical research because I intend to show that many sociological thinkers lack the creatural lessons that would deepen their understanding of human nature. Noske asks what right Marxists have to assess the capabilities of animals: "I have always wondered how humans (Marxists and others) can be so sure about their own *ability* to judge animal *inabilities.* Humans pretend to know *from within* that they themselves possess certain faculties and to know *from without* that animals do not."[2]

She does not agree with Marx's famous distinction between the "worst of architects" and the "best of bees." According to Marx, the architect creates a structure first in his imagination, whereas no bee, even the "best," is capable of abstract thought. Noske uses recent research to prove that bees make conceptual maps and transmit them to each other:

> Griffin has suggested that . . . honey-bees can be said to show language-like behaviour in their communicative dances. Their most significant dance is the so-called waggle dance which is performed inside the hive in

> total darkness by the non-reproductive female workers. The dance consists in crawling about over the surface of the honeycomb. Karl Von Frisch was the first to discover that these dances actually convey messages about the direction, distance and relative desirability of food sources. . . .
>
> James Gould has shown by controlled experiments that most of the recipients of information indeed set out to search for food in the direction indicated by their sister's dance, rather than in the direction from which she has returned. (135–136)

I like her example of the bee because it corrects Marx, and also because we are not likely to attribute language-like behavior to an insect. We tend to see them as total automatons.

Noske gives several provocative examples that go beyond conceptual maps to the realm of the imagination: "It is possible that animals, like humans, fantasize and imagine things (i.e., represent things for themselves). It is well known that they dream. Parrots have been known to talk in their sleep and dogs bark sometimes. Many animals move during their sleep as though they are running (racehorses do), biting or even copulating. Schäfer relates how a young stallion used a typical foal's voice in his sleep, a voice which he had long stopped using while awake. A mare far away heard the young horse and answered him. Schäfer believes that the horse was dreaming of his childhood" (145).

I once saw a woman on TV who told about her dog's different ways of dreaming. He had been abused by his former owners; when she first got the dog, he yelped and whined in his sleep. After about two years of loving attention, she said, as her eyes filled up with tears, when he dreamt he wagged his tail.

Noske concludes her book by encouraging anthropology to research animals as well as humans: "If the science of anthropology would shed its a priori notion of animals as beings unworthy of an anthropological approach, and would share its insights with critical ethologists [those who study animals in their natural setting], it might grow into an integrated science of humans and animals alike under the name of anthropo-zoology or zoo-anthropology. Anthropologists of all people should know that Otherness can never be an excuse for objectification and degradation either in practice or in theory" (170).

Noske boldly suggests that separate scholarly disciplines converge, a proposition that refigures the nature/culture divide. At the same time she respects animals' differences from us when she speaks of their "Otherness." I take heart from Noske's challenge to her field of anthropology; I hope to do a similar thing with my own discipline of sociology.

SEPTEMBER 11

I PICK Laska up after her operation. Would I so easily have had her fresh young uterus taken out if I still had my periods? Her belly is shaved and she has wire staples holding the incision together. The attendant who lifts her into the hatch for me forgets to have her pee and poop first. When we are already on the highway, Laska begins to howl from the depths of her being and scratches at the windows in the back of the station wagon to get out. I pull into a rest area where luckily some truckers have stopped. In her condition she can't jump in and out of the car and I am not strong enough to lift her. I run up to a young man in a T-shirt dressed up with a gold neckband and ask him to please take her out for me. I caution him to hold her around the rump and chest to protect her belly. Once out, she hunches over and promptly poops and then pees. Though I asked him to wait, the fellow is gone by the time she finishes. I run up to the only other truck at the rest stop, which is about to depart, and ask another young man for help. As he descends from the high cab, I see that unmistakable look flicker across his face—a man sizing a woman up. So unused to the attention of men at my age, I annoy myself by finding his appraising look flattering. It also makes me nervous because there is no one else around at the rest stop. However, he gently lifts Laska into the car and we go on our way.

SEPTEMBER 12

EVER since I read Serpell's tantalizing mention of women breastfeeding animals, I've wanted to know more about this esoteric subject. Jessica's research efforts did not yield anything, so a few days ago I called the reference specialist at the UVM library, Ann Luce. Each semester Ann gives electronic classrooms (lectures on how to access and use scholarly databases effectively) to my seminar students; I often introduce her as the best search engine I know of. Ann must be in her early fifties. Her wild, graying hair caught in two waist-length braids; her customary outfit of a blouse, crocheted vest, and flowing skirt; her dramatic eyebrows, lined, ruddy face, broad shoulders, and rapid, swinging stride—all these characteristics create the impression of a Wiccan woman who holds the keys to the kingdom. Ann uses this phrase to describe the "controlled vocabulary" of databases (akin to the formalized words in the *Yellow Pages*); if you master that vocabulary, treasures will be yours.

Today I am reading one of Ann's most spectacular discoveries, a 1982 anthropology journal article (by two men) titled, "Breast-Feeding of Animals by Women: Its Socio-Cultural Context and Geographic Occurrence." Several photographs even accompany the piece. Authors Frederick J. Simoons and James A.

Baldwin include eight-and-a half pages of references; most come from the nineteenth and first half of the twentieth centuries, and few are by women, even though feminist scholarship began a good twelve years before Simoons's and Baldwin's article appeared. (More about feminism and women suckling animals later.)

Simoons and Baldwin begin by noting that a quarter of a century has passed since anthropologist Carl Sauer proposed that women facilitated the domestication of dogs and pigs, two animals most frequently breastfed. Later on in the article Simoons and Baldwin unwittingly provide an explanation for anthropology's twenty-five-year silence: "That a woman should offer her breast to a young animal is looked on in some cultures around the world as bizarre, if not disgusting behavior, and the subject is often the butt of rude jokes . . . such negative attitudes prevail, particularly in Western cultures."[3] The authors cite an anthropologist writing in 1933 who called the practice a "perversion." Unfortunately, Simoons and Baldwin don't tell the reader how or why *they* became interested in animal nursing, but their compassionate discussion suggests they have no aversions to it.

Simoons's and Baldwin's research reveals that animal nursing tends to occur among cultures that lack dairy animals or do not use them as a source of milk. Geographically these societies cluster in Southeast Asia, India, northern Japan, Australia and Tasmania, Oceania (where it is a "near universal custom"), and in certain parts of the Americas, including a few isolated examples from North America. The human societies involved include both hunter-gatherers and more modern agriculturalists. Suckling animals does not always antedate exposure to Europeans; women in two hunter-gatherer societies (in India and Tasmania) began nursing puppies after Westerners introduced dogs into their cultures. In some societies the introduction of Western values brought animal suckling to an end.

The animals women most often nurse in the various cultures are dogs, pigs, and bears; baby animals are either brought in from the wild (often after the mother has been killed) or bred domestically. The first image in the book is a Japanese print of an Ainu woman from northern Japan nursing a bear cub as her husband and child look on. A number of societies venerate bears and use them for ritual, ceremonial purposes. Dogs may serve as pets; for example, the Onge of Little Andaman Island in the Bay of Bengal (Westerners introduced dogs to the Andaman Island in the mid-nineteenth century) have a "'passionate love' for their domestic dogs, stroking them, sleeping with them, and suckling puppies as if they were children" (422). Dogs may also be used for the hunt or eaten as food; pigs usually are eaten once they mature. Customarily women who've wet-nursed an animal grieve over its slaughter and may not partake of the meat.

Women throughout New Guinea so commonly nurse pigs that, as Simoons and Baldwin explain, "at least four ethnographers have felt compelled to report that the groups they studied *do not* engage in the practice" (428). The second image in the article is a photograph of a young Chimbu woman of New Guinea. She sits on the ground, wiry legs folded under her, one arm braced behind her body so that she can present her torso frontally. The woman looks at the photographer, a subtle smile on her lips. Without any support a piglet nurses from the woman's right breast, its forefeet resting on her thigh; a nursing toddler sits pressed up against the woman's left side, held close by the woman's circling arm. An older child sits in back of the woman facing the other way. Besides the three young ones (two human children and one piglet), the woman's full belly suggests that another baby is on the way. I find this image of a woman as a source of life to a human child and a creature from a different species so compelling that the tingle that occurs before the milk lets down suffuses my breasts, even though Levin weaned over twenty years ago.

Women also nurse animals for reasons related to human health. They may wish to relieve the discomfort of a too abundant supply of milk or remove colostrum from their breasts, which some cultures consider to be "bad milk." (Actually, colostrum, the thick, yellow fluid present in a woman's breasts when she gives birth, provides unparalleled nutritional and immunological benefits to the newborn.)

The third image, also a photograph, comes from North America. A staid thin Anglo-American woman sits on a stiff-backed rocking chair in the corner of a room. The plain shelves behind her in this Maine logging camp hold only a few provisions. The woman's hair is swept up in a bun, and her flowered dress comes up high around her neck, the bodice unbuttoned. She looks down tenderly at two nurslings. The human baby on her right breast wears a long-sleeved white dress that extends past its feet; on her left breast (the one closest to the heart) she suckles a tiny dark, furry bear cub. Simoons and Baldwin explain that a famous photographer, William Lyman Underwood, took this picture in 1921. A handwritten note, apparently published along with the image, reads: "Mr. Underwood took this picture of Ursula and Bruno and me with my consent and I am glad to have him use it in this book. Bruno's Foster Mother" (433). Simoons and Baldwin explain that the woman's husband had killed the bear cub's mother; the woman wished to save the baby animal's life and ended up raising it into adulthood.

Recently a number of anthropologists have expressed concern over whether their research presents "Others" on their own terms. The Maine woman's handwritten testimony allows a glimpse into her inner life; apparently she enjoys suckling the bear cub. What about the New Guinea woman? Why has she chosen to nurse a piglet, and how does she feel about this cross-species relationship? Simoons and Baldwin do not engage in primary research by talking to women who breastfeed animals; their conclusions are speculations based upon their review of other anthropologists' work, and on the whole they are highly sympathetic to animal suckling. Simoons and Baldwin believe that the overriding reason for animal suckling is "'affectionate' breast-feeding": "In this form the primary motivation for a woman to nurse a young animal, whether newly-captured from the wild, a pet, or some other household creature, is compassion, warmth of feeling, love." Other reasons include "'economic' breast-feeding," that is, "a desire to preserve the life of an animal with some economic potential, for example a hunting dog or a pig that later can be eaten"; "'ceremonial' breast-feeding, . . . in which nursing is undertaken to provide an animal for sacrifice and ritual consumption"; and "'human welfare' breast-feeding, . . . in which the act is initiated in the health interests of the human mother and child" (435).

Simoons and Baldwin affirm Sauer's proposal that animal nursing facilitated domestication. They explain that nursed animals, bonded to human society through women's milk, often hang around settlements in a loose form of domestication. The authors call this behavior a "'free-ranging,' institutionalized pet-keeping system" and assert that "the domestication of certain animals, in certain regions of the world . . . may trace back to early man's penchant . . . for keeping populations of wild creatures captive in and around his settlements or encampments, in a state of semi- or quasi-domestication." The free-ranging pet keeping that contemporary anthropologists observe represents "a survival of one phase in the historical evolution of man's relationship with the Southeast Asian world" and, by implication, certain cultures elsewhere (436).

In a fascinating footnote, Simoons and Baldwin hint at a sophisticated cultural meaning embedded in animal nursing: "It is perhaps significant to note that among at least some lowland New Guinea peoples . . . when a human is adopted into a group not his own, he must, as part of the ceremony of adoption, suck a few drops of milk from the breast of a local woman. This symbolic nurturing then enables that person to be considered a true member of the society. Could it not be that the widespread practice of wet-nursing captive wild animals, besides the obvious nutritional advantages, has *symbolic* value as well?" (436n6). On this view women hold a key position: breastfeeding becomes the threshold experience through which animals pass from nature into culture.

Earlier I mentioned that many feminists reject the idea that women have a special bond with the natural world. (Women of color often are even more reluctant than white women to identify with animals, quite understandably, as Western culture frequently depicts nonwhites as "animalistic" or "bestial.") I was not surprised when reference specialist Ann Luce found no feminist research on women breastfeeding animals. Scholar Joan Dunayer believes that feminists are wrong to distance themselves from other species, although she understands why they do. As Dunayer says in her essay "Sexist Words, Speciesist Roots," included in the anthology *Animals and Women: Feminist Theoretical Explorations:*

> When a woman responds to mistreatment by protesting "I'm a human being!" or "I want to be treated with respect, not like some animal," what is she suggesting about the acceptable ways of treating other animals? Perhaps because comparisons between women and nonhuman animals so often entail sexism, many women are anxious to distance themselves from other animals. Feminists, especially, recognize that negative "animal" imagery has advanced women's oppression. However, if our treatment and view of other animals became caring, respectful, and just, nonhuman-animal metaphors would quickly lose all power to demean. Few women have confronted how closely they mirror patriarchal oppressors when they too participate in other species' denigration. Women who avoid acknowledging that they are animals closely resemble men who prefer to ignore that women are human.[4]

How strange that *Animals and Women,* a book devoted to rethinking women's relationship to animals, overlooked animal nursing. A feminist discussion of the practice could enrich our understanding of the patriarchal origins of the human/animal boundary in Western culture and could reinstate women as major protagonists in the domestication of animals.

Discovering a knowledge gap is both frustrating and exhilarating—surely I must devote a chapter of *Creatural Lessons* to this provocative subject. I will include a tear sheet from the July/August 1988 issue of *Utne Reader* that someone sent me long ago—a full-page photograph of a native Peruvian woman nursing a lamb. She sits on the grass, legs tucked to one side; her high-necked dress is open at the bodice; her head is bent, face hidden by a wide-brimmed straw hat with a black ribbon tied in a bow around the brim, as she gazes at a curly-coated white lamb that lies across her lap. It nurses from her left breast, eyes peacefully closed. The woman cradles the baby sheep's head in her two work-hardened hands and seems to be stroking its soft ear with one finger.

The next issue of the *Utne Reader* contained numerous letters responding to the photo. One woman angrily wrote: "I am a very open-minded, liberal person, but if I saw a picture of a dog 'schtupping' a woman, I would be offended. I was just as offended when I saw the picture of the lamb at the woman's breast. Babies suckle at mother's breasts, lambs suckle at sheep's teats. To see a lamb at a woman's breast is, to me, a form of bestiality." At the other extreme a woman said: "The exquisitely tender photo is a loving visualization of an extended understanding that includes the whole earth and all its inhabitants as intimately connected. It is also a powerful antidote to the cruelty to which humans subject other species in the factory farms, slaughterhouses, and dairy industry (not to mention laboratories, fur industry, rodeos, circuses, and other 'entertainment')."[5]

The *Utne Reader* editors explain that the photographer had not been able to ascertain (perhaps because of a language barrier) why the woman nursed the lamb. This subjective information is crucial to a fuller understanding of why a woman suckles a creature belonging to another species. Simoons and Baldwin mention that right here in North America in 1979 several women offered to nurse a young chimp whose mother would not do so; the offer was refused. Clearly there is a vein of inquiry here that deserves feminist anthropological attention. I will do my best as a sociologist to discuss animal suckling; what I most would like at this moment is to find an image of a woman nursing a puppy.

SEPTEMBER 14

SINCE her spaying operation, Laska holds my fingers in her mouth and sucks on them. I imagine that she wants the soothing connection of a puppy to its mother. At the same time, she is biting me again. Both behaviors strike me as regressions. Why wouldn't she feel both insecure and at odds with me? I left her at the vet's without being able to prepare her for what would happen, which was anything but pleasant. Last spring when I took Laska for a routine visit, I went to the bathroom and passed an examining room with a partly open door. Inside a female dog lay upside down on a cloth that had been placed on the floor. The animal was still unconscious, its head flung back, its tongue protruding slightly. I could see the incision in its shaved belly and the metal staples. The staff at the hospital is warm and friendly, and I'm sure they comforted the dog when she came to, just as they would have done with Laska. All the same, I wish that I could have talked to my puppy ahead of time, the way parents are advised to nowadays when their children face surgery, about what the operation would be like. Maybe I could have stayed with Laska when she went under anesthesia and been there when she regained consciousness. I have never forgotten the tonsillectomy I had when I was about six or seven years old.

▼▼▼

I lie on a table in the operating room. Several grownups, their faces hidden behind paper masks, hover over me. Someone places a rubber mask on my face and I sink into a stupor, thick and nauseating. The descent takes the shape of a whirlpool, at the bottom of which is a pink flamingo. When I awaken, my head aches as if someone put a tight metal band around it, and for a while afterward I vomit up dark blood. The only plusses are that the nurses feed me sherbet to soothe my throat; and that I have an unexpected visit from my father.

It is evening and I sit alone in a hospital bed with metal railings on the sides. In the semi-darkness I clutch a stuffed toy bunny to my chest that one of the nurses gave me for Easter, even though I am seven years old and Jewish. The girl next to me is asleep. Suddenly, a tall familiar figure comes through the door. I drop the stuffed toy. "Daddy," I exclaim in surprise.

"They let me in off-hours because I am a professional man," he says proudly, and plants a kiss on my forehead. I put my arms around his neck and hug him tightly. When I let go, he draws a chair up to my bed, sits down, and says, "I brought you a special surprise." I didn't notice that he holds a boxed set of books.

"What are they?" I ask.

He pulls them out for me and lays them on the bedcovers. The titles read, My Friend Flicka *and* Thunderhead. *"I don't know if you can read them yet yourself," he says, "but you look at the pictures and I'll read them to you when you get home."*

"When am I going home?" I ask, more interested in knowing that than in the books, though horses are my favorite.

"I have to find out from the doc," my father says in the important tone he uses with his dental patients.

After a short while a nurse comes in the room and asks him to leave. "Well, kiddo," he says, "don't worry, we'll have you out of here soon." He gets up and bends over the criblike railings. I hug my father hard, not minding the smell of cigarettes that hangs around him, and then he is gone.

▲▲▲

I'm sure that Laska and I experienced our operations differently, but judging from her changed behavior, the surgery couldn't have been a trivial event. I wonder what she might have seen during anesthesia?

SEPTEMBER 15

TODAY Laska flies off the deck when I let her out to pee, in chase of pigeons and starlings. She seems to feel no pain after the operation and doesn't even bite at the staples in her belly. The vet said that Laska is not supposed to run or leap; such exertions could open her stitches. How can I keep a dog like Laska down?

SEPTEMBER 18

I COME home from Ma'ariv service to find Laska's crate littered with paper and paper scraps. Some months ago when James dismantled Laska's setup in the living room, he moved her crate into the studio and placed it in front of a bookcase built into the wall. I hadn't noticed that a manila envelope filled with Xeroxed pages of a book was propped on its side and stuck out into the room. Somehow Laska, whom I'd left in her crate, pulled the whole package through the widely spaced metal grid, grabbed sheets from the envelope, and chewed them up, as if she were a shredding machine. The title of the book is *Scattered Hegemonies.* Laska ingested essays about the decline of colonialism, an apt choice for a puppy who loves her independence.

SEPTEMBER 20

THE broad wavy strip of fur down Laska's back looks braided, like a beeswax Havdallah candle. Tonight is Havdallah, the service held on Saturdays at sundown to mark the end of Shabbat and separate a sacred day from the coming week. Just so, at least once a week Laska divides me from a sense of my own goodness, though the candle imprint on her back suggests that she carries ceremonial significance. The self-separation she provokes has value; it causes me to look at unlovely aspects of myself and work to change them.

SEPTEMBER 24

FALL solstice came three days ago. I am melancholy, not over the turning season, but over losing ground with Laska. Ever since I kept her quiet for two weeks so that her stitches could heal, she has resumed biting and jumping. She couldn't bear being cooped up in her crate, and I couldn't explain why she had to be. Unfortunately, *my* old habits returned along with hers. Once again I am easily alarmed and have lost my position as her leader. A contributing problem is that I feel weariness over how long our mismatch has been going on. I'm finding it hard to summon the energy to try again. When Laska and I walked with Cass and Eli at Camel's Hump on Labor Day, clouds shrouded the mountaintop. As I look back on that view, it seems to have been an omen.

Right now, Laska is lying at the far end of the yard, chewing on her potato bone. It seems she chooses not to remain close to me. I have been thinking of giving her up, accepting that we are just not right for each other. On our walk I had told Cass that I hoped I'd never want to relinquish my puppy. But Laska makes my blood pressure rise, rather than drop; and I'm sure it's not good for her to be with someone who can't make her feel calm.

Crow prefers dogs who keep their distance; she once brusquely, but kindly, called Sarah "codependent" because Sarah pestered her too much for pats. Laska is far from overly affectionate, so much so that Crow claims she isn't a typical Lab. "She's vicious," Crow said recently. I find it hard to argue with my friend, because when Crow comes over to dinner, Laska jumps up and bites at her clothes as she does with other guests. More often than not at such times, I have to put Laska in her crate.

Crow's opinion counts more than that of a person who favors butterball dogs. Yet, as I sit here in a momentary patch of fall sunlight, I am forced to take Laska's side. I look over at my puppy, who still chews away on her bone far from me. As if Crow were here, with her charge of Laska's viciousness, I pour out a defense that is a bewildering mixture of pros and cons, "Well, she *isn't* vicious. But she guards against being touched around the head and neck. She's toothy. She's very independent, has the kind of intelligence recommended for experienced dog handlers only, which I'm not, and she eats her poops."

Luckily, it is midday and my neighbors are at work, so no one hears my outburst—except Laska, who lifts her head but keeps to herself across the yard.

SEPTEMBER 25

TODAY my heart turns to ash over Laska; the embers of warmth just go out. First, she bites and then jumps on my friend Sigrid when we take a walk at Camel's Hump. Sigrid had acted as a *doula* to Laska and me long ago; she is the last person I want Laska to accost.

Now, when we get home, I discover that Laska chewed part of the rug mat and the foam rubber underneath it in the back of the station wagon. I forgot to give her a bone to relieve tension on our trip, since she doesn't like car rides; the shock absorbers are gone and she bumps around more than is comfortable. Laska's behavior with Sigrid is nothing new and I understand why she damaged the mat and the foam; but suddenly these two small infractions produce not just a thought but a conviction that we have to split up. I feel a churning inside, as if an inevitability propels me, almost against my will. Then I wonder if two divorces and the legacy of my childhood, which is one of disconnection, contribute to this feeling that Laska's and my relationship "has" to end.

SEPTEMBER 26

LEVIN calls from New York. He and his girlfriend, Michelle, had planned to come up for my birthday. "I've got good news and bad news," he says.

The bad news is that he overslept and missed the train. There is only one a day to Burlington. The good news is that if he borrows a friend's car, he can arrive late in the day.

"That sounds like too much of a schlep," I say to Levin. "Why not come next week? The trees will be at their peak."

"We can celebrate then," Levin says, and I can sense his relief.

It is not typical of Levin to miss a train. I wonder whether he had an unconscious conflict over the trip because of my parents. Levin is on good terms with my mother and father. He often goes over to their apartment for dinner and accompanies them to gallery openings, museums, and other cultural events. Despite my estrangement from my parents, I support Levin's warm relationship with them. He is their grandson and I am their daughter—two different familial positions with two different histories. The breach between me and my parents never before interfered with Levin visiting me in Vermont. But the celebration of a birthday invites inclusion of the whole family and perhaps he doesn't want to choose sides.

I take the risk of asking, "Lev, do you think you overslept because it was too hard to come up here without Arthur and Anita knowing?"

"I think so," Levin says sleepily. His answer surprises me because he often rejects my psychological interpretations.

My anger at my parents over the loss of Levin's and Michelle's company on my birthday transfers to Laska. When she starts jumping and nipping, I hit her on the top of the nose with a vehemence far in excess of the situation. That's *my* bad news. The good news is that my unconscious has become more available to my conscious mind. The flashbacks from my early childhood have allowed me to see the sources of my fear of Laska and my anger toward her. But they used to arise *after* I acted unkindly. Today, the twin dynamic of me and Laska and me and my parents becomes not a flashback, but a double exposure where both elements coexist simultaneously. One more step and I will be able to stop myself from mistreating Laska *before* anything happens. This new awareness is a fine birthday gift.

I spend the day cleaning Levin's room and filling the shelves he'd emptied when he moved out with cherished objects from our past. I bring out the "big black big engine," as he used to call it, a windup locomotive engine that I bought at a tag sale when he was two; a stuffed toy starfish and a "moon in the man," as he used to call it, both made of fleece; a blue silk flower that he decorated his bicycle with when he worked as a courier in San Francisco at the age of eighteen. These and other remnants of our history cheer the room up and make it seem inhabited. Housekeeping is a funny way to spend my fifty-sixth birthday, but I enjoy it.

As compensation for the loss of Levin's and Michelle's company, Crow takes me out to dinner. Among other things, we talk about the need for Jewish pride.

"Look at those photos on the wall," she says. "That's what we need more of."

We are surrounded by images of African Americans full of black pride—men, women, children standing straight-backed, heads turned proudly toward the camera. I can imagine *Israeli* Jews standing that way, but not us Diaspora Jews.

My thoughts wander, crossing species lines. I always knew Sarah didn't have a Jewish temperament. She was too happy. When I watched her stretch in the morning, her tail already wagging, I used to say to myself, "Every day is another fine day for Pooch." Laska doesn't have much of a Jewish sensibility, either, because she's proud. If I work on my Jewish pride, maybe *then* she'll accept me as her leader.

October 1997

New Year

OCTOBER 1

TOMORROW is Rosh Hashanah, the beginning of the Jewish New Year, just as nice a time as my birthday for Levin and Michelle to visit. Today I take time out from my preparations for a visit from Merle; I need her help, due to the setback provoked by Laska's operation. I catch myself wishing that Merle weren't coming. Why can't Laska and I leave our troubles behind in the year that is almost over?

When Merle arrives, she sits down at the kitchen table before I do. I stop to peer out the window that overlooks the yard to see what my puppy is up to. Without lifting her nose from the ground, Laska watches me in return, with that crescent moon–eyed look.

"Why are you looking out the window?" Merle asks.

As I sit down, I explain, "I'm afraid Laska will eat her poop or bittersweet and get sick." Busy monitoring my puppy, I haven't remembered to offer Merle anything to eat or drink. "Would you like an apple?" I ask.

Merle ignores my question and says in a calm but firm voice, "You have to stop trying to control Laska. You need to let her be an animal. Don't watch her when she's out in the yard. The stool and bittersweet eating will self-correct. If you don't let her be, she will not want to be around you, and then you won't be able to do anything with her."

I place my elbows on the table and take hold of my head with both hands at the temples, like a person at the end of her wits. Then, to my dismay, sobs erupt, and with them a rush of words. "Even if I let her alone outside, that won't solve the way she startles me by jumping and biting. I try to be calm but she agitates me so much. I've watched other people with her, friends when they come over. They can't stand it either. It's been going on so long. Worst of all, she makes me feel I am no good at giving love."

Merle remains quiet and makes no effort to subdue me. I appreciate that. After a long time, I stop crying of my own accord. Without any judgment in her voice she says, "You resent her, don't you?"

What a relief to be able to say yes.

Later, refreshed by my tears and by Merle's acceptance of feelings that embarrass me, I decide to keep on trying.

OCTOBER 3

LASKA and I go for a Rosh Hashanah outing at Red Rocks, the conservation woods near Lake Champlain where Sarah and I walked the evening before she died. The new year is a good time to get over my superstition about the place—that something bad will happen to Laska if we go there. Red Rocks is only ten minutes from my house, but as we enter the woods along a winding dirt path, the city seems far away. The trees are turning, their leaves less colorful just yet than those in the mountains, where the temperature is colder. I keep Laska on her leash because she does not come reliably when I call. She pulls toward the edge of the path, her body tilted sideways over her legs, nose to the ground. I move in Laska's direction so that she can more easily sniff the fascinating scents left by other dogs. Pine needles litter the path, making it soft underfoot as we follow trails that loop around in the woods; we pass large striated red rocks speckled with silver-green lichens. In spring Red Rocks has an abundant show of the three-petaled trillium; I used to come each year to see them, until Sarah died. Today I feel shielded from her death and breathe in the sharp, fall air as if it were a cleansing tonic.

Laska and I stop at a lookout point over the lake where the rocks drop off sharply just beyond a metal guardrail. Laska walks under the rail up to the very edge and peers over, bracing her paws carefully. Though she seems to be taking good care of herself, I make her sit so that I can look at the lake without worry. The water is quiet and a few sailboats drift slowly, far out from shore; beyond the lake I can see a ridge of the Green Mountains, including Camel's Hump. Laska and I proceed to the next lookout, which you get to by climbing over large, irregularly shaped rocks. I pick my way along, eyes on the ground; suddenly Laska tugs on her leash and I hear a great flapping of wings. I look up in time to see a hawk lift off the ground, long wings fanned out, each feather visible—we are that close. His talons release a little red-brown chipmunk with white stripes down its back, who drops onto the rock. My heart thumping from shock, I peer down at the chipmunk; it seems dead. I step past the inert body and pull Laska along with me. Then I stand at the guardrail, look out at the lake, and gather my wits. Some beginning to the new year, I say to myself; why in the world did I bring us here? I turn to leave and, busy watching my step on the rock, lose control of Laska. She dashes at the lifeless-looking chipmunk; suddenly the little animal springs to its feet, tail erect, and scampers off. I laugh with surprise and relief as I pull Laska back from the chase and head down the path toward the car. It seems Laska and I accidentally saved the chipmunk's life. In an instant my whole mood changes—our walk at Red Rocks turns out to be a fine way to celebrate Rosh Hashanah.

OCTOBER 4

ON their second attempt to visit me, a week later than originally planned, Levin and Michelle did not oversleep; they arrived yesterday. The moment the young couple waved at me from the ferry (the train station is on the New York side of Lake Champlain), my anger at my parents for unwittingly disrupting my birthday celebration ceased.

This morning the three of us recite a prayer and eat apples and honey (just apples for me), a tradition on Rosh Hashanah for a sweet new year. We perform this ritual a few days late, but families weren't scattered in antiquity and so could celebrate at the appointed times. Laska sits right by the table, expecting to share in the celebration. Levin tosses her a piece of apple saying, "Happy New Year, Pooch," a term of endearment he used for Sarah, and I am full of hope that on this visit Levin and Laska will get along better than they did at Martha's Vineyard.

Levin, Michelle, and I walk to the synagogue, a practice that is an ancient custom; on Shabbat, the day of rest, driving is prohibited. Today, the old parking lot is too small to accommodate the many who commute to services.

I enter OZ with Levin and Michelle, carrying the new prayer book that the synagogue recently adopted, which contains gender-neutral language for God. We stop in the vestibule, where siddurs, yarmulkes, and talliths are provided. Since I knew that Levin and Michelle would be with me this Shabbat, I had asked the rabbi if I could recite the *kohayn aliyah.* I already have on a multicolored hat that serves as a yarmulke, but I drape a tallith around my shoulders. Levin puts on a yarmulke and he and Michelle pick up siddurs. We walk into the sanctuary and sit down in a pew, Levin beside me and Michelle next to him.

I have always come to OZ without family; Levin's tall form seated beside me, even if momentarily, seems the first abundance of a good and sweet new year. The prayer book I am holding has special significance because Levin bought it for my birthday. I used to drag him to High Holy Day services until his teenage years, when he refused to come anymore. I resigned myself to the probability that he would not see himself as a Jew. According to tradition, if the mother is Jewish, the child is too; but I felt it was up to him to *choose* what, if any, religion he wanted to join, since his father's heritage is not Jewish, but Quaker and Catholic. U.S. culture is unspokenly Christian, which makes it hard to choose being a Jew. All the same, ever since I embraced the tradition for my *own* sake, I have noticed that Levin seems friendlier toward Judaism.

When the cantor calls a *kohayn* to the bimah, I get up and walk down the aisle, holding my shoulders straight. If there was ever a time to demonstrate Jewish pride, it is now. I ascend to the altar and the cantor seems to give me an especially friendly smile. Family matters. At the designated moment, I sing the prayer in a gritty, forceful voice; it feels as if I am taking hold of the tradition for the first time. As I leave the bimah, I sense that my face isn't arranged properly, but whether the expression is one of joy or sorrow I can't tell. People seated along the aisle shake my hand as I return to my seat. When I sit down, Levin leans toward me and whispers, "You sang good, Mom."

OCTOBER 5

LEVIN takes Laska out into the yard. I am delighted that he wants to throw a ball for my puppy the way he used to for Sarah. "She might not bring it back," I say. With his good throwing arm Levin hurtles the ball all the way to the stockade fence, and Laska flies off the deck in pursuit. As if she used it as a brake, her tail rotates wildly when she reaches the ball. She scoops it up competently and head held high runs back toward Levin; she leaps back onto the deck and looks at him expectantly, the ball firmly between her teeth.

"Give me the ball," Levin says. Laska trots a short distance away. "Give it," he says, impatiently now, and starts after her. Laska jumps off the deck in a high arc and circles the yard at a gallop.

"At least she brought it back," I say, apologetically.

"She's had her chance," Levin replies.

He and I go back into the house and soon Laska whines at the door to come in. Michelle is in the studio looking at Levin's somber painting of a cornfield in fall that he gave me as a present when he left Burlington. She is nearest the door and as soon as she opens it, Laska jumps on her; my puppy's claws catch on Michelle's delicate bracelet, which breaks, scattering little silvery black beads across the floor. "Oh," Michelle exclaims, loudly.

"What has that maniac done now?" Levin says, as if he were just waiting for Laska to make a mistake. He strides angrily into the studio and takes Michelle in his arms.

"It was an accident," I say. "Laska didn't mean to harm Michelle's bracelet."

"I don't care what she meant," Levin replies. Satisfied that his girlfriend is all right, he attempts to pick up the beads. I notice that his hands are shaking.

"I'll get a broom," I say.

"First put that dog in her crate."

I try to grab Laska by the collar; she counters by dropping into a play bow and making for my hand with her mouth.

"This is no time to play," I say. I lure Laska into her crate with a treat and get the broom and dustpan.

After he gathers up the beads, Levin says, "We're going out for a walk. I don't know when we'll be back."

I leave Laska in her crate and sit down at the kitchen table. I spot the spray bottle filled with water and place it next to me. Will we ever have a family visit without some calamity occurring between Levin and my puppy?

OCTOBER 7

LEVIN and Michelle are still asleep and I am sitting in the yard, reading. After just a few days of my not watching Laska when she is outdoors, my puppy carries a huge rawhide bone, knotted at both ends, close to my chair. She plops herself down in the bright sunshine, props the bone between her paws, and gnaws on it. All this I see out of the corner of my eye. I'm trying not to watch Laska, according to Merle's instructions.

OCTOBER 8

THIS morning, the day Levin and Michelle plan to leave, I bend over to sniff the stargazer lilies that I had bought in honor of their visit. They are Levin's favorites. The pink, splayed flowers with pointed petals rest in a vase from Prinknash

Abbey in England known for crafting gray-black luminescent pewter glazes. At their center the stargazers have moist mauve pistils and long parentheses-shaped stamens covered with pollen that smells like allspice. A few minutes later I go into the bathroom and notice in the mirror that the space between my nose and upper lip is dusted with cinnamon brown pollen from sniffing the flowers. Fable has it that an angel touches that indent on your face just before you are born so that your soul forgets all it knows of other, heavenly spheres. I brush the pollen off.

After breakfast Levin sets up my new sound system in the living room. We sit in Breuer chairs by a high bookcase that used to be Levin's when he was a boy; his indelible ink graffiti remains scribbled on a small portion of the wooden facing. I never had the bookcase refinished because the illegible writing reminded me of his childhood. Objects from our years fill the shelves—several of them owl related. One day when Levin was nine years old, he said, out of the blue, "You know what you are? You're a screech owl." Then as he walked safely behind my chair (we were on the screened-in porch of the camp at Martha's Vineyard), he added, "Why don't you go sharpen your beak?" A few months later Levin named me "Feefeedorici, the owl," or "Feef," for short. On one shelf rests a wooden puzzle made up of a few large pieces. A mother owl perches on a tree branch, wings outstretched, while three baby owls sit on a lower branch looking up at her. When I used to help Levin with his homework, he often fiddled with the puzzle, turning one of the babies backward and reinserting it into the space where it belonged so that all you could see of the figure was a white wooden shape. *That* little owl wasn't listening to its mother. On the highest shelf near the ceiling a large painted plastic owl, the kind you place in a garden to scare away birds, surveys the living room fiercely.

After he gets the sound system installed, Levin plays me a tape of songs recently composed and recorded with his friends in New York.

"The first song is a prayer for my friend Saul; you met him, remember?"

I nod.

"Saul's stomach cancer has come back and we created the song to make it go away. It was strange what happened when we started playing—the music seemed to come all by itself; my mind became very clear and I lost a sense of time."

"Olympic athletes call an experience like that 'the zone'; they say time slows and they become lucid and focused. A man with the unbelievable name of Mihaly Csikzentmihalyi studies the creative process and he calls what you describe a 'flow state.'"

"I've heard of that," Levin replies. "It happens to me all the time."

Levin puts the tape on and I close my eyes. Silence . . . then, summoned or unbidden, a low sound enters, at the outer limit of human hearing. Next, high silvery tinkling, leaves of a celestial tree shaking. A tambourine echoes, palpable the hand that causes the tinny clatter. A sound of breathing, of birds, of an unknown instrument's blunt plucking. These cadences hover, eddy, not yet commingling. Suddenly long notes of a flute flow in, arc high, fall, rise again. Palms fall hard upon a taut drumskin, heartbeat of singular rhythm. Strings begin a melody, sing it over and over, fresh and sweet as dawn. Unknown yearnings stir. The three instruments loosely bind together, drawing the other sounds to them. The drum and strings keep earthward. The flute soars restless, curves down. Rises again, plunges unexpectedly into a minor key, then a lull, lifts poignantly on extended wings. Shall the soul hold fast to the heartbeat and sweet pulse of mortality? Or shall it fly away too soon? The flute drops low. Bird sounds, tambourine, human breath. One last time the flute rises even higher than before, utters a shrill cry of lamentation, then subsides. As the summoned or unbidden sounds slowly disengage from the instruments, their cohesion falters, they grow quiet, gradually fade into the silence from which they came. I feel a great sadness and longing not to have to return to my living room. Levin stops the tape and I open my eyes. I have no words to say what I've heard; I also know it isn't necessary to speak. But I make myself do it anyhow because I am Levin's mother and feel that I should acknowledge his accomplishment.

All that comes out of me is, "Congratulations."

"Why did you say that?" Levin asks, looking annoyed.

"I mean congratulations for the privilege of transmitting this music. It seemed to move through your flute and all the other instruments, even the digital ones."

"Thanks," Levin replies, mollified.

"Is the song called 'Garden of Eden'?" I ask as I look over the titles he wrote down to the songs on the tape while I was listening.

"It's called 'Birds of Sand,'" he says, looking at me with his clear, gray-green eyes. The smile folds of his lower lids show amused surprise over the title, as if it emerged just then, by itself.

"Like sand spinning in a whirlwind in a desert and turning into birds and flying away," he adds, making a high, airy motion with his hand. There are sacred associations to his title: God came to the Israelites in the desert as a whirlwind of sand, and birds in many cultures are images of the soul.

In a light tone, as if it is of little consequence, I say, "The other day I read something I wrote about how we are the color of sand. Long ago I was walking at Lucy Vincent Beach as dusk came on and I felt that water and sand and consciousness were bound up in an indissoluble unity."

Levin winds up leftover copper wire, encased in clear plastic, that he used to connect the amplifier to the speakers. The radiant wires look like fibers joining him to the place where "Birds of Sand" comes from. Levin takes what I say matter-of-factly. Yet I know he is not unaware that such alignments between him and me happen often.

Finished with his task, Levin goes upstairs to pack; I remain sitting by the sound system. Suddenly a half-memory overrides the angel's touch that at my birth made me forget the soul's home—invisible words appear in parentheses, as if the parenthetic-shaped, parent-thesis-shaped stamen touches me with cinnamon brown, and I remember a primordial time of effortless communion before the divisions into self and other. A yearning arises to live in that wordless state where song titles are not needed, where no one has to say, "I was writing about sand too." Between a mother and son it probably is best that the angel makes us forget, that such moments remain within parentheses in ordinary life. For Levin must find another and I must continue on, on my own. As Brian Swimme and Thomas Berry explain in *The Universe Story,* differentiation is fundamental to all of creation: "Were there no differentiation, the universe would collapse into a homogenous smudge; were there no subjectivity, the universe would collapse into inert, dead extension; were there no communion, the universe would collapse into isolated singularities of being." Swimme and Berry talk about the costs of feeling cut off: "The loss of relationship, with its consequent alienation, is a kind of supreme evil in the universe. In the religious world this loss was traditionally understood as an ultimate mystery. To be locked up in a private world, to be cut off from intimacy with other beings, to be incapable of entering the joy of mutual presence—such conditions were taken as the essence of damnation."[1]

In the hell that Dante describes, many souls are "locked up in a private world," alone with their story. Many times in this past year with Laska I've felt a similar sense of isolation.

Levin and Michelle interrupt my reverie as they clatter down the stairs carrying their few travel bags. I put Laska in her crate so that they can pack up the car without her running into the street. Michelle hugs me and I feel her slim body, like a child's. "Take good care," she says. Levin gives me one of his A-shaped hugs and says, "Bye, Mom, thanks for everything." To Laska he adds, "Take good care of Robbie." Then they are gone. I sit down in the kitchen near the vase filled with stargazers. From infancy on, Levin restored my connection to the larger sources of being and life that I had lost in childhood. A friend once said to me, "You gave birth to your own teacher."

OCTOBER 10

A NEW year's desire arises—it is customary during the days between Rosh Hashanah and Yom Kippur to review the past year and plan for the coming one—to resolve my relationship with my parents and with Laska. I turn to psychoanalyst Alice Miller's *Thou Shalt Not Be Aware: Society's Betrayal of the Child.* I seek her support against an inner voice that makes me responsible for too much, that insists I am the cause of the estrangement from my parents. Miller explains that our culture consciously and unconsciously protects parents' feelings at the expense of their children's. This misalignment is historically rooted and so pervasive that even psychoanalysts neglect to side with the child that their patients once were. Miller states:

> If the analyst is under the sway of the Fourth Commandment [to honor his father and mother], no matter how hard he tries to reconstruct the original situation [of the patient's childhood], he will invariably take the part of his patient's judgmental parents and sooner or later try to "educate" him [the patient] by urging him to have understanding for them. Without a doubt our parents were victims, too, not of their children, but of their own parents. It is essential for us to perceive the unintentional persecution of children by their parents, sanctioned by society and called childrearing, if our patients are to be freed from the feeling imposed on them from an early age that they are to blame for their parents' suffering.
>
> In order for this to happen, the analyst has to be free from guilt feelings toward his own parents and be sensitive to the narcissistic wounds [damage to a healthy sense of self] that can be inflicted in early childhood. If he lacks this sensitivity, he will minimize the extent of the persecution. He will not be able to empathize with a child's humiliation, since his own childhood humiliation is still repressed. If, in keeping with the saying "You'll be the death of me yet," he has learned to accept all the guilt in order to spare his parents, he will try to allay his patient's aggression, which he cannot understand, by repeatedly emphasizing the parents' good sides.[2]

In my conversation with Jessica last month, I speculated that literary critics belittle memoirs, which often show parents in an unfavorable light, out of their fealty to the Fourth Commandment. I've noticed the same tendency in social historians. That day, Jessica mentioned a book that I have only recently looked at, *The History of Childhood: The Untold Story of Child Abuse.* Psychohistorian Lloyd deMause notices that social historians who study childhood cannot face their findings:

> The social historian, whose job it is to dig out the reality of social conditions in the past, . . . defends himself most vigorously against the facts he turns up. When one social historian finds widespread infanticide, he declares it "admirable and humane."
>
> When another describes mothers who regularly beat their infants with sticks while still in the cradle, she comments, without a shred of evidence, that "if her discipline was stern, it was even and just and leavened with kindness." When a third finds mothers who dunk their infants into ice water each morning to "strengthen" them, and the children die from the practice, she says that "they were not intentionally cruel," but simply "had read Rousseau and Locke." No practice in the past seems anything but benign to the social historian.[3]

DeMause cites many other examples of scholars' refusal to bear witness to parental cruelty. His findings shock me (and, I would imagine, other readers as well) to the point where I question his scholarship; yet he documents his assertions meticulously. Remarkably, deMause offers no insight into the social historians' oversight, even though he is a psychoanalyst. Miller would likely say that the scholars are unconscious adherents of the Fourth Commandment, which prohibits them from criticizing parents' actions toward their children. That same commandment governs me when I doubt deMause's perfectly sound research and when I believe that my family's discord is my fault.

OCTOBER 11

IT is customary on Yom Kippur to fast from sundown to sundown. Like the other congregants I return home to rest between the morning and afternoon services. Since developing arthritis I allow myself water during the fast; I take a full glass out into the yard and sit down in a chair, feeling somewhat weak and light-headed. Laska bounds after me and then trots off to inspect a shallow hole dug in the grass by a squirrel or skunk looking for grubs.

I should read only the siddur on Yom Kippur, but I want to review Myla and Jon Kabat-Zinn's proposal in *Everyday Blessings: The Inner Work of Mindful Parenting* for resolving adult child/parent conflict. Although Yom Kippur is drawing to a close, I still am not clear on who owes forgiveness to whom in my family. Many books on forgiveness unconsciously obey the Fourth Commandment; Myla and Jon take the child's side. They suggest that if the parents of adult children could express regret and remorse over past behavior, reconciliation would possible:

> In our view, it is never too late to try to heal relationships with grown children who may have been hurt by us through our past ignorance, however innocent or understandable, or through lack of attention, or busyness, or neglect, withholding, judgment, or abusiveness. It is never too late to work toward creating healthy new connections, even if our children are distrustful of us, or angry about past attitudes or actions, omissions, or commissions on our part, that they feel were harmful to them.
>
> One way we might begin to heal these wounds is by sharing our regrets and our awareness of the things we did that were harmful or neglectful, either by letter or in person with our adult children. Doing this in a letter may be a more sensitive way to communicate at first, particularly if a child feels we have been intrusive or thoughtless about boundaries. To be of any real value, reaching out in this way must be a genuine overture, with the well-being of our child foremost in our mind, and, as hard as it might be for us, accepting the possibility that irreparable damage may have been done and no reconciliation possible.[4]

Their words cause an unreasonable hope to arise; if my parents could shine a light of awareness on themselves the way Myla and Jon Kabat-Zinn suggest, I could open the valves of my heart to them. With Laska, improvements wait on no one but myself. I have been shining a light of awareness on my distorted reactions to my puppy, acknowledging my mistakes, and attempting to correct them. For these efforts I allow myself a moment of self-respect.

I close the book and sit quietly in the sun, doing nothing. Laska crouches a short distance from me, chewing loudly on an ash tree twig. She forsakes this project and saunters lazily up to me, her middle swaying from side to side with each step. My puppy seems more relaxed outdoors, as am I. Laska pushes her muzzle under my hand; when I don't respond she butts at me like a goat. I pat her head and neck just a few times, the way Merle suggested. Then Laska flops upside down on the ground so that I can rub her belly, a caress she favors above all others. She sticks one front leg straight up in the air, as if bracing herself against an invisible object. Her open mouth reveals jagged white teeth, but she doesn't grab at my hand; her ears splay out, showing pink-gray undersides. She looks like a bat. "Laskali, I love you anyway," I say, dizzy from hunger.

The chimes at the Ethan Allen chapel at UVM signal that it's five o'clock in the afternoon. I put Laska in her crate and walk slowly up the street to the synagogue.

OCTOBER 12

I PICK up the phone and call Cass, Cantor Aaron's wife. "Hi, Cass, this is Robbie."

"Oh hi, I've been thinking of you. I saw you at services yesterday but I didn't get a chance to say hello, there were so many people," Cass says.

"Quite a difference from the usual Shabbat service," I reply, "but I didn't call to talk about OZ. I'm sure you hear plenty on that subject from Aaron."

"Yes," Cass laughs.

"It's about you and Eli. I wondered if you would like to take another walk this weekend up at Camel's Hump."

"I'm afraid not," Cass answers, and her voice takes on an agitated tone. "When we got home last time Eli threw up grass all over the house, upstairs and downstairs. I didn't notice he had been eating it on our walk, we were so busy talking. Dogs eat grass to help their digestion and I sympathize, but what a mess it was."

"I'm sorry, Cass," I reply, disappointed because Eli is just about Laska's only friend. "They had such a good time," I add, in an attempt to make something good out of something bad.

"Yes, they did," Cass says, "but I couldn't go through that cleanup again."

"Well, maybe we could walk in the snow," I offer, and Cass agrees, but I can sense her lack of enthusiasm.

I get off the phone and say to my puppy, who is lying on her fleecy blanket by the radiator, "Laskali Raskali"—a recent term of affection—"for once it wasn't *you* who got into trouble."

OCTOBER 13

A LEAF from an ash tree twirls to the ground. Laska, who has just wandered over to where I sit, pounces on the leaf and noses it with great interest. I catch myself watching her shake the leaf from side to side as if it were a duck she'd retrieved from a pond. I want to respect Laska's privacy, but it is hard not to look at her; her antics are captivating. Tiring of her game with the leaf, Laska spots a squirrel on the stockade fence and dashes wildly across the yard. The squirrel scurries along the top of the fence, using its bushy tail for balance, and leaps to a tree. Laska runs around the tree trunk, barking, as the squirrel chatters defiantly from a high branch. Eventually Laska moves away, sniffing at the grass. Suddenly she stands erect, back to me, apparently listening to the complaining call of Canada geese. I gaze up at the sky and see them flutter in a ragged V formation as they head south, long necks outstretched. "Those are geese," I say, and lift my arm to point at the sky. Laska turns her head to look at me instead of the migrating birds and, as the sound of the geese grows faint, the distance between us carries a small charge of connection.

OCTOBER 14

NOW that the Jewish holidays are over, I can return to my research for *Creatural Lessons.* I want to learn more about the domestication of animals, a process that transformed the relationship of human culture to nature. In *Between Pets and People: The Importance of Animal Companionship,* a groundbreaking book about the physical and emotional benefits to humans of pets, Alan Beck and Aaron Katcher summarize the literature on the domestication of dogs. They agree that domestication probably arose around twelve thousand years ago with the advent of agriculture. Wolves, the ancestors of dogs, were drawn to human settlements to scavenge for food; humans in turn found the wolves beneficial as guardians, hunting aids, and sources of meat.

But Beck and Katcher reject a purely utilitarian approach to domestication. They quote Boris M. Levinson, pioneer in using pets in psychotherapy: "There is as much reason to believe that man's psychological needs were the primary cause for domestication of animals as that man needed to use animals for such material purposes as the saving of human labor and the satisfaction of a hunger for food."[5] The emotional component of pet keeping leads Beck and Katcher to agree with the theory that young animals were humans' first domesticates. Humans are genetically disposed to find juvenile traits appealing, an attraction that insures care of their own very young.

Domestication creates dependence, a condition that may be abused. Beck and Katcher call attention to the sad reality that once a kitten or puppy matures and loses its childlike features, it often is given up to a shelter. In *Returning to Eden: Animal Rights and Human Responsibility,* noted animal behaviorist Michael W. Fox discusses the responsibility that goes along with domestication: "A relatively helpless pet has a right to a good home. This *is* a burden of responsibility on us humans since to a great extent we created pets. Many breeds of dogs and varieties of cats are extremely dependent. . . . Being so created, do they not have a right to the most understanding, compassionate, and responsible care?"[6]

In *The Others: How Animals Made Us Human,* Paul Shepard shares Fox's assumption that humans created pets; this dependence provokes in Shepard, not compassion, as it did in Fox, but scorn: "What is wrong at the heart of the keeping of pets is that they are deficient animals in whom we have invested the momentum of two million years of love of the Others [wild animals who have sovereignty over themselves]. They are monsters of the order invented by Frankenstein, . . . biological slaves who cringe and fawn or perform or whatever we wish."[7]

At first glance Shepard's repugnance toward domesticates seems excessive and even inexplicable. Yet he reflects, albeit in extreme form, both our culture's ambivalence toward pet keeping and the notion (shared by many environmentalists) that only wild animals possess dignity and integrity.

The preceding accounts share the view that humans domesticated animals. Author Stephen Budiansky believes that this assumption conceals an anthropocentric bias. In *The Covenant of the Wild: Why Animals Chose Domestication,* Budiansky states: "We need to stop looking at domestication as only a human phenomenon. The direction to start looking is through the eyes of animals. The question that must be answered is not what's in it for us, but what's in it for them."[8]

Budiansky refutes Shepard's assumption that nature is only truly itself apart from the human world. Budiansky uses the example of the house mouse to make his point: "When it's in our house it already *is* in nature. By its evolutionary history, by its feeding habits, and by its nesting habits, cohabitation with man is the way of life the house mouse has adapted to" (46).

According to Budiansky, domestication occurred almost simultaneously throughout the world at the end of the Pleistocene era, around 8500 BP (an anthropological acronym that means "before the present"). Climatic upheavals, in particular the Ice Age, forced animals and humans together and favored animals who could adapt to a variety of geographic circumstances. The creatures best suited were those whose neotenic (childlike) traits evolved into permanent features, physically and temperamentally, since neoteny attracted humans. As Budiansky explains:

> This systematic neoteny, selected as a way to adapt to a changing world, would have laid an even more solid foundation for the interactions of humans and other animals. The curiosity, the lack of a highly species-

> specific sense of recognition [characteristic of the very young], and the retention into adulthood of juvenile care-soliciting behavior (such as begging for food) of neotenates would all have been powerful factors in inducing wolves, sheep, cattle, horses, and many other occupants of the Asian and European grasslands of the late glacial era to approach human encampments and to allow humans to approach them. The neoteny that is part of our own evolutionary heritage [we are drawn to babies] may have likewise made us more willing to enter into relationships with animals other than the highly specialized one of predator to prey. (80)

Thus, evolution, not humans, created the domestic animal. Budiansky disagrees sharply with animal rights advocates who believe that we should release animals from captivity (such as laboratory chimps, minks cultivated for fur, even cows). How can we expect them to search for food, he asks, when they do not have the urge or ability to forage? (He recognizes that in a pinch feral animals can survive.) Budiansky concludes his book by insisting that we accept stewardship of domestic animals for, evolutionarily, they have asked us to assume this responsibility. At the same time, he invites us to cultivate humility about our place in nature; the word "humble" occurs several times in his book:

> Looking at the family dog lying on the living room floor, we can either see what most do—that is, almost nothing except a commonplace fixture in the twentieth-century American home—or we can see a link with the very dawn of civilization, when a series of evolutionary and climatic forces brought together two species in a way that transformed the face of the planet. The drama that the science of coevolution has disclosed may be able to inspire a sense of wonder and respect for animal life in a way that the airy, strident, and absolutist stance of animal rightists fails to.
>
> The other humbling lesson that nature can teach us, if we let her, is the pretentiousness of our believing that we can even make clean moral choices about a system as complex as the natural world. (165–166)

Budiansky doesn't go into detail about how "two species . . . transformed the face of the planet." I do know that dogs aided early humans in the hunting of wild animals; by herding sheep and cattle, dogs contributed significantly to their domestication. Herbivores' need of a constant supply of food intensified humans' motivation to domesticate plants; without doubt the agricultural revolution transformed the face of the planet. One fascinating theory proposes that dogs influenced the development of human speech. Canines' sense of smell allowed them to protect human communities; dogs' olfactory vigilance may have freed human facial structure to evolve toward a capacity for speech at the expense of the nose.

Budiansky's argument about domestication touches on the subject of abuse. Animals make a covenant with us, he says, hence we owe them respect on their own terms, even if they are dependent. This moral charge is similar to the one that should guide adults in their treatment of children; the very young are not our creations (even though we conceive, gestate, and give birth to them), yet they depend on us. Proper respect of animals would include kind treatment of those we eat (assuming that only some people will choose vegetarianism) or use for our own ends (such as racehorses), and an end to cruel or neglectful care of pets. Additionally, respect would include recognition that animals have inner lives, even if they cannot express themselves in human language.

As for *my* family dog, when I place her in the ten-thousand-year stream of domestication, I notice right away that her every "wild" action comes from a desire to catch my attention. She almost insists on covenant. Perhaps she wouldn't have been the most desirable of pups to humans at the dawn of civilization. Budiansky speculates that early humans preferred docile canines, and killed or drove off the most aggressive ones, a practice that shaped domesticated traits. On the other hand, Laska is very different from the half-wolf we pass on our daily walks. The owner keeps a head collar on the animal, like the one that Vivian made Laska wear in our last obedience class. As the wolf-dog pads along with a rangy motion, his tail floating out behind him, he observes the world coolly. I can sense the wildness in that dog, as if his rough, ragged pelt carried the scent of snow draped on fir tree branches. Budiansky explains that wild animals walk differently from domesticated ones: "The tracks of wild animals such as wolves and foxes move in straight and purposeful lines; at the trot, each hind foot is cautiously placed exactly in the spot where the corresponding front foot first fell. Dog and cat tracks are a testimony to carefree fearlessness. They meander, circle, zigzag, and drag; the hind feet sloppily miss the mark" (34).

When Laska and I take a walk, she often shuffles carelessly along beside me, her nails scraping the sidewalk. This particularly happens when she is tired or hot. Her gait then indicates an absence of watchfulness and signals her domesticity. True, there is an edge of wildness to Laska, but my inner turbulence may well have interfered with her becoming a docile dog. Budiansky would do well to look into the ways the human psyche shapes the animals who choose us as their stewards.

OCTOBER 15

I AM sitting at the kitchen table, fiddling with my napkin. Merle just called to find out how Laska and I are doing. We missed last week because Levin and Michelle were visiting and this week I am flying to Washington, D.C., as a consultant on a collaborative book project about the evolution of obstetric care. Then I travel to Brandeis University to speak in a class that is reading *Bearing Meaning,* and to give a colloquium. "It's just as well we can't get together," Merle says. "You might need a break from our meetings; I get the feeling you think I am trying to control you."

I have never said as much to Merle but her understanding of me doesn't depend on words. In a recent phone conversation I let slip that I do not keep Laska on her leash at Camel's Hump. Although my tone of voice was perfectly normal, I felt defiant of Merle's earlier advice to keep Laska leashed whenever I take her for a walk.

"Perhaps we should interrupt our regular meetings for now," Merle continues. "You can call if you need me; usually I can come right over."

I thank Merle for her generosity over the last months and promise to stay in touch. When I get off the phone I feel a small current of fear but also excitement over Laska and me being on our own.

OCTOBER 16

THE leaves are "past peak," according to the Vermont Fall Foliage Hot Line, which I enjoy calling this time of year. Laska and I are on our way in the car to Vivian's house in Underhill; after I drop Laska off, I will go directly to the airport for a ten-day trip. I find it hard to imagine myself in a professional role. Since May when I stopped teaching, my wardrobe has consisted of jeans, Birkenstock sandals, and shirts with rips in them from Laska's teeth. Just now, I feel rather like a new mother who has trouble remembering what she was like before the baby came.

We pass a large maple tree in front of a dilapidated clapboard house that I've noticed before. No one is behind me so I slow the car to look at the tree; vivid reddish orange leaves lie on the ground in a circle around its trunk. The tree stands naked, its dark branches forming an intricate pattern against the gray sky. The maple's revealed form seems like the truth of the tree, and its unadorned strength gives me courage to take this trip without worrying so much about what to wear and how to act. However, I am not reassured when I think about the long separation from Laska. Will our mutual goodwill fall away like the maple leaves, as it did after she was spayed?

Laska sits in the hatch with her back to me. In the rearview mirror I watch her turn her head in search of interesting sights on either side of the road.

"Look," I say, "horses."

Off to our left, two chestnut workhorses, perhaps Suffolk Punch, with cream-colored manes and tails stand nuzzling each other's necks. Already, their coats are shaggy in preparation for winter. Laska spots them and stands up excitedly, her tail wagging in circles; she watches until they disappear from view.

"You've got good concentration," I tell Laska, "and so I want you not to forget me when I'm away. Just remember that we'll stay linked the whole time."

Once we pull up at Vivian's house, I make Laska sit before she jumps out of the hatch. With her leash around my wrist, I take out a brown paper bag stuffed with her fleecy blanket, fleecy duck, bone, cheese, and instructions about when to feed her, the vet's and my phone numbers, and how often she needs to pee and poop. Laska has stayed with Vivian before, but so many dogs pass through Vivian's house that she can't be expected to remember details about their care. I know that Vivian would never allow Laska to pull on the leash the way she is doing as we approach the house. Vivian opens the door, smiles with that foxlike look of hers, and says, "Laska, how nice to see you." Laska leaps up at Vivian, despite my efforts to keep my puppy by my side. Vivian says, "Off!" firmly but cheerfully, and takes the brown bag from me.

"I'll put her next to Danny," Vivian says, and shows me the crate intended for Laska.

Danny, Vivian's little black griffon that Laska played with last time she was here, stands eagerly on slightly bowed legs watching our approach. I put Laska's fleecy blanket inside the crate and lure her in with a treat. The crate is not high and Laska stands head level with her shoulders, looking up at me; the crescent-moon whites of her eyes show, and my heart suddenly hurts. "Just remember, we'll stay linked the *whole* time," I say, though I'm not sure whether I'm talking to Laska or to myself.

"She'll be fine," Vivian says.

"I know," I answer. "I just wish I could explain that I'll be back."

Vivian sees me to the door and the car feels empty when I get inside it. I drive away with a curiously light feeling that is not altogether unpleasant.

OCTOBER 23

I AM in Washington, D.C., but one modern hotel is so much like another, I could be anywhere in the United States. Elaborate chandeliers cast glittery light on the conference room. I lean back in a chair upholstered with black vinyl and rub my eyes, which feel dry and itchy from the closed-air system. Robbie Davis-Floyd, a cultural anthropologist who wrote a brilliant book about obstetrical care in the United States, sits beside me. Robbie is a Texan and puts herself together in a traditionally feminine way. Her rayon dress sports a large red and orange floral design, a long string of pearls circles her neck, her hair is cut in what I think of as a country-and-western style (long in the back and short in the front). I, in contrast, am wearing a skirt suit of gray, black, and tan striped linen, a white shirt with a broad collar, and a brown tie. A dozen or so people sit around the large, rectangular conference table, most of them women, several of whom have traveled from England, Europe, or Canada. The clothing styles range between the extremes of my and Robbie's attire. The midwives present favor a feminine style (long skirts and loose, flowing tops), the academics a more gender-neutral look. Perhaps Robbie and I have dressed tongue-in-cheek. Her flowery style hides a keen, analytical intellect; my tailored getup contradicts my presentation. I have just finished arguing somewhat passionately that the feminist concept of "patriarchy as a social institution" can help us understand the distortions of contemporary childbearing practices. Why would I wear masculinized clothes (a reverse version of dressing in drag) while defending such an idea?

I open the floor up for questions. Robbie interjects: "Robbie, my alter-ego, is very modest. I want you to know that she has written an award-winning book, *Bearing Meaning,* that would deepen your understanding of her talk."[9]

My editor at University of Illinois Press chose Robbie as the anonymous reader for *Bearing Meaning,* and Robbie's strong advocacy made its publication possible. Breaching academic tradition, she revealed her identity to me—this was back in 1994. Since that time Robbie and I have become collegial friends and have discovered that the coincidences go beyond our common nicknames and scholarly interests. Robbie loves horses as much as I do; like me, her favorite song as a child had been "Don't Fence Me In." However, besides the fifteen-year age difference (I am the elder), there are other disparities. After spending the war years in Texas, I grew up in a New York apartment, dreaming about horses. Robbie spent much of her youth riding on the plains of Wyoming from dawn to dusk (the very state where my favorite book *Thunderhead* took place). To make the story even more enchanting, Robbie's pony, Spot, wore a red bridle and saddle decorated with silver fittings.

I thank Robbie for mentioning my book and ask again if there are any questions. A tall, slender young woman whose translucent skin shows color easily begins. "While I appreciate your overall analysis, I don't think that the word 'patriarchy' is a good choice. Feminists nowadays use terms like 'male advantage,' which I think is a more accurate descriptor."

"I agree," says a plain-looking Dutch woman, also considerably younger than myself.

"'Patriarchy' was used when feminist scholarship began. More recent research favors a more nuanced approach."

Several other women concur, and the critique proceeds in a spirited manner. To me, these young women (I am the oldest in the group) are afraid of using a provocative term. Eager to appease those in power, who are after all mostly men, the new crop of feminists tones down their language. Is their reticence due to fear of losing social ground that women have gained over the last twenty-five years, thanks to the efforts of earlier feminists?

I listen quietly and when the objections end, I say, "I am acquainted with your critique, although I have to say I don't agree with it. I like the term 'patriarchy' because it gives a sense that this social institution is ancient, dating back to the very beginnings of Western civilization. 'Male advantage' lacks a historical dimension."

Afterward the tall woman, Susan Erikson, comes up to me, high color in her cheeks. "Please forgive me for being critical just now," she says. "You and your generation of feminists are my foremothers; my generation stands on your shoulders. I am in my thirties and can sympathize with how you must feel. As an anthropology graduate student, I have had the experience of younger feminists in the field telling me that my ideas are not current."

"I appreciate your challenge," I say, "and I'm not upset." My reassurance isn't entirely honest. I actually feel somewhat shocked; never before has anyone objected to my use of the word "patriarchy." Later I can talk to Robbie about the attack; she shares my fondness for the p-word. To Susan I say, "Well, if I am your foremother, then that makes you my intellectual daughter."

Susan smiles so warmly that I give her a hug. "What you say means a lot to me," she replies, and to my surprise her eyes fill with tears. She explains, "I don't have such a happy relationship with my real mother."

"I know what that's like," I reply. I take a copy of *Bearing Meaning* out of my bookbag and write on the subtitle page, "To my intellectual daughter, Susan, with respect and affection, Robbie."

OCTOBER 27

THE conference trip helps me remember that I am more than a dog owner of uncertain ability. Before Laska, I didn't understand when a new mother told me that she wanted a vacation from her child. I couldn't imagine being physically distant from Levin when he was a baby. Maybe that was because I nursed him for three-and-a-half years; also my part-time job varied my day.

When I get home from the airport, I drop off my suitcase and drive right out to Vivian's to pick up Laska; I call ahead and, when I arrive, Vivian has Laska on her leash.

"Hi," Vivian says, as she lets me in the front door. Vivian holds Laska firmly so that my puppy can't jump at me, the way she did at Vivian when I dropped her off.

"Sit!" Vivian says, with such authority that I want to obey her myself. Laska sits smartly, but I notice that she is focused on me, more than the last time I picked her up. When Vivian gives Laska over to me, my puppy bestows a few quicksilver licks on my hand, wriggling all over. I put my foot on her leash near the collar so that she is forced to lie down.

"How did Laska do?" I ask.

"She was not too unruly this time," Vivian says. "Also, Laska seemed to expect you to come after a few days, the way you usually do. When you didn't show up, she got a bit mopey, but Danny cheered her up."

Gratified that Laska missed me, I take her belongings, thank Vivian, and drive home. When Laska and I get in the house I try to take off her prong collar, and she gets into her teeth routine. I forget that she may be excited—forget, too, that she did seem happy to see me at Vivian's. I tap the top of her nose firmly, as I've seen Merle do. This rebuke seems to impress my puppy, perhaps because I am not in an angry state, and she quiets down and allows me to remove her leash. Later in the afternoon I feel compelled to call Merle to give her a report on Laska's and my progress. I say, "Prior to this trip Laska has stayed at Vivian's only for long weekends. Maybe after spending over a week there Laska decided that I'm not so bad after all and minded me when we got home."

"Dogs don't think as you imagine they do," Merle answers. "Laska isn't making comparisons. The trip gave you confidence and Laska is calmer as a result."

Perhaps Merle is right, although I wouldn't rule out the effect of Vivian's discipline. Cass and Aaron tell me that Eli comes back from Vivian's better behaved also.

OCTOBER 30

I stand in front of a six-gallon carboy of spring water that sits on the kitchen floor and pour myself a glass of water, using the battery operated pump. It is morning and I have on a T-shirt nightgown that ends just above the knee. Laska walks behind me on her way to her fleecy blanket by the radiator. As she passes by, she casually licks the back of my knee, the same spot she crashed into the day we took a walk with Cass and Eli.

I turn and say, "Laskali, thank you for the lick."

Settled on her blanket, my puppy looks up at me and thumps her tail.

November 1997

Reconciliation

NOVEMBER 1

SHATTERED pumpkins litter the grass along the sidewalk. I don't remember this prank being so much in fashion when Levin was young. Laska profits, carrying a large orange segment all the way home from downtown; when I let her out in the yard with it, she gobbles up the whole thing. Now, back inside the house, she lies down cautiously on her haunches in the kitchen; her belly is so swollen that I feel foolish for having let her eat it all.

I sit at the kitchen table, my favorite spot to read, and persuade myself not to worry about Laska's pumpkin consumption. The phone rings.

"Hey, Mom."

"Hi, Lev, how are you?"

"I'm OK, but there's some bad news." Levin lowers his voice. "Grandma broke her hip."

The words rush at me too fast. To slow things down, I foolishly repeat what he said. "Broke her hip?"

"Yeah. I drove Grandma and Grandpa in their car from New York to Boston for a bar mitzvah. While I visited my dad, they took the car. They got lost, the way they always do, and when Grandma got out of the car to ask directions, her foot got caught in her pocketbook strap. She fell down on the sidewalk and broke her hip."

"That's awful," I say. I forget all about the more than three-year estrangement from my parents, adding, "I'll call her right away. Where is she?"

"At the Newton Wellesley Hospital," Levin replies. "Arthur called"—Levin often calls my parents by their first names, Arthur and Anita—"and me and Eric drove right out there from Cambridge. As soon as I walked in the room, Arthur looked at me and said, 'You should never have left us.' Like it was all my fault."

Touched by the couplet "me and Eric," a phrase Levin has used to refer to himself and his father since childhood, and appalled by my parents' putting the blame for the accident on him, I say, "Oh, Lev, it *wasn't* your fault. You had a right to visit your father. Besides, don't Arthur and Anita still drive their car?" I was a little out of date as to their habits.

"Yeah, they drive up to their house in Connecticut all the time and lots of other places." His voice sounds dispirited, as if everything between him and his grandparents is ruined.

"So you see, it's not as if they needed you there. 'You never should have left us,'" I say, and as I quote my parents my heart fires up with anger. "That's the way they feel about anyone who wants to have a life separate from them. Try not to feel guilty," I add. "You look after them in New York; you are a good grandson."

"I have been," Levin says sadly. "Eric spoke up for me and said that Arthur shouldn't blame me."

"Good for him." I was surprised. In conflicts, Eric tends to appease rather than to confront. I suddenly remember about my mother and say, "I'll call Anita if you give me the number."

"Don't say anything about what I told you."

"I won't, I'll just ask how she's doing."

Levin gives me the phone number and we say goodbye.

My sense of the injustice done to Levin does not abate. Here are my parents blaming yet another generation for their misfortunes. Then I try to focus on my mother—the accident was one she dreaded. Her own mother had broken her hip in old age, and for reasons I'm not clear about, the mishap contributed to her death.

I dial the number that Levin gave me. My father picks up the phone.

"Hi, Dad, it's Robbie."

"Anita, it's Robbie," my father says, and I can hear him choke up with tears.

"Levin called to tell me that Mom broke her hip."

"Yes, Mummy and I were going to a bar mitzvah and we got lost. My knees were bothering me so she got out of the car to ask directions. Next thing I knew she went flying."

"I'm so sorry, Dad." "Went flying" is a family phrase usually reserved to describe my father's tendency to trip, fall, and end up in the Emergency Room.

"They operated the next day, put in a titanium hip ball, and so far, so good." Then he whispers into the phone, "I'm worried about blood clots." My father's medical training causes him to imagine possibilities that wouldn't occur to a layperson.

"Try not to worry, Dad, it doesn't help anything," I say, and feel as if I can see the fear on his face.

"We'll be taking her back to New York in an ambulance. It's so damn expensive. But what can you do?"

"Maybe health insurance will pay for it," I reply, amused over his Depression-mentality concern about money at such a time.

"I don't know, I can't think straight right now. Would you like to say hello to your mother?"

"Sure," I reply. Suddenly nervous, I fiddle with the pepper shaker on the kitchen table.

"Hi, Rob?" my mother says. Just as in the past, she seems to acknowledge me as a question. Her voice sounds flat but surprisingly strong.

"I'm sorry about your hip."

"I tell you, bad things happen faster than good things."

"I guess that's true," I reply; her wry tone reassures me that she's all right.

"The doctors say I can go back to New York, into a rehab hospital for a few weeks, and then home. Over a bar mitzvah, no less. Some mitzvah," she says, playing on the Hebrew word's meaning, which is "blessing."

"Well, you still have your sense of humor, that's something."

"Thanks for calling," my mother says, signaling a wish to end the conversation.

"I'll call tomorrow. Keep getting better," I say, and hang up.

I put my coat on and invite Laska to join me in the yard. She trots along the fence line as she sniffs at the bare ground. Unable to follow my own advice to Levin, I feel that I'm to blame for my mother's broken hip. *I* am the one who should never have left my parents. Look at the sacrifice she made, injuring herself, to get me to communicate with them again; this is the first conversation we've had in more than three years. I forget all about Laska and go back into the house, as if to escape my thoughts. In a moment, Laska whines at the door to come in. "I'm sorry," I say, as she wriggles through the slightly opened door. "I'm trying to get away from myself, not you."

NOVEMBER 4

THIS morning Laska let me talk on the phone without jumping and nipping. On our afternoon walk she licks the hand of a little girl on Church Street, though after a while she begins nipping the child. I even walk all the way down to Lake

Champlain with Laska on a slack leash. She stays right by my side. Her favorite place to accost me used to be outside the Nickelodeon movie theater on our way home. Perhaps the place exuded an energy because of the films it shows, with the customary amounts of violence. Today she doesn't seem to even think of jumping on me and I don't have to bribe her with treats. When we get home, I try to pat her out of gratitude; she leaves my side and comes back with her fleecy potholder in her mouth, as if to keep herself from biting me.

I can see my puppy is going to be fine in every respect, except that she still eats her poops. Nothing has worked. I actually have been thinking of calling a dog psychic as a last resort. Perhaps if someone could speak to Laska herself about the problem, she would change her ways. Her behavior dissolves boundaries that should, in my view, be honored. And it is not just me. Judaism is much concerned over the boundaries between the contaminated and the uncontaminated. I understand the Buddhist idea that birth, death, and regeneration are a continuum—the rose is the garbage and the garbage is the rose, but no one would suggest putting garbage in a vase and setting it on the kitchen table.

NOVEMBER 5

I NEED Alice Miller's help after my mother's accident. From my earliest years I was held responsible for my parents' well-being; now, I find it hard to maintain the conviction that I am not the cause of my mother breaking her hip. I turn to Alice Miller because she is my "enlightened witness." In her book *Banished Knowledge: Facing Childhood Injuries* Miller uses the term to describe someone who does "not shrink from unequivocally taking the side of the child and protecting him from power abuse on the part of adults." Miller even faults herself as an inadequate advocate of the child: "In leafing through my early books, I am struck by my constant efforts to avoid blaming parents. . . . Today I see the situation differently. It is still not my aim to reproach unknown parents, but I am no longer afraid to entertain, and express, the thought that parents are guilty of crimes against their children, *even though* they act out of an inner compulsion and as an outcome of their tragic past."[1]

One of the last times I visited my parents in New York, I found a letter I wrote to my father when I was nine years old. He had been hospitalized with pneumonia. The letter shows my fear of losing him (of the two parents, he was my shelter) and guilt that I caused his illness:

> Dear Daddy: I am very, very worried about you and I miss you very very much. Get rid of that stinky old germ real quick, so you can come up to

> the country and be with me. I sent the book New York 22 with mommy to give to you. I hope you enjoy it.
>
> Get a lot of rest so you can get better real soon. Even though you are in a hospital and you are getting the very best of care I cannot help worrying a big much.
>
> I was a real bad girl when I was griping because I could not have ice cream. I feel very bad because I made you get upset.
>
> Please get better real real quick so I can see you again. I gave mommy a kiss to give to you, and send one back to me.
>
> Loads and loads of love x x x x Robbie and Karen

At three, at nine, at fifty-six, my guilt persists. My mother has suffered an injury associated with aging. At this stage of her life oughtn't I forget about the past and forgive her and my father unconditionally? Alice Miller lists what she calls "pedagogic pronouncements" about forgiveness, notions that are "misleading and untrue yet . . . generally regarded as true because they have been around for so long" (154, 155). These moral pronouncements include:

> I am sure that was hard for you, but then it's so long ago. Isn't it time to forget?
>
> Your hatred isn't good for you; it poisons your life and prolongs your dependence on your parents. Only when you become reconciled with your parents will you be free of them.
>
> Try to see the positive aspects too: Didn't the parents whom you now call bad pay for your studies? Aren't you being unfair? (154)

Courageously, Miller challenges such commonplace assumptions, held even by most therapists. She says, "Since, to me, therapy means a sensory, emotional, and mental discovery of the long-repressed truth, *I regard the moral demand for reconciliation with parents as an inevitable blocking and paralyzing of the therapeutic process*" (154; Miller's emphasis).

Miller concludes *Banished Knowledge* with an impassioned "nonpedagogic pronouncement" that goes against the grain of our entire cultural heritage: "The notion, that parents must never be blamed no matter what they have done, has caused untold damage. Let us look at reality. With the act of conception, parents enter on a commitment to care for the child, to protect him, to satisfy his needs, and not to abuse him. If they fail to fulfill this obligation, they actually remain in some degree indebted to the child, just as they would remain indebted to a bank after taking up a loan. They remain liable, regardless of whether or not they are aware of the consequences of their actions" (142).

Alice Miller helps me realize that I must not forsake myself for my parents. For one thing if my parents arouse troubled feelings in me I might take them out on Laska, a pattern I am trying to break. Alice Miller teaches me that getting well can't be rushed; she didn't work free from her past until she was nearly sixty.

I am talking to my parents; that is a step toward reconciliation. Actually, from the time I learned about my mother's accident, I was calling every day. Eventually I told my father that my phone bill was getting out of hand, and now he has been calling me daily. A visit can wait until Thanksgiving.

NOVEMBER 6

DUSK comes early and the smell of woodstove smoke seeps into the kitchen from outdoors. I gather my plate and silverware after supper, and start to get up from my chair; as I do, Laska comes up to me and presses her chin down on my leg. At first I ignore her because I want to finish with the evening meal. She persists. I put the dishes back on the table and reach down for her. She allows me to scratch her around her muzzle and under the neck. Then she buries her head in my flannel shirt, and nuzzles back and forth as if the soft cloth were her mother's side. She curves her body in a C shape between my legs, and tilts her face upwards as I rub her chest, my hands drawn to the warmth of her body near the heart.

NOVEMBER 12

IT gets dark early, but Laska attracts attention even in the absence of sunlight. This evening a passerby on Church Street who observes Laska sitting at the curb comments, "What a well-behaved dog!"

Soon after, a woman wheeling a baby carriage says, "What a beautiful dog!" as Laska prances beside me, head high, her thought furrow accentuated in the light from a store window. At almost a year, she is close to her full height, muscular, yet delicately built. Like her body, her head is graceful, though still with a broad forehead and square muzzle. She resembles Labs of thirty or more years ago, which is why I gave her one early nickname, "Lockerbie Lady Laska," after the older line of the breed I had admired in books about the history of Labrador retrievers.

Part of our daily walk includes a stop at Bone Appetite, a store full of yuppie pet delights. Tonight, on the way in, Laska grabs a beige rubber doorstop; it is the one plain item amidst extravagant dog and cat gifts such as a box of biscuits shaped like cigars, a gumball machine filled with treats that a dog can activate with a tap of the paw, and ceramic dishes decorated with the image of a dog.

I say, "Drop it!" and Laska gives up the doorstop, but then she heads for the gumball machine; her legs splay every which way as she pulls me after her. She knows that uneaten treats often lie in the little tray beneath the spout. I get her back to my side and we walk, more or less, to the glass cabinet filled with delectables at the back of the store. There are "Great Dane" biscuits in the shape of a bone, small, round crunchy "cinnamon rolls," and seasonal turkey-shaped treats. I'm headed for the free samples on the cabinet counter; the saleswoman seems to be in the storage room. Without my asking, Laska sits and I say, in a recent term of affection, "That's my good girl, that's my Laski." She trembles with excitement as I take two broken pieces, instead of one, of a peanut butter treat (all the treats at Bone Appetite are made with natural ingredients) and give them to her.

NOVEMBER 14

I DRIVE home from Daniel's office in Bristol, a rural area forty miles from Burlington. Though summer's green and even the fall leaves are gone, color surrounds me—burnt and raw sienna, burnt and raw umber, ochre, gray brown and red brown, mauve. I need a painter's chart to name them all. There are textures too—high grasses with feathery tops, sheared cornfields with stubble poking up, low-lying bushes with tangled dry branches, meadows with pale dead stalks flattened to the ground. Behind the fields to the east rise the Green Mountains, a gray brown dusky red, their upper half catching the last sun. The Adirondack Mountains in the west cast a long shadow over the Green Mountains' lower portion. Above the mountains float clouds whose names, like the paint colors, I suddenly want to know. Some contain crests like tendrils of a boy's or girl's hair in a Minoan fresco. Round puffy clouds shake apart at the edges like cotton batten. Dark gray, blue gray, pink gray, and blue pink clouds layer the air above the mountains, catching the sun differently. I have trouble keeping the car on the road, my eyes are so given to looking.

It would be *dayenu* (enough) to see that much. But as I go up a rise, Camel's Hump comes into view. Higher than the shadow of the Adirondack Mountains encroaching on the Green Mountains as the sun sets, Camel's Hump shines a hot yet snowy pink, as if aroused by some greater radiance. Just so, Moses' face appeared when he descended Mt. Sinai after being in God's presence. The mountain shines like a newborn baby that pinks up after the gray hue (the color of a baby before it breathes) leaves. God is a Rock, Deuteronomy says. Tonight at dusk, which, like dawn, is a sacred time in Judaism, I glimpse God in a mountain's radiant breathing stone.

NOVEMBER 15

I AM sitting at my desk enjoying the sound of the rain as I write. Laska interrupts my mood; she stands on her hind legs, places her front legs on the low windowsill, and barks at a mother who has come to pick up her baby at the family day-care center across the street. Then the phone rings; it is my father. After we exchange hellos, he asks: "How is your health?" Until now our conversations have focused on my mother.

"It could be better," I reply, a little stiffly. "I work on it all the time, but there are modalities I could try if they were covered by health insurance."

"I'd be happy to pay for doctor visits," my father offers.

His words are a well-meant trap; I need my parents' financial assistance but can't afford to become dependent on them again. Our history shows that they might withdraw help abruptly, complain that the amount I need is a hardship, and delay sending funds. When I asked for the money they had promised, my mother complained, "All you ever call about is money."

"Thanks, Dad," I say, "but I could never go back to that system of reimbursements. It just wasn't working."

"I agree," he says, though I'm sure he doesn't know why I disliked it. I wonder why he thought it didn't work, but all my life he so often responded to my questions with silence that I don't ask.

"And the way it ended so abruptly, that was terrible," I continue. The words carry me along, but I feel awkward speaking about myself to him, after an estrangement of three-and-a-half years. "I was so sick in the summer of 1994 I couldn't walk. You don't just cut someone off like that. Everyone knows how fundamental economic security is to a person's well-being. If you want to stop helping someone, you need to talk it over and make a plan."

My father remains silent; maybe he doesn't remember what my needs were back then. I decide to remind him; as writers are fond of saying, everything is in the detail. "When you cut me off, there was no clapboarding on one side of the house where the carpenter had found dry rot. For a whole winter the exposed part was only covered with plastic; in the spring I had new clapboarding put on to close the hole, but the dry rot was still inside the wall and the clapboards still aren't primed or painted. There were two other big problems. The house hadn't been painted properly when I bought it, and the paint was flaking off the clapboards. Also, the front porch sagged so much I was told it could collapse.

Something else, too; I had to give up health treatments that weren't covered by insurance. I stopped getting massages even though they help connective tissue remain flexible in people with rheumatoid arthritis."

Over the past three and a half years I haven't let myself think about these derelictions. I am telling my father about them in the past tense, but nothing has changed. With unexpected confidence, perhaps born from the time apart, I say, "I can't go back to the old way, but if you ever wanted to give me a gift, I would be very grateful."

"A chunk of money," my father offers, and his voice takes on the authority of a man of means. "I'd like you to have that, and I'll talk to Mummy about it."

My mother is likely to dissuade him. In the past, I blamed her; with new insight, I realize that he is equally responsible. After all, *he* wrote the letter that cut me off.

When my mother comes to mind, I realize how atypical this conversation with my father is. He rarely speaks to me on his own; either he doesn't call at all or my mother monitors what he says on an extension phone. Surely, he's unconsciously taking advantage of my mother's weakened condition to talk to me. She restricts my father's access to me, apparently out of jealousy that I have yet to understand. Perhaps I fear her retaliation for this unsanctioned conversation; or I fear intimacy with my father, since his untutored feelings often engulfed me as a child; or maybe I don't want to be part of a crazy triangle (after all, it should be normal and natural, not a clandestine act, for a father to speak to his daughter). For whatever reason, I put a stop to our conversation. "This isn't such a good time to talk about these things, with Mom and her hip," I say.

"This *is* a good time to talk about it," he replies, "and it helps me understand." I want to know *what* he understands, but I do not ask.

After we get off the phone, I cannot quiet the anxiety that his unexpected recognition of me will vanish, even though I already know that it will. I notice as never before that I oscillate between fear that my father will become too close or too far away from me. Why is he the way he is? As if summoned by my question, a flashback from my parents' last visit to Vermont, before the estrangement, rises into consciousness.

▼▼▼

One afternoon midway in their visit my father and I drive down to the camera store to buy film. It is a hot summer day, and he keeps the windows of the Cadillac closed so that we can enjoy the air-conditioning. The fresh Vermont air is a metaphor for new beginnings, and I hope for a closer relationship with my mother and father than we've had in the past. In this spirit I decide to bring up a subject my father and I have never discussed. When my sister and I developed breasts, my father stopped hugging us and we interpreted his physical recoil in ways that compromised our development as young women. I fled my changing body through overeating; in late adolescence and adulthood, convinced that I was "too much," I tirelessly sought the company of tall men. Today for the first time I decide to take my father's side; perhaps my empathy will open a door to discussing why he acts either too hot or too cold toward me.

We drive the short distance to the photo store in silence. As we draw close to the parking lot, I rashly begin to talk. "Dad, I used to be angry at you for rejecting me and Karen when we became young women. Now that I've had a child of my own, a son, I understand. One day I looked at Levin and saw that he had become an attractive young man. I could have turned away from him, the way you did with us. But I belong to a generation that explores emotions—we probably do it too much." I look over to see if my father enjoys my self-deprecation, but he peers straight ahead, as if parking the car demands his full attention. Recklessly I continue, "In any event I realized that nothing inappropriate needed to happen between us. And so I didn't need to turn away from him."

I stop talking, and my father finishes parking the shiny black Cadillac given to him by a patient, perhaps as barter for dental work. My father loves cars. Long ago, when customers would come into my grandfather's candy store in Jersey City to buy cigars, my father would sneak into the idling parked cars and drive them around the block. I turn to look at my father and find him staring straight ahead, breathing rapidly. Abruptly, he fumbles with the electronic levers that control the windows and opens all four of them, even though it's hot outside and we are not planning to stay. He looks utterly trapped. For a moment the panic that lies in wait whenever my father gets too close to his feelings reveals itself to me. I don't know how to talk about his fear. We continue in silence until I finally say, "It's hot out there, but I guess we can't get the film unless we leave the car. You probably meant to close the windows but you opened them by mistake." Is my father relieved that I gave him an excuse for his frightened reaction? If so, he gives no sign as he closes the windows and turns off the ignition. He opens his door, I mine, and we climb out of the Cadillac into the steamy air.

▲▲▲

NOVEMBER 16

FIRST snow of winter. Laska asks to go out to pee but stops at the opened door to look at the changed, whitened world. Half of her body still inside the house, she puts out one paw and scrapes at the snow gingerly. As she moves slowly out onto the deck, she picks her feet up like a cat, her back hunched and tail drooped.

"Do you remember?" I ask her, because this is the season in which she was born.

She walks down the steps into the yard and puts her nose in the snow. When she lifts her head again her muzzle is white; white coats her back, too, from the lightly falling snow. Another poke of her nose into the snow and a skittish jump—this looks like *fun.* I run to put my boots and coat on. By the time I'm back, she's tearing around the yard. "You go run around. Be a crazy girl!" I cry out. She dips her nose into the snow, pushing like a snow plow, then explodes into wild circles of running, her tail curved against her body, legs splaying out every which way, back twisting in midair as she angles a turn, whites of her eyes showing. She spots her large, soccer-sized red plastic ball and pushes against it with her chest, back and forth in the yard, leaning her head on it sideways, fixing the ball with one eye, growling, trying to get her teeth into it. I tramp around after Laska in my big felt-lined boots. Grasses poke up through the snow like spring shoots; how joyful it is to be with her at this moment. After a short time she runs to me, leaps up with excitement but doesn't bite my jacket or my hands. We've gotten to be what Merle calls "pals."

NOVEMBER 21

I'M sitting at my kitchen table with a list of questions about Laska in front of me, and my watch. A few weeks ago I read a newspaper article about an animal communicator and decided to make a telephone appointment (secured with my credit card); the session will be thirty-five minutes long. At the appointed time I dial up the psychic, whose name is Crystal.

"Should I bring my dog, Laska, into the room with me?"

"No need, she will be aware of all that we say."

On her own, Laska wanders into the kitchen and stands under the table where I sit, something I've never seen her do before.

"Tell me your dog's name, age, breed, and color and what you would like help with." Crystal has a down-to-earth, friendly voice with a trace of a rural accent.

"Her name is Laska, she is an eleven-month-old black Labrador retriever, and she eats her stools."

"Oh, Labs," Crystal says, her tone implying that Laska's habit is normal to the breed.

"The trouble is," I protest, "I have rheumatoid arthritis and there's a theory it's caused by microorganisms. I might be picking them up from Laska's saliva.

She mouths me a lot because she was weaned at three weeks. At least I think that is the reason." I pause, wondering how much to tell Crystal. I decide to give her a complete thumbnail sketch of my life with Laska. "We got off to a difficult start," I continue. "Laska used to bite me and jump on me, which rattled and upset me and sometimes I hit her. Maybe she eats her poops out of stress."

Crystal says, "Let me speak to Laska." My puppy still stands quietly under the table, as if listening.

"Should I put the phone next to her ear?"

"No, you can keep it just where it is, she will hear me."

There is silence for some minutes, and then Crystal resumes speaking to me. "Laska says she loves you and is happy about the way things are now. She didn't know the poop eating was dangerous to *you.* She thought you wanted her to stop because it was dangerous to her, and she knew it wasn't. She says she wants to care for you and she will stop, though it might take a while."

Apparently Laska also communicated to Crystal about her biting, for Crystal continues, "Laska says her mother was taken away too soon but she is OK now. That's why she used to bite and jump."

The right side of my brain wants to believe that Laska conversed with Crystal. I especially like the part where my puppy said that she wanted to care for me. But the left side of my brain is skeptical: isn't everything that Laska allegedly said a version of what I had told Crystal myself?

Despite my doubts, I decide to ask Crystal a question that still troubles me about Sarah's death.

"Thanks for talking to Laska; it will be great if she gives up her habit, and I'm willing to wait. Addictions don't clear up overnight," I say, aware of my own eating disorder. "Since there's time left," I continue, "may I ask you a question about my previous dog, Sarah, who was also a black Lab?"

"Of course," Crystal replies sympathetically.

"Sarah died a natural death and I was with her through the whole experience. During all those hours she never looked at me, and I've never known why."

"Just a minute," Crystal says, and she falls silent.

With a shallow intake of breath I realize that Crystal has summoned Sarah for a reply.

After some minutes, Crystal says, "Sarah tells me that she didn't look at you as she was dying because it was hard for her to leave you."

I had thought this myself at the time, and so I didn't seek out her eyes, not wanting to impose my grief and fear on her.

Crystal continues, "But her body was failing. She says she feels that you think of her, and she is often with you." As Crystal tells me what Sarah said, I weep piteously, not even caring if what she says is true.

It might be true, though. I once asked Crow if she knew why Sarah didn't look at me, because my friend is a hospice care worker. Crow told me that dying people tend to look off into space rather than at those around them. She also said that people often die in the early hours of the morning. Apparently it is easier to depart when relatives, who usually want their loved ones to stay alive, are not around. Looking back on Sarah's death, I realize that each time I left Sarah's side to go to the bathroom, she let herself die a little more. This pattern suggests that it *was* hard for her to leave me; looking at each other would have made it worse.

Before we get off the phone, Crystal asks if there is anything else I want to tell Laska. I say, "Well, if she were less mischievous that would be nice, but I don't ask that of her. Everyone's entitled to something. She should just stop eating her poops, that's the important thing."

Again, silence as Crystal communicates with Laska, who went into the living room when I was talking about Sarah.

"Laska understands," Crystal tells me, and then our time is up.

Afterward, I walk into the living room to find that, as if by special permission, Laska grabbed my credit card, library card, and driver's license, which were all together in a little envelope on the living room table, and dented them sharply with her teeth.

NOVEMBER 22

JUST as my hand comes down to hit Laska on her muzzle, my puppy looks up at me, her crescent-moon eyes full of reproach.

Later, I sit in a synagogue pew at Shabbat services and ask myself why I hit Laska. True, she started the day by eating her poop, such a messy thing to do, but I'm not convinced by this reason. I listen to Cantor Aaron chanting in his deep voice and gradually am able to look more deeply at what happened. Ever since I told my father that it was too expensive for me to call every day, as I had been doing after my mother broke her hip, he telephoned me daily. Then, abruptly, he didn't call for a whole week. He stopped after I told him that I would be happy to come to New York for Thanksgiving, but that I planned to stay with my high school friend, Alicia. He cut me off the way he always had done whenever I did not behave as he wanted me to. My father is the reason I was angry at Laska today; I have to be very careful not to mix her up with him.

NOVEMBER 23

LAST night I dreamt that I saw my own conception. The fresh young egg chose a solitary sperm and took it into herself, and the genetic elements lined up and divided in a protoplasmic dance that was to become me. At the same time, I could see my parents as they lay on the floor of my father's office. My mother had told me about my conception. After their honeymoon, my parents had moved in with my father's parents, who lived in a small apartment behind my grandfather's candy store. Since they had no privacy, my parents went to my father's new dental office to make love. In the dream I saw his awkward plunging and her protective recoiling, a moment she would remember as being "knocked up," since I was conceived soon after they were married. "What did I know?" my mother often has said about the incident, referring to her dreamlike ignorance. Their drama was far away and separate from the drama of creation going on inside her body. Yet their lives would decisively stamp mine.

Beyond these fused beings (man and woman, sperm and egg) I noticed a third solitary element, my *soul.* I felt my soul enter the sperm and egg and saw that it wasn't created even by these seeds of new life. For the first time, I realized in every fiber of my being that my parents *do not own my soul.* It was a huge mistake, a deception they visited on me to make me feel that I belonged to them. My soul was sacred, as unblemished as the red heifer whose purity I had envied. I saw that my parents should have treated me respectfully, even though I had been in a peeing and pooping baby's body. There was no cause to feel shamed and humiliated. How *could* I have taken care of myself at that age? I needed them to care for me physically, but I also needed their respect. With new clarity I saw that I had no cause to feel guilt and responsibility for their unhappiness. I felt infinitely apart from them, yet not alone, embedded in what Rabbi Noah refers to each Shabbat morning as "the Holy One source of our being."

NOVEMBER 24

TONIGHT, at minyan service, I tell the rabbi that I will miss Shabbat service on Saturday because I am going to spend Thanksgiving with my parents. He raises his eyebrows and, out of habit, repositions the yarmulke on his head with one hand. He knows the visit is a big step for me, but he gives me no advice. I appreciate his silence, because he leaves what will happen up to me. Instead Rabbi Noah says, "I'm planning to ask the question in the discussion period, 'What is a person's birthright?' Do you have any thoughts about that?"

"Yes," I reply firmly, "a person's birthright is that her parents don't own her soul."

NOVEMBER 25

THIS morning when I awake, I stretch out crosswise on the bed and drop my head over the side to look for my puppy. The summer my parents cut me off I had an arthritis attack; bending my knees caused such pain that I had the short-legged bed elevated on three-foot-high cement blocks. Even though my knees recovered, I left the bed propped up, just in case. I see Laska, a black shape, curled tightly on her fleece-covered L. L. Bean bed that rests directly under mine. Last week I removed the nighttime crate she had slept in ever since I brought her home. She had been housetrained months ago (dogs regard crates as their den and tend not to eliminate in them), but I didn't trust her to behave when I was asleep. My worry was needless; when I slept, so did she (I still put her in her downstairs crate when I leave the house, though).

I call Laska over to me and watch as she rises, then drops her belly to the floor, rear end in the air, front legs extended. "What a good stretch!" I say.

Laska comes up to me. Her tail whirls like a propeller and she bangs her mouth against my cheek. I pull back onto the bed, sit up, and swing my legs over the side. She makes for my toes. I scoot one foot into a felt clog, but she grabs the other one and prances off into my writing room, which is next to the bedroom. I hobble after her and pull the shoe out of her mouth. Nowadays Laska appears mischievous to me rather than menacing.

I pack up my puppy's belongings, and we set out for Vivian's place, where Laska will stay while I'm away. I take the train to New York tomorrow afternoon. Patches of first snow cover the pale fields as we drive to Underhill, which is about forty-five minutes from Burlington. In the rearview mirror I see Laska; she faces the hatch window and braces herself against the upright section of the back seat. She shifts her weight from one front leg to the other two or three times until she feels firmly planted; I noticed this same back and forth motion when Laska first sat on my lap as a five-week-old puppy. I admire her simple act of stabilization and consider her to be an example for me to follow in New York. I want to remain balanced despite the shifting ground I will encounter when I reenter my parents' world.

When we reach Vivian's driveway, Laska loses her aplomb and barks wildly as she races from one side of the car to the other. I pull up to the house and go around to the hatch to bring Laska out. I ask her to sit and wait patiently for her to stop barking. As soon as she pauses, I praise her and bring her out, leash in my hand. As we approach the house I smell the fragrant scent of baked goods.

When Vivian answers the door, she has an apron on. She says, "I am in the middle of cooking for Thanksgiving, you'll have to forgive me."

"Oh, there's really nothing to say. You know Laska well."

Vivian takes Laska from me and puts her in the same crate she stayed in last time, alongside the tiny black griffon, Danny. Accustomed to the routine, Laska goes in willingly enough, but she turns around to face the metal door and holds my eyes with hers.

"Don't worry," I say to her, "we'll stay linked the *whole* time."

I still have to pack for my trip so I make myself turn away from Laska. I say goodbye to Vivian, who has returned to the kitchen. "Have a great Thanksgiving," she says, as she pours a bag of cranberries into a stainless-steel pot.

"You, too," I reply and let myself out of the house. As I drive home, the trip to New York enters my mind without any distractions. What will it be like? A few days ago, my mother got on the phone after I had been talking to my father. "What mischief have you been up to?" she asked.

"I don't understand what you are talking about," I replied, for the first time in my life suggesting that her assessment of me made no sense.

"What Arthur discussed with you on the phone just now."

"I was telling him that the award ceremony in Toronto was attended by two thousand people and projected onto two movie screens."

Perhaps the large audience and big screens shielded me from further belittling because her only reply was, "Oh." Our conversation ended soon after.

When I told Daniel the next day about what my mother said, he explained that the word "mischief" meant that I was escaping her control. Can I make her new perception my own?

NOVEMBER 27

THE taxi pulls up in front of my parents' apartment building that faces Riverside Drive Park in Manhattan. I did not rush to leave my friend Alicia's house this morning, and I will arrive while Thanksgiving dinner preparations already are under way. As the elevator ascends, childhood dreams of going through the roof or free-falling return to my mind. On the brass panel above the door, digits light up in red as the corresponding floor goes by; I want the trip over but am not eager for the arrival. Out of habit I stare at the brass-framed inspection certificate; it used to calm my fears, and the accustomed sound of a click as each floor goes by soothes me.

I get out on the fourteenth floor and press a new doorbell that makes a melodic sound. My sister answers the door. We both have plausible excuses for not seeing each other since 1993 in Vermont. I don't like to fly and Karen lives in California; for my sister's part, she finds it too hard, with a young son, to visit me when she comes east. But we both know that the estrangement between me and my parents affected everyone in our family.

My sister's and my births fixed our mother's view of us—I am a menace; Karen is the kindly one. "She popped out like bread from a toaster," is how my mother described Karen's birth. When my sister became pregnant in her midforties (she married at forty-two), my mother said, "I'd like to be reborn as Karen's baby." This wish echoed through Karen's and my childhoods; my mother wanted her children to take care of her. Although my mother favored Karen over me, she treated us more or less the same. And so, like me, Karen had turned to our father for love, and shared my fear of his emotional trespasses.

"Hi, Sis," Karen says as she opens the door, a phrase I never heard before. We exchange hugs, look at each other, hug again as our eyes fill with tears. It relieves me to see that Karen looks the same, dressed in a large T-shirt, black tights, white socks, and jogging shoes.

Levin comes to the door carrying his cousin, Matty, on his hip. My son is alone this Thanksgiving because Michelle went to visit her parents in Texas. "Hey, Mom," he says. I appreciate his casual greeting. He, at least, is someone I've seen recently. Long and thinned-out since I last saw him as a compact toddler, seven-year-old Matty stares at me with dark eyes; his wide mouth is open slightly. The changes in him show me how long the separation has lasted; still, his young face doesn't yet have any defining planes in the bone structure. I go up to the two of them, kiss Levin on the cheek, and ask Matty if he remembers "ahmwah." Invented by him, this word meant "kiss." I lean close, and to my surprise he repeats the word and presses his lips against my face.

I pull my suitcase into the apartment and take a look around. I have never seen my parents' newly renovated apartment, double the size of the one my sister and I grew up in. In the early nineties, my parents bought the two-bedroom apartment next door, with a layout that mirrored theirs, and connected the two. We are standing in an elegant foyer created from the two original ones. Two double-doored coat closets flank an entryway into the living room. The doors have heavy glass knobs, and interior lights turn on automatically when you open them. I hang up my coat and walk into a huge room that looks like a museum wing; Karen, Matty, and Levin follow me. In the old apartment my parents' art collection looked out of place, as if several different exhibits accidentally ended up in someone's living room. When you walked around in there, you were likely to bang your head against a mobile or trip over a large sculpture; the walls were hectic with floor-to-ceiling images. In the renovated apartment, every piece has its place and is shown off to advantage. Much of the furniture is new. I feel like a stranger, and in a certain sense I am.

"Wow!" I say, reverting to a 1960s exclamation.

"Quite something," Karen replies. "The renovation was a nightmare, but they are very happy with the way it turned out." She adds, "I'm going back to the kitchen. Mom and Dad are in the bedroom; Bill is in the study on the computer, naturally."

I walk through the dining room and into a large bedroom with wall-to-wall windows that overlook the Hudson River, offering a view of the George Washington Bridge. When my parents bought the additional apartment, I predicted that they would end up hanging out in the new bedroom around their card table, the way they did in the old place. "You grew up in small spaces; they feel cozy to you," I said. "What are you going to do with so much room? It might feel lonely." My assessment was accurate.

The same inexpensive card table stands at the foot of their side-by-side twin beds; as before, it is piled high with mail, magazines and newspapers. My mother sits on her bed leaning against a carved wood headboard, her legs extended in front of her. The rest of the bed is cluttered with new and old issues of the *New York Times.* Above the beds hangs a large Picasso print. A woman lies on her back, one arm languidly circles her head, and one fleshy leg crosses over the other; her pudenda presents itself frontally to the viewer. The image lends a bordello accent to the room that seems out of keeping with my parents' relationship. Long ago, when my mother returned from her summer in France with our downstairs neighbor, I watched with a twelve-year-old's eyes to see how she would greet my father. Why had she gone away for a whole summer? Did she still love him? My mother walked gingerly down a ramp from the ocean liner, looking stylish in a trim dark blue suit I'd never seen; when she reached her husband, she turned her head so that his eager kiss landed on her cheek. Today my mother wears a white blouse and black pants, her usual colors in recent years; a string of beads hangs from her neck, and a black bow holds her white hair back in a ponytail.

"Hi, Rob," she says in a flat tone.

"Hi," I reply. "How are you feeling and how is your hip?"

"I just want to shoot myself for falling down, that's all. You know the old joke, 'It only hurts when I laugh?' Well, this hurts when I sit, walk, and lie down."

"Mom, you shouldn't blame yourself; an accident is an accident. What does your doctor say about the pain?"

"That I can expect to be sore for some time."

"A colleague of mine had a knee replaced; it took months before the pain went away."

"You came all the way from Vermont to tell me this good news?"

I move close and kiss my mother's soft, lined face with the high cheekbones I did not inherit. All the while I can feel my father's eyes on me.

He sits in a comfortable steel-rimmed black leather chair that moves on wheels. As I walk toward him, he gets up with difficulty. Karen is right; she told me over the phone that he has become "rickety." My father is thinner and shorter than when I saw him last; he now is about my height. We meet halfway, and I notice that he balances unsteadily on deerlike legs. My sister also told me that my father suffers from arthritis in his knees. Magnified by his reading glasses, his eyes hold a childishly hopeful look; that hasn't changed.

"Good to see you," my father says, and his voice chokes with tears. He puts his long arms around me and plants a kiss on my mouth before I can turn my cheek. I smell Allenberry Pastilles on his breath. For years he has sucked on them to soothe his throat; he almost died during the Spanish flu epidemic in 1918, and the illness left his respiratory tract susceptible to infections. Piles of empty cough-drop tins clutter the bookshelves in the bedroom, saved for some imagined future use. "How do I look?" my father asks. "Like a Holocaust survivor?"

"Not at all, you still look like Dad."

"Did you hear that, Anita?"

"I heard," my mother answers, a touch of mockery in her voice.

I feel momentarily caught in the old triangle where my father recruits me to support him against my mother. Has she teased him about his weight loss? All through the years my mother had made fun of my father's thin legs, a physical trait he felt self-conscious about. She'd call him a *langa lux,* Yiddish for a "long drink of water." I disengage myself from my father's arms and say, "I'm going into the kitchen to help with dinner. We'll catch up later." As soon as the words are out of my mouth, I realize no one has asked me about myself.

I walk back through the dining room. The table is not yet set, and each of the antique wooden chairs with elegantly curved backs is covered with a dishcloth to protect the upholstery. I reach the kitchen, which is warm and fragrant from the roasting turkey. An industrial refrigerator with steel doors and an industrial stove flank the room; glossy gray marble counters, striated with pink, yellow, and white lines, surround a deep double sink. Karen's face is flushed from the heat as she cuts sweet potatoes and apples for a casserole. "Don't forget to put marshmallows on top," I say, remembering the Thanksgivings of our childhood.

"I'm not sure we have any," Karen replies.

"I don't know why I asked about them," I say. "I can't eat sugar anyhow."

Levin stands at the sink with a dishtowel tossed over his shoulder as he washes lettuce, arugula, and endive (his favorite). Matty bangs enthusiastically on an electronic keyboard in the museum-wing living room.

"What can I do to help?" I ask.

"Why don't you make salad dressing," Levin says, without turning his head. "You do it so well."

I busy myself squeezing lemons (I can't eat vinegar) and then add olive oil, salt, pepper, and dill to taste. I learn from Karen where to find the silverware and dishes, and I set the table. I want to remove the dishtowels from the chairs but decide against it; I do not want to aggravate my mother.

When dinner is ready, Bill emerges from the study, and my father walks slowly into the dining room alongside my mother, who limps with the aid of a prosthetic cane; its sturdy aluminum and rubber construction lack aesthetic grace. My heart contracts to see my parents so old and infirm.

My mother and father always sit at opposite ends of the table, with me next to my father and my sister next to my mother. Matty slides into a chair next to Levin, while Bill settles tentatively alongside me, as if he'd rather stand in the doorway—part of things, yet separate. My father stands up to slice "the bird," as he calls it, and he does a surprisingly good job, considering his age. We fill our plates; my father, who likes his food hot, begins to eat. "Dad, wait," I say, "let's offer a prayer before we start." I take his hand and Bill's and everyone around the table joins us. "Blessed Shekinah," I offer, "thank you for bringing us together this day, and please help my mother heal speedily and well." I glance at my mother; her face seems shut down, an expression New Yorkers assume as they walk among strangers on the street. I am dismayed by the chill her look creates in me, just as it used to when I was little. The prayer is over, and my father hastily returns to his food; we all dig in, chewing and swallowing. Minimal conversation accompanies a Kahn dinner. Karen encourages Matty to eat his turkey, not just sweet potatoes and buttered bread. "It's yukky," Matty protests, hunching his shoulders and screwing up his face.

"Do you want dessert?" Karen asks. Matty nods and takes a small forkful of turkey breast. "He can't just live on carbohydrates," Karen says to no one in particular as she heaps cranberry sauce on her plate.

Bill catches my attention with a question to my mother, whose withdrawn state holds us all hostage. "How's the stock market?" he asks. Like her father, my mother is financially astute and keeps daily track of the market.

Bill's query rouses my mother. She replies, wryly, "Do you have something to invest?"

My mother thinks that I lack savvy with money; however, back in the 1970s, I advised her to buy Hewlett-Packard, the company that makes electronic fetal heart monitors used on women in childbirth. She didn't listen to me and now the stock is thriving. I could tease her about this mistake, but I promised myself on the way to New York not to be provocative. I look over at Levin, who is watching Matty refuse a forkful of turkey from his mother. Matty pushes Karen's hand away, and the utensil clatters onto the table. "Remember last year when Matty hit Karen's nose by accident and she went to the hospital?" Levin says, laughing.

My father clears his throat and replies, "Usually I'm the one who ends up there." He's right. The last time my parents visited me in Vermont, he went to the hospital to have a sore toe checked out. A few years before that he tripped over the open stove door in my sister's home and went to the hospital.

Matty slips under the table and tickles my shin; he makes a yipping sound. "Laska, is that you?" I ask.

"You mean the scathing brute?" Levin says. I check the expression on his face. He is smiling, as if to say, "I'm sorry I once meant what I just said."

Despite his tacit apology, I reply earnestly, "Oh, no, Lev, Laska is turning out very well. I can prove it to you; I've got the evidence in a daily journal I'm keeping about me and her."

"You could publish that," Bill says, ever thinking about ways to make money. "Do you have a title?"

"I've thought of calling the story, 'My Puppy, Myself.'"

"That's a seller," Bill replies, with a trace of envy. "Don't tell anyone about your idea. They could steal it."

"At this point, it's far from being a book," I say.

"My daughter, the author," my father says proudly. My mother keeps her head down, face expressionless.

Even with second helpings, dinner is soon over. The absence of a sustained conversation, normal in my family, is one cause, but my mother's seemingly defiant refusal to engage is another. When she gets up and limps into the kitchen, using her cane, to put on the teakettle, my father leans toward me and in a low voice says, "Your mother has been depressed. See if you can talk to her."

I also promised myself on the trip here that I would not get drawn into the vortex of my parents' relationship. My mother's isolation grieves my father; in turn he calls upon me for help, as he has done ever since I was a child. Despite my resolve to remain disengaged, over tea and apple pie from the Fairway supermarket (topped with ice cream, my favorite, although all I can have is tea), I say, "Mom, you look really down." She doesn't answer.

It is audacious of me to address my mother directly about her feelings. She prefers to broadcast them silently. My father's request released frustration in me rather than compassion. Like Laska, I am bright with challenge; it is not right for my mother to spread a vapor of unhappiness over the meal. Karen gives me a warning look. Backing off, I resort to an old strategy, one that I've used throughout my life. I let my mother know that I am no more fortunate than she. "I can sympathize with you," I say, "because of my arthritis. It is hard to accept that your body has changed." Still no sign that my mother hears me; she keeps her head down and stares at her crumpled napkin. I remember that I neglected to acknowledge her feelings first; maybe doing that will rouse her. "It is normal to be depressed at first," I say, but I ruin the empathic gesture by lecturing her; my words and tone are less than sympathetic. I can't distinguish between my mother's present mood and her intractable unhappiness that clouded my childhood and adult life, and for which she seems to hold me responsible. "The thing to consider is how to enjoy life," I say, "even with your hip causing you pain and limiting your movement." I can't imagine that a pep talk persuades my mother any more than it does me. All she says, though, without looking my way, is, "Thanks for your advice."

Is there a hint of mockery in her voice? I can't tell, but her words feel like a turned back, and I stop talking. Mistrustful of what else I might say, I get up from the table and join Levin and Karen in the cleanup.

Later we all hang out in the living room as Levin and Matty play rowdy duets on the keyboard. My mother and father sit in twin slipcovered armchairs, their backs supported by pillows covered with sable fur. I'm restless to leave and tell them I don't want to travel late at night on the bus that takes me from midtown Manhattan to Greenwich Village, where my friend Alicia lives. Not long afterward I get up from the couch, hug and kiss everyone goodbye, and go into the foyer to get my coat. My father follows, head pitched slightly forward to steady his newborn-foal walk. He comes up to me and says, "August 14, 1998, Burlington, give me five." He holds out his right hand for a homeboy slap. I am surprised by his idea of celebrating his birthday in Vermont; it seems wildly premature. Quietly, I reply, "I don't know, I'll have to see." My father already has discounted that I am visiting for the first time since Thanksgiving 1993, pushing as ever for more and more of me. "Give me five," he repeats. I look at him, not knowing how to respond. Then without consciously thinking about it, I extend my left index finger and put it lightly against his right one. His eyes light with a hope painful to see. It stirs me to forget my own well-being in favor of his, an old family pattern. I say goodnight and leave.

NOVEMBER 28

TONIGHT when my father says, "Give me five," as I get ready to leave, I offer him two fingers. "Five," he says.

"Arthur, *genug*" (the Yiddish word for "enough"), says my mother. Ever the monitor of my father's emotions, she often cuts him off from me; this time I am grateful.

NOVEMBER 29

AT the end of the evening, I open the front door to leave and my father says, "Let's see, last night it was two fingers." I hold up three and we touch. His face lights with that same pleading hope, and I am moved that he does not press for more.

NOVEMBER 30

WHEN I depart tonight, the last evening of my visit, my father forgets about our "give me five" ritual. All my life his attention has come and gone like an intermittent circuit. I grew accustomed to waiting and developed an unhealthy attraction to living in a state of longing. Although my father doesn't remember "give me five," he uncharacteristically offers to walk me to the bus stop. We go down the elevator and up the street in silence. When we reach the cold, windy corner of West End Avenue and Seventy-second Street, I turn to him and say, "It's only the fourth night, but since I'm going home tomorrow, here's five." Our gloved fingers touch. My father's face lacks animation and, seeing his expression, the exchange I initiated becomes lifeless to me. Ever since I was little, I learned to be a cipher to my father's emotions; I should have foreseen that he could not continue the ritual of "give me five," once I set the pace. When my father leaves me, I watch him walk spindly-legged, head pitched forward in the strong wind blowing off the Hudson River. He does not look back. I hope he won't fall down. I want to help him, which would be more appropriate, given his age. But I realize that I need to let him be the caretaker tonight. It is a restitution of sorts. From the beginning, our parents had found Karen and my emotional and physical needs burdensome, as if we were to be *their* parents. (For instance, they enlarged the opening to my then baby sister's bottle nipple to shorten her time in their arms.) I stand at the empty bus stop remembering how I used to walk behind my father down that street on windy winter days. By holding onto the back of his scratchy overcoat I protected myself from the cold that was so strong it made my forehead ache. Those had been rare moments of feeling sheltered by him. Now I watch my father grow smaller as he walks down the street, and the habit of longing for his love returns; with it comes the admission that I *do* love him.

The bus arrives and sinks pneumatically for me to enter. I am grateful for its uncomplicated kindness and make my way down the aisle, smelling the hot damp air I remember from girlhood. I take a seat far from the only other passenger. In the dark I bring out the homemade roasted sunflower seeds I took on my trip to New York for comfort, if needed. Although there is no reason to be secretive, I eat them furtively as I look out the window at the brightly lit New York streets. The seeds are tasty and filling; but they do not replace the lost years of a father's love.

December 1997

"Good Days Coming"

DECEMBER 1

VIVIAN begins to open her front door and Laska pushes her face between it and the doorjamb; she sniffs wildly at my slacks, the whites of her eyes showing. Vivian asks Laska to sit and my young dog obeys, although she trembles all over with excitement. I admire Laska's coat, fluffy and shinier than usual from the bath Vivian gave her. Out of respect for Laska's eagerness to reunite with me, Vivian ceremoniously hands me the leash before we even exchange greetings. I shove my hand through the loop at the end of it as if I were attaching myself to a lifeline. "It's good to be back from New York," I say, as we head toward the kitchen for Laska's belongings.

"Not my idea of a place to spend time, that city," Vivian replies, echoing a sentiment I often hear from Vermonters.

"Every time I saw a dog being walked, I missed Laska," I say. "But I would never bring her with me to Manhattan; it's so hectic there that dogs ignore each other, the same way New Yorkers do, to have some peace of mind. I'm glad she was with you."

"Laska is better every time she comes here," Vivian says.

My heart beats with pride and at that very moment Laska jumps on me.

"Down!" I say, amused that she isn't living up to her reputation, adding, "You are such a contrary one." Laska drops onto all fours and eyes me brightly.

The drive home will be long, and I ask Vivian to hold Laska for me while I use the bathroom. When I return I find Laska sitting alertly by Vivian's side.

Laska looks with great concentration in my direction, head up, soft ears pricked forward; her tail sweeps back and forth across the floor in a semi-circle.

"Laska watched for you the whole time you were gone," Vivian says. "She's much more bonded with you than in the past."

"We owe a lot to your help," I reply, as Vivian sees us to the door; secretly I hope that the change in Laska does not depend on any outside influence.

I drive home on a two-lane road that winds between cornfields; stalks sheared off close to the root stick up through the snow. In spring they disappear, turned under by a plow, and where they stood, rows of dark earth swell softly. After some months feathery light green plants appear; they become "knee high by Fourth of July" and over the summer mature into sturdy stalks with slender, ripply leaves that fork sharply downward along the tall stems. Where the leaf meets the stalk, sheathed heads of corn cluster, glistening silky hairs protruding from their tops. Laska and I have almost completed our first seasonal round together. For us, spring seems to be coming in wintertime.

DECEMBER 4

TODAY, Laska's birthday, we take our customary walk, which includes a visit to the yuppie pet store, Bone Appetite. Usually we stop only for a free treat; but today I have a different plan. I want to buy a present for Laska's birthday. Bone Appetite sells a special version of the flat, oversized, bone-shaped biscuit called Great Dane. This one has "Happy Birthday" written on it in blue confectioner's sugar paste; a green candle sticks straight up from the biscuit, just as it would on a cake. As I eye that treat, I argue with myself. The birthday greeting is addressed to me, taking advantage of my sentimental attachment to my pet. I decide on the plain Great Dane biscuit, pretty fancy, really, since it is made with chicken and carob and costs $1.50. Laska, meanwhile, sits trembling with excitement as the salesperson hands the present over to me in a paper bag. "Not for now, Laska," I say. "Later."

On the way home I ruminate. When I celebrate Laska's birthday, am I showing respect for her or am I anthropomorphizing my dog? Another question: Am I observing Laska's birthday because I live alone and have turned her into a significant other? I prefer to believe that Laska is not a substitute for human companionship, that her traits are distinctive and irreplaceable. I love her silence, her enthusiastic greeting when I return home, her awareness of the natural world. As if to interrupt my self-interrogation, Laska touches her nose to my knee. On this celebratory day I am grateful for the reminder to quiet my mind.

After supper I say to Laska, "Guess what?" Whenever I put this question to her, she regards me with the utmost attention. "Today is your birthday, and here is your birthday gift." I catch myself hoping that she will sit down beside me and eat her Great Dane biscuit civilly while I have my dessert. But she runs off to a corner with her treat and wolfs it greedily.

DECEMBER 12

DURING the night I dream of a big house, many chambered, with walls of stone. I descend into a dirt cellar where a seven-year-old girl named Rusty lives. She is gamine and smudgy, and dressed in a dusty Peter Pan outfit with orange tights and green buskins and jacket. Rusty is wild and untutored in human ways from living down in that cellar for so long; nevertheless she follows me willingly. We try to ascend by a set of spiral stairs but someone has shut a slatted wood trapdoor. I manage to pry it open and rebuke my father for confining me down there; whether "me" is Rusty, myself, or both of us isn't clear. I awake feeling vividly alive.

Surely the wild girl I rescued symbolizes the rude life force I forfeited to gain my parents' acceptance. Rusty reminds me of a little girl quoted in a book called *Bring Me the Ocean.* As she watched a fox, the girl told her mother something I would never have dared say to either parent: "She [the fox] has a very wild place inside her. We need to respect this wildness. . . . I have that place too, and you should know about it." Rusty, too, fiercely embodies creatural life, and her emergence alters my relationship with Laska. This morning I find myself actually liking the way Laska thrashes around upside down, teeth showing, jagged as new mountains, legs thrusting fiercely to keep me from patting her. Rusty's arrival makes plain that a roughhouse puppy, rather than a gentle one, was just what the doctor ordered.

DECEMBER 15

RUSTY'S appearance provokes a flashback.

▼▼▼

Leather straps loop over my shoulders like suspenders; a horizontal buckle strap crosses my upper chest to keep the shoulder ones from slipping off. The shoulder straps also attach to a broad leather belt with a buckle that circles my stomach; this belt in turn fastens to a child's toilet seat that clips onto the regular one. A book rests on my short legs as I look up at my father, who is taking my picture. "Look at you," he says, with a laugh that sounds slightly wild. "I've got to get a shot of this pose. I can just see it on the cover of the Saturday Evening Post." I smile but my mouth won't work right, and my eyes cross. That is because even though I'm only one year old, I don't like being tied down and made fun of. The cold draught of the toilet hole on my bottom makes me afraid that I will be sucked down the watery opening, out of sight.

▲▲▲

How was it that my parents could buy a toilet-training harness in the first place? This "training aid" may have been an offshoot of devices developed by a physician, Daniel Gottlieb Moritz Schreber, one of the most influential writers on child rearing and discipline in Germany in the mid-nineteenth century. Psychohistorian Philip Greven explains that Schreber had invented contraptions that were "designed to shape and control children's bodies and physical movements, including head and neck braces, straps for shoulders, and harnesses to keep sleeping children from turning over in bed (a device still used in the mid-twentieth century in at least one Philadelphia household)."[1]

Greven's historical account, *Spare the Child,* traces parental control over the "wills, bodies, and selves" of children in the West. According to Greven, the authoritarian behavior of parents arises from the coercive experiences of their own childhoods; one generation transmits this legacy to another down through time. Although the harness example might seem extreme today, most parents still spank their children (in a survey taken in 1994, 84 percent of parents used this disciplinary technique), as if the word "spank" meant something different from "hit."[2] Recently, several U.S. states passed laws that sanction spanking. Parents rarely question their control of children because they have forgotten much of what happened to them in their own childhoods. Greven explains that we develop "selective amnesia" about the insults we suffered, a capacity "rooted in the astonishing ability of children to deny their own rage, aggression, hatred, and revengefulness when they are being forced to suffer in the name of discipline by the parents or other adults whom they love and on whom they must depend."[3]

Laska disturbed my selective amnesia; her "assaults" provoked anger and fear rooted in the past. Now she provides a friend for the child Rusty inside me who remained alive, though hidden in the cellar. I understand why Rusty resembles Peter Pan. My parents took me to see the play on Broadway when it first came out in the 1950s, with Mary Martin in the starring role. Peter Pan was a spirited, defiant boy who believed that growing up destroyed creatural aliveness;

he sang, "If growing up means it will be beneath my dignity to climb a tree, I'll never grow up, never grow up never grow up, not me!"[4] Because Rusty was unacceptable to my parents, I had hidden her away in the cellar (an underground place that is a metaphor for the unconscious); she remained there all these years, unaffected by time. As Greven explains: "The psychic past is also the psychic present, time being absent in the unconscious."[5] As I shed the past, I grow as young and rascally as Laska. *Imagine* that I refused my father's insistence that I "give him five"!

DECEMBER 16

IN September I wrote about anthropologist and philosopher Barbara Noske, who criticizes the Western tendency to place humans above nature and other animals (I say "other" for we, too, are animals). Toward the end of her book, *Beyond Boundaries,* she challenges recent scientific efforts to explore the species boundary. Researchers take humans as the standard to measure animals by; for instance, scientists test primate intelligence by how well they can adopt human language. Noske asserts: "There is a way things look, taste, smell, feel or sound to an animal, a way of which we will have no idea as long as we insist that the only things worth knowing about are our own social constructions of the world. Although I do acknowledge that there is a sense in which we cannot know the Other (whether it be other species, other cultures, the other sex or even each other) we must remind ourselves that other meanings exist, even if we may be severely limited in our understanding of them."[6]

This quote precedes the final chapter of *Beyond Boundaries,* a finale that takes the dissolution of boundaries very far. In that chapter, called "Meeting the Other: Towards an Anthropology of Animals," Noske explores examples of *Homo ferus,* feral or "wolf" children, who have been raised by animals. Research about such youngsters neglects to study the social influence of *animals* upon humans: "The notion that animals culturally construct their own world some people already find hard to digest, let alone that animals could actively imprint humans with their culture! Most children found among animals were indeed displaying marked animal features: they often walked on all fours, used animal communicative signs, exhibited animal behaviours and had no verbal language" (161).

There have been some fifty cases of animal-reared children in the last six hundred years, most of them in Europe and Asia and some in Africa; some of the adoptive animals were domestic, some wild—wolf, bear, leopard, panther, lion, monkey, sheep, pig, cow, bird, and gazelle.

Noske accuses most scientists of asking anthropocentric questions about feral children, such as: "How human is this child and how can we rehumanize it, i.e. de-animalize it?" (164). She contrasts this narrow approach to that of Jean-Claude Armen. In 1976, he published a book called, *Gazelle Boy: A Child Brought Up by Gazelles in the Sahara Desert,* which recounts the time the author Armen spent with the "gazelle boy" and his adoptive herd. I found one story particularly poignant, given that when I was young I had longed for an "animal childhood." Noske writes: "At dusk he [the author Jean-Claude Armen] would see the boy lie down under the neck of a large old female gazelle who seemed to have a particular predilection for him: there was almost incessant nose-muzzle rubbing between them. Would this female be his old wet-nurse and adoptive mother?" (165).

Noske does not tell us what ultimately became of the boy, only that when Armen returned to the herd two years later, he found that the old female gazelle had disappeared (perhaps died) and that the boy had risen to a rank just beneath that of the leader.

According to Noske, Armen attempted to answer the right questions: "How did the child succeed in becoming animal with the animals? How did the two species learn to communicate with each other and understand each other's meanings, considering they were born with different means of communication?" Armen discovered that the boy and the gazelles constructed their own discourse, one that took their physical differences into account. The boy would: "imitate gazelle ear signals with his facial muscles and some tail signs with finger movements, having no tail of his own and his ears being covered with hair. The gazelles seemed to have had no trouble decoding these signs" (164, 166).

Noske hauntingly points out that research like Armen's may never occur again: "The rate at which humans are presently encroaching upon animal habitats makes it extremely unlikely that any human being will ever 'get lost' among animals again. Our future world threatens to be human-controlled rather than animal-shaped, with concrete rather than natural jungles and deserts" (167). She praises those scientists, mostly nonmainstream, who participate in animal societies and attempt to understand the meaning animals give to the world. Of course, engaging in empathic research is different from being *raised* by animals. Just now, Rusty's emergence from the cellar and my growing enjoyment of Laska's wildness makes an animal childhood seem like the best way to experience the creatural. On the other hand, so-called feral children face challenges I can only guess at—being different, having to connect, then being a pariah in human society; I must be careful not to romanticize.

DECEMBER 21

TODAY is the winter solstice. As if to celebrate the dead season with aliveness, Laska takes my mittens off the kitchen counter; a little later she drags my felt clogs across the room, grabs my pen off the table, then the keys; later still she pulls a cardboard cylinder from a toilet paper roll out of the bathroom wastebasket, pounces on it, and then bites it into pieces. On a low bookshelf in my writing room she finds crocheted red wool booties. Guaranteed not to be able to be pulled off by a restless child—they were for Levin when he was a baby, made according to my own pattern, now lost to my memory. Laska must *not* destroy those booties. I can't catch her, so I throw a pen on the floor and retrieve my treasures. Laska dents the pen top, rendering it useless.

As aggravating as these assaults on my possessions may be, none of them makes me want to hit her. Only her attacks upon *me* set off transference from the past. Both Merle and Daniel have often said, "You are angry at your mother and father, not at Laska. Try to direct your anger toward them." Nowadays I do. Yesterday morning Laska jumped up at me when I tried to put her leash on. I tapped her on the muzzle. I say "tap" because I have been trying to do it symbolically, a reminder rather than a real slap. Yet I'd rather not hit her at all, because even tapping her on the nose, a "gentle" punishment, can be demeaning.

I remember a Sunday morning in Texas when I was about four years old. After breakfast my mother walked into my bedroom to pick out a dress for me to wear. If I had had a choice, it would have been overalls. I hung back in the gloomy dining room even though we were going on my favorite outing, to visit a lion cub mascot at the air force base. I loved the baby lion's big furry head, round eyes and ears, and clumsy paws. Every day a soldier took the cub for a walk, his leash attached to a harness that reminded me of the one my parents used to strap me into when I sat on the toilet seat. Even though I was looking forward to seeing the baby lion again, I didn't want my parents to rush me, and I didn't want to wear a dress. So I dawdled by the claw-foot dining room table, ignoring my mother's call. Impatient with me, my father swatted me on the backside and I ran into the bedroom.

Such disrespectful moments, repeated many times over the years, are the real source of my anger at Laska when she jumps on me.

DECEMBER 22

I HAVE been watching a program called *Woof* that features dog trainer, "Uncle Matty." A lean man dressed in suburban clothes with the mobile, open face of a stand-up comic, Uncle Matty talks to dogs as if he is working a crowd in the Catskills. Today he trains a female golden retriever whose bad habit is that she pulls on the leash. The training area is a suburban sidewalk, flanked by heavily fertilized stretches of green grass. Uncle Matty croons to the dog in a falsetto voice, "Come on, sweetheart, come on and heel for Uncle Matty." When she obliges, he adds, "*Oh,* what a good girl." And again, "Uncle Matty is *so* proud of you, that's right, honey, come to Uncle Matty." His voice switches from disapproval to approval as *soon* as the dog obeys. After demonstrating his training method, Uncle Matty hands the dog over to her owner, a slightly overweight young woman dressed in stretch jeans and a jersey top. With an impassive face and humorless voice, the dog owner issues the command, "Heel!" while she uses Uncle Matty's technique of snapping the leash to get her dog's attention and make her follow. Although the retriever does exactly as her owner asks, the woman forgets to praise her dog, so much has her resentment over chronic bad behavior built up. When Uncle Matty reminds her that praise is important, the woman says glumly, "Good dog."

I am rather like that dog owner, although less so than in the past. I decide to try out Uncle Matty's technique, and I don't have to wait long. Laska grabs my pen off the kitchen table, and I say sternly, "Drop it!" When she complies, in the blink of an eye I switch to a bright, sunny, "*Good* drop it."

The rapid change of mood reminds me of a poem written by the North Vietnamese leader Ho Chi Minh during a time when he was a prisoner of war. I first read his poem "Good Days Coming" almost thirty years ago; he showed me a different way of living from the one I was accustomed to since childhood. Difficulties can be resolved, there can be an end to unhappiness:

> Everything changes, the wheel
> of the law turns without pause.
>
> After the rain, good weather.
>
> In the wink of an eye
>
> The universe throws off
> its muddy clothes.
>
> For ten thousand miles
> the landscape
>
> Spreads out like
> a beautiful brocade.

Gentle sunshine.
Light breezes. Smiling flowers.

High in the trees, amongst the
sparkling leaves,

All the birds sing at once.

Men and animals rise up reborn.

What could be more natural?
After sorrow comes happiness.[7]

DECEMBER 23

CROW comes into the kitchen. Her straight short black hair gleams, and she is wearing a handsome oversized batik shirt. "Where did you get that?" I ask, already knowing the answer.

"Battery Street Jeans," Crow replies and smiles, showing her white teeth.

"As usual," I say. "I wish I could shop secondhand the way you do. For some reason the clothes look tired to me, not fresh. My thing is to order from L. L. Bean. I even got a credit card from them so that the postage is free."

"No judgment," Crow says, which refers to her disapproval of L. L. Bean's conservative politics.

"Well, if there is a boycott," I reply defensively, "I'll stop buying from them."

While we talk, Laska barks in her crate. Normally when I have dinner guests I leave her in there, but tonight Chanukah begins, a Jewish festival of independence, and so I let her out. Chanukah commemorates the right to religious cultural diversity within a nation. In 165 B.C.E., the Syrian king Antiochus, embroiled in political struggles with other states, demanded that diverse groups within his sphere of influence forsake their own traditions. A small group of Jews led by Judah Maccabeus revolted. They restored the temple, which had been sacked and defiled. As legend goes, a small amount of oil was found to rekindle the eternal light that used to burn at the altar. By a miracle the oil burned for eight days. Jews celebrate this wondrous event by lighting a menorah. Each night, with the shammes, or helping candle, you light as many candles as the day requires until, at the end of Chanukah, eight burn brightly.

When I let Laska out of her crate, she dashes up to Crow and jumps up on her nice shirt. As a puppy Laska was frightened of Crow, and I enjoy the excitement with which my young dog now greets my friend. But I can't let Laska rip Crow's clothes. I decide to try the head collar that Vivian insisted Laska wear the night we graduated from obedience class. The device looks like a muzzle; but if I put the head collar on Laska, she might not have to go back in her crate. I manage to get the contraption on, and it does keep her from jumping up and nipping. Reassured, I give the leash to Crow so that I can finish making supper. Earlier, I prepared buttercup squash stuffed with curried turkey pieces mixed with quinoa; right now, I am steaming collard greens and making the salad dressing. For a while Laska forgets about the head collar and watches for food scraps that might fall on the floor. Then, when Crow isn't paying attention, Laska cleverly slips the collar off her muzzle by rubbing at it with her paws. I take the collar off altogether; to my surprise Laska leaves Crow alone.

"Wow, Crow," I say, "here we are, two friends and a dog, enjoying a normal evening together." Crow bends over to pat Laska's back, and Laska wags her tail and looks up at Crow.

Crow lights the candles, after which we recite the traditional Chanukah blessing in Hebrew. When Laska hears the guttural sounds she jumps up excitedly, the whites of her eyes showing, as if she can tell that we speak in a different language. "What a smart dog!" I brag. "Laska knows that we aren't speaking English."

"Let's eat," Crow says, not sharing my interest in Laska's canniness. We sit down to our meal, but now Laska circles the table, her nose lifted so that it is level with our plates.

"She reminds me of a shark, cruising," Crow jokes.

"Just ignore her," I say, but soon Laska swipes Crow's napkin; I return my dog to her crate.

"What are you going to do on Christmas Eve?" I ask Crow. Some Jews call this time of year "the December dilemma"; the phrase refers to the difficulty Jews experience during a Christian holiday celebrated by the whole culture.

"Luckily this year Chanukah and Christmas happen at the same time; I'm going to a Chanukah party and you are welcome to come."

"Thank you, that sounds like a great idea."

We hurry through dinner so that we can watch a video called *Fly Away Home* that my sister told me about. Orphaned Canada goslings bond with a little girl. When winter comes, the goslings need to migrate south but have no parents to guide them on the journey. The girl's father, who is a handy sort, rigs a small plane to look like a goose with which he and his daughter lead the geese to their winter home.

When the movie is over, I tell Crow how my sister's seven-year-old boy, Matty, reacted to the film. "When they came into the theater lobby, Matty extended his arms and 'flew' around the space, not saying a word. Karen tried to get him to stop so that they could go out for dinner but he would not. To me, it was Matty's way of joining the birds, being one with them."

"You know how I kid you about your insights," Crow says. "Maybe Matty was just having fun running around, after sitting in a seat for so long."

"Well, what about this?" I add. "When Levin was about two years old, I happened to be parent-helping in his day-care group the day we went to the Peabody Museum to see the stuffed animals."

"Where is that?"

"At Harvard University," I reply. "We got to a big room filled with glass cases. Inside them were stuffed deer, gazelles, and other such creatures. The taxidermy was pretty crude—you could see seams in the skin. But the kids saw something else. Without a word, all six or eight of them got down on their hands and knees and *crawled.* They joined or, since many of them had only recently learned to walk, you could say they rejoined the four-legged ones, just the way Matty became a bird."

"That's a sweet story," Crow says. "Who knows, you might be right."

We hug goodnight. After Crow leaves, I let Laska out of her crate and say affectionately, "Hi, my four-legged one."

DECEMBER 24

LASKA jumps on the living-room couch. I surprise myself by chiding her humorously, rather than scolding. I say, "Oh, Laska, you *know* you aren't supposed to be on the couch."

Tonight, as I sit in a Breuer chair watching the news in the living room, Laska sticks her head between my arms, which rest on my knees; Steely did the same thing with Merle long ago. Merle said that this gesture showed trust. Afterward, Laska sits down tidily in front of me, and I say, "We're getting to be a *family.*"

DECEMBER 25

A DAY more quiet outside than any other. Everywhere families are indoors, opening Christmas presents. This morning Laska gives me one, too. She lies on her side in a patch of sunlight on the kitchen floor. I lean over from my chair and stroke her sleek side. Her eyes close; her black, blunt lashes are visible in a peaceful line instead of the watchful, wary, sideways glance I usually see. For the first time, she falls asleep to my touch.

DECEMBER 30

I HAVE a new phrase. "For *heaven's* sake, Laska," I say in a good-natured tone whenever she commits mischief. I look back on Laska's and my past with horrified respect for the power of transference to distort reality. How could I have felt threatened by Laska when, at two months, she ate a ficus leaf and bared her teeth? She was so small that I held her in my two hands as I carried her away from the plant, yet she seemed a monster to me.

Laska has given me a creatural lesson I never planned on when I outlined my sabbatical project. I now know what it *feels* like to be abusive. To feel what novelist Jane Smiley, speaking of a father's incest, calls "the goad of an unthinkable urge" that wraps you in "an impenetrable fog of self."[8] I must have been a child very like Laska—intelligent, curious, perhaps with the same heightened sensitivity to stimulus, and an unwillingness to conform. In her memoir *Home to the Wilderness*, naturalist Sally Carrighar explains that babies who undergo high-forceps births (as she and I both did) often suffer subtle birth injuries to the autonomic nervous system. Oxygen deprivation or trauma caused by the instruments themselves can cause excessive sensitivity in babies, making it difficult to comfort them. Carrighar explains that if parents act soothingly, such babies can learn how to be calm. What a mismatch I was for my mother (as she once told me, she had "little patience") and a father who derived pleasure from overstimulating and frightening me! (My sister, who had an easy birth, was a placid baby.) Laska's mother, Nancy, was six years old when she gave birth, and it took her all day. I gather from Stacey, Laska's breeder, that the labor was longer than usual. Perhaps Laska, too, had a minimal birth trauma that made it hard for her to be quieted.

Laska's creatural lesson allows me to understand my parents from the inside out. I still hold them responsible for their actions, just as I do myself with Laska. But I no longer feel a gulf between "them" (those who abuse) and "us" (those who don't), as I did when I was raising Levin. I cherish the startling sentence with which Jane Smiley ends her novel *A Thousand Acres*, about incest and family disintegration (she models the story loosely on Shakespeare's *King Lea*r). Through the urges of the narrator, Ginny, to murder her sister Rose out of jealousy over a man, Ginny gains insight into her father's "unthinkable" incest. The difficult knowledge remains with her as "the gleaming obsidian shard I safeguard above all the others."[9] Shiny black Laska becomes the obsidian mirror in which I see myself.

January 1998

Anniversary

JANUARY 5

ALTHOUGH I don't use words that belonged to Sarah like "Sweet Pea" or "Pooch" (if, by mistake, I do, it causes a pang in my heart), I now have a set of affectionate terms for Laska. She has become "Laski, Laskali Raskali, Sweetness Girl, Crescent Moon–Eyed One, Good Girl, Ms. Tiptoes, Shufflefoot." Laska has her own way of expressing affection nowadays; she's apt to bump against my leg when we are out for a walk, so closely does she stick by my side.

JANUARY 7

A WARM, dense, steady rain has come from the South, apparently due to El Niño. When the rain hits the ground, it freezes. The driving rain bends trees to the ground; when the water turns to frost it encases the branches in sleek ice sheaths. Any time you go outside you hear trees snapping—sharp cracking sounds—without being able to identify the exact source.

Laska won't go out into the back yard because the deck is too slippery. So I take her on a leash out the front way; while I stand on the protected front porch, she gingerly steps into the small yard right near the house and eliminates there. Whenever we go outside, she stands still at first, tail drooped, head up, ears flattened as she listens to the unfamiliar sounds.

JANUARY 8

TODAY ice coats all that we see; there are grass blades with knobby tips of ice and sleek clumps of leathery-looking brown leaves that have frozen one over the another. Although Laska is getting no exercise, she is surprisingly cooperative, as if, in the face of nature's harsh side, we should stick together.

JANUARY 9

THE half-inch-thick glaze of ice begins to melt off the trees and clatters to the ground, gleaming strangely. According to many Vermonters, this ice storm is the worst natural disaster they can remember.

JANUARY 10

BY now it is reasonably safe to assume that a branch or power line won't fall on you, so Laska and I take a walk. We keep to the street since the sidewalks are still covered with ice. Trees stand broken, their trunks snapped in half, the raw yellow-white wood showing. Heavy clusters of branches drape toward the ground like lamentations. In this desolate landscape I feel lucky to be warm and alive with Laska beside me, and I can tell how bonded we've become after surviving the unnatural disaster of our first year.

JANUARY 23

TODAY is the first anniversary of my bringing Laska home as a pup. A light dry snow falls and, in the cold still air, retains the footprints of passersby. Hardly anyone is about, so when Laska and I go out for a second walk, I recognize the biting tread of my hiking boots in the snow, like footprints on the moon. Alongside these marks I see Laska's earlier prints. Her front paws left rosette shapes. The shuffle-foot gait of her back legs made rosette shapes from which a tail extrudes; these prints resemble comets.

Increasingly, the metaphors I choose to describe Laska are happy ones. A few days ago, when Laska stretched her front legs, sinking her body close to the ground except for her rump, which stuck up in the air, her blunt front paws splayed out into what I saw as four-pointed stars.

As the metaphors accumulate, they become an offering—a grateful expression of my growing love for Laska.

Tonight Laska hangs back in the unlit studio, which opens onto the deck and yard, after I let her into the house. I keep the door between the kitchen and studio closed during the winter because the double-high space doesn't heat properly, especially now that the radiator is broken. I stand waiting, just over the threshold into the kitchen. Lately Laska does not come when I call (in the past she sometimes came). Is this the so-called adolescent period (she is almost fourteen months old)? I am tired and want to go to bed. I peer into the studio. In the dark all I can see of Laska is the crescent slip of the whites of her upturned eyes. They come into view and then fade as she looks at me intermittently to see if I still mean what I said. Seeing her eyes, my closed heart opens and I laugh.

Epilogue

March 2001

LASKA MEETS MY MOTHER

EVEN though I "gave him five," my father did not come to Vermont to celebrate his birthday in August 1998. Instead, he and my mother flew out to the West Coast for the opening of an art show to which they had lent major pieces from their collection. However, they did come to Burlington in September, which coincided with my birthday, their trip largely prompted by an about-to-expire plane ticket. In October of the previous year, when I was still estranged from my parents, out of the blue my mother had FedExed a letter to me announcing that she was coming to Vermont three days hence and planned to stay with me. She and my father had been invited to a dinner at UVM's Fleming Museum, to which they had donated a few paintings; my father was out of town lecturing on reconstructive dentistry and so my mother planned the trip on her own. I had quickly FedExed back to say that I'd be happy to find a hotel accommodation for her and to accompany her to the dinner; I did not respond to my mother's demand to stay with me. Consequently my mother had chosen to remain in New York, and her unused plane ticket would have gone to waste had she and my father not come to Vermont for my birthday. I am grateful for the airline company's one-year expiration rule, because my parents' visit that fall proved to be their last. My father died a year later, in September 1999.

Of all the people I have described in my journal, my mother seems the most difficult to like. Whenever I reread *Anna Karenin,* I appreciate Tolstoy's ability to evoke sympathy for all of his characters. I could easily dislike Anna's cold bureaucrat of a husband, Karenin; his decision not to divorce Anna so that she could her marry her lover, Vronsky, contributes to her suicide. But Tolstoy provides insights into Karenin's limited inner life that stir some compassion in the reader. In a powerful scene that takes place in the close quarters of a horse-drawn carriage, Anna tells Karenin that she fears and hates him and that she loves Vronsky. After making this confession she begins to sob. In response, Karenin's "whole face suddenly" assumes "the solemn immobility of the dead."[1] The chill expression on Karenin's face is disturbing. Later, Tolstoy explains why Karenin responded the way he did: "None but those who knew Karenin most intimately was aware that, while on the surface the coldest and most rational of men, he had one weakness quite inconsistent with the general trend of his character. Karenin could not with equanimity see or hear a child or woman crying. The sight of tears upset him and made him lose all power of reflection" (300). This insight alters the unfavorable impression formed by Karenin's behavior.

I do not pretend to have discovered a master key to my mother's emotional life, but an encounter between her and Laska gave me new insights. I picked my parents up at the airport when they visited to celebrate my birthday. I watched through the glass doors as they disembarked from a small commuter plane parked a short distance from the airport building. They climbed down the steep, narrow stairs slowly; each of them now used prosthetic canes. Despite their age (my father was eighty-eight and my mother seventy-nine), they looked slender and stylish. My mother wore a white beret, black peacoat, and long black skirt with a red, white, and black plaid scarf tied around her neck. She had a Zabar's shopping bag looped over one arm. My father wore a brown-gray cashmere car coat and black pants, a woven scarf wrapped around his neck. He held a copy of the *New York Times* against his chest. His thin, gray-black hair was long (my mother thought the uncut look gave him an artistic air), and as they walked toward the terminal from the plane a strong wind blew his hair back off his face. When they came through the door, I hugged each of them; I felt their bony shoulders beneath their coats, and tears started from my eyes but I hid them. Their arrival in Burlington after a more than three-year interruption seemed less like a continuation than an epilogue, or a return to the beginning. My sister had been born when I was five years old; until then it had been just us three. I took the Zabar's bag from my mother; we picked up the luggage at the claims station and went to the car for the short ride to my house.

Before I left home I had put Laska in her crate. She had never met my parents (although she has felt their influence in the way I have treated her) and was apt to be more excited than usual. I didn't want her to jump on them, what with my father's unsteadiness on his legs and my mother's hip replacement. When my parents came through the door, Laska stood up in her crate and barked wildly; her wagging tail banged against the metal bars, making them vibrate with a tinny sound. I ignored her because I wanted to help my parents bring their luggage inside and up the stairs. They would sleep in my bedroom, to have the benefit of the raised bed, and Laska and I would sleep in Levin's old room.

After they got settled in my room, my mother and father came back downstairs for a cup of tea. When they were seated safely at the kitchen table, I let Laska out of her crate. I offered her a bone stuffed with cheese, which I'd prepared ahead of time; it calmed Laska to chew on it. She lay down on the fleecy mat behind my chair, put one paw on top of the bone, bent her head sideways, and licked at the cheese noisily. After about ten minutes Laska got up and casually walked over to my mother. Apparently self-absorbed, it took my mother a minute to notice Laska. When she did, a current seemed to pass between them. Laska stiffened into a canine position of dominance—head alert, mouth open, tail curved up. She stood there and stared. My mother stared back, laughed nervously, then said, "Dictator."

Laska stood even more stiff-legged.

"She wants to make me her slave," my mother said. Then to my father, she added, "You be her favorite."

He called Laska over and soon she lay upside down, one front leg extended so that her paw rested on his arm as he rubbed her belly. Oddly enough, my father, so often governed by unruly emotions, possessed at the deepest level a reservoir of great calm. In childhood, I had clung onto rare peaceful moments with him the way a toddler grasps her parent's forefinger in her plump fist.

"Boy, I wish she'd be that relaxed with me," I said, out of an old habit of self-deprecation. In fact I had been able to make Laska feel peaceful.

I turned my attention back to my mother. I suddenly understood her apparent fear of being controlled, and it fit with the few facts I knew about her early life. My mother had been an only child and, in her early years, in weak health. Before antibiotics, and without good housing, nutrition, and medical attention, a poor family had few ways to insure that a child would survive. (My father's mother had given birth to six children, but only three lived into adulthood.) Out of anxiety, my grandfather Morris saw to it that every moment of my mother's life was supervised. He insisted that my grandmother Pauline follow my mother to school to close any open windows that might give her daughter a draft and cause her to catch a cold. Morris demanded of Pauline that she make sure my mother ate all her food. This tedious job did not suit my grandmother, who was a gifted, vain woman perhaps not meant for motherhood. "With her voice she could have been an opera singer," my mother often said, lamenting the pinched opportunities available to an immigrant (Pauline worked as a seamstress). On one occasion, my grandmother became so vexed with feeding her baby that she poured a bowl of eggs on top of my mother's head.

Of my mother's two parents, Morris was the loving one; this father-daughter dyad repeated itself in my childhood relationship with my father. Even when my mother was in high school, Morris would wait for her on rainy days so that he could drive her home in his car. When at twenty-one my mother left college to marry my father (who was nine years older and had just graduated from dental school), she had had little opportunity to exercise control over her life, and little experience of motherly love.

My mother's generation was raised to respect its elders; hence, I have seldom heard my mother speak critically of her parents. But impermissible feelings do not just vanish. It seemed that my mother transferred her frustration and rage at being controlled as a child onto me (and to a lesser extent onto Karen), misperceiving us as overbearing because we needed her care and her love. In the encounter with Laska, my mother seemed to react as she would have with one of her children. Initially, Laska simply wanted to connect. When my mother exhibited power by withholding herself, Laska challenged her. I understood with terrible clarity how my mother likely would have interpreted a baby's relentless needs as a "dictatorship." I could imagine why she had shunted me off to my father when I was a child ("You be her favorite"), then become jealous, wanting his attention back.

My mother's apparent resourcelessness, when faced with needs or claims upon her, hinted at a feeling of inner emptiness. In this way she reminded me of Karenin. About halfway through *Anna Karenin*, the reader learns a small amount about Karenin's childhood, which provides insight into his diminished ability to feel: "Karenin had grown up an orphan. There were two brothers. They did not remember their father, and their mother died when Alexei Alexandrovich was ten years old. Their means were small. Their uncle, Karenin, a distinguished Government official and at one time a favourite of the late Emperor, had brought them up" (534).

Although Tolstoy allows us this inner glimpse, he does not falsify Karenin's capacity to love. Anna's aunt arranges a marriage with Karenin, and Tolstoy writes with unsparing honesty that Karenin "made the offer, and bestowed on his betrothed and wife all the feeling of which he was capable" (535). Like Karenin's, my mother's limited ability to give and receive love seems rooted in her history; as with Karenin, the effects of this impoverishment are real.

After the extraordinary scene between my mother and Laska, we had lunch. It wasn't until the following day that I had the opportunity to learn more about my mother.

MY MOTHER AND I TALK

It was early afternoon and the sun poured into the living room where my mother and I sat. My father was upstairs napping in my bedroom. That night we would go out to dinner at Mona's, a restaurant that overlooked Lake Champlain, to celebrate my birthday. I almost felt peaceful. My mother looked relaxed as well as she sat slumped in a chair. She wore a V-necked white blouse with wide lapels, a multicolored vest that she had bought at a New York crafts fair, and a long black skirt. Laska snored lightly in her crate at the far end of the room. I had been telling my mother about a former student who had decided to become a midwife after taking my Sociology of Reproduction class, when my mother suddenly said, "I should have sent you away after you were born, the way I was when I was born."

"I never knew about that," I answered, ignoring her rejection of me.

"Well, you never asked," my mother said, reversing the blame with characteristic humor. "Grandma Pauline had a very hard childbirth, just as I did. Afterwards they kept her in the hospital and my father took me, a little nothing in his arms, that's all I was, on a train to Aunt Molly's house in Philadelphia. You remember Molly, Grandma's sister?"

"Sure I do." What I remembered most was that she lived in a brick town house, was friendly, had blue-white hair, and kept a bowl of chocolates on a side table in the living room next to an armchair.

"What did Molly know about babies? She was only eighteen years old. Grandpa Morris didn't come to pick me up until a few months later. It would have been better if I'd had time away from you after you were born."

I sat quietly, trying to be both daughter and counselor.

My mother continued, "I was only twenty-one when your father knocked me up. You were a month late and came out with long hair and fingernails. While I was in labor, your father's sister-in-law Aunt Bobby, treated him to dinner. God knows she wasn't much of a cook, but your father eats anything put in front of him. It wasn't like today in the hospital; I was all alone and you tore my body coming out. When I got home from the hospital and saw that hi-fi set your father bought to celebrate, I wanted to throw it out the window."

For a moment I pictured the hi-fi set sailing out the fourteenth story window of their apartment. Then I returned to consider all that my mother had told me. She had called herself "a little nothing," a phrase that suggested a diminished sense of self. What must it have been like for her, as a newborn, to be taken away from her mother and placed with an inexperienced young woman? She had used the phrase "your father" the same way my father would say "your mother," as if somehow I was to blame for their actions. How strange that my mother had said "knocked me up," even though she was married when I was conceived. Why had she said, "You tore my body," when it was the high forceps that had injured her? I leaned forward in my chair, placed a certain distance from hers, and said, "But, Mom, don't you see it wasn't me? It was patriarchy that treated you so badly, a medical system shaped by men with no sensitivity to your needs as a woman. I was just a helpless, innocent baby. My whole book *Bearing Meaning* is intended to protect women from what you went through."

My mother's pale, lashless eyes looked at me impassively. She continued as if I hadn't spoken. "You are lucky you weren't aborted."

I sat up, shocked into the same hyperclarity that a strong winter wind can produce when you step outside from a heated house. Her words gave meaning to feelings I'd never fully understood. Now I knew why I had felt that I oughtn't be alive at all, why I felt my life was at the expense of another's, why I became frightened every time my life became plentiful or touched by joy. In a curious way her double story—sending me away for a while, aborting me—was a strange birthday gift. I said, "It helps me understand why you've hated me all my life."

"I'd prefer you didn't use that word," my mother said, not denying the sentiment the word expressed.

"Disliked me."

She did not object.

My mother's story fragments about her own birth and about giving birth to me expanded the narrative of her life I had put together over the years based on things she and others had told me. Surely my mother's prolonged separation as a newborn from her mother, my grandparents' well-meaning but stultifying control of their only child, and the suffering my mother endured giving birth to her first child help explain her initial "dislike" of me. But these historical facts do not explain her persistent antipathy toward me over the years (the conversation about my birth occurred on my fifty-seventh birthday). What seemingly unquenchable element, impervious to reason, inhabits my mother's psyche and shapes her perceptions of me? In *Home to the Wilderness*, author Sally Carrighar quotes a British psychiatrist, Susan Isaacs, who provides insight into Sally's mother. As Dr. Isaacs explains, a psychological disturbance can be severe and yet cause no more than "'a narrow gap in an otherwise perfectly rational mind.'"[2] This "narrow gap" is not inborn, Dr. Isaacs adds. "'Usually it is the result of some highly traumatic experience.'" Sally's mother and mine suffered trauma giving birth to us and, postpartum, were faced with taking care of homely newborns (besides my long hair and nails, I had forceps bruises on my face) who were difficult to comfort. Because "wide areas of her mind were entirely normal," Sally's mother, like mine, functioned at a high level of competence in the world, even though she acted irrationally toward her daughter (16). From Dr. Isaacs's and Sally's own studies, she learned that a decisive "'tear in the psyche' may be 'too deep to heal'" (17, 15). Based on this knowledge, Sally says: "Behavior which originates in such a scarred mind will be blameless, and I only wish that I could have understood the true situation much earlier" (17). Although I share Sally's compassion, I find it hard not to hold my mother responsible for raising me without love and for blaming me, right into the present, for her unhappiness. In a memoir about his mother, *All Over but the Shoutin'*, Rick Bragg describes the effect of his tormented relationship with his father: "Somewhere between understanding and forgiveness, there is another wall too wide to get around."[3] I search for a way past that wall.

FAREWELL

Shortly after my parents' visit to Vermont for my birthday, my father found it harder and harder to breathe. Increasingly, his bronchial tubes, injured by the Spanish flu, filled with fluid that he had to cough up. As the year progressed, he began to spend a good part of the day breathing through a nebulizer, a device that temporarily clears the airways. I visited him in April and in July of 1999, and both times saw with sorrow his increasing weight loss and inability to remain engaged in conversation, so much did coughing and breathing claim his attention.

During the July visit, I sat beside my father on his bed and showed him photographs of the house renovations and the new car he and my mother had made possible. My mother chose to remain on her bed, where she scanned the pictures briskly.

When she apparently decided I'd had enough time with my father, she said, "Robbie, you better go check the rice."

"I will when I'm done," I replied, annoyed at the chill of anxiety I felt in opposing her desire to cut short my time with my father.

My parents never did give me a "chunk of money," and our financial negotiations resembled those of the past more than I wished. But my father took genuine pleasure in seeing pictures of the new front porch, the fresh clapboarding and paint (ochre with white trim), and the gray Volvo station wagon parked alongside the house (my rusted-out 1984 Volvo had gone 150,000 miles).

One night in September 1999, my father hardly could breathe at all and would have died had he not been taken by ambulance to New York Cornell Hospital in Manhattan. For a few days he used a breathing mask; then his doctor suggested that he take a "vacation" from his troubles by going on a respirator. My father accepted.

Over the next three weeks I traveled to New York on weekends to visit him in the hospital. The last time I saw my father was on September 26, my birthday. As I walked down the long corridor of the intensive care unit, I was as shocked by the inhospitable atmosphere as I had been the first time I had come here, weeks before. Now, as then, the staff person on duty at the nursing station gazed fixedly at a computer screen, ignoring my arrival. To my left, a row of doors opened onto rooms in which patients lay prone and unmoving, attached to life-support systems. The machines recorded vital signs that sent tiered rows of colored waves across a screen. At frequent, unpredictable intervals one machine or another would begin beeping as urgently as a fire alarm, while a red light at the top of the machine blinked in rhythm to the sound. I later learned that a machine went into high alert whenever it malfunctioned, wasn't attached properly to the person, or the person began to fail. The loud noises were intended to be heard anywhere in the ICU, which made rest or peace of mind impossible, since the machines went off frequently.

At the far end of the corridor was my father's room, which looked out over the East River rather than offering his accustomed view of the Hudson River on the West Side. The phone was ringing, and as I was about to enter the room I heard a nurse say to another attendant, "No one's home." What if my father could hear her disrespectful remark? Crow had told me that the last of the senses to go is the ability to hear. I should have rebuked the nurse for her insensitivity, but I was afraid to antagonize her, since my father was in her care. Shortly after I arrived, the nurses left the room.

On my previous visits to the hospital I had not been alone with my father, but today my mother, sister, and son would be arriving later than usual. As before, my father's gaunt face was turned toward the bright window; his body under the sheet was improbably thin. So many tubes were inserted into him that it was hard to get close. But over the last few visits, I'd eked out a spot for myself. I leaned over the metal railing and cupped one hand around his shoulder bone. I looked into my father's eyes. His gaze was unfocused yet seemingly on a quest, and this expression reminded me of the great idealist Don Quixote. My father's aristocratic, aquiline nose, long hair that trailed on the pillow as if blown by the wind, and brows raised in what seemed to be melancholic suffering, strengthened the comparison. I was afraid to remind him about my birthday. What if he died today? Forever after, my birth would be merged with his death, an annual event that would symbolize his unstoppable desire to be close to me. Instead he would die three days later, on September 29, the date of his mother Katy's memorial service following the "unveiling" of her gravestone. (A faded newspaper clipping I later found among his papers provided me with this information.)

I gazed at my father the way a mother looks at a baby, a perceptual activity called "entrainment" (being utterly engrossed by the "other"). These were the first moments in my life when my father didn't run away from me or come too close. Even if he had not been sedated and suffering from what a nurse called "ICU psychosis" (a severely dissociative state induced by the harsh lights that were on twenty-four hours a day and by the agitating alarms), my father could not have talked to me, because a fat respirator tube was stuck down his throat. The hospital physician had asked a dentist friend of my father's to remove the bridges in my father's lower jaw; I assume the reasons for taking them out were convenience and safety. Already sedated, my father had no say over whether they performed this procedure. Alex, a young dentist greatly influenced by my father's work, told me that when he began removing the bridges, my father tried to bite him. "Good for him," I had said. After the removal, just a few yellowed teeth remained in the front and back of my father's mouth. I never had known that my father was missing most of his bottom teeth; perhaps he kept the loss a secret out of shame. More than any story my father had ever told me, the empty spaces in his mouth educated me about the deep poverty of his childhood, and I understood why, all his professional life, he passionately advocated against tooth extraction.

As on earlier visits, I tried to ignore the tinny sound of the respirator as it breathed for my father and to erase from my mind a scene my father had once described to me, when I was a child, that came from the city streets of his childhood. A monkey, held fast by a harness, perched atop a hurdy-gurdy; his narrow-brimmed hat, encircled by a braid, sat jauntily on his head. A thickset, unshaven organ grinder cranked the instrument and the monkey's body, like my father's on the respirator, moved in time to the tinny music.

This vision had horrified me as a child because I had often felt kin to the monkey—little more than a tool forced into animation by a power indifferent to my real aliveness. To escape the hurdy-gurdy vision now, I told my father a story. "Dad, listen. Before I left Vermont I had a dream. I took all the tubes out of you very carefully and carried you to Camel's Hump, the place where I walk with Laska. You lay so lightly across my arms. It was nighttime and you leaned your head back and looked up at the dark sky embedded with shining stars. You had the same questing look on your face that you have now. Overhead the Milky Way, loosely folded like a transparent white scarf, streamed across the heavens. You smelled the rich, damp earth and the fragrant grasses. You breathed the fresh air that blew softly against your skin and I breathed with you, in and out, in and out, in and out, and our breath was part of all that was around us, all of nature breathing together." I stopped talking and once again the tinny sound of the respirator filled the room. I repeated my vision over and over. Then I fell silent, and for a long time just gazed into my father's faraway eyes. I said softly, "You and I and all of nature breathing together." Careful not to dislodge any tubes, I slowly withdrew my hand from his shoulder and left the room.

Although I returned later, the rest of my family was crowded around the bed; and so the dream I shared with my father became my true farewell. I left for Vermont the next day. Two days after that, on the night of September 29, my mother called to say that just a few minutes before, my father's heart had slowed, and slowed, and finally stopped. The next morning I took a bus back to New York; my sister and her family arrived four days later from California in time for the funeral. With Rabbi Noah's help, I found a wonderful rabbi in the city, helped my mother plan the funeral, and took care of her for a week following the burial. The first seven months after my father's death, I visited my mother every two to three weeks and dared to believe that the loss of him might create a mother/daughter closeness where little had existed before. More recently, though, the opposite has happened. My mother and I seem to have drifted apart, as if it had been my father who had kept us, however tenuously, together. Although she suffers some residual discomfort from the hip replacement, my mother walks without the aid of a cane and is otherwise in excellent health. She appears to be adjusting well to the loss of her husband. Eminent people in the art world invite my mother out to dinner, and she regularly attends museum and gallery events, as well as the theater and ballet. Were my mother to need me, I would, of course, help her out (I live closer to New York than my sister does), but I get the feeling that our cordial distance is a temporary relief to both of us.

In the month following my father's death the nightly changes of the moon surprised me. How could nature continue without my father alive? Happily, the moon and the yellow, white, and purple crocuses that poked up out of the ground in early spring corrected my delusion. There remains an unripeness to my father's presence in my life; the satisfying times came too seldom, and now no more such moments will ever come. At the same time I feel a certain release; my father will never again overwhelm me with his desires, or abandon me.

On the first anniversary of my father's death, I went to the synagogue to recite the Jewish prayer for the dead, Kaddish. When I returned home, I lit a yarzheit candle, which burns for twenty-four hours; standing before it, I conducted a somewhat pagan ritual by reading Mary Oliver's poem "In Blackwater Woods," which celebrates the incessant, incandescent dying and regeneration of the natural world:

In Blackwater Woods
Look, the trees
are turning
their own bodies
into pillars

of light,
are giving off the rich
fragrance of cinnamon
and fulfillment,

the long tapers
of cattails
are bursting and floating away over
the blue shoulders

of the ponds,
and every pond,
no matter what its
name is, is

nameless now.
Every year
everything
I have ever learned

in my lifetime
leads back to this: the fires
and the black river of loss
whose other side

is salvation,
whose meaning
none of us will ever know.
To live in this world

you must be able
to do three things:
to love what is mortal;
to hold it

against your bones knowing
your own life depends on it;
and, when the time comes to let it go,
to let it go.[4]

COZIES

I draw muslin Shaker curtains across plain wood dowels to shut out the night. An industrial lamp suspended over the large, round table fills the living room with soft light. "Laska," I say, "would you like to have our cozies?"

I settle myself on the orange futon and adjust the back support that leans up against the couch. The setup I created almost two years ago so that Laska and I could hang out together has had nightly use. Laska walks over to me, head down, ears flat, tail held low and wagging. She climbs into the crook of my legs, circles once, and then folds herself into a tidy circle with her two front paws draped across my right thigh; she holds her head erect with characteristic dignity. Although she does not look at me, I can tell that she is listening for what I might say.

In the prologue, I wrote about the very first time Laska and I had what I took to calling "our cozies." Was she really once so "wild" that I did not dare to invite her close?

"Do you remember when I used to call you a little pup?" I ask Laska, now slightly over three years old.

Laska swings her head around and regards my face, the whites of her eyes showing.

"I used to say, 'Hi, puppy,'" I add, as the phrase returns to my memory.

Laska's tail thumps against the futon; she tilts her muzzle up and licks my chin rather than banging against it with her open mouth, a rowdy practice that even now is her custom. I had left the word "puppy" behind because it didn't carry the association of the cuddly moments you imagine with a young dog. Apparently the term remains in Laska's lexicon with affection.

SLIPPERS

Gray dawn light filters through the bedroom window. Lying on my stomach, I lean over the edge of my bed to look for Laska. She is curled tightly on her bed, which rests under mine.

"Laskali, would you like to say good morning? Would you like me to rub your belly?"

She lifts her head and in the gray dawn light her dark eyes look at me, the thin crescent moon of white showing underneath. She doesn't move, though. This is a game we play.

"No? You don't want me to rub your belly?" I bring my head and shoulders back onto the bed. As soon as I am out of sight, she gets up, pauses—which I know is for a stretch—and then comes over to me on tiptoes, mincing her steps. I put my face over the side of the bed again, and she bumps her mouth against my cheek. I should not allow this but I will be washing my face soon. I reach one arm down. With a solemn expression on her face Laska sits, swivels in a 360-degree circle with one leg held open to expose her flank, and then flops upside down on the floor. I rub her warm belly and the thick winter fur (which has not yet begun to shed) across her chest. Her ears splay out on the floor, and her mouth is slightly open, revealing her teeth. As usual, she resembles a bat.

"Laska, you know what?" Her body becomes absolutely still, as it does when I put this question to her. "We're going for a walk in the mountains today." Her thick otter tail swishes across the floor. "First you'll have your supper." More tail swipes. (For some reason I call her morning and evening meals "supper.") "And then we'll go in the car on our trip to the mountains, where you can go run around." At this Laska wags her tail vigorously, turns her head, and takes my hand, gently enough, between her teeth.

I say, ungrammatically, "Where's my shoes?" For years Laska has enjoyed running off with my shoes and gloves. She doesn't chew on them and as soon as I lose interest in her mischief, so does she; the sole purpose of her retrieval in reverse is to get my attention. Long ago Merle told me, "When Laska takes something, turn it into a game. Ask her to bring it to you." Her advice worked, and for over a year Laska has brought me my felt clogs in the morning. Today, she leaps to her feet with catlike agility and pads across the room. I watch her upside down from where I lie on my stomach, my head hanging over the side of the bed. When she finds the shoe, she pounces on it and slides across the floor. "Bring it," I say.

With the shoe hanging jauntily from her mouth, tail held high and waving, Laska prances back to me.

"Good girl," I say, as I take the clog from her mouth. "Where's my other shoe?" Laska casts around, nose to the ground, in a classic retriever motion. She spots the shoe, this time on the far side of the bed, and pounces on it. Looking over the edge of the bed from where I lie on my stomach, all I can see are four legs moving briskly past the raised bed frame, preceded by a dangling shoe. "Good girl," I say enthusiastically as she reaches me.

Philosopher and animal trainer Vicki Hearne explains that fetching is not just a mechanical act. As she puts it: "'Fetch!' cannot be said meaningfully unless it is said with reverence. Its coherence requires that retrieving be sacred for both members of the community." When Hearne uses the words "reverence" and "sacred," she encourages dog owners to respect the freedom of the one whom they command. Obedience should be regarded as a gift rather than a right. A gift always contains an element of surprise. Hearne explains that a correct response on the part of the trainer is not approval but recognition, because the dog is doing something that arises from its own impulses: "Full-blown retrieving demands full-blown love of the activity itself. Salty doesn't (can't) retrieve for me, she can only retrieve with me."[5] (Salty is the name of her dog.) Hearne says an act of free obedience should arouse "awe" in the owner, an emotion I have been cultivating.

A few months after Laska started fetching my slippers, she learned to bring me my jogging shoes. One morning after breakfast Laska and I stood in the living room. I said, "Shall we go for a walk?" I never got to ask for my jogging shoes because Laska gave me a discerning look, wheeled, raced across the living room, and grabbed one of them between her teeth; she understood that the word "walk" was connected to fetching my shoes. At that moment, I comprehended what Hearne meant by "awe." A few weeks later Laska again aroused awe in me when she fetched each jogging shoe from a whole clump of shoes in the mudroom. Retrieving a ball never held much interest for Laska. She needed to initiate an action, such as pilfering a shoe, for retrieval to capture her heart.

While I shower, Laska goes back to sleep on her bed. After I dress, I head down the hall to the stairs, with Laska by my side. But when I reach the first floor, I am alone. Laska remains on the top step, her ears drooped down on either side of her face. This is another game. "Aren't you coming downstairs?" I ask, looking up at her. She doesn't move. I sit down on the second step, the same spot I chose the day I brought Laska home as a puppy. My back to her, I say, "Well, then, I guess I'll just have to sit down right here and wait for my little girl." As Laska clatters down the steps, her toenails clicking on the pine wood, I add, "I'll wait for her as long as it takes"; Laska arrives by my side just as the string of words ends. Her back legs on the third step, her front legs on the first, she wags her tail madly and makes for my face with her open mouth, all the while wriggling with excitement as I scratch her back. "OK," I say as I stand up, "let's go get your supper."

THE MOOSE

Sunlight glints off the snow, as if shattered by infinite prisms. Tiny flashes of reddish orange, green, and blue surround me as I trudge along on my snowshoes. Laska trots ahead, keeping to the cross-country ski tracks for better footing. She is as unfamiliar with the trail as I am, so she stops frequently and looks back at me, as if we were connected by an invisible tether. This network of trails in the foothills of Camel's Hump is less traveled by skiers than the ones we usually frequent. Here there is less chance that Laska will knock someone down by jumping on them. A small wooden sign nailed to a tree trunk told me that we are on Skunk Brook Trail, which winds among widely spaced deciduous trees—maple, poplar, and birch.

I pause on a small footbridge to listen to the faint sound of water flowing. Many streambed rocks create lumps under the snow cover; larger stones poke through the whiteness and are surrounded by irregularly shaped ice crusts formed by the eddying stream as it froze. Small openings around the ice allow me to see the stream moving darkly, as it forces its way past the cover of late winter.

When the trail we are on meets up with Dead River Run, Laska waits at the crossroads. "We go this way," I say, motioning to the left, and she sets out jauntily, her head up and pink tongue visible in a slight pant; her breath looks like steam as it comes out of her mouth. Although I have on only silk long johns, a fleece jacket and pants, and Gortex shells over these, I, too, am hot and enjoy the warmth in the dead season around us. We continue along, going up hill and down. Slender saplings protrude from the deep snow to either side of the trail; snow lies heavily across the length of an old tree, the dead one supported by the trunk of a younger tree. Above, the blue of the sky appears condensed, the color is so vivid. We reach a place where the trail dips into a small valley between the mountains and then rises. Laska suddenly tears down the hill, her tail held in a tight tuck, legs splaying out every which way, the whites of her eyes showing.

When she gets to the bottom she wheels sharply, sending up a plume of snow that sparkles in the air, and begins to race back toward where I stand laughing.

"That's right, you go on and be a crazy girl," I say, planting my snowshoe poles and lifting my arms. Laska is headed straight for me, but at the last minute she passes on the left, circles behind me, and then dashes back down the hill. Again, she wheels, as snow sprays and glints; then she returns. She does this over and over. Eventually, Laska comes up to me, panting heavily as if it were a summer day, and sits smartly.

"Laska, you nutcake, would you like a treat?" She watches me excitedly, ears pricked forward, as I fish for a treat in the fanny pack strapped around my waist. Because she has expended so much energy, I give her two or three cubes of fresh apple, and then we set out again. A hill rises steeply to the right of us, and through the tree trunks I see a small log cabin, perhaps belonging to a hunter. For the first time, I feel alone in the woods, even though I am with Laska. The sight of human habitation returns me to a self-conscious awareness I temporarily shed on the walk. I suddenly see myself through the eyes of a man, a hunter, standing at the threshold of the cabin, and I fear him. But the cabin is deserted, and we pass on. Before long the vigorous physical activity that warms my body, the naked trees, fresh snow, and Laska's happiness cause my apprehension to disappear.

Laska reaches the end of the trail before I do. We have never gone this far, and I wonder if there is another way back or whether we will have to return the way we came. We head down Stagecoach Road just as the late afternoon sun passes behind tall, closely spaced evergreens. The trail falls into shade and the air chills, creating a somber feeling. Once again anxiety stirs in me, but it is of a different kind than my fear of the imaginary hunter. Winter temperatures are unforgiving should you lose your way and unexpectedly have to spend a night in the woods. I move along stolidly on my snowshoes with Laska not far ahead. In a short while, we reach a trail that looks like it heads in right direction. I stop and unfold a large map of the Camel's Hump Nordic ski trails. The map shows a tangle of trails that traverse the hills surrounding the mountain. I find Bear Cat Draw to our left and am happy to see that it will take us back to the lower trails.

Suddenly I sense that Laska, who stopped when I did, has left me. I lift my eyes from the map to see her running back up Stagecoach Road. In shadow, no more than perhaps sixty feet away, stands a large creature, looking intently at us. The bulk of him is supported by long, slender, knobby-kneed legs. His broad chest, massive head with a wide drooped-over nose, and fanned-out span of heavy antlers appear to spread sideways, as if visually distorted in a mirage. I often enough have seen large moose tracks on the trails, especially during spring when the heavy-bodied animals leave imprints of their hooves deep in the muddy earth. Only the sign, never the creature itself. I could have been afraid, yet the quality of the moose's attention, so different from the imaginary hunter's stare, holds me fast. The big animal gives off a regal, even patriarchal air, but he neither challenges my sovereignty over myself nor turns away from me. Later I would wonder if, by enchantment, the moose gave me something I had always longed for from my father, a parent unable to respect my separate life who would either violate my integrity or desert me if I attempted independence from him. Enlivened by the wild creature's gaze, I continue to peer at him as the shadows deepen.

After her initial dash in his direction, Laska has stopped about halfway between the moose and me. She, too, stands and stares. Then suddenly, she charges at him.

"Laska, come," I say hoarsely. For the first time I am afraid. I turn, and clumsily but rapidly head down Bear Cat Draw. I look back; to my astonishment my black dog, who rarely comes when I call, is racing toward me as the moose flees, its improbably long hind legs forking up, disappearing into the gray gloom of the upper trail.

When Laska reaches my side, we descend Bear Cat Draw, which turns out to be a steep but quick way back to the lower trails that take us to the snow-covered road where I parked my car. The sun, glowing orange, sinks behind the hills as we head for home.

Postscript

IN our family it was usually one person's well-being at the expense of another's. This economy of scarcity seems active right now, as I consider the effect on my mother and me of publishing *Milk Teeth*. In the last few years my mother has changed. She has extended newly thoughtful expressions of consideration, as well as much-needed financial help. The transformation seemed to follow a yearlong illness I suffered in 2004–2005. During that period my mother called me her "firstborn," as she expressed her worry to my sister. Such different words from "lucky you weren't aborted." I am deeply grateful to my mother for her change of heart and for her generosity. In deference to her, should I toss *Milk Teeth* into Lake Champlain, as if to drown the past?

True, my mother complains virtually every month when I ask for a check in accordance with her commitment to assist me. There never seems to be a right time to bring the subject up. I usually wait until the end of a phone conversation or a visit to New York City. Once in 2006, I stood at the steel front door of my mother's apartment, on my way out, carry-on suitcase with wheels and retractable handle by my side. Levin had bought the suitcase on Canal Street for twenty-five dollars. My right hand already grasped the handle when I finally told my mother the previous month's expenses. She said, half-joking, "Oh, you are shtupping me again" (Yiddish for "screwing"). "Mom," I said, looking hard into her eyes. Suddenly my mother's face brightened, as if she'd been struck by a new idea. She said, "I'm glad to be in a position to help you out." The words hung in the air like a vision of a different life history. I removed my hand from the suitcase and took my mother's slight figure into my arms as I replied, "That's the nicest thing you've ever said."

Novelist and clinical psychologist Lucy Daniels dedicates her memoir *With a Woman's Voice: A Writer's Struggle for Emotional Freedom* to "all those whose emotional struggles have kept them silent." In Daniels's note to the reader she explains that she changed many names to protect people's privacy. I have done the same. Daniels adds, "There are, however, people whose names could not be changed." (Here I insert my own list: my mother, sister, son, and first husband.) Daniels continues with a quote I write as if it were my own: "I hope that this telling of my story will not cause them hardship. Not telling it would have been damaging to me."[1]

Notes

PROLOGUE

1 Swimme and Berry 1992, 41.
2 Greven 1990, 149.
3 Kahn 1995, 114.
4 Giddens 1991, 180.
5 Alighieri 1961, 23.
6 For an enlightening discussion about the nature of memory, see Siegel 1999, 23–66.
7 Karr-Morse and Wiley 1997, 117.
8 Ibid., 118.
9 Hardyment 1983, 173–174.
10 Simpson 2000, 4.
11 Oliver 1983, 44.

JANUARY

1 Stevens 1953, 116, 118.
2 O'Hara 1943, 17.
3 Terhune 1919, 150.
4 Tolstoy 1978, 111.

FEBRUARY

1 Marx 1975, 329.
2 Goldberg 1986, 38.

MARCH

1 Kowalski 1991, 105–106.
2 Stevens 1953, 119.

APRIL

1 Favre and Tsang 1993, 31.
2 In memory of Alex Chirelstein, songwriter and cofounder of Baby's Nickel Bag. "Mr. DJ," music and lyrics by Alex Chirelstein.
3 Morgan 1996, 7.
4 Ibid., 5.
5 Mead 1962, 182.
6 Masson 1995, 42.
7 Ibid., 20.
8 Hearne 1986, 108–109.
9 Thomas qtd. in Masson 1995, 44.
10 Ibid., 116.
11 Ibid.
12 Cohen 1961, 7.

MAY

1 Warwick 1986, 20.
2 Proulx 1993, 32–33.
3 Tolstoy 1978, 623.

JUNE

1 Sogyal Rinpoche, Gaffney, and Harvey 1992, 263, 275.
2 Nhat Hanh 1987, 40, 41.
3 Ibid., 75, 76.

JULY

1 Serpell 1996, xvii.
2 Ibid., 62, 65, 81.

AUGUST

1 Grossman 2, 57.
2 Miller 1984, 106.
3 Mehr qtd. in Miller 1986, 45. Mariella Mehr prefers the unpublished translation of these lines by Roger Russi: "the god of my childhood wears black robes, horns on the head and an ax in his hand. how

then was it still possible for me to squeeze past him? all my life i had to sneak, through my landscape, with a bit of life beneath my arm, a bit of life i feel i have stolen." From Mehr, *Steinzeit* [Stone Age], 1981, 83, 34.

4 ASA Awards Ceremony, ninety-second annual meeting of the American Sociological Association, Toronto, August 10, 1997.

5 Hearne 1986, 47. Succeeding cites of this book appear as page numbers in parentheses in the text.

6 Homer 1990, book 17, 389–394.

7 Masson 1990, 82–83.

8 Ibid., 82.

September

1 Torgovnick 1997, 4. Succeeding cites of this book appear as page numbers in parentheses in the text.

2 Noske 1997, 78. Succeeding cites of this book appear as page numbers in parentheses in the text.

3 Simoons and Baldwin 1982, 434. Succeeding cites of this article appear as page numbers in parentheses in the text.

4 Dunayer 1995, 19.

5 "Readers Respond to Catalin Valentin's Lamb," *Utne Reader,* September/October 1988, 6.

October

1 Swimme and Berry 1992, 72–73, 78.

2 Miller 1986, 22.

3 deMause 1988, 4.

4 Kabat-Zinn, M. and J. Kabat-Zinn 1997, 376–377.

5 Levinson, qtd. in Beck and Katcher 1996, 166–167.

6 Fox 1980, 81.

7 Shepard 1996, 151.

8 Budiansky 1992, 41. Succeeding cites of this work appear as page numbers in parentheses in the text.

9 "The Evolution of Obstetric Care: Toward an Understanding of the Relationship between Culture, Medicine, and Women's Health," Raymond De Vries, convener, International Book Project Seminar, Washington, D.C., October 1997.

November

1 Miller 1990, 7, 25–26. Succeeding cites of this work appear as page numbers in parentheses in the text.

December

1 Greven 1990, 170.

2 Straus 1994, 20.

3 Greven 1990, 172.

4 Charlap and Leigh 1982, 22–23.

5 Greven 1990, 166.

6 Noske 1997, 160. Succeeding cites of this work appear as page numbers in parentheses in the text.

7 Ho Chi Minh 1968, 63.

8 Smiley 1991, 370–371.

9 Ibid., 371.

Epilogue

1 Tolstoy 1978, 232. Succeeding cites of this work appear as page numbers in parentheses in the text.

2 Carrighar 1973, 15. Succeeding cites of this work appear as page numbers in parentheses in the text.
3 Bragg 1997, xxi.
4 Oliver 1983, 82–83
5 Hearne 1986, 65, 71.

POSTSCRIPT

1 Daniels 2001, front matter.

Bibliography

The interested reader may wish to look at some of the following references. Milk Teeth *draws upon all the books and articles listed below, but the notes cite only a selection.*

Adams, C. J., and J. Donovan, eds. 1995. *Animals and Women: Feminist Theoretical Explorations*. Durham: Duke University Press.

Alighieri, Dante. 1961. *The Divine Comedy*. Translated by J. D. Sinclair. 3 vols. New York: Oxford University Press.

"Animal Consciousness." 2000. *Inside the Animal Mind*. 3rd VHS. Directed and narrated by Steve Kroft. Produced by Sanjida O'Connell for the BBC, 13/WNET New York, and Green Umbrella.

Ascione, F. R., and P. Arkow, eds. 1999. *Child Abuse, Domestic Abuse, and Animal Abuse: Linking the Circles of Compassion for Prevention and Intervention*. West Lafayette, Ind.: Purdue University Press.

Beck, A. M., and A. Katcher, 1996. *Between Pets and People: The Importance of Animal Companionship*. New York: Purdue University Press.

Bell, D., and R. Klein, eds. 1996. *Radically Speaking: Feminism Reclaimed*. North Melbourne: Spinifex Press.

Bernard, J. 1981. *The Female World*. New York: Free Press.

Boston Women's Health Book Collective. 1976. *Our Bodies, Ourselves: A Book by and for Women*. New York: Simon and Schuster.

Bragg, R. 1997. *All Over but the Shoutin'*. New York: Vintage.

Buber, M. 1970. [1923]. *I and Thou*. New York: Scribner.

Budiansky, S. 1992. *The Covenant of the Wild: Why Animals Chose Domestication*. New Haven: Yale University Press.

Carrighar, S. 1973. *Home to the Wilderness*. Boston: Houghton Mifflin.

Charlap, M., and C. Leigh. 1982. "I Won't Grow Up." *Vocal Selections from Peter Pan: Broadway's Musical Hit*. Milwaukee: Hal Leonard.

Chirelstein, A. 1994. "Mr. DJ." *Baby's Nickel Bag*. SPCD1001.

Christ, C. 1980. *Diving Deep and Surfacing: Women Writers on Spiritual Quest*. Boston: Beacon Press.

Cohen, A., ed. 1961. *The Five Megilloth: Hebrew Text, English Translation, and Commentary*. London: Soncino Press.

Collard, A. 1983. *The Rape of the Wild: Man's Violence against Animals and the Earth*. Bloomington: Indiana University Press.

The Color Purple. 1985. Directed by Steven Spielberg, with Danny Glover and Whoopi Goldberg. Amblin Entertainment.

Cool Hand Luke. 1967. Directed by Stuart Rosenberg, with Paul Newman and George Kennedy. Jalem Productions.

Csikzentmihalyi, M. 1990. *Flow: The Psychology of Optimal Experience*. New York: Harper and Row.

Daly, M. 1985. *Beyond God the Father: Toward a Philosophy of Women's Liberation*. Boston: Beacon Press.

Daniels, L. 2001. *With a Woman's Voice: A Writer's Struggle for Emotional Freedom*. Lanham, Md.: Madison Books.

deMause, L. 1988. *The History of Childhood: The Untold Story of Child Abuse*. New York: Peter Bedrick Books.

Dunayer, J. 1995. "Sexist Words, Speciesist Roots." In *Animals and Women: Feminist Theoretical Explorations*, ed. C. J. Adams and J. Donovan, 11–31. Durham: Duke University Press.

Fantasia. 1942. Directed by James Algar, et al. Walt Disney Pictures.

Farley, W. 1941. *The Black Stallion*. New York: Random House.

Favre, D., and V. Tsang. 1993. "The Development of Anti-Cruelty Laws during the 1800s." *Detroit College of Law Review* 1:1–35.

Fly Away Home. 1996. Directed by Carroll Ballard, with Jeff Daniels and Anna Paquin. Sony. VHS.

Fox, M. W. 1980. *Returning to Eden: Animal Rights and Human Responsibility*. New York: Viking Press.

Franklin, A. 1999. *Animals and Modern Cultures: A Sociology of Human-Animal Relations in Modernity*. London: Sage.

Freud, S. 1963. *General Psychological Theory: Papers on Metapsychology*. Edited by Philip Rieff. New York: Collier/Macmillan.

Giddens, A. 1991. *Modernity and Self-Identity: Self and Society in the Late Modern Age*. Stanford: Stanford University Press.

Gilgamesh Epic. N.d. Xerox handout based on translation of available tablets, compiled by University Studies, School of the Humanities, Brandeis University.

Goldberg, N. 1986. *Writing Down the Bones: Freeing the Writer Within*. Boston: Shambhala.

Goldstein, J. 1976. *The Experience of Insight: A Simple and Direct Guide to Buddhist Meditation*. Boston: Shambhala.

Goode, C. 1993. *Labrador Retrievers Today*. New York: Howell Book House.

Greven, P. 1990. *Spare the Child: The Religious Roots of Punishment and the Psychological Impact of Physical Abuse*. New York: Vintage.

Grossman, A. 2002. *Sweet Youth: Poems by a Young Man and an Old Man, Old and New*. New York: New Directions.

Hardyment, C. 1983. *Dream Babies: Three Centuries of Good Advice on Child Care.* New York: Harper and Row.

Ho Chi Minh. 1968. "Prison Poems." Translated by K. Rexroth. *Avant-Garde* 3:63.

Hearne, V. 1986. *Adam's Task: Calling Animals by Name*. New York: Alfred A. Knopf.

Homer. *The Iliad.* 1974. Translated by R. Fitzgerald. Garden City: Anchor.

———. *The Odyssey.* 1990. Translated by R. Fitzgerald. New York: Vintage Classics.

Hurston, Z. N. 1978. *Their Eyes Were Watching God.* Urbana: University of Illinois Press.

Kabat-Zinn, M., and J. Kabat-Zinn. 1997. *Everyday Blessings: The Inner Work of Mindful Parenting.* New York: Hyperion.

Kahn, R. P. 1995. *Bearing Meaning: The Language of Birth.* Urbana: University of Illinois Press.

———. 1996. "Though It's Your Heart's Passion: Healing from the Death of a Family Dog." Paper presented at refereed roundtable, Sociology of Emotions. Ninety-first annual meeting of the American Sociological Association, New York, August.

———. 1999. "Family Album/1943." *Journal of the Association for Research on Mothering* 1 (1): 107–108.

———. 2000. "Family Strut." *Journal of the Association for Research on Mothering* 2 (1): 152–155.

Karr-Morse, R., and M. S. Wiley. 1997. *Ghosts from the Nursery: Tracing the Roots of Violence.* New York: Atlantic Monthly Press.

Kipling, R. 1942. *The Elephant's Child.* Garden City, N.Y.: Garden City Publishing.

Knapp, C. 1998. *Pack of Two: The Intricate Bond between People and Dogs.* New York: Dial.

Kowalski, G. A. 1991. *The Souls of Animals.* Walpole: Stillpoint.

———. 1997. *Goodbye, Friend: Healing Wisdom for Anyone Who Has Ever Lost a Pet.* Walpole: Stillpoint.

Lawrence, D. H. 1959. *Lady Chatterley's Lover.* New York: Pocket Books.

Lerner, Alan Jay, and Frederick Loewe. *Brigadoon (1947 Original Broadway Cast).* RCA Victor Broadway B000002W1D.

Lindisfarne Gospels. Late seventh or early eighth century. Cotton MS Nero D.IV, f.211, British Library, London.

Marx, Karl. 1975. "Economic and Philosophical Manuscripts, 1843–1844." *Early Writings.* Translated by R. Livingstone and G. Benton, 279–400. New York: Vintage.

Masson, J. M. 1990. *Final Analysis: The Making and Unmaking of a Psychoanalyst.* Reading: Addison-Wesley.

———. 1995. *When Elephants Weep: The Emotional Lives of Animals.* New York: Delta.

McCullers, C. 1965. *The Member of the Wedding.* New York: Time.

Mead, G. H. 1962. *Mind, Self, and Society: From the Standpoint of a Behaviorist.* Chicago: University of Chicago Press.

Miller, A. 1984. *For Your Own Good: Hidden Cruelty in Child-rearing and the Roots of Violence.* New York: Farrar, Straus and Giroux.

———. 1986. *Thou Shalt Not Be Aware: Society's Betrayal of the Child.* New York: New American Library.

———. 1990. *Banished Knowledge: Facing Childhood Injuries.* New York: Doubleday.

The Monks of New Skete. 1978. *How to Be Your Dog's Best Friend: A Training Manual for Dog Owners.* Boston: Little, Brown.

———. 1991. *The Art of Raising a Puppy.* Boston: Little, Brown.

Morgan, R. 1996. "Light Bulbs, Radishes, and the Politics of the 21st Century." In *Radically Speaking: Feminism Reclaimed,* ed. D. Bell and R. Klein, 5–8. North Melbourne: Spinifex Press.

Myers, G. 1998. *Children and Animals: Social Development and Other Connections to Our Species.* Boulder: Westview Press.

Nhat Hanh, T. 1987. *Being Peace.* Berkeley: Parallax Press.

Noske, B. 1997. *Beyond Boundaries: Humans and Animals.* Montreal: Black Rose Books.

Oakley, A. 1974. *The Sociology of Housework.* New York: Pantheon.

O'Hara, M. 1941. *My Friend Flicka.* New York: J. B. Lippincott.

———. 1943. *Thunderhead.* New York: J. B. Lippincott.

Oliver, M. 1983. *American Primitive.* Boston: Little, Brown.

Proulx, A. 1993. *The Shipping News.* New York: Scribner.

Rahv, P. 1957. "Attitudes toward Henry James." In *Image and Idea: Twenty Essays on Literary Themes.* ed. P. Rahv, 77–86. New York: New Directions.

"Readers Respond to Catalin Valentin's Lamb." 1988. *Utne Reader,* September/October, 5–6.

Reynolds, R. A. 1995. *Bring Me the Ocean: Nature as Teacher, Messenger, and Intermediary.* Acton, Mass.: VanderWyk and Burnham.

Rich, A. 1977. *Of Woman Born: Motherhood as Experience and Institution.* New York: Bantam.

Salten, F. 1931. *Bambi.* Translated by W. Chambers. New York: Grosset and Dunlap.

Schmemann, S. 1997. "A Red Heifer, or Not? Rabbi Wonders." *New York Times,* June 14.

Serpell, J. 1996. *In the Company of Animals: A Study of Human-Animal Relationships.* Cambridge: Cambridge University Press.

Sewell, A. 1927. *Black Beauty: The Autobiography of a Horse.* Philadelphia: John C. Winston.

Shepard, P. 1996. *The Others: How Animals Made Us Human.* Washington, D.C.: Island Press.

Shock Theater. 1957–1960. Hosted by John K. Zacharle. WABC-TV.

Siegel, D. J. 1999. *The Developing Mind: Toward a Neurobiology of Interpersonal Experience.* New York: Guilford Press.

Simoons, F. J., and J. A. Baldwin. 1982. "Breast-feeding of Animals by Women: Its Socio-Cultural Context and Geographic Occurrence." *Anthropos* 77:421–448.

Simpson, J. C. 2000. "It's All in the Upbringing." *Johns Hopkins Magazine.* April. Accessed May 15, 2001, at www.jhu.edu/~jhumag/0400web/35.htm.

Singer, P. 1975. *Animal Liberation: A New Ethics for Our Treatment of Animals.* New York: Random House.

Smiley, J. 1991. *A Thousand Acres.* New York: Alfred A. Knopf.

Sogyal Rinpoche, P. Gaffney, and A. Harvey. 1992. *The Tibetan Book of Living and Dying.* San Francisco: HarperSanFrancisco.

Solomon, R. 1998. "Catalin Valentin's Lamb, Callejon de Conchucos, Ancash, Peru." *Utne Reader,* July/August, 128. Photograph.

Stevens, W. 1953. *Harmonium.* New York: Alfred A. Knopf.

Straus, M. A. 1994. *Beating The Devil out of Them: Corporal Punishment in American Families.* San Francisco: Jossey-Bass.

Swimme, B., and T. Berry. 1992. *The Universe Story: From the Primordial Flaring Forth to the Ecozoic Era: A Celebration of the Unfolding of the Cosmos.* San Francisco: HarperSanFrancisco.

Terhune, Albert Payson. 1919. *Lad: A Dog.* New York: E. P. Dutton.

Thompson, W. I. 1996. *The Time Falling Bodies Take to Light: Mythology, Sexuality, and the Origins of Culture.* New York: St. Martin's Press.

Tolstoy, L. 1978. *Anna Karenin.* Translated by R. Edmonds. Harmondsworth: Penguin.

Torgovnick, M. 1997. *Primitive Passions: Men, Women, and the Quest for Ecstasy.* New York: Alfred A. Knopf.

Tousey, S. 1941. *Chinky Joins the Circus.* Garden City, N.Y.: Doubleday, Doran.

Warwick, H. 1986. *The New Complete Labrador Retriever.* 3rd ed. New York: Howell Book House.

When the Bough Breaks. 1986. Directed by Waris Hussein, with Ted Danson and Richard Masur. Westlake. VHS.

Winnicott, D. W. 1964. *The Child, the Family, and the Outside World.* Reading, Mass.: Addison-Wesley.

Woof! It's a Dog's Life with Matthew Margolis. 1998. Produced by Laurie Donnelly. Hosted by Matthew Margolis. WGBH.

Yellow Submarine. 1968. Directed by George Dunning, with the Beatles and Paul Angelis. Apple Corps.

Index

About the Author

ROBBIE PFEUFER KAHN is associate professor of sociology at the University of Vermont. Her first book, *Bearing Meaning: The Language of Birth* (1995), received the 1997 Jesse Bernard Award of the American Sociological Association. Kahn also won the 2006 Innovative Course Award from the Center for Respect of Life and Environment and the Humane Society of the United States for her course Sociology of Animals and Society. Kahn has published in *Tikkun,* the *Women's Review of Books,* and *Inquiring Mind.*

Kahn received her M.A. and Ph.D. from Brandeis University, as well as a B.A. in English and American literature. As a graphic designer, she won the American Institute of Graphic Arts Fifty Best Books of the Year Award for *The Movement toward a New America* (1970), edited by Mitchell Goodman. After the birth of her son, Levin Morrell Pfeufer, in 1972, Kahn turned her attention to childbirth activism. She was a contributing author to the 1976 and 1984 editions of the women's health classic *Our Bodies, Ourselves* and received an M.P.H. from the Boston University School of Public Health. Kahn believes that her interest in the very young (principle subjects in *Bearing Meaning* and *Milk Teeth*) comes from a desire to grant respect to those who lie outside the human "language community."